Fodor's 96
Bermuda

"When it comes to information on regional history, what to see and do, and shopping, these guides are exhaustive."

—*USAir Magazine*

"Usable, sophisticated restaurant coverage, with an emphasis on good value."

—Andy Birsh, *Gourmet Magazine* columnist

"Valuable because of their comprehensiveness."

—*Minneapolis Star-Tribune*

"Fodor's always delivers high quality...thoughtfully presented...thorough."

—*Houston Post*

"An excellent choice for those who want everything under one cover."

—*Washington Post*

Fodor's Travel Publications, Inc.
New York • Toronto • London • Sydney • Auckland

Fodor's Bermuda 1996

Editor: Amy McConnell

Contributors: Steven K. Amsterdam, Rob Andrews, Lori Lincoln, Laura M. Kidder, Honey Naylor, Peter Oliver, Mary Ellen Schultz, M. T. Schwartzman (Gold Guide editor), Dinah Spritzer, Judith Wadson

Creative Director: Fabrizio La Rocca

Cartographer: David Lindroth

Cover Photograph: Andrew McKim/Masterfile

Text Design: Between the Covers

Copyright

Special Sales

CONTENTS

Contents

ON THE ROAD WITH FODOR'S

A GOOD TRAVEL GUIDE is like a wonderful traveling companion. It's charming, it's brimming with sound recommendations and solid ideas, it pulls no punches in describing lodging and dining establishments, and it's consistently full of fascinating facts that make you view what you've traveled to see in a rich new light. In the creation of Fodor's *Bermuda '96*, we at Fodor's have gone to great lengths to provide you with the very best of all possible traveling companions—and to make your trip the best of all possible vacations.

About Our Writers

Lori Lincoln, cruise editor at *Travel Weekly*, has been on at least 14 cruises. From her Manhattan apartment she can hear the cruise horns blow as ships pull out from the Port Authority harbor, en route to Bermuda and beyond.

Honey Naylor's featured articles have appeared in *Travel & Leisure, Travel Holiday, USA Today, The Times-Picayune,* and *New Orleans Magazine.* She has traveled extensively throughout the Caribbean, but there's no place she prefers to Bermuda, which she calls the most civilized of the islands.

Peter Oliver, a Vermont-based freelance writer specializing in sports and the out doors, won the Lowell Thomas Award for print journalism in 1995. His articles have appeared in *Backpacker,* the *New York Times, Skiing,* and *Travel Holiday.* His latest book, *Bicycling, Touring, and Mountain Bike Basics,* was published by Norton in July, 1995.

Judith Wadson, a native Bermudian, has written freelance travel pieces about her island home for the *New York Times,* the *San Francisco Examiner,* and *Islands* magazine. Her photographic prints of Bermuda's architecture and landscapes are sold in select island galleries. *Seasons of Bermuda,* Judith's book about Bermudian traditions, was published in winter, 1995.

What's New

A New Design

If this is not the first Fodor's guide you've purchased, you'll immediately notice our new look. More readable and easier to use than ever? We think so—and we hope you do, too.

Travel Updates

Just before your trip, you may want to order a Fodor's Worldview Travel Update. From local publications all over Bermuda, the lively, cosmopolitan editors at Worldview gather information on concerts, plays, opera, dance performances, gallery and museum shows, sports competitions, and other special events that coincide with your visit. See the order blank at the back of this book, call 800/799–9609, or fax 800/799–9619.

And in Bermuda

Bermuda continues to recover from the effects of the same recession that has troubled the U.S. economy in the last few years. High numbers of overseas tourists—many of them repeat visitors—continue to fly or sail to this traditionally popular destination, but relatively few changes have been made in recent years to the island's hotels and attractions. Because of this and because prices are high and bargains scarce, Bermuda has not been able to reignite the kind of boom it enjoyed in the 1980s.

Events

Sunday in Bermuda has traditionally been a day of closed stores and quiet. The **Royal Naval Dockyard,** at the western end of the island, has changed that tradition. Retail outlets there are now open 11–5 on Sunday throughout the year; and special events, including art exhibit openings, a food festival, cycling tours, and cultural festivals, are regularly scheduled. The shopping area has been expanded from the Clocktower Building to the new Victorian Mall, where boutiques, specialty items, and branches of Hamilton stores are now thriving.

The highly successful spring and summer **Harbour Nights,** instituted in 1993, continue to draw crowds. The best place to be for this event is in Hamilton on Wednesdays, when visitors and locals stroll down Front Street, which is closed to motorized traffic for the event. Gombey dancers and local bands entertain passers-by, street vendors sell fish chowder, and local craftspeople display their wares. Most stores are open late on these nights, in case you should have the urge to splurge. The event also takes place on Tuesdays in St. George's.

Hotels

Annual refurbishments of rooms and public guest areas are the norm in Bermuda. Of the resort hotels, the **Sonesta Beach Hotel & Spa** reopened at the end of March, 1995, after an $18 million–dollar refurbishment of its guest rooms and public areas. **Pink Beach Club & Cottages** has expanded its room capacity, making it the largest cottage colony on the island. On a smaller scale, **Cambridge Beaches** has introduced an aerobics class and a weekly catamaran trip available to guests.

Restaurants

Hamilton continues to hold sway as the restaurant capital of Bermuda; new restaurants open here every year. The latest addition to the culinary scene is a small **sushi bar** built inside the already established Harbourfront Restaurant, on Front Street. Sushi lovers will be happy to dispense with the trek to Tucker's Town, where Marriott's Mikado held a sushi monopoly for years. Now you can start your dining experience at the sushi bar in the Harbourfront, then proceed to a corner table in the elegant, adjoining dining room.

If you want to dine casually under the stars while enjoying the sound of the surf as it breaks along the island's southern coast, head to **Calaban's,** the new dining room at Ariel Sands Beach Club in Devonshire. Since opening in June, Calaban's has become a frequent meeting place for locals who enjoy the lighter international fare on its dinner menu. At breakfast and lunchtime, you can eat in your bathing suit on the ground level.

Newly redecorated interiors enhance two of the island's most elegant dining rooms—Horizons and Waterloo House—both Relais et Châteaux properties. Waterloo House now has deep raspberry walls, rich chintzes, and elegant candle sconces. Dining at Horizons is less formal, with a fresh, plantation-style ambience of West Indian chintzes and pink and green decor. Renowned Swiss chef Anton Mosimann continues as culinary advisor to these restaurants, which are both so popular that it's sometimes necessary to book reservations a month in advance.

Tom Moore's Tavern has expanded its *al fresco* dining capacities so that more guests can enjoy nights under the stars, overlooking Walsingham Bay. Dining in this historic tavern (it was built in 1652) is peaceful and romantic: Savor fresh Bermuda fish or boneless quail stuffed with goose liver and truffles while listening to the gently lapping waters of the bay.

Attractions

The top of the tower at the Cathedral of the Most Holy Trinity—the seat of the island's Anglican Church—is once more accessible to tourists. Don't let the 150-or-so-step climb deter you; the view of Hamilton's skyline is one of Bermuda's best.

Construction of Bermuda's newest attraction—the Bermuda Underwater Exploration Institute—began last year, and the state-of-the-art medley of visitor-participant exhibits is set to open to the public in February 1997. On the outskirts of Hamilton, the 12,000-square-foot complex will be devoted to a range of interactive displays on various aspects of the ocean. Visitors will be able to board a submarine simulator; take a mock dive; watch real, underwater expeditions; and view the institute's collections of shipwreck artifacts, shells, and other sea-related objects via video camera. Internationally renowned scientists and explorers will make guest appearances at different times throughout the year.

The Bermuda Society of Arts has opened an additional outlet for its artists' wares. The Harbour Gallery, on Pitt's Bay Road (also known as Front Street East), is the island's newest gallery. With original works by local artists as well as less expensive prints, it's open Monday through Friday from 9 to 4 and weekends from 1 to 4.

The Bermuda Triangle Brewery, which opened in 1995, makes three varieties of beer—Wilde Hogge, Spinnaker, and Full Moon draft—available at many locations throughout the island. No brewery tours are available, but look for the beer.

How to Use This Guide

Organization

Up front is the **Gold Guide,** comprising two sections on gold paper that are chock-full of information about traveling within your destination and traveling in general. Both are in alphabetical order by topic. **Important Contacts A to Z** gives addresses and telephone numbers of organizations and companies that offer destination-related services and detailed information or publications. Here's where you'll find information about how to get to Bermuda from wherever you are. **Smart Travel Tips A to Z,** the Gold Guide's second section, gives specific tips on how to get the most out of your travels, as well as information on how to accomplish what you need to in Bermuda.

At the end of the book you'll find Portraits, wonderful essays about Bermuda's hidden landscapes and its historic Railway Trail, as well as an essay by William Zuill—a native Bermudian who was a member of the Bermuda House Assembly—on Bermuda's role in the American War of Independence. These are followed by suggestions for pretrip reading, both fiction and nonfiction.

Stars

Stars in the margin are used to denote highly recommended sights, attractions, hotels, and restaurants.

Restaurant and Hotel Criteria

Restaurants and lodging places are chosen with a view to giving you the cream of the crop in each location and in each price range.

Hotel Facilities

Note that in general you incur charges when you use many hotel facilities. We wanted to let you know what facilities a hotel has to offer, but we don't always specify whether or not there's a charge, so when planning a vacation that entails a stay of several days, it's wise to ask what's included in the rate.

Hotel Meal Plans

Assume that hotels operate on the **European Plan** (EP, with no meals) unless we note that they use the **American Plan** (AP, with all meals), the **Modified American Plan** (MAP, with breakfast and dinner daily), or the **Continental Plan** (CP, with a Continental breakfast daily).

Dress Codes in Restaurants

Look for an overview in the introduction to Chapter 7, Dining. In general, we note a dress code only when men are required to wear a jacket or a jacket and tie.

Credit Cards

The following abbreviations are used: **AE,** American Express; **DC,** Diners Club; **MC,** MasterCard; and **V,** Visa. Discover is not accepted outside the United States.

Please Write to Us

Everyone who has contributed to Fodor's *Bermuda '96* has worked hard to make the text accurate. All prices and opening times are based on information supplied to us at press time, and Fodor's cannot accept responsibility for any errors that may have occurred. The passage of time will bring changes, so it's always a good idea to call ahead and confirm information when it matters—particularly if you're making a detour to visit specific sights or attractions. When making reservations at a hotel or inn, be sure to speak up if you have a disability or are traveling with children, if you prefer a private bath or a certain type of bed, or if you have specific dietary needs or any other concerns.

Were the restaurants we recommended as described? Did our hotel picks exceed your expectations? Did you find a museum we recommended a waste of time? We would love your feedback, positive and negative. If you have complaints, we'll look into them and revise our entries when the facts warrant it. If you've happened upon a special place that we haven't included, we'll pass the information along to the writers so they can check it out. So please send us a letter or postcard (we're at 201 East 50th Street, New York, New York 10022.) We'll look forward to hearing from you. And in the meantime, have a wonderful trip!

Karen Cure

Karen Cure
Editorial Director

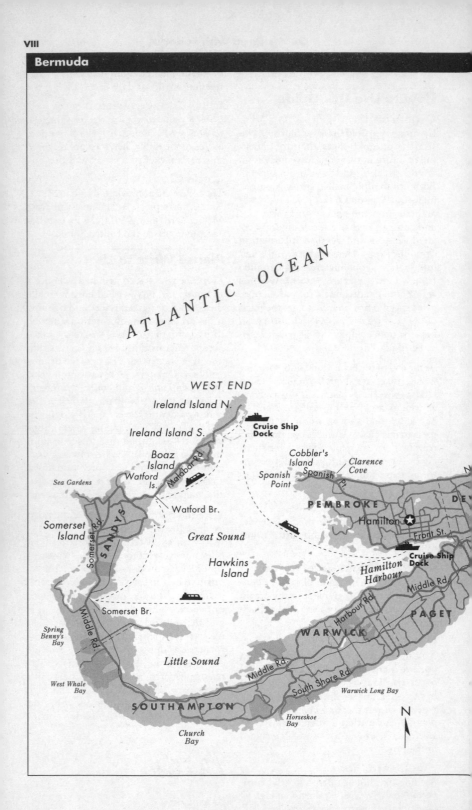

ATLANTIC OCEAN

WEST END

Ireland Island N.

Cruise Ship Dock

Ireland Island S.

Boaz Island

Watford Is.

Cobbler's Island

Clarence Cove

Spanish Point

Spanish Pt.

Sea Gardens

Maldbar Rd.

PEMBROKE

DE

Hamilton

Somerset Island

Somerset Rd.

SANDYS

Watford Br.

Great Sound

Hawkins Island

Front St.

Cruise Ship Dock

Hamilton Harbour

Middle Rd.

PAGET

Spring Benny's Bay

Middle Rd.

Somerset Br.

Little Sound

Harbour Rd.

WARWICK

West Whale Bay

Middle Rd.

South Shore Rd.

Warwick Long Bay

SOUTHAMPTON

Church Bay

Horseshoe Bay

N

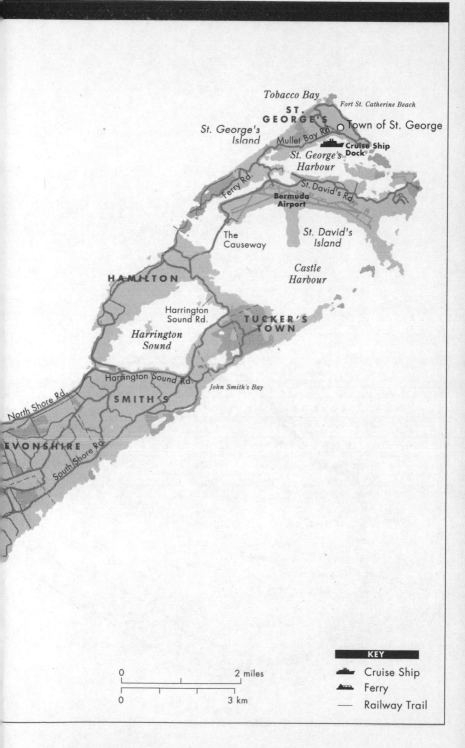

Tobacco Bay

Fort St. Catherine Beach

ST. GEORGE'S

St. George's Island

Mullet Bay Rd.

○ Town of St. George

Cruise Ship Dock

St. George's Harbour

Ferry Rd.

St. David's Rd.

Bermuda Airport

St. David's Island

The Causeway

Castle Harbour

HAMILTON

Harrington Sound Rd.

TUCKER'S TOWN

Harrington Sound

Harrington Sound Rd.

John Smith's Bay

North Shore Rd.

SMITH'S

DEVONSHIRE

South Shore Rd.

0   2 miles

0   3 km

KEY

⛴ Cruise Ship

⛴ Ferry

— Railway Trail

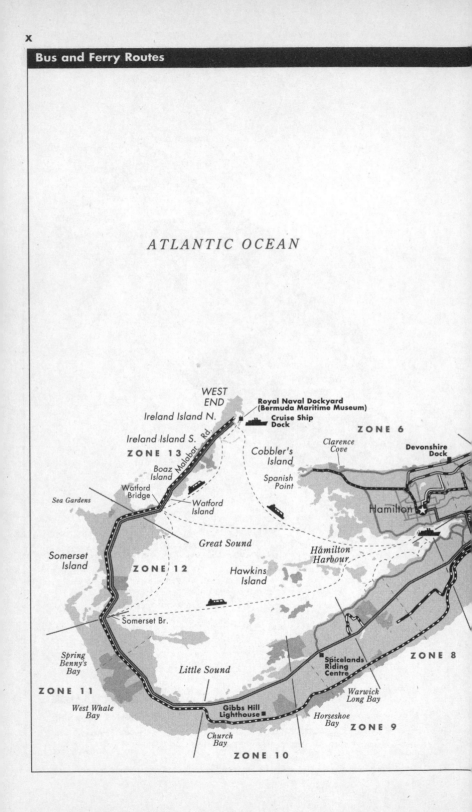

ATLANTIC OCEAN

WEST
END
Ireland Island N.

Royal Naval Dockyard
(Bermuda Maritime Museum)
Cruise Ship
Dock

ZONE 6

*Clarence
Cove*

Devonshire
Dock

Ireland Island S.

ZONE 13

Cobbler's
Island

*Boaz
Island*

*Spanish
Point*

Watford
Bridge

Watford
Island

Hamilton

Sea Gardens

Great Sound

*Hamilton
Harbour*

*Somerset
Island*

ZONE 12

*Hawkins
Island*

Somerset Br.

*Spring
Benny's
Bay*

Little Sound

Spicelands
Riding
Centre

ZONE 8

ZONE 11

*West Whale
Bay*

Gibbs Hill
Lighthouse ■

*Warwick
Long Bay*

*Horseshoe
Bay*

ZONE 9

*Church
Bay*

ZONE 10

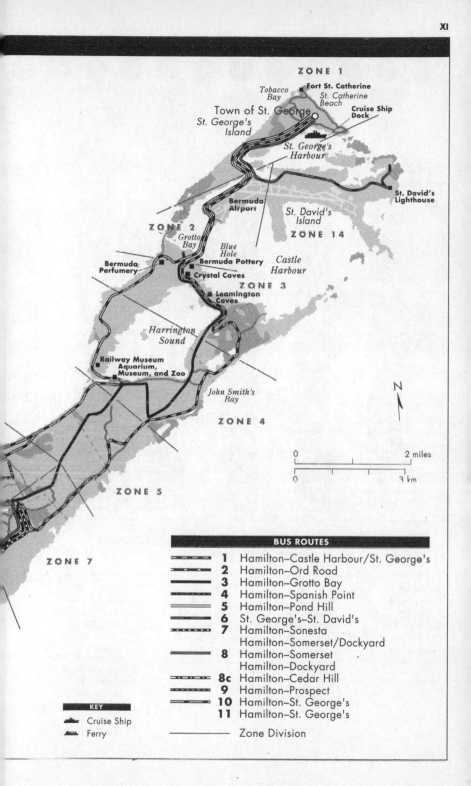

ZONE 1

Tobacco Bay

Fort St. Catherine
St. Catherine Beach
Cruise Ship Dock

Town of St. George
St. George's Island

St. George's Harbour

St. David's Lighthouse

Bermuda Airport

St. David's Island

ZONE 14

ZONE 2

Grotto Bay

Blue Hole

Bermuda Pottery

Castle Harbour

Bermuda Perfumery

Crystal Caves

ZONE 3

Leamington Caves

Harrington Sound

Railway Museum
Aquarium, Museum, and Zoo

John Smith's Bay

ZONE 4

N

| 0 | | 2 miles |
| 0 | | 3 km |

ZONE 5

ZONE 7

BUS ROUTES		
	1	Hamilton–Castle Harbour/St. George's
	2	Hamilton–Ord Road
	3	Hamilton–Grotto Bay
	4	Hamilton–Spanish Point
	5	Hamilton–Pond Hill
	6	St. George's–St. David's
	7	Hamilton–Sonesta
		Hamilton–Somerset/Dockyard
	8	Hamilton–Somerset
		Hamilton–Dockyard
	8c	Hamilton–Cedar Hill
	9	Hamilton–Prospect
	10	Hamilton–St. George's
	11	Hamilton–St. George's
		Zone Division

KEY	
	Cruise Ship
	Ferry

World Time Zones

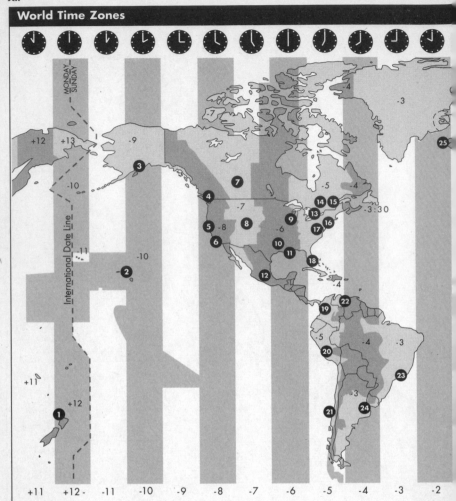

Numbers below vertical bands relate each zone to Greenwich Mean Time (0 hrs.).
Local times frequently differ from these general indications,
as indicated by light-face numbers on map.

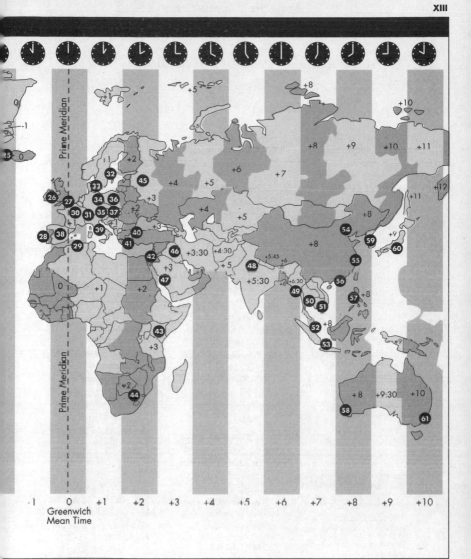

THE GOLD GUIDE / IMPORTANT CONTACTS

IMPORTANT CONTACTS A TO Z

An Alphabetical Listing of Publications, Organizations, and Companies That Will Help You Before, During, and After Your Trip

No single travel resource can give you every detail about every topic that might interest or concern you at the various stages of your journey—when you're planning your trip, while you're on the road, and after you get back home. The following organizations, books, and brochures will supplement the information in Fodor's *Bermuda '96*. For related information, including both basic tips on visiting Bermuda and background information on many of the topics below, study Smart Travel Tips A to Z, the section that follows Important Contacts A to Z.

A

AIR TRAVEL

The major gateway to Bermuda is the **Civil Air Terminal** (Kindley Field Rd., St. George's, ☎ 441/293–1640, FAX 441/293–2417), on the east end of the island, approximately 9 miles from Hamilton and 17 miles from Somerset. Flying time from New York, Boston, Raleigh/Durham, and Baltimore is about 2 hours; from Atlanta, 2¾ hours; from Toronto, 3 hours; and from London, 7 hours.

CARRIERS

Carriers serving Bermuda include **Ameri-can Airlines** (☎ 441/293–1420 or 800/433–7300) from New York and Raleigh/Durham; **Continental** (☎ 441/293–3092 or 800/231–0856) from Newark; **Delta Airlines** (☎ 441/293–2000 or 800/241–4141) from Boston and Atlanta; **USAir** (☎ 800/428–4322 in U.S., 800/423–7714 in Bermuda) from Baltimore, Charlotte, Boston (in summer only), Philadelphia, and New York; and **Air Canada** (☎ 441/293–2121 or 800/776–3000) from Toronto and Halifax, with connections throughout Canada.

Only **British Airways** (☎ 0171/897–4000 or 0345/222111 outside London) flies direct to Bermuda from the United Kingdom, with two to three flights a week from Gatwick.

COMPLAINTS

To register complaints about charter and scheduled airlines, contact the U.S. Department of Transportation's **Office of Consumer Affairs** (400 7th St. NW, Washington, DC 20590, ☎ 202/366–2220 or 800/322–7873).

CONSOLIDATORS

Established consolidators selling to the public include **TFI Tours International** (34 W. 32nd St., New York, NY 10001, ☎ 212/736–1140 or 800/745–8000). **FLY-ASAP** (3824 E. Indian School Rd., Phoenix, AZ 85018, ☎ 800/359–2727) isn't a discounter, but gets good deals from among published fares as well as discount tickets from consolidators.

PUBLICATIONS

For general information about charter carriers, ask for the Office of Consumer Affairs' brochure **"Plane Talk: Public Charter Flights."** The Department of Transportation also publishes a 58-page booklet, **"Fly Rights"** (Consumer Information Center, Dept. 133-B, Pueblo, CO 81009; $1.75).

For other tips and hints, consult the Consumers Union's monthly **"Consumer Reports Travel Letter"** (Box 53629, Boulder CO 80322, ☎ 800/234–1970; $39 a year) and the newsletter **"Travel Smart"** (40 Beechdale Rd., Dobbs Ferry, NY 10522, ☎ 800/327–3633; $37 a year;); *The Official Frequent Flyer Guidebook,* by Randy Petersen (4715-C Town Center Dr., Colorado Springs, CO 80916, ☎ 719/597–8899 or 800/487–8893; $14.99 plus $3 shipping); *Airfare Secrets Exposed,* by Sharon Tyler and Matthew Wonder

(Universal Information Publishing; $16.95 plus $3.75 shipping from Sandcastle Publishing, Box 3070-A, South Pasadena, CA 91031, ☎ 213/255–3616 or 800/655–0053); and **202 Tips Even the Best Business Travelers May Not Know,** by Christopher McGinnis (Irwin Professional Publishing, 1333 Burr Ridge Pkwy., Burr Ridge, IL 60521, ☎ 800/634–3966; $10 plus $3 shipping).

AIRPORT
TRANSFERS

Taxis are readily available at the airport. The approximate fare, not including tip, to Hamilton is $17; to St. George's, $9; to south shore hotels, $25; and to the West End, $33. A surcharge of 25¢ is added for each piece of luggage stored in the trunk or on the roof. Between 10 PM and 6 AM and on Sundays and public holidays fares are 25% higher. Depending on traffic, the driving time to Hamilton is about 30 minutes; it's about one hour to the West End.

Bermuda Hosts Ltd. (☎ 441/293–1334, FAX 441/293–1335) offers round-trip transportation to hotels and guest houses aboard air-conditioned six- and 18-seat vans. Reservations are recommended. One-way fares, based on zones, are as follows: Zone 1 (to Grotto Bay Beach Hotel), $5; Zone 2 (to the Flatts Village area), $7; Zone 3 (to Cobb's Hill Road), $9; Zone 4 (to Church Rd.), $11; and

Zone 5 (westward to Dockyard), $13.

B
BETTER BUSINESS
BUREAU

For local contacts in the home town of a tour operator you may be considering, consult the **Council of Better Business Bureaus** (4200 Wilson Blvd., Arlington, VA 22203, ☎ 703/276–0100).

BICYCLING

Push bikes, as Bermudians call bicycles, are a pleasant way to travel around the island, if you don't mind hilly terrain (see Chapter 6, Sports and Fitness). Bikes can be rented at **Eve's Cycle Livery** (Middle Rd., Paget, ☎ 441/236–6247), **Oleander Cycles** (Valley Rd., Paget, ☎ 441/236–5235; Gorham Rd., Hamilton, ☎ 441/295–0919; and Middle Rd., Southampton, ☎ 441/234–0629); and **Georgiana Cycles** (Cambridge Rd., Somerset, ☎ 441/234–2404). Rentals cost $10–$15 for the first day and $5–10 for each subsequent day.

BUS TRAVEL

Hamilton buses arrive and depart from the **Central Bus Terminal** (Washington and Church Sts., Hamilton, ☎ 441/292–3854 or 441/295–4311), a small kiosk that is open Monday–Friday 7:15–5:30, Saturday 8–5:30, and Sunday 9:15–4:45 and is the only place to buy money-saving tokens.

In the West End, **Sandys Taxi Service**

(☎ 441/234–2344) has taxi service to all points on the island between 8 AM and 11 PM. It also operates a minibus between Somerset Bridge and the Royal Naval Dockyard between 8:30 and 4:30 Tuesday through Friday, 10 to 1:00 weekends, and 8:30 to 1:00 Mondays. The minibus fare depends upon the destination, but it's never more than $3 ($1 for senior citizens). Minibuses will pick you up anywhere on the island if you summon them by phone, though you can also flag them down from the road; they will take you wherever you want to go along their routes. They operate daily 8:30–5 from April 1–October 31; call for service at other times.

C
CAR RENTAL

Cars cannot be rented in Bermuda. A popular alternative is to rent mopeds or scooters (see Mopeds and Scooters, below), which are better for negotiating the island's narrow roads and sand dunes.

CHILDREN
AND TRAVEL

FLYING

Look into **"Flying with Baby"** (Third Street Press, Box 261250, Littleton, CO 80126, ☎ 303/595–5959; $5.95 plus $1 shipping), cowritten by a flight attendant. **"Kids and Teens in Flight,"** free from the U.S. Department of Transportation's Office of

Consumer Affairs, offers tips for children flying alone. Every two years the February issue of *Family Travel Times* (*see* Know-How, *below*) details children's services on three dozen airlines.

KNOW-HOW

Family Travel Times, published 10 times a year by Travel with Your Children (TWYCH, 45 W. 18th St., New York, NY 10011, ☎ 212/206–0688; annual subscription $55), covers destinations, types of vacations, and modes of travel. Travel with Your Children also publishes Cruising with Children ($22).

The *Family Travel Guides* catalogue (Carousel Press, Box 6061, Albany, CA 94706, ☎ 510/527–5849; $1 postage) lists about 200 books and articles on family travel. *Traveling with Children—And Enjoying It,* by Arlene K. Butler (Globe Pequot Press, Box 833, 6 Business Park Rd., Old Saybrook, CT 06475, ☎ 203/395–0440 or 800/243–0495, 800/962–0973 in CT; $11.95 plus $3 shipping) helps plan your trip with children, from toddlers to teens. Globe Pequot also publishes *Recommended Family Resorts in the United States, Canada, and the Caribbean,* by Jane Wilford with Janet Tice ($12.95), and *Recommended Family Inns of America* ($12.95). Also check *Take Your Baby and Go! A Guide for Traveling with Babies,*

Toddlers and Young Children, by Sheri Andrews, Judy Bordeaux, and Vivian Vasquez (Bear Creek Publications, 2507 Minor Ave., Seattle, WA 98102, ☎ 206/322–7604 or 800/326–6566; $5.95 plus $1.50 shipping).

Weeklong cruises to Bermuda leave from New York, Boston, and other east coast U.S. ports. For a complete rundown on the ships, *see* Cruising in Bermuda, Chapter 2.

U.S. CITIZENS

The **U.S. Customs Service** (Box 7407, Washington, DC 20044, ☎ 202/927–6724) can answer questions on duty-free limits and publishes a helpful brochure, "Know Before You Go." For information on registering foreign-made articles, call 202/927–0540.

CANADIANS

Contact **Revenue Canada** (2265 St. Laurent Blvd. S, Ottawa, Ontario, K1G 4K3, ☎ 613/993–0534) for a copy of the free brochure **"I Declare/ Je Déclare"** and for details on duties that exceed the standard duty-free limit.

U.K. CITIZENS

HM Customs and Excise (Dorset House, Stamford St., London SE1 9NG, ☎ 0171/202–4227) can answer questions about U.K. customs regulations and publishes **"A Guide for Travellers,"** detailing

standard procedures and import rules.

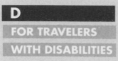

COMPLAINTS

To register complaints under the provisions of the Americans with Disabilities Act, contact the U.S. Department of Justice's **Public Access Section** (Box 66738, Washington, DC 20035, ☎ 202/514–0301, FAX 202/307–1198, TTY 202/514–0383).

LOCAL INFO

The Bermuda Chapter of the **Society for the Advancement of Travel for the Handicapped** (SATH, 347 5th Ave., Suite 610, New York, NY 10016, ☎ 212/447–7284) publishes the *Access Guide to Bermuda for the Handicapped Traveler.* You can also send away for the free guide by writing to Kitson & Company, Ltd. (Box HM 449, Hamilton HM BX, Bermuda, ☎ 441/295–2525, FAX 441/295–5682) or any Bermuda Department of Tourism office.

Public buses in Bermuda are not equipped for wheelchairs; however, the **Bermuda Physically Handicapped Association** (BPHA) has a volunteer-operated bus with a hydraulic lift. Arrangements for its use must be made in advance by contacting Mr. Willard Fox, (BPHA, Box HM 08, Hamilton HM AX, ☎ 441/292–5025) or Mr. Keith Simmons (☎ 441/295–7376).

LODGING

Those in search of a vacation apartment suitable for a traveler with a disability should contact **Mrs. Ianthia Wade** ("Summer Haven," Box HS 30, Harrington Sound HS BX, ☎ 441/293–2099). Mrs. Wade can also assist with sightseeing arrangements.

ORGANIZATIONS

FOR TRAVELERS WITH HEARING IMPAIRMENTS➤ Contact the **American Academy of Otolaryngology** (1 Prince St., Alexandria, VA 22314, ☎ 703/836–4444, FAX 703/683–5100, TTY 703/519–1585).

FOR TRAVELERS WITH MOBILITY PROBLEMS➤ Contact the **Information Center for Individuals with Disabilities** (Fort Point Pl., 27–43 Wormwood St., Boston, MA 02210, ☎ 617/727–5540, 800/462–5015 in MA, TTY 617/345–9743); **Mobility International USA** (Box 10767, Eugene, OR 97440, ☎ and TTY 503/343–1284, FAX 503/343–6812), the U.S. branch of an international organization based in Belgium (*see below*) with affiliates in 30 countries; **MossRehab Hospital Travel Information Service** (1200 W. Tabor Rd., Philadelphia, PA 19141, ☎ 215/456–9603, TTY 215/456–9602); the **Society for the Advancement of Travel for the Handicapped** (347 5th Ave., Suite 610, New York, NY 10016, ☎ 212/447–7284, FAX 212/725–8253); the **Travel Industry and Disabled Exchange**

(TIDE, 5435 Donna Ave., Tarzana, CA 91356, ☎ 818/344–3640, FAX 818/344–0078); and **Travelin' Talk** (Box 3534, Clarksville, TN 37043, ☎ 615/552–6670, FAX 615/552–1182).

FOR TRAVELERS WITH VISION IMPAIRMENTS➤ Contact the **American Council of the Blind** (1155 15th St. NW, Suite 720, Washington, DC 20005, ☎ 202/467–5081, FAX 202/467–5085) or the **American Foundation for the Blind** (15 W. 16th St., New York, NY 10011, ☎ 212/620–2000, TTY 212/620–2158).

PUBLICATIONS

Several free publications are available from the U.S. Information Center (Box 100, Pueblo, CO 81009, ☎ 719/948–3334): **"New Horizons for the Air Traveler with a Disability"** (address to Dept. 355A), describing legally mandated changes; the pocket-size **"Fly Smart"** (Dept. 575B), good on flight safety; and the Airport Operators Council's worldwide **"Access Travel: Airports"** (Dept. 575A).

The 500-page *Travelin' Talk Directory* (Box 3534, Clarksville, TN 37043, ☎ 615/552–6670; $35) lists people and organizations who help travelers with disabilities. For specialist travel agents worldwide, consult the *Directory of Travel Agencies for the Disabled* by Helen Hecker (Twin Peaks Press, Disability Bookshop, Box 129, Vancouver,

WA 98666, ☎ 206/694–2462 or 800/637–2256; $19.95 plus $3.50 shipping and handling).

TRAVEL AGENCIES AND TOUR OPERATORS

The Americans with Disabilities Act requires that travel firms serve the needs of all travelers. However, some agencies and operators specialize in making group and individual arrangements for travelers with disabilities, among them **Access Adventures** (206 Chestnut Ridge Rd., Rochester, NY 14624, ☎ 716/889–9096), run by a former physical-rehab counselor; and **Travel Trends** (2 Allan Plaza, 4922–51 Ave., Box 3581, Leduc, Alberta, Canada, T9E 6X2, ☎ 403/986–9000 or 800/661–2109 in Canada), which has group tours and is especially good for cruises. In addition, many general-interest operators and agencies (*see* Tour Operators, *below*) can also arrange vacations for travelers with disabilities.

FOR TRAVELERS WITH MOBILITY PROBLEMS➤ A number of operators specialize in working with travelers with mobility impairments: **Accessible Journeys** (35 W. Sellers Ave., Ridley Park, PA 19078, ☎ 610/521–0339 or 800/846–4537, FAX 610/521–6959), a registered nursing service that arranges vacations; **Hinsdale Travel Service** (201 E. Ogden Ave., Suite 100, Hinsdale, IL

THE GOLD GUIDE / IMPORTANT CONTACTS

60521, ☎ 708/325–1335 or 800/303–5521), a travel agency that will give you access to the services of wheelchair traveler Janice Perkins; and **Wheelchair Journeys** (16979 Redmond Way, Redmond, WA 98052, ☎ 206/885–2210), which can handle arrangements worldwide.

FOR TRAVELERS WITH DEVELOPMENTAL DISABILITIES➤ Contact the nonprofit **New Directions** (5276 Hollister Ave., Suite 207, Santa Barbara, CA 93111, ☎ 805/967–2841) as well as the general-interest operations above.

IN THE U.K.

Contact the **Royal Association for Disability and Rehabilitation** (RADAR, 12 City Forum, 250 City Rd., London EC1V 8AF, ☎ 0171/250–3222) or **Mobility International** (Rue de Manchester 25, B–1070 Brussels, Belgium, ☎ 00–322–410–6297), an international clearinghouse of travel information for people with disabilities.

DISCOUNT CLUBS

Options include **Entertainment Travel Editions** (Box 1068, Trumbull, CT 06611, ☎ 800/445–4137; fee $28–$53 annually, depending on destination); **Great American Traveler** (Box 27965, Salt Lake City, UT 84127, ☎ 800/548–2812; $49.95 annually); **Moment's Notice Discount Travel Club** (163 Amsterdam Ave., Suite 137, New York, NY 10023, ☎ 212/486–

0500; $25 annually, single or family); **Privilege Card** (3391 Peachtree Rd. NE, Suite 110, Atlanta GA 30326, ☎ 404/262–0222 or 800/236-9732; $74.95 annually); **Travelers Advantage** (CUC Travel Service, 49 Music Sq. W, Nashville, TN 37203, ☎ 800/548–1116 or 800/648–4037; $49 annually, single or family); and **Worldwide Discount Travel Club** (1674 Meridian Ave., Miami Beach, FL 33139, ☎ 305/534–2082; $50 annually for family, $40 single).

E

EMERGENCIES

Police, fire, or ambulance (☎ 911). **Air/Sea Rescue** (☎ 441/297–1010). The Government Emergency Broadcast Station is FM 100.1 MHz.

DOCTORS AND DENTISTS

Contact the hospital or the **Government Health Clinic** (67 Victoria St., Hamilton, ☎ 441/236–0224 or 441/236–3095) for referrals.

HOSPITALS

The **King Edward VII Memorial Hospital** (7 Point Finger Rd., outside Hamilton near the Botanical Gardens, ☎ 441/236–2345) is open 24 hours.

PHARMACIES

Bermuda Pharmacy (near Bus Depot, Church St., Hamilton, ☎ 441/295–5375 or 441/296–8515; open Mon.–Sat. 8–6); **Clarendon Pharmacy** (Clarendon Building,

Bermudiana Rd., Hamilton, ☎ 441/295–9137 or 441/295–6144; open Mon.–Sat. 8–6); **Collector's Hill Apothecary** (South Shore Rd. and Collector's Hill, Smith's, ☎ 441/236-8664 or 441/236–9878; open Mon.–Sat. 8–8, Sun. 2–9, closed holidays); **Hamilton Pharmacy** (Church and Parliament Sts., Hamilton, ☎ 441/295–7004 or 441/292–7986; open Mon.–Sat. 8–9); **Paget Pharmacy** (Rural Hill Plaza, Middle Rd., Paget, ☎ 441/236–2681 or 441/236–7275; open Mon.–Sat 8–8, 2–6 Sun., closed holidays); **Phoenix Centre** (3 Reid St., Hamilton, ☎ 441/295–3838 or 441/295–0698; open Mon.–Sat. 8–6, Sun. and holidays noon–6:30, closed Christmas Day); **Phoenix Store at Marriott's Castle Harbour** (Paynter's Rd., Tucker's Town, ☎ 441/293–8119; open Mon.–Sat. 9–1, Sun. and holidays, 6–8:30); **Robertson's Drug Store** (cnr. York St. and Customs House Sq., ☎ 441/297–1736 or 441/297–1828; open Mon.–Sat. 8–7:30, Sun. 4–6); **Woodbourne Chemist** (Woodbourne Ave., Pembroke—on the outskirts of Hamilton— ☎ 441/295–1073 or 441/295–2663; open Mon.–Sat. 8–8).

G

GAMES

The gamemeister, Milton Bradley, has games to help keep little (and not so little) children from getting fidgety while riding in planes, trains, and automobiles. Try packing the Travel

Battleship sea battle game ($7), Travel Connect Four, a vertical strategy game ($8), the Travel Yahtzee dice game ($6), the Travel Trouble dice and board game ($7), and the Travel Guess Who mystery game ($8).

GAY AND LESBIAN TRAVEL

ORGANIZATIONS

The **International Gay Travel Association** (Box 4974, Key West, FL 33041, ☎ 800/448–8550), a consortium of 800 businesses, can supply names of travel agents and tour operators.

PUBLICATIONS

The premier international travel magazine for gays and lesbians is *Our World* (1104 N. Nova Rd., Suite 251, Daytona Beach, FL 32117, ☎ 904/441–5367; $35 for 10 issues). The 16-page monthly *"Out & About"* (☎ 212/645–6922 or 800/929–2268; $49 for 10 issues), covers gay-friendly resorts, hotels, cruise lines, and airlines.

TOUR OPERATORS

Cruises and resort vacations are handled by **RSVP Travel Productions** (2800 University Ave. SE, Minneapolis, MN 55414, ☎ 800/328–7787) for gay travelers and **Olivia** (4400 Market St., Oakland, CA 94608, ☎ 800/631–6277) for lesbian travelers. For mixed gay and lesbian travel, contact **Atlantis Events** (8335 Sunset Blvd., West Hollywood, CA 90069, ☎ 800/

628–5268. **Toto Tours** (1326 W. Albion, Suite 3W, Chicago, IL 60626, ☎ 312/274–8686 or 800/565–1241) has group tours worldwide.

TRAVEL AGENCIES

The largest agencies serving gay travelers are **Advance Travel** (10700 Northwest Freeway, Suite 160, Houston, TX 77092, ☎ 713/682–2002 or 800/695–0880); **Islanders/Kennedy Travel** (183 W. 10th St., New York, NY 10014, ☎ 212/242–3222 or 800/988–1181); **Now Voyager** (4406 18th St., San Francisco, CA 94114, ☎ 415/626–1169 or 800/255–6951); and **Yellowbrick Road** (1500 W. Balmoral Ave., Chicago, IL 60640, ☎ 312/561–1800 or 800/642–2488). **Skylink Women's Travel** (746 Ashland Ave., Santa Monica, CA 90405, ☎ 310/452–0506 or 800/225-5759) serves lesbian travelers.

H

HEALTH ISSUES

MEDICAL-ASSISTANCE COMPANIES

Contact **International SOS Assistance** (Box 11568, Philadelphia, PA 19116, ☎ 215/244–1500 or 800/523–8930; Box 466, Pl. Bonaventure, Montréal, Québec H5A 1C1, ☎ 514/874–7674 or 800/363–0263); **Medex Assistance Corporation** (Box 10623, Baltimore, MD 21285, ☎ 410/296–2530 or 800/573-2029), **Near Travel Services** (Box 1339, Calumet City, IL 60409, ☎ 708/868–

6700 or 800/654–6700); and **Travel Assistance International** (1133 15th St. NW, Suite 400, Washington, DC 20005, ☎ 202/331–1609 or 800/821–2828). Because these companies also sell death-and-dismemberment, trip-cancellation, and other insurance coverage, there is some overlap with the travel-insurance policies sold by the companies listed under Insurance, *below*.

HELICOPTER TOURS

Bermuda Helicopters Limited (Box 109, Southampton SN BX, ☎ 441/293–4800 or, after hours, 441/238–0551; FAX 441/295–2539) provides up to four passengers with tours of the dramatic southern coast, surrounding reefs, and the island itself. The rides last approximately 20 minutes and cost $75 per passenger. To rent the helicopter by the hour is $950.

I

INSURANCE

Travel insurance covering baggage, health, and trip cancellation or interruptions is available from **Access America** (Box 90315, Richmond, VA 23286, ☎ 804/285–3300 or 800/284–8300); **Carefree Travel Insurance** (Box 9366, 100 Garden City Plaza, Garden City, NY 11530, ☎ 516/294–0220 or 800/323–3149); **Near Travel Services** (*see* Medical-Assistance Companies, *above*); **Tele-Trip** (Mutual of Omaha Plaza, Box

THE GOLD GUIDE / IMPORTANT CONTACTS

31716, Omaha, NE 68131, ☎ 800/228–9792); **Travel Insured International** (Box 280568, East Hartford, CT 06128, ☎ 203/528–7663 or 800/243–3174); **Travel Guard International** (1145 Clark St., Stevens Point, WI 54481, ☎ 715/345–0505 or 800/826–1300); and **Wallach & Company** (107 W. Federal St., Box 480, Middleburg, VA 22117, ☎ 703/687–3166 or 800/237–6615).

IN THE U.K.

The **Association of British Insurers** (51 Gresham St., London EC2V 7HQ, ☎ 0171/600–3333; 30 Gordon St., Glasgow G1 3PU, ☎ 0141/226–3905; Scottish Provident Bldg., Donegall Sq. W, Belfast BT1 6JE, ☎ 01232/249176; and other locations) gives advice by phone and publishes the free **"Holiday Insurance,"** which sets out typical policy provisions and costs.

L
LODGING

APARTMENT AND VILLA RENTAL

Among the companies to contact are **At Home Abroad** (405 E. 56th St., Suite 6H, New York, NY 10022, ☎ 212/421–9165); **Property Rentals International** (1008 Mansfield Crossing Rd., Richmond, VA 23236, ☎ 804/378–6054 or 800/220–3332); **Rent-a-Home International** (7200 34th Ave. NW, Seattle, WA 98117, ☎ 206/789–9377 or 800/488–7368); **Vacation Home Rentals Worldwide** (235 Kensington Ave., Norwood, NJ 07648, ☎ 201/767–9393 or 800/633–3284); **Villas and Apartments Abroad** (420 Madison Ave., Suite 1105, New York, NY 10017, ☎ 212/759–1025 or 800/433–3020); and **Villas International** (605 Market St., Suite 510, San Francisco, CA 94105, ☎ 415/281–0910 or 800/221–2260). Members of the travel club **Hideaways International** (767 Islington St., Portsmouth, NH 03801, ☎ 603/430–4433 or 800/843–4433; $99 annually) receive two annual guides plus quarterly newsletters, and arrange rentals among themselves.

HOME EXCHANGE

Principal clearinghouses include **HomeLink International/Vacation Exchange Club** (Box 650, Key West, FL 33041, ☎ 305/294–1448 or 800/638–3841; $60 annually), which gives members four annual directories, with a listing in one, plus updates; and **Loan-a-Home** (2 Park La., Apt. 6E, Mount Vernon, NY 10552, ☎ 914/664–7640; $35–$45 annually), which specializes in long-term exchanges.

M
MAPS

For a copy of the *Bermuda Islands Guide,* an atlas of every road, alley, lane, and landmark on the island, contact the **Bermuda Book Store** (Queen and Front Sts., Hamilton, ☎ 441/295–3698) or most bookshops island-wide; it's well worth the $4.95 price tag.

MONEY MATTERS
ATMS

For specific foreign **Cirrus** locations, call 800/424–7787; for foreign Plus locations, consult the **Plus** directory at your local bank.

WIRING FUNDS

Funds can be wired via **American Express MoneyGram℠** (☎ 800/926–9400 from the United States and Canada for locations and information) or **Western Union** (☎ 800/325–6000 for agent locations or to send using MasterCard or Visa, 800/321–2923 in Canada).

MOPED AND SCOOTER RENTAL

Recommended liveries are **Oleander Cycles** (Valley Rd., Paget, ☎ 441/236–5235, Gorham Rd., Hamilton, ☎ 441/295–0919 and Middle Rd., Southampton, ☎ 441/ 234–0629); **Eve's Cycle Livery** (Middle Rd., Paget, ☎ 441/236–6247); **Devil's Hole Cycles** (Harrington Sound Rd., Smith's, ☎ 441/293–1280); and **St. George's Cycles** (Water St., St. George's, ☎ 441/297–1463).

P
PASSPORTS AND VISAS

U.S. CITIZENS

For fees, documentation requirements, and other information, call the **Office of Passport Services** information line (☎ 202/647–0518).

CANADIANS

For fees, documentation requirements, and other information, call the Ministry of Foreign Affairs and International Trade's **Passport Office** (☎ 819/994–3500 or 800/567–6868).

U.K. CITIZENS

For fees, documentation requirements, and to get an emergency passport, call the **London Passport Office** (☎ 0171/271–3000).

PHOTO HELP

The **Kodak Information Center** (☎ 800/242–2424) answers consumer questions about film and photography. Pick up the *Kodak Guide to Shooting Great Travel Pictures* (Fodor's, ☎ 800/733–3000; $16.50), which gives you tips on how to take travel pictures like a pro.

S

SENIOR CITIZENS

EDUCATIONAL TRAVEL

The nonprofit **Elderhostel** (75 Federal St., 3rd Floor, Boston, MA 02110, ☎ 617/426–7788), for people 60 and older, has offered inexpensive study programs since 1975. The nearly 2,000 courses cover everything from marine science to Greek myths and cowboy poetry. Fees for two- to three-week international trips—including room, board, and transportation from the United States—range from $1,800 to $4,500.

ORGANIZATIONS

Contact the **American Association of Retired Persons** (AARP, 601 E St. NW, Washington, DC 20049, ☎ 202/434–2277; $8 per person or couple annually). Its Purchase Privilege Program gets members discounts on lodging, car rentals, and sightseeing, and the AARP Motoring Plan furnishes domestic trip-routing information and emergency road-service aid for an annual fee of $39.95 per person or couple ($59.95 for a premium version).

For other discounts on lodgings, car rentals, and other travel products, along with magazines and newsletters, contact the **National Council of Senior Citizens** (1331 F St. NW, Washington, DC 20004, ☎ 202/347–8800; membership $12 annually) or *Mature Outlook* (6001 N. Clark St., Chicago, IL 60660, ☎ 312/465–6466 or 800/336–6330; subscription $9.95 annually).

PUBLICATIONS

The 50+ Traveler's Guidebook: Where to Go, Where to Stay, What to Do, by Anita Williams and Merrimac Dillon (St. Martin's Press, 175 5th Ave., New York, NY 10010, ☎ 212/674–5151 or 800/288–2131; $12.95), offers many useful tips. **"The Mature Traveler"** (Box 50400, Reno, NV 89513, ☎ 702/786–7419; $29.95), a monthly newsletter, covers travel deals.

SIGHTSEEING

BOAT TRIPS

Bermuda Island Cruises (☎ 441/292–8652, FAX 441/292–5193) operates a 130-passenger boat, which leaves Albuoy's Point in Hamilton at 7:30 PM on Tuesday, Wednesday, Friday, and Saturday for a "Pirate Party Cruise." Two-hour tours of Sea Gardens ($30 adults, $15 children, free for children under 5) in glass-bottom boats leave twice daily from the ferry terminal in Hamilton. A 6½-hour island cruise ($60 adults, $30 children under 12) departs from Albouy's Point in Hamilton Monday through Saturday at 10 AM.

The **Submarine** *Enterprise* (☎ 441/234–3547) takes passengers on dives off the West End in a 44-passenger air-conditioned submarine with large viewing windows. The 2½-hour excursion ($65 adults, $32.50 children under 16) includes travel from Dockyard (three hours from the dock in Hamilton) to the submarine and back. Weather conditions must be good; call ahead for reservations and to find out whether the submarine will be operating. The *Enterprise* does not run in January or February.

Bermuda Water Tours (☎ 441/236–1500, FAX 441/292–0801) operates the 65-foot *Ovation* and the 50-foot *Bottom Peeper*, which depart daily on a variety of excursions from the dock next to the Ferry Terminal in Hamilton. A two-hour sightseeing trip in a glass-bottom boat ($30) leaves at 10, 1:30, and 6:15; a three-hour snorkeling excursion ($45) leaves at 1:15 and 3; the three-hour combination snorkeling and glass-bottom sightseeing tour ($45) leaves at 9:20 and 4. A daylong outing ($65) leaves at 9:20, and includes snorkeling, viewing fish through the boat's glass bottom, sightseeing, and time out for lunch and shopping. Three-hour barbecue dinner, glass-bottom-boat sightseeing, and stargazing cruises feature live entertainment and an open bar ($65); they leave at 5 and 6:30. A two-hour, open-bar cocktail cruise ($35) leaves at 6:30.

Butterfield Travel Ltd., Bee-Line Transport, and **Destination Bermuda Ltd.** (*see* Bus Tours, *below*) also arrange boat trips.

BUS AND MINIBUS TOURS

Contact **Bee-Line Transport Ltd.** (Box HM 2270, Hamilton HM, ☎ 441/293–0303, FAX 441/293–8015); **Bermuda Hosts Ltd.** (Box CR 46, Crawl, Hamilton CR, ☎ 441/293–1334, FAX 441/293–1335); **Butterfield Travel** (Box HM 656, Hamilton HM CX, ☎ 441/292–1520, FAX 441/292–1243); **Destination Bermuda Ltd.** (Box HM 1822, Hamilton HM HX, ☎ 441/292–2325, FAX 441/292–2252); and **PenbossMeyer** (Box

HM 510, Hamilton HM CX, ☎ 441/295–9733 or 800/468–3310, FAX 441/292–8251) for three-hour narrated tours of the island ($35 per person) in the big pink buses that are chartered from the Bermuda Government.

HORSE-DRAWN CARRIAGES

Carriages can be hired on Front Street in Hamilton; for special itineraries, contact **Terceira's Stables** (☎ 441/236–3014). Rates for a one- or two-horse carriages for up to four passengers are $20 for the first 30 minutes, and $20 for each additional 30 minutes; an additional $5 is charged for each adult per half-hour when more than five people ride in a carriage.

In spring, the **Garden Club of Bermuda** arranges tours that visit three different houses each Wednesday between 2 and 5. Admission is $10, $5 children. Contact President Garden Club (☎ 441/292–4575).

Free guided tours of the **Botanical Gardens** (441/236–4201) leave at 10:30 AM from the visitor center just inside the Berry Hill Road entrance. These 75-minute tours are conducted April 1 through October 31 on Tuesday, Wednesday, and Friday and November 1 through March 31 on Tuesday and Friday. Tours can be taken at other times by special arrangement with the curator of the gardens on the condition that a

donation be made to the Botanical Society.

SNORKELING

Bermuda Barefoot Cruises (Box DV 525, Devonshire, ☎ 441/236–3498) aboard the 32-foot *Minnow* leave Darrell's Wharf in Warwick. Captain Shirley tours the inshore waterways before ducking into his favorite local snorkeling site in shallow waters off Somerset, where no other charters go.

Bermuda's Multihull Sailing Adventures (☎ 441/234–8149 or 441/234–1434) offers the island's only regularly scheduled sail-snorkel charters. Owned and operated by the experienced Captain Kirk Ward and his wife, Joan, two vessels are available for private or regularly scheduled trips, daily at 10 and 2, April through October.

Hayward's Snorkeling and Glass Bottom Boat Cruises (☎ 441/292–8652 from 9 to 5 or 441/236–9894 after hours, FAX 441/236–2608) offers one of the island's best sightseeing-snorkeling excursions ($45 including instruction and gear) aboard the 54-foot glass-bottom *Explorer*. The cruise departs from the dock adjacent to Hamilton Ferry Terminal. Special excursions are arranged during the spring migration of the humpback whales; call for prices.

Pitman's Snorkeling (☎ 441/234–0700) offers excellent sightseeing-snorkeling excursions with informative ecological lectures aboard the glass-bottom *Fathom*. The $45, four-hour outing, which includes snorkeling instruction and gear, departs every morning (May–October) from the Robinson's Marina dock.

Jessie James Snorkeling & Sightseeing Cruises (☎ 441/236–4804, FAX 441/236–9208) offers half-day snorkeling cruises ($40 adults, $20 children 5–12) aboard its 40-passenger luxury Chris-Craft *Rambler* from Albuoy's Point in Hamilton, Darrell's Wharf and Belmont Hotel dock in Warwick. Cruises depart daily at 9:15 and 2:15

Salt Kettle Boat Rentals Ltd (☎ 441/236–4863, FAX 441/236–2427) offers motorboat snorkeling cruises for $40 per person. The four-hour trips depart Salt Kettle, Paget Monday through Saturday at 9:30 and 1:30. The price includes complimentary rum swizzles, soft drinks, and snorkeling gear.

WALKING TOURS

The **Bermuda Department of Tourism** (☎ 441/292–0023) publishes brochures detailing self-guided tours of Hamilton, St. George's, the West End, and the Railway Trail. **"The Bermuda Nature Guide,"** also issued by the Bermuda Department of Tourism, has details about the island's flora, fauna, and pink coral sand. Available free at all visitor service bureaus and at hotels and guest houses, these

brochures also contain detailed directions for walkers and cyclists and historical notes and anecdotes.

HOSTELING

Contact **Hostelling International–American Youth Hostels** (733 15th St. NW, Suite 840, Washington, DC 20005, ☎ 202/783–6161) in the United States; **Hostelling International–Canada** (205 Catherine St., Suite 400, Ottawa, Ontario K2P 1C3, ☎ 613/237–7884) in Canada; and the **Youth Hostel Association of England and Wales** (Trevelyan House, 8 St. Stephen's Hill, St. Albans, Hertfordshire AL1 2DY, ☎ 01727/855215 and 01727/845047) in the United Kingdom. Membership ($25 in the United States, C$26.75 in Canada, and £9 in the United Kingdom) gets you access to 5,000 hostels worldwide that charge $7–$20 nightly per person.

ID CARDS

To be eligible for discounts on transportation and admissions, get the **International Student Identity Card** (ISIC) if you're a bona fide student or the **International Youth Card** (IYC) if you're under 26. In the United States, the ISIC and IYC cards cost $16 each and include basic travel accident and illness coverage, plus a toll-free travel hot line. Apply through the Council on International Educational Exchange (*see* Organizations, *below*). Cards are avail-

able for $15 each in Canada from **Travel Cuts** (187 College St., Toronto, Ontario M5T 1P7, ☎ 416/979–2406 or 800/667–2887) and in the United Kingdom for £5 each at student unions and student travel companies.

ORGANIZATIONS

A major contact is the **Council on International Educational Exchange** (CIEE, 205 E. 42nd St., 16th Floor, New York, NY 10017, ☎ 212/661–1450) with locations in Boston (729 Boylston St., 02116, ☎ 617/266–1926); Miami (9100 S. Dadeland Blvd., 33156, ☎ 305/670–9261); Los Angeles (1093 Broxton Ave., 90024, ☎ 310/208–3551); 43 other college towns nationwide; and the United Kingdom (28A Poland St., London W1V 3DB, ☎ 0171/437–7767). Twice a year, it publishes *Student Travels* magazine. The CIEE's Council Travel Service is the exclusive U.S. agent for several student-discount cards.

Campus Connections (325 Chestnut St., Suite 1101, Philadelphia, PA 19106, ☎ 215/625–8585 or 800/428–3235) specializes in discounted accommodations and airfares for students. The **Educational Travel Centre** (438 N. Frances St., Madison, WI 53703, ☎ 608/256–5551) offers rail passes and low-cost airline tickets, mostly for flights departing from Chicago.

In Canada, also contact **Travel Cuts** (*see above*).

THE GOLD GUIDE / IMPORTANT CONTACTS

T

TAXIS

For radio-dispatched taxis, contact **Radio Cabs Bermuda** (☎ 441/295–4141) and **Bermuda Taxi Operators** (☎ 441/292–5600).

TOUR OPERATORS

Among the companies selling packages to Bermuda, the following have a proven reputation, are nationally known, and offer plenty of options.

Independent vacation packages are available from major tour operators and airlines. Contact **Adventure Tours** (10612 Beaver Dam Rd., Hunt Valley, MD 21030, ☎ 410/785–5300 or 800/638–9040); **American Airlines Fly AAway Vacations** (☎ 800/321–2121); **Apple Vacations** (in the eastern United States: 7 Campus Blvd., Newton Square, PA 19073, ☎ 215/359–6500 or 800/727–3550; in the western United States: 25 Northwest Point Blvd., Elk Grove Village, IL 708/640–1150 or 800/365–2775); **Certified Vacations** (Box 1525, Ft. Lauderdale, FL 33302, ☎ 305/522–1414 or 800/233–7260); **Delta Dream Vacations** (☎ 800/872–7786); **Friendly Holidays** (1983 Marcus Ave., Lake Success, NY 11042, ☎ 516/338–1200 or 800/221–9748); **Globetrotters** (139 Main St., Cambridge, MA 02142, ☎ 617/621–9911 or 800/999–9696); **GWV International** (300 1st Ave., Needham, MA 02194, ☎ 617/449–5460 or 800/225–5498); **Haley/TNT Tours** (2 Charlesgate W, Boston, MA 02215, ☎ 617/262–0123 or 800/232–5565); and **Travel Impression/Cavalcade** (465 Smith St., Farmingdale, NY 11735, ☎ 516/845–7000 or 800/284–0044).

ORGANIZATIONS

The **National Tour Association** (546 E. Main St., Lexington, KY 40508, ☎ 606/226–4444 or 800/755–8687) and **United States Tour Operators Association** (USTOA, 211 E. 51st St., Suite 12B, New York, NY 10022, ☎ 212/750–7371) can provide lists of member operators and information on booking tours.

PUBLICATIONS

The National Tour Association (*see* Organizations, *above*) publishes **"On Tour,"** which has a current list of member operators. Also get a copy of the **"Worldwide Tour & Vacation Package Finder"** from the USTOA (*see* Organizations, *above*) and the Better Business Bureau's **"Tips on Travel Packages"** (Publication No. 24-195, 4200 Wilson Blvd., Arlington, VA 22203, ☎ 703/276–0100; $2).

THEME TRIPS

GOLF➤ Bermuda's finest courses and resorts can be booked through **ITC Golf Tours** (4134 Atlantic Ave., Suite 205, Long Beach, CA 90807, ☎ 310/595–6905 or 800/257–4981).

SCUBA DIVING➤ For programs at resorts or on live-aboard boats, contact **Sea Safaris** (3770 Highland Ave., Suite 102, Manhattan Beach, CA 90266, ☎ 310/821–6670 or 800/821–6670).

FROM THE U.K.

Contact **British Airways Holidays** (Astral Towers, Betts Way, London Rd., Crawley, West Sussex RH10 2XA, ☎ 01293/518–022).

TRAVEL AGENCIES

For names of reputable agencies in your area, contact the **American Society of Travel Agents** (1101 King St., Suite 200, Alexandria, VA 22314, ☎ 703/739–2782).

The American Express agent in Bermuda is **L. P. Gutteridge Ltd.** (opposite City Hall, 16 Church St., Hamilton, ☎ 441/295–4545, FAX 441/295–2261). Thomas Cook is represented by **Butterfield Travel Ltd.** (75 Front St., Hamilton, ☎ 441/292–1510, FAX 441/292–1243).

U

U.S.

GOVERNMENT

TRAVEL BRIEFINGS

The U.S. Department of State's Overseas Citizens Emergency Center (Room 4811, Washington, DC 20520; enclose SASE) issues **Consular Information Sheets,** which cover crime, security, political climate, and health risks as well as embassy locations, entry requirements, currency regulations, and other routine matters. For the latest information, stop in at any U.S. passport office, consulate, or embassy; call the interactive hot line (☎ 202/647–5225 or fax 202/647-3000); or, with your PC's modem, tap into the Bureau of Consular Affairs' computer bulletin board (☎ 202/647–9225).

V
VISITOR INFO

Contact the **Bermuda Department of Tourism** in the United States at 310 Madison Avenue, Suite 201, New York, NY 10017–6083, ☎ 212/818–9800 or 800/223–6106, FAX 212/983–5289; 245 Peachtree Center Avenue NE, Suite 803, Atlanta, GA 30303–1223, ☎ 404/524–1541, FAX 404/586–9933; 44 School Street, Suite 1010, Boston, MA 02108, ☎ 617/742–0405, FAX 617/723–7786; Randolph-Wacker Building, 150 North Wacker Drive, Suite 1070, Chicago, IL 60606, ☎ 312/782–5486, FAX 312/704–

6996; Tetley/Moyer & Associates, 3151 Cahuenga Boulevard West, Suite 111, Los Angeles, CA 90068, ☎ 213/436–0744 or 800/421–0000 (800/252–0211 in CA), FAX 213/436–0750. In Canada, contact the department at 1200 Bay Street, Suite 1004, Toronto, Ontario M5R 2A5, ☎ 416/923–9600.

In the United Kingdom, contact **Bermuda Tourism,** BCB Ltd., 1 Battersea Church Road, London SW11 3LY, ☎ 0171/734–8813, FAX 0171/352–6501.

IN BERMUDA

Visitors Service Bureaus, which provide tourist information and assistance with reservations and ticketing, can be found in Hamilton (Ferry Terminal Bldg., 8 Front St., ☎ 441/295–1480; open Apr. 1–Oct. 31 Mon.–Sat. 9–4 and Nov. 1–Mar. 31 Mon. Sat. 9:30–2); at the Civil Air Terminal-Airport (2 Kindley Field Rd., ☎ 441/293–0736 or 441/293–0030; open daily, hours depending on plane arrival

times); at the Royal Naval Dockyard (opposite the ferry stop, ☎ 441/234–3824; open Apr. 1–Oct. 31 Mon.–Fri. 9–4 and Sun. 10–3; Nov. 1–Mar. 31 Mon.–Fri. 9:30–2 and Sun. 11–3); in St. George's (7 King's Sq., next to Town Hall, ☎ 441/297–1642; open Apr. 1–Oct. 31 Mon.–Sat. 9–4 and Nov. 1–Mar. 31 Mon.–Sat. 9:30–2); and in Somerset (86 Somerset Rd., near St. James's Church, ☎ 441/234–1388; open Apr–Nov weekdays 9–3, closed the rest of year).

You can also contact the **Bermuda Department of Tourism** (43 Church St., Hamilton, ☎ 441/292–0023, FAX 441/292–7537).

W
WEATHER

For current conditions and forecasts, plus the local time and helpful travel tips, call the **Weather Channel Connection** (☎ 900/932–8437; 95¢ per minute) from a Touch-Tone phone.

SMART TRAVEL TIPS A TO Z

Basic Information on Traveling in Bermuda and Savvy Tips to Make Your Trip a Breeze

The more you travel, the more you know about how to make trips run like clockwork. To help make your travels hassle-free, Fodor's editors have rounded up dozens of tips from our contributors and travel experts all over the world, as well as basic information on visiting Bermuda. For names of organizations to contact and publications that can give you more information, *see* Important Contacts A to Z, *above.*

A
AIR TRAVEL

If time is an issue, **always look for nonstop flights,** which require no change of plane. If possible, **avoid connecting flights,** which stop at least once and can involve a change of plane, although the flight number remains the same; if the first leg is late, the second waits.

ALOFT

AIRLINE FOOD➤ If you hate airline food, **ask for special meals when booking.** These can be vegetarian, low-cholesterol, or kosher, for example; commonly prepared to order in smaller quantities than standard catered fare, they are usually tastier.

SMOKING➤ Smoking is banned on all flights within the United States of less than six hours' duration and on all Canadian flights; the ban also applies to domestic segments of international flights aboard U.S. and foreign carriers. Delta has banned smoking system-wide. On U.S. carriers flying to Bermuda and other destinations abroad, a seat in a no-smoking section must be provided for every passenger who requests one, and the section must be enlarged to accommodate such passengers, if necessary, as long as they have complied with the airline's deadline for check-in and seat assignment. If smoking bothers you, request a seat far from the smoking section.

Foreign airlines are exempt from these rules but do provide no-smoking sections; some nations have banned smoking on all domestic flights, and others may ban smoking on some flights. Talks continue on the feasibility of broadening no-smoking policies.

CUTTING COSTS

The Sunday travel section of most newspapers is a good source of deals.

CHARTER FLIGHTS➤ Charters usually have the lowest fares and the most restrictions. Departures are limited and seldom on time, and you can lose all or most of your money if you cancel. (The closer to departure you cancel, the more you lose, although sometimes you will be charged only a small fee if you supply a substitute passenger.) The flight may be canceled for any reason up to 10 days before departure (after that, only if it is physically impossible to operate). The charterer may also revise the itinerary or increase the price after you have bought the ticket, but only if the new arrangement constitutes a "major change" do you have the right to a refund. Before buying a charter ticket, **read the fine print** about the company's refund policies. Money for charter flights is usually paid into a bank escrow account, the name of which should be on the contract, and if you don't pay by credit card, **make your check payable to the carrier's escrow account** (unless you're dealing with a travel agent, in which case, his or her check should be payable to the escrow account). The U.S. Department of Transportation's Office of Consumer Affairs has jurisdiction.

Charter operators may offer flights alone or with ground arrangements that constitute a charter package. You typically must book charters through your travel agent.

CONSOLIDATORS➤ Consolidators, who buy tickets at reduced rates from scheduled airlines, sell them at prices below the lowest available from the airlines directly—usually without advance restrictions. Sometimes you can even get your money back if you need to return the ticket. Carefully read the fine print detailing penalties for changes and cancellations. If you doubt the reliability of a consolidator, **confirm your reservation with the airline.**

MAJOR AIRLINES➤ The least-expensive airfares from the major airlines are priced for round-trip travel and are subject to restrictions. You must usually **book in advance and buy the ticket within 24 hours** to get cheaper fares, and you may have to **stay over a Saturday night.** The lowest fare is subject to availability, and only a small percentage of the plane's total seats are sold at that price. It's good to **call a number of airlines,** and **when you are quoted a good price, book it on the spot**—the same fare on the same flight may not be available the next day. Airlines generally allow you to change your return date for a $25 to $50 fee, but most low-fare tickets are nonrefundable. However, if you don't use it, you can apply the cost toward the purchase price of a new ticket, again for a small charge.

B

BUS TRAVEL

Bermuda's modern pink-and-blue buses travel the island from east to west. Bus tickets are sold at most post offices. Finding a bus stop outside Hamilton can be difficult; some are easily identifiable stone shelters, but others are marked only by striped poles by the road. These poles can be short or tall, pink and blue, green and white, or black and white. Remember to **wait on the proper side of the road**—driving in Bermuda is on the left. Bus drivers will not make change, **so carry plenty of coins**; the fare depends on your destination. Bermuda is divided into 14 bus zones, each about 2 miles long. Within the first three zones, adults pay $2.50 (coins only). For greater distances, the fare is $4. Children 3–12 pay $1 for all zones. If you plan to do much bus travel, **buy a booklet of tickets** (15 14-zone tickets for $22 or 15 three-zone tickets for $13). Ticket booklets and packets of discounted tokens are available at the Hamilton bus terminal and at post offices. Three-and seven-day passes ($20 and $32.50, respectively) are available at the bus terminal and the visitors bureau in Hamilton. Buses run about every 15 minutes, except on Sunday, when they usually come every hour. Bus schedules, which also contain ferry timetables, are available at the bus terminal in Hamilton and at many of the hotels. Bermudian bus drivers are sometimes rude, but they do answer questions about fares and destinations; upon request, they will also tell you when you've reached your stop.

In addition to the public buses to and from Hamilton, private minibuses serve the western end of the island. The minibus fare depends upon the destination, although you won't pay more than $3 ($1 for senior citizens). Minibuses, which you can flag down on the road, drop passengers wherever they want to go between Somerset Bridge and Royal Naval Dockyard. They operate daily 8:30 to 5 from April 1 through October 31; call for service at other times.

BUSINESS HOURS

BANKS

Branches of the Bank of Bermuda and the Bank of Butterfield are open Monday through Thursday 9:30 to 3, Friday 9:30 to 4:30. Bermuda Commercial Bank (opposite Anglican Cathedral, Church St., Hamilton) operates Monday through Thursday 9 to 3, Friday 9 to 4:30.

MUSEUMS

Hours vary greatly, but generally museums are open Monday through Saturday from 9 or 9:30 until 4:30 or 5; some museums close on Saturday. Check with the museum for exact hours.

STORES

Most stores are open Monday through Saturday from around 9 until 5 or 5:30. Some Hamilton stores keep evening hours when cruise ships are in port; during high season (March through November) many Front Street retailers that participate in Harbour Nights are open late on Wednesday, and many street vendors sell their wares that evening only. Shops at the Royal Naval Dockyard are generally open Monday through Saturday 10 to 5, and Sunday 11 to 5.

C

CAMERAS, CAMCORDERS, AND COMPUTERS

LAPTOPS

Before you depart, **check your portable computer's battery,** because you may be asked at security to turn on the computer to prove that it is what it appears to be. At the airport, you may prefer to **request a manual inspection,** although security X-rays do not harm hard-disk or floppy-disk storage. Also, **register your foreign-made laptop with U.S. Customs.** If your laptop is U.S.-made, call the consulate of the country you'll be visiting to find out whether or not it should be registered with local customs upon arrival. You may want to **find out about repair facilities at your destination** in case you need them.

PHOTOGRAPHY

If your camera is new or if you haven't used it for a while, **shoot and develop a few rolls of film** before you leave. Always **store film in a cool, dry place**—never in the car's glove compartment or on the shelf under the rear window.

Every pass of film through an X-ray machine increases the chance of clouding. To protect it, carry it in a clear plastic bag and **ask for hand inspection at security.** Such requests are virtually always honored at U.S. airports, and usually are accommodated abroad. Don't depend on a lead-lined bag to protect film in checked luggage—the airline may increase the radiation to see what's inside.

VIDEO

Before your trip, **test your camcorder, invest in a skylight filter to protect the lens, and charge the batteries.** (Airport security personnel may ask you to turn on the camcorder to prove that it's what it appears to be).

Videotape is not damaged by X-rays, but it may be harmed by the magnetic field of a walk-through metal detector, so **ask that videotapes be hand-checked.**

CHILDREN AND TRAVEL

BABY-SITTING

For recommended local sitters, **check with your hotel desk.** The charge is $4–$8 per hour, and sitters expect paid transportation.

FLYING

Always **ask about discounted children's fares.** On international flights, the fare for infants under age 2 not occupying a seat is generally either free or 10% of the accompanying adult's fare; children ages 2 through 11 usually pay half to two-thirds of the adult fare. On domestic flights, children under 2 not occupying a seat travel free, and older children currently travel on the lowest applicable adult fare. Some routes, including a few in the Caribbean, are considered neither international nor domestic and have different rules.

BAGGAGE➤ In general, the adult baggage allowance applies for children paying half or more of the adult fare. Before departure, **ask about carry-on allowances,** if you are traveling with an infant. In general, those paying 10% of the adult fare are allowed one carry-on bag, not to exceed 70 pounds or 45 inches (length + width + height) and a collapsible stroller; you may be allowed less if the flight is full.

FACILITIES➤ When making your reservation, **ask for children's meals or freestanding bassinets** if you need them; the latter are available only to those with seats at the bulkhead, where there's enough legroom. If you don't need a bassinet, **think twice before requesting bulkhead** seats—the only storage for in-flight necessities is in the inconveniently distant overhead bins.

SAFETY SEATS➤ According to the Federal Aviation Administration (FAA), it's a good idea to **use safety seats aloft.** Airline policy varies. U.S. carriers allow FAA-approved models, but airlines usually require that you buy a ticket, even if your child would otherwise ride free, because the seats must be strapped into regular passenger seats.

LODGING

Most hotels allow children under a certain age to stay in their parents' room at no extra charge, while others charge them as extra adults; be sure to **ask about the cutoff age.**

CRUISES

Bermuda has long been a favorite destination of cruise lines and, except for a few cruises that continue down to the Caribbean, is usually a ship's only port of call. Most ships make seven-day loops from New York, with three days spent at sea and four days in port; other cruises leave from Baltimore; Philadelphia; Boston; Charleston, SC; Newport News, VA; Wilmington, NC; and Port Everglades, FL. The cruise season in Bermuda runs from March to October.

Cruising to Bermuda combines the benefits of an inclusive package (all your transportation, meals, and lodging are usually included in the cruise fare with a typical land package

(the ship acts as your hotel while you explore the island). Not all cruises to Bermuda are the same, however; **check where in Bermuda you will dock.** The traditional port is Hamilton, the capital and the most commercial area on the island. If you like to shop, this is where most stores are. Many ships tie up at St. George's, where passengers walk off the vessel into Bermuda's equivalent of Colonial Williamsburg, a charming town of 17th-century buildings, narrow lanes, and a smattering of small boutiques. The West End, Bermuda's third port of call, is fast becoming the preferred place to be. Here passengers find the Royal Naval Dockyard, an erstwhile shipyard that was the British Royal Navy's headquarters until March 1995. It has been beautifully restored as a minivillage with shops, restaurants, a maritime museum, an art gallery, and a crafts market. There is a marina with rental boats, submarine cruises, parasailing excursions, and a snorkeling area; special events take place here, too.

To get the best deal on a cruise, **consult a cruise-only travel agency.** (*See* Cruising in Bermuda, Chapter 2.)

CUSTOMS
AND DUTIES

IN BERMUDA

Visitors entering Bermuda may bring in duty-free up to 50

cigars, 200 cigarettes, and 1 pound of tobacco; 1 quart of wine and 1 quart of liquor; 20 pounds of meat; and other goods with a total maximum value of $30. You may not import plants, fruit, vegetables, or animals without an import permit from the **Department of Agriculture, Fisheries and Parks** (Box HM 834, Hamilton HM CX, ☎ 441/236–4201, FAX 441/236–7582). Remember, though, that merchandise and sales materials for use at conventions must be cleared with the hotel concerned before you arrive.

BACK HOME

IN THE U.S.➤ Usually, you may bring home $400 worth of foreign goods duty-free if you've been out of the country for at least 48 hours and haven't already used the $400 exemption, or any part of it, in the past 30 days.

Travelers 21 or older may bring back 1 liter of alcohol duty-free, provided the beverage laws of the state through which they reenter the United States allow it. In addition, 100 non-Cuban cigars and 200 cigarettes are allowed, regardless of your age. Antiques and works of art more than 100 years old are duty-free.

Duty-free, travelers may mail packages with a total value $200 or less to themselves and $100 or less to others, with a limit of one parcel per addressee per day (and no alcohol or tobacco products or perfume valued at more than $5); outside, identify the package as being for personal use or an unsolicited gift, specifying the contents and their retail value. Mailed items do not count as part of your exemption.

IN CANADA➤ Once per calendar year, when you've been out of Canada for at least seven days, you may bring in C$300 worth of goods duty-free. If you've been away less than seven days but more than 48 hours, the duty-free exemption drops to C$100 but can be claimed any number of times (as can a C$20 duty-free exemption for absences of 24 hours or more). You cannot combine the yearly and 48-hour exemptions, use the C$300 exemption only partially (to save the balance for a later trip), or pool exemptions with family members. Goods claimed under the C$300 exemption may follow you by mail; those claimed under the lesser exemptions must accompany you.

Alcohol and tobacco products may be included in the yearly and 48-hour exemptions but not in the 24-hour exemption. If you meet the age requirements of the province through which you reenter Canada, you may bring in, duty-free, 1.14 liters (40 imperial ounces) of wine or liquor *or* 24 12-ounce cans or bottles of beer or ale. If you are 16 or older, you may bring in, duty-free, 200 cigarettes, 50 cigars or cigarillos, and 400 tobacco sticks or 400 grams of manufactured tobacco. Alcohol and tobacco must accompany you on your return.

An unlimited number of gifts valued up to C$60 each may be mailed to Canada duty-free. These do not count as part of your exemption. Label the package "Unsolicited Gift— Value under $60." Alcohol and tobacco are excluded.

IN THE U.K.➤ From countries outside the European Union (EU), including Bermuda, you may import duty-free 200 cigarettes, 100 cigarillos, 50 cigars or 250 grams of tobacco; 1 liter of spirits or 2 liters of fortified or sparkling wine; 2 liters of still table wine; 60 milliliters of perfume; 250 milliliters of toilet water; plus £136 worth of other goods, including gifts and souvenirs.

D
FOR TRAVELERS WITH DISABILITIES

When discussing accessibility with an operator or reservationist, **ask hard questions.** Are there any stairs, inside *or* out? Are there grab bars next to the toilet *and* in the shower/tub? How wide is the doorway to the room? To the bathroom? For the most extensive facilities, meeting the latest legal specifications, **opt for newer accommodations,** which have usually been designed with access in mind. Older properties or ships must usually be retrofitted and may offer more limited facilities as a result. Be sure to **discuss your needs before booking.**

GUIDE DOGS

If you plan to bring a guide dog to Bermuda, you must **obtain a permit in advance.** Application forms are available at all Bermuda Department of Tourism offices. Once approved, the Department of Agriculture, Fisheries, and Parks will send an import permit to the traveler; the permit must accompany the dog at the time of arrival.

LODGING

The best hotels for travelers with disabilities are the large resorts, such as the Belmont Hotel, Elbow Beach, Marriott's Castle Harbour, the Sonesta Beach, the Hamilton Princess and the Southampton Princess.

DISCOUNT CLUBS

Travel clubs offer members unsold space on airplanes, cruise ships, and package tours at as much as 50% below regular prices. Membership may include a regular bulletin or access to a toll-free hot line giving details of available trips departing from three or four days to several months in the future. Most also offer 50% discounts off hotel rack rates. Before booking with a club, **make sure the hotel or other supplier isn't offering a better deal.**

DIVERS' ALERT

Scuba divers take note: **Do not fly within 24 hours of scuba diving.**

F

FERRY TRAVEL

Quick and enjoyable, ferries sail every day from the Ferry Terminal (☎ 441/295–4506) in Hamilton, with routes to Paget, Warwick, and across the Great Sound to Somerset in the West End. On weekdays, most ferries run until 11 PM, although the last ferry from Hamilton to Somerset leaves at 5:20 PM; on Sunday, ferry service is limited and ends around 7 PM. A one-way fare to Paget or Warwick is $2, $3.50 to Somerset; children under 12 ride on any ferry for $1. Bicycles can be brought aboard free, but passengers must pay $3.50 extra to take a motor scooter to Somerset; scooters are not allowed on the smaller Paget and Warwick ferries. The friendly and helpful ferry operators will answer questions about routes and schedules, and they'll even help get your bike aboard. Schedules, posted at each landing, are available at the ferry terminal, central bus terminal, and most hotels.

H

HEALTH CONCERNS

Sunburn and sunstroke are problems for summer visitors to Bermuda. On a hot, sunny day, wear a long-sleeve shirt, a hat, and long pants or a beach wrap. These are essential for a day on a boat, but are also advisable for midday at the beach. Carry sunscreen for your nose, ears, and other sensitive areas. Drink liquids and, above all, **limit the amount of time you spend in the sun** until you become acclimated.

The Portuguese man-of-war is an occasional visitor to Bermuda's waters. These nasty sea critters are not numerous hereabouts but show up usually in summer or whenever the water is particularly warm. They are recognizable by a purple, balloonlike float sack of perhaps 8 inches in diameter, below which dangle 20- to 60-inch tentacles armed with powerful stinging cells. Contact with these stinging cells causes immediate, severe pain. A serious sting can put a person in shock, and medical attention should be sought immediately. Even if you don't think the sting is severe, you should still go to a doctor. In the meantime—or if getting to a doctor will take a while—liberally treat the affected area with ammonia. Although usually encountered in the water, Portuguese man-of-wars may also wash up on shore, and if you spot one on the sand, steer clear—the sting is just as severe when they're out of the water.

I

INSURANCE

Travel insurance can protect your investment, replace your luggage and its contents, or provide for medical coverage should you fall ill during your trip. Most tour operators, travel agents, and insurance agents sell specialized health-and-accident, flight, trip-cancellation, and luggage insurance as well as comprehensive policies with some or all of these features. Before you make any purchase, **review your existing health and homeowner's policies** to find out whether they cover expenses incurred while traveling.

BAGGAGE

Airline liability for your baggage is limited to $1,250 per person on domestic flights. On international flights, the airlines' liability is $9.07 per pound or $20 per kilogram for checked baggage (roughly $640 per 70-pound bag) and $400 per passenger for unchecked baggage. Insurance for losses exceeding the terms of your airline ticket can be bought directly from the airline at check-in for about $10 per $1,000 of coverage; note that it excludes a rather extensive list of items, shown on your airline ticket.

FLIGHT

You should **think twice before buying flight insurance.** Often purchased as a last-minute impulse at the airport, it pays a lump sum when a plane crashes, either to a beneficiary if the insured dies or sometimes to a surviving passenger who loses eyesight or a limb. Supplementing the airlines' coverage described in the limits-of-liability paragraphs on your ticket, it's expensive and basically unnecessary. Charging an airline ticket to a major credit card often automatically entitles you to coverage and may also embrace travel by bus, train, and ship.

HEALTH

If your own health insurance policy does not cover you outside the U.S., **consider buying supplemental medical coverage.** It can cover from $1,000 to $150,000 worth of medical and/or dental expenses incurred as a result of an accident or illness during a trip. These policies also may include a personal-accident, or death-and-dismemberment, provision, which pays a lump sum ranging from $15,000 to $500,000 to your beneficiaries if you die or to you if you lose one or more limbs or your eyesight, and a medical-assistance provision, which may either reimburse you for the cost of referrals, evacuation, or repatriation and other services, or may automatically enroll you as a member of a particular medical-assistance company.

TRIP

Without insurance, you will lose all or most of your money if you must cancel your trip due to illness or any other reason. Especially if your airline ticket, cruise, or package tour is nonrefundable and cannot be changed, it's essential that you **buy trip-cancellation-and-interruption insurance.**

When considering how much coverage you need, look for a policy that will cover the cost of your trip plus the nondiscounted price of a one-way airline ticket should you need to return home early. Read the fine print carefully, especially sections defining "family member" and "preexisting medical conditions." Also **consider default or bankruptcy insurance,** which protects you against a supplier's failure to deliver. However, such policies often do not cover default by a travel agency, tour operator, airline, or cruise line if you bought your tour and the coverage directly from the firm in question.

FOR U.K. TRAVELERS

You can buy an annual travel-insurance policy valid for most vacations during the year in which it's purchased. If you go this route, make sure it covers you if you have a preexisting medical condition or are pregnant.

L
LODGING

APARTMENT AND VILLA RENTALS

If you want a home base that's roomy enough for a family and comes with cooking facilities, **consider a furnished rental.** It's generally but not always cost-wise; some rentals are luxury properties that are economical only when your party is large. Home-exchange directories do list rentals—often second homes

owned by prospective house swappers—and some services search for a house or apartment for you (even a castle if that's your fancy) and handle the paperwork. Some send an illustrated catalogue and others send photographs of specific properties, sometimes at a charge; up-front registration fees may apply.

HOME EXCHANGE

If you would like to find a house, an apartment, or other vacation property to exchange for your own while on vacation, **become a member of a home-exchange organization,** which will send you its annual directories listing available exchanges and will include your own listing in at least one of them. Arrangements for the actual exchange are made by the two parties to it, not by the organization.

M
MAIL

Airmail letters and postcards to the United States and Canada require 60¢ postage per 10 grams, and 75¢ per 10 grams to the United Kingdom.

RECEIVING MAIL

If you have no address in Bermuda, you can **have mail sent care of General Delivery** (General Post Office, Hamilton HM GD, Bermuda).

MONEY AND EXPENSES

The Bermudian dollar is on a par with the U.S. dollar, and the two currencies are used interchangeably. American money can be used anywhere, but change is often given in Bermudian currency. Try to **avoid accumulating large amounts of local money,** which is difficult to exchange for U.S. dollars in Bermuda and expensive to exchange in the United States. Canadian and British currency must be converted.

In Bermuda, most shops and some restaurants accept credit cards, but the majority of hotels on the island insist on other forms of payment, such as cash or traveler's checks, so **check in advance whether or not your hotel takes credit cards.** Some take personal checks by prior arrangement (a letter from your bank is sometimes requested).

ATMS

Cirrus, Plus and many other networks connecting automated-teller machines operate internationally. Chances are that you can **use your bank card at ATMs** to withdraw money from an account and get cash advances on a credit-card account if your card has been programmed with a personal identification number, or PIN. Before leaving home, **check on frequency limits** for withdrawals and cash advances. Also **ask whether your card's PIN must be reprogrammed** for use in Bermuda. Four digits are commonly used overseas. Note that Discover is accepted only in the United States.

On cash advances you are charged interest from the day you receive the money, whether from a teller or and ATM. Although transaction fees for ATM withdrawals abroad may be higher than fees for withdrawals at home, Cirrus and Plus exchange rates are excellent because they are based on wholesale rates only offered by major banks.

COSTS

Since Bermuda imports everything from cars to cardigans, prices are high; the most common complaint of visitors to Bermuda is the high cost of a vacation on the island. At an upscale restaurant, for example, be prepared to pay as much for a meal as you would in New York, London, or Paris. The average cost of dinner in a chic restaurant is $60 to $80 per person—$120 with drinks and wine. Up scale restaurants, however, are not your only option. The island is full of coffee shops, where locals and thrift-minded tourists can eat hamburgers and french fries for about $7. The same meal at a restaurant costs about $15.

A cup of coffee costs between $1.50 and $3; a mixed drink $4 to $6; a bottle of beer $2.25 to $6; and a can of Coke about $1.50. A 15-minute cab ride will set you back about $25 including the tip, and a pack of Kodak 110 cartridge film with 12 exposures costs about $4.30. A 36-exposure roll of 35mm 100 ASA

print film costs about $8. Smokers pay $5 to $7 for a pack of cigarettes.

TAXES

Hotels add a 6% government tax to the bill and most add a 10% service charge or a per diem dollar equivalent in lieu of tips. Other extra charges sometimes include a 5% "energy surcharge" (at small guest houses) and a 15% service charge (at most restaurants).

TRAVELER'S CHECKS

Whether or not to buy traveler's checks depends on where you are headed; **take cash to rural areas and small towns, traveler's checks to cities.** The most widely recognized are American Express, Citicorp, Thomas Cook, and Visa, which are sold by major commercial banks for 1% to 3% of the checks' face value—it pays to **shop around.** Both American Express and Thomas Cook issue checks that can be countersigned and used by you or your traveling companion. Record the numbers of the checks, cross them off as you spend them, and keep this information separate from your checks.

WIRING MONEY

You don't have to be a cardholder to send or receive funds through MoneyGram[SM] from American Express. Just go to a MoneyGram agent, located in retail and convenience stores and in American Express Travel Offices.

Pay up to $1,000 with cash or a credit card, anything over that in cash. The money can be picked up within 10 minutes in the form of U.S.-dollar traveler's checks or local currency at the nearest Money-Gram agent, or, abroad, at the nearest American Express representative (in Hamilton, 809/295–4545). There's no limit, and the recipient need only present photo identification. The cost runs from 3% to 10%, depending on the amount sent, the destination, and how you pay.

You can also send money using Western Union. Money sent from the United States or Canada will be available for pickup at agent locations in 100 countries within 15 minutes. Once the money is in the system, it can be picked up at any one of 25,000 locations. Fees range from 4% to 10%, depending on the amount you send.

MOPEDS AND SCOOTERS

Because car rentals are not allowed on Bermuda, many visitors choose to get around by moped or scooter. Bermudians routinely use the words "moped" and "scooter" inter-changeably, even though a scooter is actually a type of moped. The difference between the two is horsepower and passen-ger capacity. Mopeds have 3-hp engines and scooters 6-hp. Unless you request otherwise, what generally happens

is that those riding with a passenger get a 6-hp scooter, and solo riders are given a 3-hp moped.

Riding a moped, how-ever, is not without hazards—especially for first-time riders. The often rough-surface roads are narrow, winding, and full of blind curves. Also, many Bermudians are bad drivers, and it is wise to **think twice before renting** a moped, as accidents occur frequently and are sometimes fatal. The best ways to avoid mishaps are to **drive defensively, obey the 20-mph (35 km) speed limit,** remember to **stay on the left-hand side of the road**—especially at traffic circles—and **avoid riding in the rain and at night.**

Helmets are required by law. Single- or double-seat mopeds and scoot-ers can be rented from cycle liveries by the hour, the day, or the week. The liveries will show first-time riders how to operate the vehicles. Rates vary, but single-seat mopeds cost about $32 per day or $113 per week (plus a mandatory $12 repair waiver). The fee in-cludes helmet, lock, key, third-party insurance, breakdown service, pickup and delivery, and a tank of gas. A $20–$50 deposit is required for the lock, key, and helmet, and you must be at least 16 and have a valid driver's license to rent. Major hotels have their own cycle liveries, and all hotels and guest houses will make rental

arrangements. Many gas stations are open daily 7–7, and a few stay open until 11 PM; most are closed on Sunday. Gas for cycles is $3 to 4 per liter.

P PACKAGES AND TOURS

A package or tour to Bermuda can make your vacation less expensive and more convenient. Firms that sell tours and packages purchase airline seats, hotel rooms, and rental cars in bulk and pass some of the savings on to you. In addition, the best operators have local representatives to help you out at your destination.

A GOOD DEAL?

The more your package or tour includes, the better you can predict the ultimate cost of your vacation. Make sure you know exactly what is included, and **beware of hidden costs.** Are taxes, tips, and service charges included? Transfers and baggage handling? Entertainment and excursions? These can add up.

Most packages and tours are rated deluxe, first-class superior, first class, tourist, and budget. The key differ-ence is usually accom-modations. If the package or tour you are considering is priced lower than in your wildest dreams, **be skeptical.** Also, **make sure your travel agent knows the hotels** and other services. Ask about location, room size, beds, and whether the facility has a pool, room service, or programs for children, if you care about these. Has your agent been there or sent others you can contact?

BUYER BEWARE

Each year consumers are stranded or lose their money when operators go out of business—even very large ones with excellent reputations. If you can't afford a loss, take the time to **check out the operator**—find out how long the company has been in business, and ask several agents about its reputation. Next, **don't book unless the firm has a consumer-protection program.** Members of the United States Tour Operators Association and the National Tour Association are required to set aside funds exclusively to cover your payments and travel arrangements in case of default. Nonmember operators may instead carry insurance; look for the details in the operator's brochure—and the name of an underwriter with a solid reputation. Note: When it comes to tour operators, **don't trust escrow accounts.** Although there are laws governing those of charter-flight operators, no governmental body prevents tour operators from raiding the till.

Next, **contact your local Better Business Bureau and the attorney general's office** in both your own state and the operator's; have any complaints been filed?

Last, **pay with a major credit card.** Then you can cancel payment, provided you can document your complaint. Always **consider trip-cancellation insurance** (*see* Insurance, *above*).

BIG VS. SMALL➤ An operator that handles several hundred thousand travelers annually can use its purchasing power to give you a good price. Its high volume may also indicate financial stability. But some small companies provide more personalized service; because they tend to specialize, they may also be experts on an area.

USING AN AGENT

Travel agents are an excellent resource. In fact, large operators accept bookings only through travel agents. But it's good to **collect brochures from several agencies,** because some agents' suggestions may be skewed by promotional relationships with tour and package firms that reward them for volume sales. If you have a special interest, **find an agent with expertise in that area;** the American Society of Travel Agents can give you leads in the United States. (Don't rely solely on your agent, though; agents may be unaware of small-niche operators, and some special-interest travel companies only sell direct).

SINGLE TRAVELERS

Prices are usually quoted per person, based on two sharing a room. If traveling solo, you may be required to

pay the full double occupancy rate. Some operators eliminate this surcharge if you agree to be matched up with a roommate of the same sex, even if one is not found by departure time.

PACKING FOR BERMUDA

Bermudians are more formal than most Americans when it comes to dress. Although attire tends to be casual during the day—Bermuda shorts are acceptable, even for businessmen—cutoffs, short shorts, and halter tops are inappropriate. Swimsuits should not be worn outside pool areas or off the beach; you'll need a cover-up in the public areas of your hotel. Joggers may wear standard jogging shorts but should avoid appearing on public streets without a shirt. Bare feet and hair curlers in public are also frowned upon. In the evening, many restaurants and hotel dining rooms require that men wear a jacket and tie and that women dress comparably. Recently, some hotels have been setting aside one or two nights a week for "smart casual" attire, when jacket-and-tie restrictions are loosened. For women, tailored slacks with a dressy blouse or sweater are fine, although most Bermudian women wear dresses or skirts and blouses. Bermudian men often wear Bermuda shorts (and proper knee socks) with a jacket and tie.

THE GOLD GUIDE / SMART TRAVEL TIPS

During the cooler months, you should bring lightweight woolens or cottons that you can wear in layers, depending on the vagaries of the weather; a few sweaters and a lightweight jacket are always a good idea, too. Regardless of the season, you should **pack a swimsuit, a cover-up, sunscreen and sunglasses,** as well as an umbrella and raincoat. Comfortable walking shoes and a bag for carrying maps and cameras are a must. If you plan to play tennis, be aware that many courts require proper whites and that tennis balls in Bermuda are extremely expensive—bring your own if possible.

Pack light, because porters and luggage trolleys can be hard to find. Bring an extra pair of eyeglasses or contact lenses in your carry-on luggage, and if you have a health problem, **pack enough medication** to last the trip or have your doctor write a prescription using the drug's generic name, because brand-names vary from country to country (you'll then need a prescription from a local doctor). **Don't put prescription drugs or valuables in luggage to be checked,** for it could go astray. To avoid problems with customs officials, carry medications in original packaging. Also don't forget the addresses of offices that handle refunds of lost traveler's checks.

LUGGAGE

Free airline baggage allowances depend on the airline, the route, and the class of your ticket; ask in advance. In general, on domestic flights and on international flights between the United States and foreign destinations, you are entitled to check two bags—neither exceeding 62 inches, or 158 centimeters (length + width + height), or weighing more than 70 pounds (32 kilograms). A third piece may be brought aboard; its total dimensions are generally limited to less than 45 inches (114 centimeters), so it will fit easily under the seat in front of you or in the overhead compartment. In the United States, the FAA gives airlines broad latitude to limit carry-on allowances and tailor them to different aircraft and operational conditions. Charges for excess, oversize, or overweight pieces vary.

If you are flying between two foreign destinations, note that baggage allowances may be determined not by piece but by weight—generally 88 pounds (40 kilograms) in first class, 66 pounds (30 kilograms) in business class, and 44 pounds (20 kilograms) in economy. If your flight between two cities abroad *connects* with your transatlantic or transpacific flight, the piece method still applies.

SAFEGUARDING YOUR LUGGAGE➤ Before leaving home, **itemize your bags' contents** and their worth, and label them with your name, address, and phone number. (If you use your home address, cover it so that potential thieves can't see it.) Inside your bag, **pack a copy of your itinerary.** At check-in, **make sure that your bag is correctly tagged** with the airport's three-letter destination code. If your bags arrive damaged or not at all, file a written report with the airline before leaving the airport.

PASSPORTS AND VISAS

If you don't already have one, **get a passport.** While traveling, **keep one photocopy of the data page** separate from your wallet and leave another copy with someone at home. If you lose your passport, promptly call the nearest embassy or consulate and the local police; having the data page can speed replacement.

U.S. CITIZENS

You do not need a passport or visa to enter Bermuda if you plan to stay less than six months, although you must have onward or return tickets and proof of identity (original birth certificate with raised seal or voter's registration card, along with photo ID; a driver's license is unacceptable). If you have a passport, bring it to ensure quick passage through immigration and customs. U.S. passports are valid 10 years. New and renewal application forms are available at any of the 13 U.S. Passport Agency offices and at some post offices and courthouses. Passports are usually mailed within four weeks; allow five weeks or more in spring and summer.

CANADIANS

Canadians do not need a passport to enter Bermuda, though a passport is helpful to ensure quick passage through customs and immigration. A birth certificate or a certificate of citizenship is required, along with a photo ID. Passport application forms are available at 28 regional passport offices as well as post offices and travel agencies. Whether for a first or a renewal passport, you must apply in person. Passports are valid for five years and are usually mailed within two to three weeks of application.

U.K. CITIZENS

Citizens of the United Kingdom need a valid passport to enter Bermuda for stays of up to 30 days. Applications for new and renewal passports are available from main post offices as well as at the passport offices, located in Belfast, Glasgow, Liverpool, London, Newport, and Peterborough. You may apply in person at all passport offices, or by mail to all except the London office. Children under 16 may travel on an accompanying parent's passport. All passports are valid for 10 years. Allow a month for processing.

S

SENIOR-CITIZEN DISCOUNTS

To qualify for age-related discounts, **mention your senior-citizen status up front** when booking hotel reservations, not when checking out, and before you're seated in restaurants, not when paying your bill. Note that discounts may be limited to certain menus, days, or hours. When renting a car, **ask about promotional car-rental discounts**—they can net lower costs than your senior-citizen discount.

SIGHTSEEING

BOAT TOURS

A host of boats offers sightseeing, snorkeling, and swimming excursions. Major attractions include the Sea Gardens, with their splendid underwater scenes, and the coral-wrapped wreck of HMS *Vixen*, both of which lie off the West End. Many of the boats operate only during high season, so call in advance for schedules.

CARRIAGE TOURS

The few horse-drawn carriages on the island are a romantic way to see the sights. The raconteurs at the reins dispense local lore, information, and misinformation. Even though their tales stretch the truth, you'll enjoy the telling.

HOUSE AND GARDEN TOURS

For six weeks each spring, a collection of Bermudian homes and gardens is open for public tours. On show are some of the island's most beautiful residences, the grounds of which are perfectly manicured and showcase Bermuda's beautiful flora.

TAXI TOURS

For an independent tour of the island, a taxi is a good but more expensive alternative to a group tour. A blue flag on the hood of a cab indicates that the driver is a qualified tour guide. These cabs can be difficult to find, but most of their drivers are friendly, entertaining—they sometimes bend the truth for a good yarn—and well informed about the island and its history. Ask your hotel to arrange a tour with a knowledgeable driver.

Cabs are four- or six-seaters, and the legal rate for island tours is $20 per hour for one to four passengers and $30 per hour for five and six passengers; two children under 12 equal an adult. A 25% surcharge is added between 10 PM and 6 AM, and on Sunday and public holidays.

WALKING TOURS

From November 1 to March 31, the **Bermuda Department of Tourism** coordinates 45-minute to two-hour walking tours of Hamilton's Session House, St. George's, Spittal Pond Nature Reserve, the Royal Naval Dockyard, and Somerset. The tours of St. George's and the Royal Naval Dockyard take in the large number of 17th- and 18th-century buildings, while the Spittal Pond and Somerset tours focus on the island's flora. The Session House tour begins outside the historic Hamilton building on the corner of Parliament and Church streets every Monday at 11:15 AM. The tour of Spittal Pond, its endemic flora and their healing qualities is conducted on Tuesday at 10:30 AM, while another walk that covers the bird sanctuary and other points of interest, including Spanish Rock, starts on Friday at 1 PM; both meet in the east parking lot. The St. George's walk leaves from King's Square at 10:30 AM and 2 PM on Wednesday and 10:30 AM on Saturday. The Somerset walk departs at 10:00 AM on Thursday from the Country Squire restaurant; a slide show is held afterwards at 11:15 AM. Tours of the Royal Naval Dockyard leave from the Clocktower Building on Thursday at 2:15 PM and Sunday at 11 AM; the 2:15 PM Sunday walk leaves from the Craft Market.

STUDENTS ON THE ROAD

Like other travelers, students arriving in Bermuda must have confirmation of hotel reservations, a return plane ticket, a photo ID, and proof of citizenship, such as a passport, birth certificate, or a signed voter registration card. There are no youth hostels, YMCAs, or YWCAs on the

island. During Bermuda Spring Break Sports Week (*see* Festivals and Seasonal Events *in* Chapter 1, Destination: Bermuda), however, special student rates are offered at some hotels and guest houses, restaurants, pubs, and nightclubs.

To save money, **look into deals available through student-oriented travel agencies.** To qualify, you'll need to have a bona fide student ID card. Members of international student groups also are eligible. *See* Students *in* Important Contacts A to Z, *above*.

T

TAXIS

Taxis are the fastest and easiest way around the island—and also the most costly. Four-seater taxis charge $4 for the first mile and $1.40 for each subsequent mile. A 3-hour trip costs $20 per hour, excluding tip. Between 10 PM and 6 AM, or on Sunday and public holidays, a 25% surcharge is added to the fare. There is a 25¢ charge for each piece of luggage stored in the trunk or on the roof.

For information on taxi-tours, *see* Sightseeing, *above*.

TELEPHONES

Pay phones, identical to those found in the United States, are found on the streets of Hamilton, St. George's, and Somerset, as well as at ferry landings, some bus stops, and public beaches. Deposit 20¢ (U.S. or Bermudian) in the meter as soon as

your party answers. Most hotels charge 20¢–$1 for local calls.

LONG DISTANCE

The long-distance services of AT&T, MCI, and Sprint make calling home relatively convenient and let you avoid hotel surcharges; typically, you dial a local number. Before you go, **find out the local access codes** for your destinations.

Direct dialing is possible from anywhere on the island. Most hotels impose a surcharge for long-distance calls, even those made collect. Many of the small guest houses and apartments have no central switchboard; if you have a phone in your room, it's a private line from which you can make only collect, credit-card, or local calls. Some of the small hotels have a telephone room or kiosk where you can make long-distance calls. Specially marked AT&T USADirect phones can be found at the airport, the cruiseship dock in Hamilton, and at King's Square and Ordnance Island in St. George's. International calls with a calling card can also be made from the main post office (Church and Parliament Sts., Hamilton, ☎ 441/295–5151). Prepaid international calls may be made from the Cable & Wireless Office (20 Church St., opposite City Hall, Hamilton, ☎ 441/297–7000), which also offers international telex, cable, and fax services Monday through Saturday 9 to 5.

To call the United States, Canada, and most Caribbean countries, dial 1 (or 0 if you need an operator's assistance), plus the area code and the number. For all other countries, dial 011 (or 0 for an operator), the country code, the area code, and the number. Using an operator for an overseas call is more expensive than dialing direct. For calls to the United States, rates are highest from 10 AM to 7 PM and discounted from 7 PM to 11 PM; the lowest rates are from 11 PM to 7 AM. Calls to Alaska and Hawaii are not discounted. Calls to Canada are cheapest from 9 PM to 7 AM and to the United Kingdom from 6 PM to 7 AM.

TIPPING

A service charge of 10% (or an equivalent per diem amount), which covers everything from baggage handling to maid service, is added to your hotel bill. Most restaurants tack on a 15% service charge; if not, a 15% tip is customary (more for exceptional service). Porters at the airport expect about a dollar a bag, while taxi drivers usually receive 15% of the fare.

TRANSPORTATION

Despite its small size, Bermuda does pose some transport problems. Rental cars are not allowed, so visitors must travel by bus, taxi, ferry, moped, bike, or on foot. More than 1,200 miles of narrow, winding roads and a 20-mph speed limit (35 km) make moving around the island a time-consuming process. Traveling the length of this long, skinny island takes particularly long: The trip from St. George's to Hamilton takes an hour by bus, and the journey onward to the West End takes another hour, although an express bus from Hamilton to the West End takes only 40 minutes. Hiring a taxi can cut down the amount of time you spend on the road, but the cost may discourage you. Fortunately, Hamilton, St. George's, and Somerset are all manageable on foot.

W
WHEN TO GO

Bermuda has a remarkably mild climate that seldom sees extremes of either heat or cold. During the winter (December through March), temperatures range from around 55°F at night to 70°F in the early afternoon. High, blustery winds can make the temperature feel cooler, however, as can Bermuda's high humidity. The hottest part of the year is between May and mid-October, when temperatures range from 75°F to 85°F; 90°F is not uncommon in July and August. The summer months are somewhat drier, but rainfall is spread fairly evenly throughout the year. Bermuda depends solely on rain for its supply of fresh water, so residents usually welcome the brief storms. In August and September, hurricanes moving northward from the Caribbean sometimes batter the island.

During summer, the island teems with activities. Hotel barbecues and evening dances complement daytime sightseeing excursions, and the public beaches are always open. The pace during the off-season slows considerably. A few of the hotels and restaurants close, some of the sightseeing boats are dry-docked, and only the taxis and the St. George's minibus operate tours of the island. The majority of hotels remain open, however, slashing their rates by as much as 40% from November to March. The weather at this time of year is often perfect for golf and tennis, and visitors can still rent boats, tour the island, and take advantage of the special events and walking tours offered (see Festivals and Seasonal Events in Chapter 1, Destination: Bermuda).

What follows are average daily maximum and minimum temperatures for Bermuda.

Climate in Bermuda

Jan.	68F	20C	May	76F	24C	Sept.	85F	29C
	58	14		65	18		72	22
Feb.	68F	20C	June	81F	27C	Oct.	79F	26C
	58	14		70	21		70	21
Mar.	68F	20C	July	85F	29C	Nov.	74F	23C
	58	14		74	23		63	17
Apr.	72F	22C	Aug.	86F	30C	Dec.	70F	21C
	59	15		76	24		61	16

1 Destination: Bermuda

A BASTION OF BRITAIN, WITH A TROPICAL TWIST

BASKING IN THE ATLANTIC, 508 miles due east of Cape Hatteras, Bermuda is one of the wealthiest countries in the world—average per capita income is $20,000. Bermuda has no income tax, no sales tax, no slums, no unemployment, and no major crime problem. Don't come to Bermuda expecting a tropical paradise where laid-back locals wander around barefoot drinking piña coladas. On Bermuda's 20 square miles, you will find neither towering mountains, glorious rain forests, nor exotic volcanoes. Instead, pastel cottages, quaint shops, and manicured gardens are indicative of a more staid, suburban way of life. As a British diplomat once said, "Bermuda is terribly middle-age"—and in many ways he was right. Most of the island is residential; the speed limit is 20 mph; golf and tennis are popular pastimes; the majority of visitors are over 40 years old; restaurants and shops are expensive; and casual attire in public is frowned upon. The population of 58,000 is 61% black and 39% white, but Bermudians speak the Queen's English in the Queen's own accent. White Bermudians, in particular, have strived to create a middle-class England of their own. And like almost all colonies, the Bermudian version is more insular, more conservative, and more English than the original. Pubs, fish-and-chips, and cricket are just outward manifestations of a fierce loyalty to Britain and everything it represents (or used to represent). A self-governing British colony, with a Parliament that dates from 1620, Bermuda loves pomp and circumstance, British tradition, and Bermudian history. Great ceremony attends the convening of Parliament; marching bands parade through the capital in honor of the Queen's official birthday; regimental bands and bagpipers reenact centuries-old ceremonies; and tea is served each afternoon.

Bermuda wears its history like a comfortable old coat—land is too valuable to permit the island's legacy to be cordoned off for mere display. A visitor need only wander through the 17th-century buildings of St. George's, now home to shops and private residences, to realize that Bermudian history remains part of the fabric of life, with each successive generation adding its own thread of achievement and color. Indeed, the island's isolation and diminutive size have forged a continuity of place and tradition almost totally missing in the United States. Walk into Trimingham's or A. S. Cooper & Son department stores, and you are likely to be helped by a descendant of the original founders. The same names from history keep cropping up—Tucker, Carter, Trott—and a single lane in St. George's can conjure up centuries of memories and events. Even today, the brief love affair in 1804 between Irish poet Thomas Moore and the married Hester Tucker—the "Nea" of his odes—is gossiped about with a zeal usually reserved for the transgressions of a neighbor. Bermuda's attachment to its history is more than a product of its size, however. Through its past, Bermuda invokes its own sense of identity and reinforces its relationship with Britain. Otherwise, cast off in the Atlantic more than 3,445 miles from London (yet only 508 miles from the United States), Bermuda would probably have succumbed to American cultural influences long ago.

Since the very beginning, the fate of this small colony in the Atlantic has been linked to that of the United States. The crew of the *Sea Venture,* whose wreck on Bermuda during a hurricane in 1609 began the settlement of the island, was actually on its way to Jamestown in Virginia. Indeed, the passenger list of the *Sea Venture* reads like a veritable *Who's Who* of early American history. Aboard were Sir Thomas Gates, deputy governor of Jamestown; Christopher Newport, who had led the first expedition to Jamestown; and John Rolfe, whose second wife was Princess Pocahontas. In succeeding centuries, Bermuda has been a remarkable barometer of the evolving relationship between the United States and Britain. In 1775, Bermuda was secretly forced to give gunpowder to George Washington in return for the lifting of a trade blockade that threatened the island with starvation. In the War of 1812, Bermuda was the staging post for the British fleet's attack on Washington, DC. With Britain facing a national crisis in 1940, the United States was given land on Bermuda to build a Naval Air Station in exchange for ships and supplies; then in 1990, Prime Minister Thatcher and President Bush held talks on the island.

The fact that Bermuda—just two hours by air from New York—has maintained its English character through the years is obviously part of its appeal for the more than half-million Americans (89% of all tourists) who flock here each year. More importantly, however, Bermuda means sun, sea, and sand. This bastion of Britain boasts a mild climate year-round, pink beaches, turquoise waters, coral reefs, 17th-century villages, and splendid golf courses (Bermuda has more golf courses per square mile than anywhere else in the world).

Bermuda did not always seem so attractive. After all, more than 300 wrecks lie submerged on those same reefs where divers now frolic. William Strachey, secretary-elect for Virginia and a passenger on the *Sea Venture* in 1609, wrote that Bermuda was "a place so terrible to all that ever touched on them—such tempests, thunders and other fearful objects are seen and heard about those islands that they are called The Devils Islands, feared and avoided by all sea travellers above any place in the world." For the crew of the *Sea Venture*, however, the 181 small islands that comprise Bermuda meant salvation. Contrary to rumor, the islands proved to be unusually fertile and hospitable, supporting the crew during the construction of two new ships, in which they departed for Jamestown on May 10, 1610.

Shakespeare drew on the accounts of the survivors in *The Tempest*, written in 1611. The wreck of the *Sea Venture* on harsh yet beneficent Bermuda—"these infortunate (yet fortunate) islands," as one survivor described them—contained all the elements of Shakespearean tragicomedy: That out of loss something greater is often born. Just as Prospero loses the duchy of Milan only to regain it and secure the kingdom of Naples for his daughter, Admiral Sir George Somers lost a ship but gained an island. Today, Bermuda's motto is "Quo Fata Ferunt" (Whither the Fates

Carry Us), an expression of sublime confidence in the same providence that carried the *Sea Venture* safely to shore.

That confidence has largely been justified over the years, but concerns have recently been raised about congestion, overfishing, reef damage, and a declining quality of life. Nearly 600,000 visitors a year are the golden eggs that many Bermudians feel are now killing the goose. In the face of such an influx of tourists, the behavior of some service employees, particularly bus drivers and young store clerks, has become sullen and rude. Traffic jams leading into Hamilton, the island's capital, are no longer a rarity, despite the fact that families can have only one car and car rentals are prohibited. In 1990, the government restricted the number of cruise ship visits to four per week, citing the large numbers of passengers who add to the congestion but contribute little to the island's coffers. Instead, the Bermuda Department of Tourism hopes to attract a wealthier clientele (Bermuda's tourists are already among the most affluent anywhere), preferably during the less-frequented winter season, when golf and tennis are the island's major attractions.

When all is said and done, however, Bermuda's problems stem from a surfeit of advantages rather than a dearth, and almost every island nation would gladly inherit them. The "still-vexed Bermoothes" is how Shakespeare described this Atlantic pearl, but the author of *The Tempest* may have changed his tune if he had had a chance to swim at Horseshoe Bay, or hit a mashie-niblick to the 15th green at Port Royal. Who knows, instead of referring to a storm-wracked island, *The Tempest* might have been Shakespeare's reaction to a missed putt on the 18th.

—*William Zuill*

William Zuill was a native Bermudian who was a member of the Bermuda House of Assembly, wrote several historical works about the island. Mr. Zuill died in July 1989.

WHAT'S WHERE

Hamilton

As the capital of Bermuda since 1815, the city of Hamilton is home to most of the island's government buildings; here visitors may watch the Parliament in session or visit the grand City Hall, home to two major art galleries. The Soaring Cathedral of the Most Holy Trinity, seat of the Anglican Church of Bermuda, is in Hamilton, as is Ft. Hamilton, a moated fortress with underground passageways. But most people know Hamilton as the hub of shopping and dining, with colorful Front Street as the main thoroughfare. The departure point for ferries heading to other parts of the island, Hamilton is also one of the smallest, busiest port cities in the world.

St. George

Bermuda's original capital (from the early 17th century until 1815) is steeped in history; settled in 1609, it was the second English settlement in the New World (after Jamestown, VA). Today its little alleys and walled lanes are packed with small museums and historical sights, starting with King's Square—where a cedar replica of the stocks and pillory originally used to punish criminals serves as a prop for tourist photos.

The West End

The West End of Bermuda, encompassing Somerset and Ireland islands, is a bucolic area of nature reserves, wooded areas, and beautiful harbors and bays. In addition to its natural beauty, the area's big attraction is the Royal Naval Dockyard, a former bastion of the Royal British Navy, now a major tourism center with a maritime museum and a shopping arcade.

The Parishes

Bermuda's many other parishes harbor diverse attractions: from the historic smugglers' town of Flatts Village to the coveted beaches of Paget. Scattered across the island, the parishes of Southampton, Warwick, Paget, Pembroke, Devonshire, Smith's, and Tucker's Town are best visited by bicycle or moped—but don't try to see them all in one day.

PLEASURES AND PASTIMES

Beaches

The fine, pink sand of Bermuda's beaches—a result of the many particles of shells, calcium carbonate, and bits of crushed coral that's mixed with the sand—gives them a pastel, ephemeral look. This is amplified by their picturesque surroundings, which include dramatic cliff formations, coconut palms, and gently rolling dunes that slope toward the shimmering blues of the Atlantic. The island's 34 beaches range from long, unbroken expanses of shoreline such as that at Warwick Long Bay, to small, secluded coves divided by rock cliffs such as those found at Whale Bay Beach and Jobson's Cove.

Cricket

The popularity of cricket in Bermuda can only be comprehended when you consider that the annual Cup Match Cricket Festival, a two-day event, is a national holiday. Traditionally held the Thursday and Friday before the first Monday in August, Cup Match draws an average of 12,000 people, including zealous supporters who "decorate" the batsman by running out onto the field and slipping a little cash in his pocket. Other cricket games can be viewed throughout the summer, from April through September.

Diving and Snorkeling

Reefs; shipwrecks; underwater caves; a variety of coral and marine life; and warm, clear water make Bermuda an ideal place for underwater exploration. Around Bermuda's many sheltering reefs, snorkelers may encounter parrot fish, angelfish, trumpet fish, or grouper, while divers enjoy a visibility range of 70 to 150 feet—the longest in the Western Atlantic.

Shopping

For shoppers, Bermuda has everything from sophisticated department stores and top-quality boutiques to art galleries with works by resident artists for sale, as well as fun, quirky products such as Outerbridge's Sherry Peppers and Bermuda rum. On the high end, European-made crystal and china, British-made clothing (especially woolen sweaters), and fine jewelry are popular (and expensive) products. On the artsy side, galleries throughout the island offer sculptures and paintings, handblown glass, handmade dolls, and other works by local artists and artisans.

Tennis

With more than 80 tennis courts in its 22-square miles, Bermuda has been a tennis capital since 1873. That was the year when Sir Bronlow Gray, the island's chief justice, introduced the game and built a grass tennis court at his Paget Parish home; the court still stands today. With its semitropical climate, Bermuda is still a perfect place to play tennis year-round, day or night (many courts are lit).

FODOR'S CHOICE

Beaches

★ The tiny adjacent beaches of **Chaplin Bay,** which almost disappear at high tide, are blissfully secluded.

★ Fine, pink sand, clear water, and a vibrant social scene make **Horseshoe Bay** a Bermudian favorite.

★ The quiet, low-key **Somerset Long Bay** is shielded by undeveloped parkland, grass, and brush.

★ **Warwick Long Bay,** the island's longest beach, has a beautiful sculpted coral outcropping that seems to balance on the surface of the water.

Favorite Outdoor Activities

★ **Offshore wreck diving** is a dramatic way to contemplate the storm-tossed past that's responsible for Bermuda's 300 wrecks, one of which inspired Shakespeare's *The Tempest.*

★ For a leisurely tour of the nooks and crannies of a coral-cliff wall, try **snorkeling in Church Bay.**

★ With a 16th hole that sits on a treeless promontory overlooking the waters of Whale Bay, the **Port Royal Golf & Country Club** is justifiably famous.

★ The hard-packed trails through the dunes of **South Shore Park** are ideal territory for runners and horseback riders.

Lodging

★ The island's original cottage colony, 100-year old **Cambridge Beaches,** remains a favorite among royalty and commoners alike. *$$$$*

★ A Relais & Châteaux property, **Horizons & Cottages** has the elegant feel of an 18th-century home—which, in fact, it once was. *$$$$*

★ The pink lanais of **The Reefs,** a small, casually elegant resort, are set in cliffs above Christian Bay. *$$$$*

★ **Waterloo House,** another Relais & Châteaux property, is in an early-19th-century white-column house that faces Hamilton Harbour. *$$$$*

★ The traditional, slightly formal **Princess,** in business since 1884, is regarded as the mother of Bermuda's tourist industry. *$$$–$$$$*

★ In a quiet residential area near Hamilton Harbour, the two cottages of **Little Pomander Guest House** are a find for budget travelers. *$$*

★ The secluded **Pretty Penny** guest cottages have bright, colorful rooms, kitchen and dining areas, and private patios. *$$*

★ The cozy **Salt Kettle House,** with its water views, fireside lounge, and hearty English breakfast, attracts repeat visitors year after year. *$*

Restaurants

★ Superior French cuisine and a 1670–manor house setting combine to make the **Waterlot Inn** one of the island's finest restaurants. *$$$$*

★ Nestled between high cliff rocks and a pristine beach, **Coconuts** is a lovely place to enjoy grilled fish, charbroiled steak, and of course, coconut tart. *$$$*

★ At **Plantation,** a plant-filled, glass-enclosed atrium is the perfect setting in which to enjoy freshly caught fish and tropical specialties. *$$$*

★ **Black Horse Tavern** is the place to try curried conch stew, Bermuda lobster, amberjack, rockfish, and—a true Bermuda original—shark hash. *$$*

★ The eclectic menu at **Paw-Paws,** a bistro with a cozy dining room and outdoor seating, includes everything from homemade lobster ravioli to shark hash with Creole sauce. *$$*

★ At **Dennis's Hideaway,** you'll find the eccentric Dennis Lamb offering everything from conch fritters to mussel pie to bread-and-butter pudding, among homemade picnic tables and a yapping dog or two. *$*

Special Moments
★ The **ferry ride from Hamilton to Somerset** gives you a fish's eye view of the island.

★ There's no better way to explore the parishes than on a **Vespa,** which you can ride in and out of coves and over the dunes.

★ Book lovers spend hours browsing through the **Bermuda Book Store,** a musty old place with stacks of books about the island.

★ Watch for the colorfully costumed **Gombey Dancers,** a troupe whose tradition blends African, West Indian, and American Indian influences.

FESTIVALS AND SEASONAL EVENTS

Precise dates and information about the events listed below are available from the Bermuda Department of Tourism (*see* Important Contacts A to Z *in* the Gold Guide).

WINTER

DEC.➤ The **Hamilton Jaycees Santa Claus Parade** brings Father Christmas to Front Street, along with bands, floats, majorettes, and other seasonal festivities. St. Nick also appears at the West End Junior Chamber Santa Claus Parade and the St. George's Junior Chamber Silver Bells Santa Comes to Town Parade. Contact the Bermuda Department of Tourism.

DEC.➤ The **Bermuda Goodwill Tournament for Men (Golf)** is played on four courses. Contact Tournament Director (Box WK 127, Warwick, WK BX, ☎ 441/238–3118).

DEC. 24➤ **Christmas Eve** is celebrated with midnight candlelight services in churches of all denominations.

DEC. 25➤ **Christmas** is a public holiday.

DEC. 26➤ **Boxing Day** is a public holiday for visiting friends and family. A variety of sports activities are held, and the Bermuda Gombey Dancers perform around town.

JAN.1➤ **New Year's Day** is a public holiday.

EARLY JAN.➤ The **ADT International Marathon & 10K Race,** in which top international runners participate, is open to all. Contact Pat Lake, Secretary, Bermuda Track & Field Association (Box DV 397, Devonshire DV BX, ☎ 441/236–3629, FAX 441/236–3555).

EARLY JAN.➤ The **Bermuda Senior Golf Classic,** open to visitors and residents, is played on the Port Royal Golf Course, the St. George's Golf Club, and the Ocean View Golf Course. Contact Kim Swan, Tournament Chairman, Bermuda Golf Company (Box GE 304, St. George's GE BX, ☎ 441/297–8067, FAX 441/297–2273).

EARLY JAN.➤ The **Annual Photographic Exhibition** features the work of local amateur and professional photographers. Particularly strong representation of underwater shots reveals the island's beauty beneath the surface. It is organized by the Bermuda Society of Arts in its City Hall gallery (☎ 441/292–3824).

JAN.–MAR.➤ The **Bermuda Festival** attracts internationally known artists for concerts, dance and theatrical performances. Contact Bermuda Festival Ltd. (Box HM 297, Hamilton HM AX, ☎ 441/295–1291, FAX 441/295–7403; and *see* Art and Nightlife, Chapter 9).

JAN.–MAR.➤ **Regimental Musical Display** is a captivating recreation of a retreat ceremony that lures both locals and visitors. It is performed by the Bermuda Regiment Band and the Bermuda Isles Pipe Band with dancers in Hamilton. Contact the Regimental Band (☎ 441/238–2470).

FEB.➤ The **Golden Rendezvous Month** includes special events designed for travelers over 50.

FEB.➤ The **Bermuda International Open Chess Tournament,** open to visitors and residents, takes place at one of Bermuda's major hotels. Contact the Bermuda Chess Association (Box HM 1705, Hamilton HM GX, ☎ 441/234–2322).

FEB.➤ The **Annual Regional Bridge Tournament** is held at a major hotel. Contact Bermuda Bridge Club (7 Pomander Rd., Paget PG 05, ☎ 441/236–0551).

FEB.➤ The **Lobster Pot Pro-Amateur Golf Tournament** is an annual event played at one of the island's top courses. Contact Tournament Director (Box HM 1154, Hamilton HMEX, ☎ 441/292–8822 or 441/292–6898).

FEB.➤ The **Bermuda Valentine's Mixed Foursomes,** couples' tournaments open to all golfers, are played at the St. George's Golf Club, Ocean View Golf Course, and the Port Royal Golf Course. Contact Tournament Chairman, the Bermuda Golf Company (Box GE 304, St. George's GE BX, ☎ 441/297–8067, FAX 441/297–2273).

FEB.➤ The **Annual Bermuda Rendezvous Bowling Tournament,** open to all bowlers, is sanctioned by the ABC and WIBC. Cash prizes are awarded. Contact Warwick Lanes (Box WK 128, Warwick WK BX, ☎ 441/236–5290).

FEB.➤ The **Bermuda Amateur Golf Festival,** a two-week event at five courses, includes tournaments for all. Contact the Bermuda Golf Festival, Robustelli Sports Marketing (4 Summer St., Stamford 06901, ☎ 203/352-5000) or the Bermuda Department of Tourism.

SPRING

MAR.➤ The **Bermuda All Breed Championship Dog Shows & Obedience Trials** (☎ 441/293–2128) draw dog lovers from far and wide to the Botanical Gardens in Paget. The same event also takes place in November.

MAR.➤ A **street festival** on Front Street in Hamilton includes marching bands, the Gombey Dancers, and a variety of activities. Contact the Bermuda Department of Tourism.

MAR.➤ The **Bermuda Super Senior Invitational Tennis Tournament** is a USTA-sanctioned event held at the Coral Beach & Tennis Club in Paget. Contact the Coral Beach Tennis Shop (☎ 441/236–6495).

MAR.➤ The **Bermuda Horse & Pony Association Spring Show Horse Trials** features a range of equestrian events, including dressage, jumping, West-

ern, and driving classes at National Equestrian Centre, Vesey St., Devonshire (contact Michael Cherry, ☎ 441/234–0485). **Bermuda Horse & Pony Association Trials** takes place at one of the island's equestrian arenas. Contact Michael Cherry (☎ 441/234– 0485).

MAR.➤ The **Bermuda Men's Amateur Golf Championship** is played at the Mid Ocean Club in Tucker's Town. Contact the Secretary, Bermuda Golf Association (Box HM 433, Hamilton HM BX, ☎ 441/238–1367, FAX 441/238–0983).

MAR.➤ The **Bermuda Rugby 10's Tournament** is played by teams from the United States, Canada, and Bermuda at the National Sports Club, Devonshire. Contact the Bermuda Rugby Football Union (Box HM 1909, Hamilton HM HX, ☎ 441/236–6994).

MAR.➤ The **Bermuda Cat Fanciers Association Championship Cat Show** features pedigree felines and household pets judged by All Breed American judges at various locations. Contact Morag Smith, Bermuda Cat Fanciers Association (Box HM 1306, Hamilton HM FX, ☎ 441/238–0112).

MAR.–APR.➤ The **Palm Sunday Walk** is an annual stroll. Contact the Bermuda National Trust (☎ 441/236–6483).

MAR.–APR.➤ **Good Friday** is a public holiday and traditionally a kite-flying day. A spectacular display of locally made kites can be seen at the **Bermuda Kite Festival** at Horeshoe Bay in Southampton between 11 AM and 4 PM.

Contact Young United Bermuda (☎ 441/295–0729).

MAR.–APR.➤ The **Easter Rugby Classic** features international competitions at the National Sports Club in Devonshire. Contact the National Sports Club (Middle Rd., Devonshire, ☎ 441/236–6994 or 441/295–8495).

MAR.–APR.➤ The **Bermuda Easter Lily Pro-Am Invitational Golf Tournament for Ladies** takes place at St. George's Golf Club and Port Royal Golf Course. Contact the Tournament Chairman, Bermuda Golf Company (Box GE 304, St. George's GE BX, ☎ 441/297–8067, FAX 441/297–2273).

MAR.–APR.➤ The **Bermuda Spring Break Sports,** an action-packed event for American college students, was started in 1994 to replace the party-oriented College Weeks that had been held for decades. Coaches, teams, and athletes are invited to participate in lacrosse, golf, tennis, and rugby. Contact Wayne Smith, Bermuda Department of Tourism (Global House, 43 Church Street, Hamilton HM 12, ☎ 441/292–0023).

MAR.–APR.➤ The **Bermuda Youth Soccer Cup** attracts teams from the United Kingdom, the United States, Canada, and several Caribbean nations. Matches are played at several fields on the island. Contact the Bermuda Department of Tourism.

MAR.–APR.➤ **Harvard's Hasty Pudding Club** has presented its satirical theatricals in Bermuda for more than 30 years; it's

the club's only perfor-
mance site outside the
United States. Call City
Hall Theatre in Hamilton
(☎ 441/295–1727).

MAR.–OCT.➤ The **Beat
Retreat Ceremony** is
usually performed twice
monthly by the Bermuda
Regiment Band, the
Bermuda Isles Pipe Band
with Dancers, and mem-
bers of the Bermuda Pipe
Band. The historic cere-
mony is performed alter-
nately on Front Street in
Hamilton, King's Square
in St. George's, and
Dockyard in the West
End. No performances
are given in August.
Contact the Bermuda
Department of Tourism.

APR.➤ The **Agricultural
Exhibition,** similar to a
county or state fair, takes
place at the Botanical
Gardens in Paget (☎ 441/
236–4201).

APR.➤ The **Peppercorn
Ceremony** celebrates—
amid great pomp and
circumstance—the pay-
ment of one peppercorn
in rent to the government,
by the Masonic Lodge of
St. George No. 200 of the
Grand Lodge of Scotland,
for their headquarters
in the Old State House
in St. George's. Contact
the Bermuda Department
of Tourism.

APR.➤ The **Bermuda Open
Tennis Classic** is an ATP
Tour, USTA–Sanctioned
Event of the world's top
professional players.
Tickets are available in
advance through Bermuda
Tennis Promotions
(☎ 441/236–1975) or the
Coral Beach and Tennis
Club (☎ 441/236–6495).

APR.➤ The **Bermuda End-
to-End Scenic Railway Trail
Walk for Charities** is a
terrific way to see the

island and meet plenty of
active residents. The 26-
mile course begins in
King's Square, St.
George's and finishes at
the Royal Naval Dock-
yard amid a range of
festive activities. An
alternate 15-mile course
begins at Albouy's Point,
Hamilton. Visitors may
sign up 30 minutes before
either starting point.
Proceeds go to four local
charities. A pasta loading
banquet takes place the
night before. Contact
Johnson & Higgins
(☎ 441/297–9715).

APR.➤ The **Bermuda
Mixed Foursomes Ama-
teur Championship** is a
36-hole stroke play com-
petition played at the Port
Royal Golf Course. Con-
tact Tom Smith, Bermuda
Golf Association (Box
HM 433, Hamilton HM
BX, ☎ 441/238–1367,
FAX 441/238–0983).

APR. 13–27➤ The 1996
**International Senior
Games** will take place in
Bermuda. Competitions
from a range of active
sports such as swimming,
cycling, squash, and tennis
are open to participants
ages 50-plus. Cultural
activities—art, poetry
readings, and creative
writing—will complement
the sports program. Con-
tact the Bermuda Depart-
ment of Tourism.

APR.–MAY➤ The **open
houses and gardens tours,**
sponsored by the
Bermuda Garden Club,
give visitors the chance to
walk through some of
Bermuda's private homes
and gardens not usually
open to the public. Con-
tact the Chairman (☎
441/236–6425).

APR.–MAY➤ **International
Race Week** pits sailors

from around the world
against Bermudians in a
series of races on the
Great Sound. Contact the
Royal Bermuda Yacht
Club (☎ 441/295–2214).

MAY➤ The **Bermuda
Heritage Month** features a
host of cultural, commem-
orative, and sporting
activities. The crescendo is
Bermuda Day (May 24), a
public holiday that in-
cludes a parade at Bernard
Park, a cycling race, a half-
marathon (13 miles) for
Bermuda residents only,
and Bermuda dinghy races
in St. George's Harbour.
Contact the Department of
Cultural Affairs (☎ 441/
292–9447).

MAY➤ The **Bermuda
Senior Amateur Champi-
onships for Men & Ladies,**
which takes place at
Riddells Bay Golf &
Country Club, requires
that women be at least 50
years old and men at least
55. Contact Tom Smith,
Bermuda Golf Association
(Box HM 433, Hamilton
HM BX, ☎ 441/238–
1367, FAX 441/238–0983).

SUMMER

JUNE➤ **Queen Elizabeth
II's Birthday** is a public
holiday celebrated in mid-
June with military march-
ing bands parading down
Front Street in Hamilton.
Contact the Bermuda
Department of Tourism.

JUNE➤ The Open Air
Pops Concerts, presented
by the Bermuda Philhar-
monic Society at King's
Square, St. George's and
Clocktower Centre at the
Royal Naval Dockyard,
are free and a great way

to meet residents. Contact the Organizer (☎ 441/293–0024).

JUNE➤ A host of **sailing races** take place in June, alternating between odd- and even-numbered years. Races that attract power-house yachtsmen during even-numbered years include the spectacular Newport to Bermuda Ocean Yacht Race and the Onion Patch Series (contact the Royal Bermuda Yacht Club, ☎ 441/295–2214), as well as the Bermuda Ocean Race from Annapolis, Maryland (contact St. George's Dinghy & Sports Club, ☎ 441/297–1612). Events in alternate years include the Bermuda 1-2 Single-Handed Race, from Newport to Bermuda and back (contact St. George's Dinghy & Sports Club (☎ 441/297–1612), the Marion (MA)–Bermuda Cruising Yacht Race (contact the Royal Hamilton Amateur Dinghy Club (☎ 441/236–5432), and the Trans-At Daytona–Bermuda Yacht Race (contact St. George's Dinghy & Sports Club (☎ 441/297–1612).

JUNE➤ The **Bermuda Amateur Stroke Play Championship for Men and Ladies** are two simultaneous events played at the Port Royal Golf Course. Men and women play 72- and 54–hole strokes, respectively. Contact Tom Smith, Bermuda Golf Association (Box 433, Hamilton HM BX, ☎ 441/238–1367, FAX 441/238–0983).

JULY➤ **Marine Science Day** at the Bermuda Biological Station for Research (11 Biological La., Ferry Reach, St. George's,

☎ 441/297–1880) gives visitors an opportunity to learn about marine research from the perspective of a mid-ocean island.

JULY➤ The **Bermuda Angler's Club International Light Tackle Tournament,** organized by the Spanish Point Boat Club, draws a large crowd of spectators to its 5 PM weigh-in (☎ 441/295–1030).

JULY OR AUG.➤ The **Cup Match Cricket Festival** is a public holiday, with matches between East and West End cricket clubs. Held at the Somerset Cricket Club (Broome St., Sandys, ☎ 441/234–0327) or the St. George's Cricket Club (Wellington Slip Rd., St. George's, ☎ 441/297–0374), the match is one of the most festive occasions of the year, attracting thousands of fans who gather to picnic, chat, and dance.

AUG.➤ Landlubbers in homemade contraptions compete in the hilarious **Non-Mariners Race,** a spectacle held on Mangrove Bay. Contact the Race Organizer (☎ 441/236–3683).

AUG.➤ The **Flybridge Tackle Junior Tournament** is open to children who fish from the shoreline or a boat, using hand lines or a rod and reel. Register with Flybridge Tackle (Reid St., Hamilton, ☎ 441/295–1845).

AUTUMN

SEPT.➤ **Labour Day** is a public holiday featuring a wide range of activities,

including a march from Union Square in Hamilton to Bernard Park. Local entertainers and specialty food stalls featuring local fare are included in the festivities. Contact the Bermuda Department of Tourism.

SEPT.➤ The **Annual Bermuda Triathlon** is open to visiting and local teams who compete in a one-mile swim, 15-mile cycle, and six-mile run. Contact the Bermuda Triathlon Association (Box HM 1002, Hamilton HM DX, ☎ 441/293–2765).

OCT.➤ The **Columbus Day Regatta Weekend,** sponsored by the Royal Bermuda Yacht Club, features keel boats competing in the Great Sound. Contact the Royal Bermuda Yacht Club (☎ 441/295–2214).

OCT.➤ The **Omega Gold Cup International Match Race Tournament** is an exciting series of one-on-one yacht races in Hamilton Harbour that attracts top sailors from around the world. Contact the Royal Bermuda Yacht Club (☎ 441/295–2214).

NOV.➤ **Remembrance Day** is a public holiday in memory of Bermuda's and its allies' fallen soldiers. A parade with Bermudian, British, and U.S. military units, the Bermuda Police, and war veterans' organizations begins at Front Street in Hamilton. Contact the Bermuda Department of Tourism.

NOV.➤ The **Convening of Parliament** on the first Friday of the month is preceded by the arrival of His Excellency The Governor, in plumed hat and full regalia, at the Cabinet Building on Front Street in Hamilton. Contact the House of Assembly (☎ 441/292–7408).

Nov.➤ The **Bermuda Four Ball Stroke Play Amateur Championship for Men and Ladies** are two simultaneous events at the Port Royal Golf Course. Contact Tom Smith, Bermuda Golf Association (Box HM 433, Hamilton HM BX, ☎ 441/238–1367, FAX 441/238–0983).

Nov.➤ The **World Rugby Classic** pits former international rugby players against the best players from Bermuda, in a match at the National Sports Club (Middle Rd., Devonshire). Contact the Chairman (☎ 295–8495).

2 Cruising in Bermuda

CHOOSING YOUR CRUISE

THE RIGHT SHIP IS ONE THAT MAKES YOU comfortable. Every ship has its own personality, depending upon its size, when it was built, and for what purpose. Big ships are more stable and offer a huge variety of activities and facilities. Smaller ships feel intimate, like private clubs. Each type of ship satisfies a certain type of passenger, and for every big-ship fan there is somebody who would never set foot aboard one of these "floating resorts."

But when choosing your cruise, the type of ship isn't the only factor to consider. You also need to find out about the nature of the experience you will have—the lifestyle and activities available by day and after dark, the mealtime hours and dining-room dress codes, how roomy the ship is, and how good the service is apt to be. Equally important are your itinerary, the accommodations, and the cost of the cruise.

Types of Ships

Although all ocean liners are equipped with swimming pools, spas, nightclubs, theaters, and casinos, there are three distinct types: classic liners, cruise liners, and megaships. Many **classic liners,** ships constructed between 1950 and 1969 for transatlantic or other ocean crossings, are still sailing in the fleets of many cruise lines. Beginning in the 1960s, ship lines began to create vessels specifically for cruising. Some of these **cruise liners** were brand-new; others were converted ferries or freighters. Vessels known as **megaships,** the biggest cruise ships ever built, first appeared in the late 1980s and, with their immense proportions and passenger capacities, immediately established a new standard of cruise ship design.

Classic Liners

With their long, sweeping hulls and stepped-back passenger decks, these vessels defined passenger ship design for decades. Now serving cruise duty, they were originally configured to keep passengers happy during long ocean crossings. Typically, their cabins and closets are larger than those on vessels built for cruising. Deck space is sheltered, with fully or partially enclosed promenades that allow you to relax on deck even during foul weather. A few are still steam powered, without the vibrations sometimes associated with diesel power. Rich wood panels the walls, and fixtures may be the original brass. Smaller ships may feel cramped because of low ceilings in the lobby and corridors. But on the most opulent vessels, public spaces designed to inspire still do. There are balconies above the dining room where musicians serenade diners; stained glass graces the cinemas and other public spaces; and grand staircases lead from one deck to another. Such traditional features have proved so enduring they have been incorporated in the plans for some of today's newest vessels.

Although classic ships typically carry between 600 and 1,000 passengers and weigh between 20,000 and 30,000 tons, a couple of them are among the largest passenger ships afloat.

Cruise Liners

When shipbuilders stopped constructing vessels for transportation and started designing them for vacationing, the cruise liner entered the scene. On these ships, outdoor deck space is plentiful; stateroom space is not. Many have a wraparound outdoor promenade deck that allows you to stroll or jog the perimeter of the ship. Older cruise liners resemble the transatlantic ships from which they are descended: Decks are stacked one atop the other in steps, and the hull amidships may appear to droop, so the bow and stern seem to curve upward. In the newest cruise liners, where traditional meets trendy, you'll find atrium lobbies and expansive sun and sports decks, picture windows instead of portholes, and cabins that open onto private verandas. The smallest cruise liners carry 500 passengers and weigh in at 10,000 tons, while the largest accommodate 1,500 passengers, register 50,000 tons, and are stuffed with diversions—almost like megaships.

Megaships

The centerpiece of most megaships is a three-, five-, or seven-story central atrium. However, these giant vessels are most easily recognized by their boxy profile: The hull and superstructure rise straight out of the water, as high as 14 stories tall, topped out by a huge sun or sports deck with a jogging track and swimming pool, which may be Olympic size. Some megaships, but not all, also have a wraparound promenade deck. Like the latest cruise liners, picture windows are standard equipment, and cabins in the top categories have private verandas. From their casinos and discos to their fitness centers, everything is proportionally bigger and more extravagant than on other ships. Between 1,500 and 2,500 passengers can be accommodated, and tonnage ranges from 60,000 to 70,000 or more.

The Cruise Experience

Your cruise experience will be shaped by several factors, and to determine whether a particular ship's style will suit you, you need to do a bit of research. Is a full program of organized activities scheduled by day? What happens in the evening? Are there one or two seatings in the dining room? If there is more than one, you will not be allowed to arrive and exit as the spirit moves you. Instead, you must show up promptly when service begins—and clear out within a specified time. What kind of entertainment is offered after dark? And how often do passengers dress up for dinner? Some cruises are fancier than others.

Equally important are the space ratio and the passenger-to-crew ratio. The latter indicates the number of passengers served by each crew member—the lower the ratio, the better the level of service. The space ratio, the gross tonnage of a ship divided by its passenger capacity, allows you to compare ships' roominess. The higher the ratio, the more spacious the vessel feels; it will feel quite large if the ratio is 40:1 or higher, cramped if the ratio is less than 25:1.

Although no two cruises are quite the same, even aboard the same ship, cruise experiences tend to fall into three categories.

Formal

Formal cruises embody the ceremony of cruising, recalling the days when traveling by ship was an event in itself. By day, shipboard lifestyle is generally unstructured, with few organized activities. Tea and bullion may be served to the accompaniment of music from a classical trio in the afternoon. Meals in the dining room are served in a single seating, and passengers are treated to the finest cuisine afloat. Jackets and ties for men are the rule for dinner, tuxedos are not uncommon, and the dress code is observed faithfully throughout the evening. Pianists, cabaret acts, and local entertainers provide nighttime diversion. Service is extremely attentive and personalized. Passenger-to-crew and space ratios are best. Because these cruises tend to attract destination-oriented passengers, shore excursions sometimes are included in the fare, as are pre- or post-cruise land packages and sometimes even tips.

Semiformal

Semiformal cruises are a bit more casual than their formal counterparts. Meals are served in two seatings, menu choices are plentiful, and the cuisine is on a par with that available in better restaurants. Men tend to wear a jacket and tie to dinner most nights. Adding a distinct flair to the dining room is the practice of many cruise lines to hire waiters of a single nationality. Featured dishes may be prepared table-side, and you often are able, with advance notice, to order a special diet, such as kosher, low-salt, low-cholesterol, sugar-free, or vegetarian. There is a daily program of scheduled events, but there's time for more independent pursuits; passengers with similar interests are often encouraged to meet at appointed times for chess or checkers, deck games, and other friendly contests. Production-style shows are staged each evening, but the disco scene may not be too lively. Passenger-to-crew and space ratios assure good service and plenty of room for each passenger.

Casual

Casual cruises are the most popular. Shipboard dress and lifestyle are informal. Meals in the dining room are served in two seatings; menus are usually not extensive, and the food is good but not extraordinary; your options may be limited if you have special dietetic requirements. Men dress in sport shirts and slacks for dinner most nights, in jackets and ties only two or three evenings of a typical seven-day sailing. Aboard casual ocean liners, activities are more diverse than on formal and semiformal ships, and there is almost always something going on, from bingo to beer chugging contests. Las Vegas-style variety shows or Broadway revues headline the evening entertainment. Discos bop into the wee hours. Passenger-to-crew and space ratios are generally good, but service tends to be less personal.

Cost

For one all-inclusive price, a cruise gives you what many have called the trip of a lifetime. The only extras are tips, shore excursions, shopping, bar bills, and other incidentals. The axiom "the more you pay, the more you get" doesn't always hold true: While higher fares do prevail for better ships, which have more comfortable cabins, more attractive decor, and better service, the passenger in the least expensive cabin eats the same food, sees the same shows, and shares the same amenities as one paying more than $1,000 per day for the top suite on any given ship. (A notable exception is aboard the *Queen Elizabeth 2*, where your dining room assignment is based on your cabin category.) To some, a larger cabin is not worth the extra money, since it is used mainly for sleeping and dressing.

A handy way to compare costs of different ships is to look at the per diem—the price of a cruise on a daily basis per passenger, based on double occupancy. (For instance, the per diem is $100 for a seven-day cruise that costs $700 per person when two people share the same cabin.) In addition to your cabin fare, consider the following expenses when budgeting for your cruise.

For each ship reviewed in Chapter 3, average per diems are listed in three cabin categories: suites, outside cabins, and inside cabins (*see* Accommodations, *below*). These average per diems are meant for comparative purposes only; for actual cruise fares, which can vary wildly and are subject to widespread discounting, you'll need to contact your travel agent or cruise specialist. When booking your cruise, don't forget to consider these expenditures:

Pre- and post-cruise arrangements: If you plan to arrive a day or two early at the port of embarkation, or linger a few days for sightseeing after debarkation, estimate the cost of your hotel, meals, car rental, sightseeing, and other expenditures. Cruise lines sell packages for pre- and post-cruise stays that may or may not cost less than arrangements you make independently, so shop around.

Airfare: Airfare and transfers are often included in the basic cruise fare; however, the cruise line chooses your airline and flight. Lines sometimes give passengers who make their own arrangements an air transportation credit of $200–$300 for Bermuda cruises. You may find a better airfare or more convenient routing or use frequent-flyer miles.

Pretrip incidentals: These may include trip or flight insurance, the cost of boarding your pets, airport or port parking, departure tax, visas, long-distance calls home, clothing, film or videotape, and other miscellaneous expenses.

Shore excursions and expenses: Costs for ship-organized shore excursions in Bermuda range from less than $25 for the cheapest city tour to $50 or more for the most expensive diving or snorkeling packages.

Amusement and gambling allowance: Video games, bingo, and gambling can set you back a bundle. If you plan to bet, budget for your losses—you'll almost certainly have them. You must be over 18 to gamble on a cruise ship.

Shopping: Include what you expect to spend for both inexpensive souvenirs and pricey duty-free purchases.

On-board incidentals: Most cruise lines recommend that passengers tip their cabin steward, dining room waiter, and assistant waiter a total of $7.50 per person, per day. Tips for bartenders and others who have helped you will vary. Also figure in the bar tabs and the cost of wine with meals, laundry, beauty parlor services, purchases in the gift shop, and other incidentals.

Accommodations

Where you sleep matters only if you enjoy extra creature comforts and are willing to pay for them; on most of today's one-class cruise ships no particular status or stigma is attached to your choice of cabin. Having said that, there's certainly an advantage to personally selecting the best cabin within your budget, rather than having your travel agent or cruise line representative simply book you into the next available accommodation. The earlier you book, the better the selection.

Cabin Size
The term "stateroom," used on some ships, is usually interchangeable with "cabin." Price is directly proportional to size and location, and the overwhelming majority of cabins are tiny. The higher you go in the ship, the larger the quarters tend to be; outside cabins are generally bigger than inside ones (*see* Location, *below*).

Suites are the roomiest and best-equipped accommodations, but even aboard the same ship, they may differ in size, facilities, and price. Steward service may be more attentive to passengers staying in suites; top suites on some ships are even assigned private butlers. Most suites have a sitting area with a sofa and chairs; some have two bathrooms, occasionally with a whirlpool bath. The most expensive suites may be priced without regard to the number of passengers occupying them.

Location

On all ships, regardless of size or design, the bow (front) and stern (back) pitch up and down on the waves far more than the hull amidships (middle). Ships also experience a side to side motion known as roll. The closer your deck is to the true center of the ship—about halfway between the bottom of the hull and the highest deck and midway between the bow and the stern—the less you will feel the ship's movement. Some cruise lines charge more for cabins amidships; most charge more for the higher decks.

Outside cabins have portholes or windows (which cannot be opened); on the upper decks, the view from outside cabins may be partially obstructed by lifeboats or overlook a public promenade. Because outside cabins are more desirable, newer ships are configured with mostly outside cabins or with outside cabins only. Increasingly, an outside cabin on an upper deck comes with a private veranda. Windows are mirrored in cabins that overlook a public promenade so that passersby can't see in—at least by day; after dark, you need to draw your curtains.

Inside cabins on older vessels are often smaller and oddly shaped. On newer ships, the floor plans of inside cabins are virtually identical to those of outside cabins. Providing you don't feel claustrophobic without a window—and most lines hang curtains on the wall to create the illusion of one—inside cabins represent an excellent value.

Cruise brochures show the ship's layout deck by deck and the approximate location and shape of every cabin and suite. Use the deck plan to make sure the cabin you pick is not near public rooms or the ship's engine, which may be noisy, and make sure that you are near stairs or an elevator to avoid walking down long corridors every time you return to your cabin. If detailed layouts of typical cabins are printed, you can determine what kind of beds the cabin has, whether it has a window or a porthole, and what furnishings are provided.

Furnishings

All ocean liner cabins are equipped with individually controlled air conditioning, limited closet space, and a private bathroom—usually closet-size, with a toilet, small shower, and washbasin. More expensive cabins, especially on newer ships, may have a bathtub. Most cabins also have a small desk or dresser, a reading light, and, on many ships, a TV and sometimes even a VCR. Except on some older ocean liners, all cabins also come with a phone.

Sharing

Most cabins are designed to accommodate two people. When more than two share a cabin, the third and fourth passengers are usually offered a substantial discount, thereby lowering the per-person price for the room for the entire group. An additional discount is sometimes offered when children share a cabin with their parents. There's usually a premium on smaller, one-person cabins—when you can find them. When none are available, as is frequently the case, passengers traveling on their own must pay a single supplement, which usually ranges from 125% to 200% of the double-occupancy per-person rate. On request, many cruise lines will match up two strangers of the same sex in a cabin at no additional surcharge.

BOOKING YOUR CRUISE

Timing is important when booking your cruise. Since most cruise ships sail at or near capacity, especially during high seasons, you get the greatest choice and sometimes a discount if you make a reservation six months to a year in advance. If you book close to the sailing date, your choices may be more limited, but you may get an even better deal.

Getting the Best Cruise for Your Dollar

Like everything in retail, each cruise has a list price. However, the actual selling price can vary tremendously: These days, if you ask any 10 passengers on almost any given ship what they're paying per diem, they'll give you 10 different answers. Discounts on the same accommodation can range from 5% on a single fare to 50% on the second fare in a cabin. On really soft sailings, you may see newspaper ads offering fares that allow two passengers to sail for the price of one.

Approach deep discounts with skepticism. Fewer than a dozen cabins may be offered at the discounted price, they may be inside cabins, and the fare may not include air transportation or transfers between the airport and the ship. Some may require that you leave almost immediately.

A single, sure-fire path to whopping savings may not exist, but you can maximize your chances in several ways.

Full-Service Travel Agents

Consider booking with a full-service travel agent. He or she can make your arrangements and deal directly with airlines, cruise companies, car-rental agencies, hotels, and resorts. You won't be charged a service fee—agents make money on commissions from the cruise lines and other suppliers—and you'll eliminate the expenses of long-distance phone calls and postage. Some agents even throw in complimentary flight bags and champagne.

But you may not wish to rely solely on your agent when selecting your ship and itinerary. Because most travel agencies book everything from cruises to business flights to theme-park vacations, your local agent may not have a full knowledge of the cruise industry. Some agents may have sailed on some ships and seen some ports, but most have acquired their knowledge of competing cruise lines from the same brochures and videotapes that are available to the public. Because agents work on commission, there is some potential conflict of interest. Fortunately, disreputable agents remain relatively scarce.

Cruise-Only Travel Agents

"Cruise-only" travel agencies constitute one of the fastest-growing segments of the travel industry, and most major towns and cities have at least one. Their knowledgeable employees may have sailed on many ships. But that's only one of their strengths. Working in conjunction with specific cruise lines, cruise-only agencies obtain significant discounts by agreeing to sell large blocks of tickets. To make their quotas, they pass along savings to their clients. The discount you get depends on the agency, cruise line, season, current demand, and the popularity of the ship you have chosen. Cruise-only agencies cannot issue airline tickets because they are not accredited by the airlines, but they can still make your flight arrangements. If the basic cost of your cruise does not include airfare, a cruise-only agency can sell you a fly-cruise package from the cruise line that includes your ship accommodations and transportation to and from the points of embarkation and debarkation. Similarly, cruise-only agencies can make your pre- or post-cruise vacation arrangements with a land package from the cruise line.

Cruise Travel Clubs

Some cruise-only agencies are run as private clubs, and for an annual fee of $25–$50 offer members a newsletter, flight bags or other gifts, special benefits to repeat clients, and sometimes, if the agency negotiates a group price with the cruise line, better rates.

Haggling

Shopping around may or may not get you a better deal. One agency may sell at fixed prices, while another may charge whatever supply and demand will allow. Some cruise-only travel agencies discount every cruise they sell. Even when an agent quotes a particular price, go ahead and try for a further discount—you have absolutely nothing to lose. If you don't *ask* for the lowest price, you're probably not going to get it.

Last-Minute Booking

When cruise companies have cancellations or unsold cabins, they use cruise-only agencies and cruise specialists to recoup revenue. The closer the sailing date, the bigger the savings. Typically, you can save more than 25% for booking at the last minute, usually only from two weeks to a month ahead. For the best discount, you have to be flexible, prepared to leave on as little as 24 hours' notice. You might end up spending your vacation at home—or you might luck into the travel bargain of a lifetime.

There's a downside. Cabin choice is limited, air transportation may not be included, and you may not get the meal seating you prefer. Also, think about why those cabins haven't been sold. Do you want to sail for less on the leftovers, or pay more to sail on a ship that is consistently full because it is consistently good?

Early Booking Discounts

More and more cruise lines are offering discounts to customers who book early. In addition to the discount, an early booking gives you a better choice of cabin and sailing date. Some lines guarantee that passengers who book early will receive any lower rate that the line subsequently posts on that particular cruise. Some lines offer an additional discount for paying the full fare in advance.

Spotting Swindlers

Always be on the lookout for a scam. Although reputable agencies far outnumber crooks, a handful of marketers use deceptive and unethical tactics. The best way to avoid being fleeced is to deal with an agency that has been in business for at least five years. If you have any doubts about its credibility, consult your Better Business Bureau or consumer protection agency *before* you mail in any deposits. Or call the cruise line to verify the agent's reliability. Do not send money for a voucher that may be redeemed for a cruise at some later, unspecified date. Be wary of bait-and-switch tactics: If you're told that an advertised bargain cruise is sold out, do not be persuaded to book a more expensive substitute. Also, if you're told that your cruise reservation was canceled because of overbooking and that you must pay extra for a confirmed rescheduled sailing, demand a full refund. Finally, if ever you fail to receive a voucher or ticket on the promised date, place an inquiry immediately.

Choosing the Right Agency or Club

How do you find an honest, competent travel agent? Solicit recommendations from friends, family, and colleagues, especially those who have cruised before. Or look in the Yellow Pages for agencies identified as members of CLIA (Cruise Lines International Association), NACOA (National Association of Cruise-Only Agencies), or ASTA (American Society of Travel Agents). Agents of the 20,000 CLIA affiliates nationwide have had extensive training, have cruised on several ships and inspected others, and have the background and resources to carefully match prospective passengers with the appropriate cruise line; agents who are CLIA Accredited Cruise Counselors or Master Cruise Counselors are most knowledgeable. Larger, well-established travel agencies—especially those that are cruise-only or are NACOA members—are more likely to employ experienced cruisers, but smaller agencies may give you more personal attention. Check around and weigh your options carefully. Then phone for an appointment to interview a few prospects.

One point is critical: To have a wonderful cruise, you need to pick the right ship. Bon vivants will find long cruises on certain formal ships boring; foodies and highbrows will be miserable on most casual cruises. A romantic getaway cannot be had in the company of families with howling children. Thus, an agent's first step should be to ask *you* questions about *your* lifestyle, vacation preferences, and expectations. If an agent places promotion of a specific ship or cruise line over consideration of your particular needs, move on.

Agencies to Contact

The agencies listed below specialize in booking cruises, have been in business at least five years, and emphasize customer service as well as price. Publications such as *Cruise Travel Magazine* and *Cruises & Tours,* available at most newsstands and bookstores, also list agencies.

CRUISE ONLY

Cruise Fairs of America (2029 Century Park E, Suite 950, Los Angeles, CA 90067, ☎ 310/556–2925 or 800/456–4386, FAX 310/556–2254), established in 1987, has a fax-back service for information on the latest deals. The agency also publishes a twice-yearly newsletter with tips on cruising.

Cruise Headquarters (4225 Executive Sq. Suite 1600 La Jolla, CA 92037, ☎ 619/453–1201 or 800/424–6111, FAX 619/453–0653), established in 1988, specializes in creating personalized shoreside arrangements.

Cruise Line, Inc. (4770 Biscayne Blvd., Penthouse 1, Miami, FL 33137, ☎ 305/576–0036 or 800/777–0707, FAX 305/576–0073), established in 1983, publishes *World of Cruising* magazine and a number of brochures, including a "Guide to First Time Cruising," and a "Guide to Shipboard Wedding Packages."

Cruise Pro (2527 E. Thousand Oaks Blvd., Thousand Oaks, CA 91362, ☎ 805/371–9884, 800/222–7447, or 800/258–7447 in CA; FAX 805/371–9084), established in 1983, has special discounts for members of its Voyager's Club ($15 to join).

Cruise Quarters of America (1241 E. Dyer Rd., Suite 110, Santa Ana, CA 92705, ☎ 714/754–0280 or 800/648–2444, FAX 714/850–1974), established in 1986, is a division of Associated Travel International, one of the country's largest travel companies, and has a VIP club (☎ 800/517–5391) for upscale cruise planning.

Crui$e Value (c/o Golden Bear Travel, 16 Digital Dr., Suite 100, Box 6115, Novato, CA 94948, ☎ 415/382–8900 or 800/551–1000 outside CA, FAX 415/382–9086) is the cruise-only division of a full-service travel company that also acts as general sales agent for a number of foreign cruise ships. The agency's Mariner Club runs hosted cruises for passengers who would like to travel as part of a group.

CruiseMasters (3415 Sepulveda Blvd., Suite 645, Los Angeles, CA 90034, ☎ 310/397–7175 or 800/242–9000, FAX 310/397–3568), established in 1987, gives each passenger a personalized, bound guide to his or her ship's ports of call. The agency's Family Cruise Club is for parents cruising with their children. A world cruise desk is dedicated to booking very long cruises.

Cruises of Distinction (93 Dorsa Ave., Livingston, NJ 07039, ☎ 201/716–0088 or 800/634–3445, FAX 201/716–9893), established in 1984, publishes a free 80-page cruise catalogue four times a year. For a fee ($39), you can receive notification of unadvertised specials by mail or fax.

Don Ton Cruise Tours (3151 Airway Ave., E–1, Costa Mesa, CA 92626, ☎ 714/545–3737 or 800/432–3491, FAX 714/545–5275), established in 1972, features a variety of special-interest clubs, including a short-notice club, singles club, family cruise club, and an adventure cruise club. Call for a complete list.

Kelly Cruises (1315 W. 22nd St., Suite 105, Oak Brook, IL 60521, ☎ 708/990–1111 or 800/837–7447, FAX 708/990–1147), established in 1986, publishes a quarterly newsletter highlighting new ships and special rates. Passengers can put their names on a free mailing list for last-minute deals.

Vacations at Sea (4919 Canal St., New Orleans, LA 70119, ☎ 504/482–1572 or 800/749–4950, FAX 504/486–8360), established in 1983, puts together its own pre- and post-cruise land packages and hosted tours.

FULL SERVICE
Ambassador Tours (120 Montgomery St., Suite 400, San Francisco, CA 94104, ☎ 415/981–5678 or 800/989–9000, FAX 415/982–3490), established in 1955, devotes 80% of its business to cruises.

Time to Travel (582 Market St., San Francisco, CA 94104, ☎ 415/421–3333 or 800/524–3300, FAX 415/421–4857), established in 1935, devotes 90% of its business to cruises.

Trips 'n Travels, (1024 Kane Concourse, Bay Harbor, FL 33154, ☎ 305/864–2222 or 800/331–2745, FAX 305/861–8809) devotes 80% of its business to cruises. The agency's concierge service arranges theater tickets and other amenities in ports of call.

White Travel Service (127 Park Rd., West Hartford, CT 06119, ☎ 860/233–2648 or 800/547–4790, prerecorded cruise hot line 860/236–6176, FAX 860/236–6177), founded in 1972, does most of its business in cruises.

Payment

Handing money over to your travel agent constitutes a contract, so before you pay your deposit, study the cruise brochure to find out the provisions of the cruise contract. What is the payment schedule and cancellation policy? Will there be any additional charges before you can board your ship, such as transfers, port fees, or local taxes? If your air connection requires you to spend an evening in a hotel near the port before or after the cruise, is there an extra cost?

If possible, pay your deposit and balance with a credit card. This gives you some recourse if you need to cancel, and you can ask the credit card company to intercede on your behalf in case of problems. Don't forget to get a receipt.

Deposit

Most cruises must be reserved with a refundable deposit of between $200 and $500 per person, depending upon how expensive the cruise is; the balance is due 45–60 days before you sail. Don't let a travel agent pressure you into paying a larger deposit or paying the balance earlier. If the cruise is less than 45 days away, however, it may be legitimate for the agency to require the entire amount immediately.

Cancellation

Your entire deposit or payment may be refunded if you cancel your reservation between 45 and 60 days before departure; the grace period varies from line to line. If you cancel later than that, you will forfeit some or all of your deposit. An average cancellation charge is $100 one month before sailing, $100 plus 50% of the ticket price between 15 and 30 days prior to departure, and $100 plus 75% of the ticket price between 14 days and 24 hours ahead of time. If you simply fail to show up when the ship sails, you will lose the entire amount. Many travel agents also assess a small cancellation fee. Check their policy.

WAIVERS AND INSURANCE

Cruise lines sell two types of policies that protect you in the event of cancellation or trip interruption. **Waivers** provide a full refund if you cancel your trip for any reason, usually up to 72 hours before sailing; the cost to cover a seven-day cruise is about $65. **Insurance** protects against cancellation for specified reasons plus trip delay, interruption, medical expenses, emergency evacuation, and lost, stolen, or damaged luggage; the cost to cover a seven-day cruise is about $99. Neither of these cruise-line programs protects you against cruise-line default.

BEFORE YOU GO

Tickets, Vouchers, and Other Travel Documents

After you make the final payment to your travel agent, the cruise line will issue your cruise tickets and vouchers for airport–ship transfers. Depending on the airline, and whether you have purchased a fly-cruise package, you may receive your plane tickets or charter flight vouchers at the same time; you may also receive vouchers for any shore excursions, although most cruise lines issue these aboard ship. Should your travel documents not arrive when promised, contact your travel agent or call the cruise line directly. If you book late, tickets may be delivered directly to the ship.

Planning for Expenses

Some ships will not cash personal checks or take certain credit cards. Check your cruise documents to determine which forms of payment are accepted aboard ship. The purser's office usually cashes traveler's checks, and on some ships, you can even open an account there and get cash when you need it; it will be added to your bill along with on-board purchases, and you pay at the end of the cruise. Cashiers at on-board casinos also cash traveler's checks and dispense cash advances on your credit card, even to those who don't intend to gamble.

ON BOARD

Checking Out Your Cabin

The first thing to do upon arriving at your cabin or suite is to make sure that it is the one you booked. If there are two twin beds instead of the double bed you wanted, or other serious problems, ask to be moved *before* the ship disembarks. Unless the ship is full, you can usually persuade the chief housekeeper or hotel manager to allow you to change cabins. It is customary to tip the stewards who assist you in moving to another cabin.

Since your cabin is your home away from home for a week, everything should be to your satisfaction. Take a good look around. Is the cabin clean and orderly? Do the toilet, shower, and faucets work? Check the telephone and television. Again, major problems should be addressed immediately. Minor concerns, such as not enough bath towels or pillows, can wait until the frenzy of embarkation has subsided.

Your dining time and seating assignment card may be in your cabin; now is the time to check it and immediately request any changes.

Shipboard Accounts

Virtually all cruise ships operate as cashless societies. Passengers charge onboard purchases and settle their accounts at the end of the cruise with a credit card, traveler's checks, or cash. You can sign for wine at dinner, drinks at the bar, shore excursions, gifts in the shop—virtually any expense you may incur aboard ship. On some lines, an imprint from a major credit card is necessary to open an account. Otherwise, a cash deposit may be required and a positive balance maintained to keep the shipboard account open. Either way, you will want to open a line of credit soon after settling into your cabin if an account was not opened for you at embarkation. You can arrange this by visiting the purser's office, located in the central atrium or main lobby.

Tipping

For better or worse, tipping is an integral part of the cruise experience. Most companies pay their cruise staff nominal wages and expect tips to make up the difference. A number of lines have replaced "voluntary" tipping with a mandatory 15% service charge, which is added to every bar bill. Tipping of dining room staff and cabin stewards on these ships is still left to the discretion of the passenger.

Whom to Tip

Lines that encourage tipping advertise a recommended tipping policy in their brochures and even on information sheets left on your pillow (along with envelopes addressed to Steward, Waiter, Busboy, and so on). These are guidelines only; you may tip as little or as much as you wish. On most cruise ships it is customary to tip on the last night at sea. Always tip in cash, preferably in U.S. dollars. Generally, tip your regular waiter and cabin steward. On some ships you should also tip the busboy, but on others the waiter shares his tips with the busboy. If the maître d' provides any special services, such as moving you to another table, he should be tipped a nominal amount, usually between $5 and $15. If you order wine with your meals, the wine steward should be tipped 15% of the total bill, unless a service charge is added automatically. You may wish to tip a bartender or steward who has been especially friendly or gracious. Do not tip any of the officers, the entertainers, or the cruise staff.

Dining

Restaurants
The chief meals of the day are served in the dining room. Most ships' dining rooms and kitchens are too small to serve all passengers simultaneously, so there are usually two mealtimes—early (or main) and late (or second) seatings—usually from 1½ to 2½ hours apart. Early seating for dinner is generally between 6 and 6:30, late seating between 8 and 8:30.

Most cruise ships have a Lido deck, adjacent to the swimming pool, where fast food and snacks are served cafeteria-style. Entrées available in the regular dining room may also be served here. Most Lidos are open only for sunrise coffee, breakfast, morning snacks, lunch, and afternoon tea. Many ships provide self-serve coffee or tea on the Lido around the clock, as well as buffets at midnight.

Special Diets
With notification well in advance, many ships can provide a kosher, low-salt, low-cholesterol, sugar-free, vegetarian, or other special menu. However, there's always a chance that the wrong dish will somehow be handed to you. Especially when it comes to soups and desserts, it's a good idea to ask about the ingredients.

An increasing number of cruise ships offer an alternative "light" or "spa" menu based upon American Heart Association guidelines, using less fat, leaner cuts of meat, low-cholesterol or low-sodium preparations, smaller portions, salads, fresh-fruit desserts, and healthy garnishes. Some smaller ships may not be able to accommodate special dietary needs. Vegetarians generally have no trouble finding appropriate selections on ship menus.

CRUISE SHIPS

Chart Symbols. *The following symbols are used in the cabin charts that accompany each ship's evaluation.* **D:** *Double bed;* **K:** *King-size bed;* **Q:** *Queen-size bed;* **T:** *Twin bed;* **U/L:** *Upper and lower berths;* ●: *All cabins have this facility;* ○: *No cabins have this facility;* ◐: *Some cabins have this facility. Per diems listed are average per diems. Lower/higher priced fares exist.*

Celebrity Cruises

MV Zenith
SPECIFICATIONS

Type of ship: Cruise liner
Cruise experience: Semiformal

Size: 47,255 tons
Number of cabins: 687
Outside cabins: 84%

Passengers: 1,374
Crew: 670 (international)
Officers: Greek
Passenger/crew ratio: 2.1 to 1
Year built: 1992

ITINERARY
Seven-night Bermuda loops depart New York Saturdays, April through October, calling at Hamilton and St. George's.

Bermuda Cruise Fleet

	Dreamward	Zenith	Meridian	Queen Elizabeth 2	Royal Majesty	Song of America
Child Care	●	●	●	●	●	○
Video Arcade	●	●	●	●	○	○
Boutiques/Gift Shops	●	●	●	●	●	●
Library	●	●	●	●	●	○
Cinema/Theater	●	○	●	●	○	●
Disco	●	●	●	●	●	●
Casino	●	●	●	●	●	●
Deck Sports	●	●	●	●	○	●
Sauna/Massage	●	●	●	●	●	●
Whirlpool	●	●	●	●	●	○
Swimming Pool	2	2	2	3	1	2
Walking/Jogging Circuit	●	●	●	●	●	●
Health Club	●	●	●	●	●	●
Special Dietary Options	●	●	●	●	●	◐
Accessibility	●	●	◐	◐	●	◐
Sanitation Rating*	98	91	94	91	88	95
Passenger/Crew Ratio	2.6:1	2.1:1	1.9:1	1.8:1	2.1:1	2.6:1
Number of Passengers	1,242	1,379	1,106	1,850	1,056	1,402
Length of Cruise	7 days	7 days	7 days	5 days	7 days	7 days
Per Diem Rates	$249–$354	$215–$381	$175–$528	$215–$656	$193–$371	$189–$447
Cruise Experience	Casual	Semiformal	Semiformal	Formal–Semiformal	Semiformal	Casual
Type of Ship	Cruise liner	Cruise liner	Classic liner	Classic liner	Cruise liner	Cruise liner
Size (in tons)	41,000	47,255	30,440	57,139	32,400	37,584
Cruise Line	Norwegian Cruise Line	Celebrity Cruises	Celebrity Cruises	Cunard Line	Majesty Cruise Line	Royal Caribbean Cruise Line
Ship	Dreamward	Zenith	Meridian	Queen Elizabeth 2	Royal Majesty	Song of America

*Sanitation ratings are provided by the Vessel Sanitation Program, Center for Environmental Health and Injury Control. Ships are rated on water, food preparation and holding, potential contamination of food, and general cleanliness, storage, and repair. A score of 86 or higher indicates an acceptable level of sanitation. According to the center, "a low score does not necessarily imply an imminent outbreak of gastrointestinal disease." Chart ratings come from the center's July 28, 1995, report.

With a navy band of paint encircling its white hull, the Zenith cuts a sharp profile at sea. Inside, the ship is indisputably gracious, airy, and comfortable, with an abundance of oversize windows that make the most of natural light. The nine passenger decks sport several bars, entertainment lounges, and ample deck space. Wide corridors, broad staircases, seven elevators, and well-placed signs make it easy to get around. Decor is contemporary and attractive, the artwork pleasant rather than memorable.

Cabins and Rates

	Beds	Phone	TV	Sitting Area	Fridge	Tub	Per Diem*
Suite	D	●	●	●	○	●	$381
Outside	D or T/K	●	●	●	○	○	$270
Inside	D or T/K	●	●	○	○	○	$215

Rates are cruise only for Bermuda itineraries. Airfare and port taxes are extra.

The cabins are modern and quite roomy. Furnishings include a nightstand, a desk, and a small, glass-top coffee table. Closets are reasonably large, as are bathrooms. Bedtime readers will find the lone lamp on the nightstand insufficient, especially in rooms with double beds. The 20 suites are enormous, with large sitting areas, tubs with whirlpool jets, 24-hour room service, and a private butler. The view from many outside cabins on the Bahamas Deck is partially obstructed by lifeboats.

Outlet voltage: 110/220 AC.

Single supplement: 150%–200% of double-occupancy rate.

Discounts: A third or fourth passenger in a cabin pays $135 per diem for Bermuda cruises. Children 2–12 traveling with two full-paying adults pay $77 per diem for Bermuda cruises. Children under two travel free. Early booking discounts available.

Health club: Bright, sunny upper-deck spa with sauna, massage, weight machines, stationary bicycles, rowing machine, stair climber, treadmill, separate mirrored aerobics area, facial/body treatments.

Walking/jogging: Unobstructed circuit on Marina Deck (5 laps=1 mile).

Other sports: Exercise classes, putting green, shuffleboard, snorkeling, trapshooting, table tennis, two pools, three whirlpools.

Public rooms: Seven bars and lounges, showroom, disco, casino, two restaurants, library/reading room, card room, video-game room.

Shops: Gift shop, boutique, perfume shop, cigarette/liquor store, photo shop.

Health care: Hospital staffed by doctor and nurse, limited dispensary for prescriptions.

Child care: Playroom, preteen and teen youth programs supervised by counselors as needed, baby-sitting arranged with crew member.

Services: Photographer, laundry service, beauty shop/barber.

Other: Safe-deposit boxes.

ACCESSIBILITY

Four cabins with 39½″ doorways are accessible to wheelchair users. Specially equipped public elevators are 35½″ wide, but certain public areas may not be wide enough for wheelchairs. Passengers with mobility problems must provide their own small, collapsible wheelchairs and travel with an able-bodied companion.

SS Meridian

SPECIFICATIONS

Type of ship: Classic liner

Cruise experience: Semiformal

Size: 30,440 tons

Number of cabins: 553

Outside cabins: 53%

Passengers: 1,106

Crew: 580 (international)

Officers: Greek

Passenger/crew ratio: 1.9 to 1

Year built: 1967

ITINERARY

Seven-day Bermuda loops depart New York (or, occasionally, Baltimore, Boston, Charleston, Newport News, Philadelphia, or Fort Lauderdale), April through October, calling at Somerset.

SHIP'S LOG

The *Meridian* radiates a relaxed, personable charm—it's like staying in someone's home. The dining room food is even better than on the *Zenith,* although the same cannot be said about the lunch and breakfast buffets. Two crowds seem to prefer this ship: Families take advantage of the children's program, which is broken down into three age groups; older passengers appreciate the ship's lineage, its traditional design, and intimate public areas—most of which are on the same deck, allowing easy access. Two drawbacks discourage singles and young couples, however: The health club is neither as large nor as bright as the one aboard the *Zenith,* and the Marina Cafe doubles as a dreary disco at night.

Cabins and Rates

	Beds	Phone	TV	Sitting Area	Fridge	Tub	Per Diem*
Suite	T	●	●	●	○	●	$328
Outside	T or D	●	◑	◑	○	○	$247
Inside	T, D, or U/L	●	○	○	○	○	$175

*Rates are cruise only for Bermuda itineraries. Not all categories are listed. Airfare and port taxes are extra.

Cabins are similar in size and amenities to those aboard the Zenith; however, they are decorated in a somewhat jarring scheme of orange, red, and purple sunset hues. Bathtubs in the Presidential, Starlight, and Deluxe suites have whirlpool jets. Outside cabins on the Horizon Deck have floor-to-ceiling windows. Obstructed or partially obstructed views are a drawback to many of the outside cabins on the Atlantic Deck.

Outlet voltage: 110/220 AC.

Single supplement: 150%–200% double-occupancy rate.

Discounts: A third or fourth passenger in a cabin pays $135 per diem for Bermuda cruises. Children 2–12 sharing a cabin with two full-paying adults pay $59 to $99 per diem for Bermuda cruises. Children under two travel free. You get a discount for booking early.

SPORTS AND FITNESS
Health club: Stationary bikes, weight machines, treadmills, rowing machines, sauna, massage, facial/body treatments.

Walking/jogging: Unobstructed circuit on Captain's Deck (8 laps=1 mile).

Other sports: Exercise classes, putting green, golf driving range, shuffleboard, snorkeling, trapshooting, table tennis, pool, children's pool, three outdoor whirlpools.

FACILITIES
Public rooms: Seven bars, four entertainment lounges (including main showroom), card room/library, casino, chapel/synagogue, cinema, dining room, disco, Lido Deck, video arcade.

Shops: Boutique, perfumery, drugstore, photo shop, beauty salon/barber.

Health care: Doctor on call.

Child care: Playroom with large windows, patio, and wading pool; youth programs with counselors in three age groups; baby-sitting arranged privately with crew members.

Services: Photographer, laundry service, beauty shop/barber.

Other: Safe-deposit boxes.

ACCESSIBILITY
Two cabins are accessible to wheelchair users. Celebrity requires that passengers using wheelchairs travel with an able-bodied adult who will take full responsibility in case of emergency.

FOR MORE INFORMATION
Celebrity Cruises (5200 Blue Lagoon Dr., Miami, FL 33126, ☎ 800/437–3111, ℻ 800/437–9111.

Cunard Line Limited

RMS Queen Elizabeth 2
SPECIFICATIONS
Type of ship: Classic liner
Cruise experience: Semiformal/Formal
Size: 67,139 tons
Number of cabins: 900
Outside cabins: 70%
Passengers: 1,850

Crew: 1,000 (international)
Officers: British

Passenger/crew ratio: 1.8 to 1
(varies according to cabin price)
Year built: 1969

ITINERARY
Several five-day Bermuda loops depart New York, calling at Hamilton.

SHIP'S LOG
The *Queen Elizabeth 2* is the last of its kind: Put into service in 1969 as a transatlantic liner, it's the only cruise ship that still makes regularly scheduled crossings of the Atlantic between New York and England and that still assigns passengers to dine according to their cabin class, in one of five restaurants. A recent $45 million renovation has resulted in several new public rooms, including the Golden Lion, styled after a traditional English pub, and a new Lido which, with its gener-

ous use of blond woods, floor-to-ceiling glass, and brass finishing, brings a contemporary touch to the very traditional ship. Celebrating that tradition is a new "Heritage Trail" exhibit, which showcases Cunard memorabilia and artifacts. Despite the recent major investment, the *QE2* continues to show its age like a fine old hotel.

Thirteen stories high and three football fields long, the *QE2* still possesses a grace that eludes most new megaships. Almost every passenger need has been thought of, and though some passengers find the ship too large, and others find it too stuffy, the wealth of space, good service, and wide range of activities make the *QE2* a dazzling gem worthy of British royalty.

Cabins and Rates

	Beds	Phone	TV	Sitting Area	Fridge	Tub	Per Diem*
Queen's Grill	Q or T/D	●	●	●	●	●	$656
Princess/ Britannia Grill	Q or T	●	●	●	●	●	$470
Caronia	Q or T	●	●	○	○	◐	$302–386
Mauretania	T or U/L	●	●	○	○	○	$215

Rates are for Bermuda itineraries and include airfare from East Coast cities. Port taxes are extra. The wide range of rates reflects differences among cabins in the lower-priced categories.

The *QE2* has the most varied cabin configurations of any ship afloat. Suites accommodate up to four passengers, at no extra charge per passenger, making them more economical for a family of four than two luxury cabins. Penthouse suites, with verandas and whirlpools, are the largest, most luxurious accommodations afloat; first-class cabins (all with VCRs) compare with those of any luxury ship. Luxury cabins, except No. 8184, have private verandas. Lifeboats partially obstruct the view from some cabins on the Sports Deck, and Boat Deck cabins look onto a public promenade.

Most but not all cabins received new bathrooms during the recent refit. Before booking, make sure your cabin's bathroom has been renovated.

Outlet voltage: 110 AC.

Single supplement: 175%–200% of double-occupancy rate; several single cabins are available at $319–$655 a day.

Discounts: A third or fourth passenger in a cabin pays half the minimum fare in the cabin's restaurant grade.

SPORTS AND FITNESS

Health club: Thalassotherapy pool, inhalation room, French hydrotherapy bath treatment, computerized nutritional and lifestyle evaluation, aerobics and exercise classes, weight machines, Lifecycles, rowers, Stairmasters, treadmills, sauna, whirlpools, hydrocalisthenics, massage.

Walking/jogging: There is no unobstructed circuit.

Other sports: Putting green, golf driving range, paddle tennis, table tennis, shuffleboard, tetherball, trapshooting, volleyball, one outdoor and one indoor pool, whirlpools, sports area with separate clubhouses for adults and teens.

FACILITIES

Public rooms: Six bars, five entertainment lounges, card room, casino, chapel/synagogue, cinema, art gallery, Epson computer center, disco, executive boardroom, library/reading room, piano bar, video game room.

Shops: Arcade with men's formal rental shop, Harrods, designer boutiques (Burberry, Pringle, Wedgwood), florist, beauty center, barbershop.

Health care: Extensive hospital with full staff of doctors and nurses.

Child care: Playroom, wading pool, teen center, nursery staffed with British nannies, baby-sitting by counselors.

Services: Full-service laundry, dry-cleaning, valet service, laundromat, ironing room, photographer, film processing.

Other: Foreign exchange and cash center, garage, kennel, safe-deposit boxes.

ACCESSIBILITY

Ramps were installed in public corridors during the most recent refit, but many public rooms have a step or two up and down. Four cabins have been refitted to accommodate wheelchair users.

FOR MORE INFORMATION

Cunard Line Limited (555 5th Ave., New York, NY 10017, ☎ 800/221–4770, FAX 212/949–0915).

Majesty Cruise Line

MV Royal Majesty

SPECIFICATIONS

Type of ship: Cruise liner
Cruisee xperience: Semiformal

Size: 32,400 tons
Number of cabins: 528
Outside cabins: 65%

Passengers: 1,056
Crew: 500 (international)
Officers: Greek
Passenger/crew ratio: 2.1 to 1
Year built: 1992

ITINERARY

Seven-night Bermuda loops depart Boston May through October, calling at St. George's.

SHIP'S LOG

The "royal" theme reigns throughout Majesty Cruise Line's sole ship. From its Queen of Hearts Card Room to the House of Lords Executive Conference Room to the Royal Fireworks Lounge, the excellent use of light and space creates bright, inviting public areas with fine sea views. The Royal Observatory Panorama Bar is a favorite perch from which to watch the ship pull into and out of ports of call. From the Cafe Royale, over breakfast or lunch, you can see all that lies ahead; at the end of the ship, the Piazza San Marco draws visitors with its sweeping views aft (not to mention its ice cream/pizza parlor).

The *Royal Majesty* was the first cruise ship to declare its dining room smoke-free, and a number of staterooms have been set aside for nonsmokers as well.

As in the rest of the ship, cabin decor is tasteful and classy: Understated earth tones complement wood furnishings and moldings. Each stateroom comes with robes, color TV, five channels of music, direct-dial ship-to-shore telephones, hair dryers, security safes, and ironing boards.

Cabins and Rates

	Beds	Phone	TV	Sitting Area	Fridge	Tub	Per Diem*
Suite	D	●	●	●	●	○	$428
Outside	T/D	●	●	○	◐	○	$257
Inside	T/D	●	●	○	○	○	$193

Rates are cruise only for Bermuda itineraries. Port taxes are extra.

Suites and some outside cabins have a minibar, a queen-size bed, and an enormous ocean-view picture window. Views from many cabins on Queen's Deck are obstructed by lifeboats; cabins on the Princess Deck look out onto a public promenade.

Outlet voltage: 110 AC.

Single supplement: 150% of double-occupancy rate.

Discounts: A third or fourth passenger in a cabin pays $86 per diem for Bermuda cruises. Discounts are given for early booking.

SPORTS AND FITNESS
Health club: Fitness center with circuit training, weights, stair climber, stationary bikes, rowing machines, treadmills, and sauna.

Walking/jogging: Unobstructed wraparound promenade on Princess Deck.

Other sports: Pool, two whirlpools.

FACILITIES
Public rooms: Showroom, dining room, outdoor cafe, pizza/ice cream parlor, three bars, casino, disco, meeting rooms, card room, library.

Shops: Gift shop, beauty salon.

Child care: Playroom, splash pool, baby-sitting, youth program with counselors.

Services: Photographer.

ACCESSIBILITY
The ship is fully accessible to wheelchair users, including four elevators, rest rooms on various decks, and four specially equipped staterooms.

FOR MORE INFORMATION
Majesty Cruise Line (901 South America Way, Miami, FL 33132, ☎ 800/532–7788, FAX 305/358–4807).

Norwegian Cruise Line

MS Dreamward

SPECIFICATIONS

Type of ship: Cruise liner
Cruise experience: Casual
Size: 41,000 tons
Number of cabins: 623
Outside cabins: 85%

Passengers: 1,242
Crew: 483 (international)
Officers: Norwegian
Passenger/crew ratio: 2.6 to 1
Year built: 1992

ITINERARY
Seven-day Bermuda loops depart New York, April through October, calling at St. George's and Hamilton.

Terraced decks give panoramic views forward and aft, and walls of glass line the length of the ship. Multilevel public rooms include the Terraces dining room, the show lounge, and the two-deck-high Casino Royale, where the action includes roulette, craps, blackjack, and slot machines. Instead of one big dining room, four smaller restaurants create a more intimate ambiance. Even the biggest, the Terraces, seats only 282 on several levels and has windows on three sides. Matching these two ships' variety of eateries is a variety of special menus, theme meals, and children's menus. Dinner has two assigned seatings, but breakfast and lunch are open, so you can try the other restaurants or opt for hamburgers and hot dogs at the casual Sports Bar & Grill.

Showroom productions are the usual festive affairs, including the full-length Broadway-style shows that NCL is famous for. A proscenium stage makes these productions NCL's most elaborate yet. The Sports Bar & Grill transmits live ESPN and NFL broadcasts on multiple screens. There's plenty of space for relaxing on the five-tier Sun Deck, and the especially broad Promenade Deck is good for walking and jogging.

Cabins and Rates

	Beds	Phone	TV	Sitting Area	Fridge	Tub	Per Diem*
Suite	T/Q	●	●	●	●	◑	$354
Outside	T/Q	●	●	●	○	○	$289
Inside	T/Q	●	●	○	○	○	$249

Rates include airfare and are for Bermuda itineraries. Port taxes are extra.

The *Dreamward* has an unusually high percentage of outside cabins, most with picture windows. Standard cabins, with their Caribbean villa look and feel, are among the prettiest at sea. The suites have floor-to-ceiling windows; some have private balconies and special amenities that include daily fruit baskets, champagne, trays of hors d'oeuvres, and concierge service. Adjoining suites are available on the Norway, International, and Star decks. Outside cabins have couches that convert into beds. Deluxe suites can accommodate up to four people and adjoining U-shape suites work well for families of up to six. Some cabins on the Norway deck have obstructed views.

Outlet voltage: 110 AC.

Single supplement: 150%–200% of double-occupancy rate.

Discounts: A third or fourth passenger in a cabin (including children) pays $107 per diem for Bermuda cruises. Early booking discounts are available.

Health club: Lifecycles, Lifesteps, exercise equipment, Jacuzzis, a variety of massage treatments.

Walking/jogging: Unobstructed, padded circuit on wraparound Promenade Deck.

Other sports: Basketball court, exercise course, two pools, golf driving range.

Public rooms: Four restaurants, eight bar/lounges, showroom/theater, disco/observation lounge, casino, ice cream parlor (at extra cost), library, video game room, conference center.

Shops: Gift shops and boutiques, beauty salon/barber.

Health care: Doctor on call.

Child care: Supervised children's playroom with organized kids' program year-round.

Other: Safe-deposit boxes.

ACCESSIBILITY
All decks and activities are accessible to wheelchair users, except the Sky Deck and public lavatories. An able-bodied companion must accompany the passenger. Six specially-equipped cabins are accessible to wheelchair users, and 28 are designed for passengers with hearing impairments.

FOR MORE INFORMATION
Norwegian Cruise Line (95 Merrick Way, Coral Gables, FL 33134, ☎ 800/327–7030, FAX 305/443–2464).

Royal Caribbean Cruise Line

MS Song of America

SPECIFICATIONS

Type of ship: Cruise liner
Cruise experience: Casual
Size: 37,584 tons
Number of cabins: 701
Outside cabins: 57%

Passengers: 1,402
Crew: 535 (international)
Officers: Norwegian
Passenger/crew ratio: 2.6 to 1
Year built: 1982

ITINERARY
Seven-day Bermuda loops depart New York Sundays, May through October, calling at St. George's and Hamilton.

SHIP'S LOG
The *Song of America* is unusually handsome. Despite its size, it looks more like a yacht than a cruise ship, though its width gives it space and stability that a yacht could never manage. Plentiful chrome, mirrors, and overhead lights give the ship a flashier look than other RCCL vessels, but the overall effect is clean, crisp, and airy. A refurbishment finished in 1994 ensured that the *Song of America* kept its youthful appearance.

Cabins and Rates

	Beds	Phone	TV	Sitting Area	Fridge	Tub	Per Diem*
Suite	D or T	●	●	●	●	●	$397
Outside	T/D	●	●	○	○	○	$293
Inside	T or T/D	●	●	○	○	○	$242

*Rates include airfare and are for Bermuda itineraries. Port taxes are extra.

Standard outside cabins are done in nautical blue; inside cabins are a bright orange. Suites on the Promenade Deck look onto a public area.

Outlet voltage: 110/220 AC.

Single supplement: 150% of double-occupancy rate; however, less expensive singles are available if you are willing to wait for your cabin assignment until embarkation time.

Discounts: A third or fourth passenger in a cabin pays $107 per diem. Senior citizen discounts are offered on specific sailings. You get a discount of $200 off total price per person for arranging your own airfare for Bermuda cruises, and discounts for booking early on standard inside and outside cabins only.

SPORTS AND FITNESS

Health club: Rowing machines, treadmills, stationary bikes, massage, men's and women's saunas.

Walking/jogging: Unobstructed circuits on Compass Deck and wraparound Promenade Deck.

Other sports: Aerobics, table tennis, ring toss, snorkeling lessons, shuffleboard, skeet shooting, two pools.

FACILITIES

Public rooms: Six bars, four entertainment lounges, casino, card room, cinema, disco.

Shops: Gift shop, drugstore, beauty salon/barber.

Health care: Doctor on call.

Child care: Youth programs with counselors during holidays and in summer, baby-sitting arranged privately with crew member, cribs available but must be requested at time of booking.

Services: Full-service laundry, dry-cleaning, photographer, film processing.

ACCESSIBILITY

Accessibility aboard this ship is limited. Doorways have lips, and public bathrooms are not specially equipped. Passengers with mobility problems must bring a portable wheelchair and be escorted by an able-bodied companion. Tenders are easy to board; if seas are rough, crew members will carry passengers and their wheelchairs.

FOR MORE INFORMATION

Royal Caribbean Cruise Line (1050 Caribbean Way, Miami, FL 33132, ☎ 800/327–6700, 𝖥𝖠𝖷 800/722–5329).

3 Exploring Bermuda

BERMUDA IS NOTHING if not colorful. The streets are lined with hedges of hibiscus and oleander, and rolling green hills are shaded by tall palms and casuarina trees. The limestone buildings are painted in pretty pastels (pink and white seem to be most popular), and their gleaming white roofs are steeply pitched to channel the rain upon which Bermudians depend—the island has no freshwater lakes or streams. In addition, many houses have quaint butteries, miniature cottages that were once used to keep food cool. House numbers are a relatively new phenomenon on the island, although most houses have names, such as Tranquillity, Struggle, and Last Penny. Another architectural feature commonly seen in Bermuda is moon gates. These Chinese-inspired freestanding stone arches, which have been popular since the late 18th century, can be found in gardens all over the island, and Bermudians favor them as backdrops for wedding pictures.

For exploring purposes, we've divided Bermuda into four separate tours. The first tour is of Hamilton, the island's capital. Hamilton is of primary interest for its harbor, its shops—housed in small pastel-colored buildings—and the government buildings, where visitors can watch sessions of Parliament. In addition, the town is the major departure point for sightseeing boats, ferries, and the pink-and-blue buses that ramble all over the island. Don't confuse Hamilton town with the parish of the same name—Hamilton town is adjacent to Pembroke Parish. The second tour is of the Town of St. George on the eastern end of the island, near the site of Bermuda's first settlement. History mavens will find much of interest in St. George's, which boasts several noteworthy 17th-century buildings. The third tour explores the West End, the site of the sleepy hamlet of Somerset and the Royal Naval Dockyard, a former British naval shipyard that is home to the Maritime Museum and a developing tourist center. The West End is in Sandys Parish, which can be pronounced either "Sandies" or "Sands."

The fourth tour is a rambling journey through the island's other parishes that is best done by moped, bicycle, or taxi. The parishes date back to 1616, when Bermuda was first surveyed and the island was divided into eight tribes or parishes, each named for an investor in the Bermuda Company, an offshoot of the Virginia Company, which controlled the island until 1684. The parishes are Sandys, Southampton, Warwick, Paget, Smith's, Hamilton, Pembroke, and Devonshire. St. George's, which was considered public land in the early days, is the ninth parish and includes the Town of St. George. Bermudians customarily identify sites on the island by the parish in which they are located: "It's in Pembroke," a resident will say, or "It's in Warwick." The main roads connecting the parishes are self-explanatory: North Shore Road, Middle Road, South Road, and Harbour Road. Almost all traffic traversing the island's 21-mile length uses these roads, although some 1,200 smaller roads crisscross the island. Visitors will see several "tribe roads" that date back to the initial survey of the island; many of these are now no more than country lanes, and some are dead ends. As you travel around the island you'll see small brown-and-white signs pointing to the Railway Trail. Built along the route of Bermuda's old railway line, the trail is now a peaceful route reserved for pedestrians and cyclists (*see* Off the Beaten Path, *below; see also* Portraits of Bermuda, Chapter 10).

Tour 1: Hamilton

Numbers in the margin correspond to points of interest on the Tour 1: Hamilton map.

Historically, Bermudians were seafarers. For revenues, the government relied on the duties paid on ship's cargoes. Ships were required by law to anchor in the harbor at St. George's to declare their goods, but most captains preferred to anchor closer to their homes, and the law was largely ignored. To combat the loss of revenues, legislation was passed in 1790 to establish a second port and customs house at Crow Lane Harbour (now Hamilton Harbour). Largely because of Hamilton's excellent harbor and central location, the seat of government was moved from St. George's to Hamilton in January 1815.

❶ Your first stop should be the **Visitors Service Bureau** in the Ferry Terminal Building, where the friendly staff can provide you with maps and brochures. Step out of the bureau onto the capital's main avenue, **Front Street.** Running alongside the harbor, Front Street bustles with small cars, mopeds, bicycles, buses, pedestrians, and the occasional horse-drawn carriage. It's fun to imagine what the street must have looked like prior to the arrival of automobiles in 1946. From 1931 to 1946, railroad tracks ran along Front Street, carrying "Old Rattle and Shake," as the Bermuda Railway was called. Today, Front Street is lined with colorful little buildings, many with balconies and arcades that house shops and boutiques selling everything from imported woolens to perfumes and cosmetics. This is the main shopping area on the island, and shoppers will probably want to spend plenty of time—and money—here (*see* Chapter 4, Shopping).

The docks behind the Ferry Terminal are the departure points for ferries making the short trip to Paget and Warwick parishes, or the longer trip across the Great Sound to the West End. Next to the terminal, the glass-bottom boats and other sightseeing vessels pick up passengers for excursions to the Sea Gardens, St. George's, and Dockyard. Beyond these is **No. 1 Shed,** the pink passenger-ship terminal (two other terminals are situated farther east on Front Street). During high season, one or two cruise ships are usually moored alongside the docks—all but the largest ships, such as the *QE2,* can sail right into Hamilton Harbour. During the low season (November through March), No. 1 Shed is the site of regularly scheduled afternoon teas, art and fashion shows, and performances by the Gombey Dancers (*see* Chapter 9, The Arts and Nightlife).

The oddly shaped traffic box at Heyl's Corner, at the intersection of Front and Queen streets, is known as the **"Birdcage,"** from which the police (locally known as "bobbies" as in Great Britain) sometimes direct traffic. Named for its designer, Michael "Dickey" Bird, the traffic box has been a Hamilton landmark for more than 30 years. The corner itself is named for J. B. Heyl, a Southerner who came to Bermuda in the 19th century and opened an apothecary shop on this site.

❷ Visitors interested in coins should cross Point Pleasant Road and go up to the mezzanine of the **Bank of Bermuda.** British and Spanish coins, many of them ancient, are displayed in glass cases. The collection includes some pieces of "hog money," Bermuda's first currency, which was issued by the Bermuda Company in 1616. Pigs were the only inhabitants encountered by Sir George Somers and his crew when his ship, the *Sea Venture,* foundered on Bermuda's shores in 1609; thus the coin is appropriately stamped on one side with a wild hog ringed with the

Tour 1: Hamilton

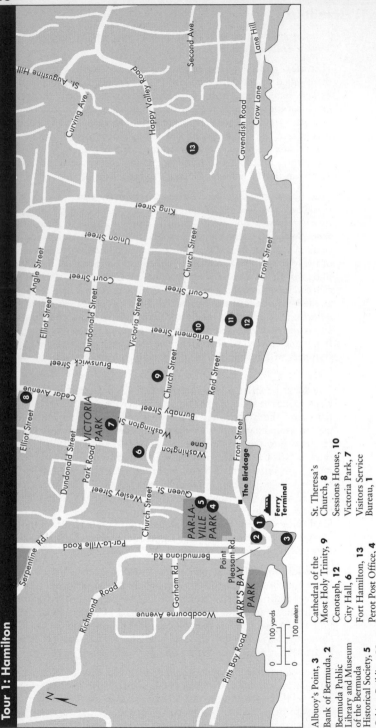

Albuoy's Point, **3**
Bank of Bermuda, **2**
Bermuda Public Library and Museum of the Bermuda Historical Society, **5**
Cabinet Building, **11**

Cathedral of the Most Holy Trinity, **9**
Cenotaph, **12**
City Hall, **6**
Fort Hamilton, **13**
Perot Post Office, **4**

St. Theresa's Church, **8**
Sessions House, **10**
Victoria Park, **7**
Visitors Service Bureau, **1**

words "Somer Ilands" and on the other with a replica of Sir George's ruined ship. Hog money is the oldest of all British colonial coins. *6 Front St.,* ☎ *441/295–4000.* ☞ *Free.* ⊗ *Mon.–Thurs. 9:30–3, Fri. 9:30–4:30.*

③ Following Point Pleasant Road toward the water, you'll come to **Albuoy's Point,** a pleasant waterfront park with benches, trees, and a splendid view of the activity in the harbor. Nearby is the **Royal Bermuda Yacht Club,** which was built in the 1930s. The idea for the yacht club was conceived in 1844 beneath the Calabash Tree at Walsingham (*see* Tom Moore's Tavern *in* Tour 4, *below*), and Prince Albert gave permission for the club to use the word "Royal" in 1845. Today, royalty, international yachting celebrities, and the local elite hobnob at the posh club, which sponsors the Newport–Bermuda Ocean Yacht Race and the Omega Gold Cup International Match Race Tournament.

Barr's Bay Park to the west also affords a good view of the yacht club and the harbor. Just beyond Bermudiana Road on Pitts Bay Road (a continuation of Front Street), steps and a ramp lead from the street to the park's vast expanse of green grass, its benches, and its scenic vistas.

If you plan to do a lot of independent exploring, visit the **Bermuda Book Store,** on Queen Street, to buy a copy of the *Bermuda Islands Guide* ($4.95). This paperback atlas contains every lane, tribe road, alley, and landmark on the island. The bookstore, a marvelous Dickensian place with creaky wood floors, is filled with books about the island.

④ From the bookstore, continue along Queen Street to the **Perot Post Office,** a white two-story edifice that dates back to around 1840. Still a post office, this shuttered building is where Bermuda's first postage stamps originated (in 1848). The island's first postmaster was William Bennet Perot. Appointed in 1818, Perot would meet arriving steamers to collect the mail, stash it in his beaver hat, and then stroll around Hamilton to deliver it. Customers wishing to post a letter paid Perot, who hand-stamped each letter. Obviously, the postmaster had to be at his station to do this, which annoyed Perot, who preferred pottering around in the garden. Local historians credit Perot's friend, the pharmacist J B. Heyl, with the idea for Bermuda's first book of stamps. Heyl suggested that Perot make a whole sheet of postmarks, write "Wm B. Perot" on each postmark, and sell the sheet for a shilling. People could then tear off a postmark, paste it on a letter, and post it—without having to extricate Mr. Perot from the garden shrubbery. The extremely rare Perot stamps, some of which are in the Queen's Royal Stamp Collection, are now coveted by collectors. At press time, the record price for an 1848 Perot stamp was £225,000 ($350,000). *Queen St.,* ☎ *441/295–5151.* ☞ *Free.* ⊗ *Weekdays 9–5.*

TIME OUT The garden where Perot liked to pass his time is now **Par-la-Ville Park,** a pleasant spot that occupies a large portion of Queen Street. The Queen Street entrance (there's another on Par-la-Ville Road) is next to the post office. Paths wind through the luxuriant gardens, and the park benches are ideal for picnicking or a short rest. At noon you may have trouble finding a place to sit, because this is a favorite lunch spot of Hamilton office workers. Half a block along Queen Street is a Kentucky Fried Chicken franchise (open Sun.–Thurs. 11–11; Fri., Sat. 11–midnight).

Next to the post office is a giant rubber tree from British Guiana (now Guyana) that was planted by Perot. On a visit to Bermuda, Mark Twain lamented that the rubber tree didn't bear fruit in the form of hot-water bottles and rubber overshoes. The tree is in the front yard of the Georgian house where Mr. Perot and his family lived. Now the **Bermuda Pub-**

★ **⑤**

lic **Library** and **Museum of the Bermuda Historical Society,** the house is a wonderful find for history buffs. The library, which was founded in 1839, moved to its present quarters in August, 1916. One early librarian was an eccentric gentleman with the Pickwickian name of Florentius Frith, who rode in from the country on horseback and struck terror into the heart of anyone who interrupted his chess games to check out a book. The reference section of the library has virtually every book ever written about Bermuda, as well as a collection on microfilm of Bermudian newspapers dating back to 1784. The collection of rare books contains a 1624 edition of John Smith's *Generall Historie of Virginia, New England and the Somers Isles*. In the museum's entrance hall are portraits of Sir George Somers and his wife, painted about 1605; portraits of Postmaster Perot and his wife can be seen in the back room. Notice Admiral Sir George Somers's lodestone (circa 1600), used for magnetizing compass needles, and a Bermuda map from 1622 that shows the division of the island into 25-acre shares by the original Bermuda Company. The museum also contains an eclectic collection of old English coins and Confederate money; Bermuda silver; Oriental porcelains; portraits of the major investors in the Bermuda Company; and pictures of horse-and-buggy Bermuda juxtaposed with modern-day scenes. There are several cedar pieces, including two Queen Anne chairs from about 1740; a handsome grandfather clock; a Waterford chandelier; handmade palmetto hats; and a recently restored sedan chair from around 1770. Ask to see the letter from George Washington, written "to the inhabitants of Bermuda" in 1775, asking for gunpowder. *13 Queen St. Library:* ☎ *441/295–2905.* ☛ *Free (donations appreciated).* ☉ *Weekdays 9:30–6, Sat. 9:30–5. Museum:* ☎ *441/295–2487.* ☉ *Weekdays 9:30–3:30. 15-minute closure at lunchtime, depending on number of visitors in museum.*

TIME OUT **Fourways Pastry Shop** (Reid St., at the entrance to Washington Mall, ☎ 441/295–3263) and the **Gourmet Store** (Windsor Place Mall, across Queen St. and north of the library, ☎ 441/295–4085), both operated by Fourways Inn, are great places to relax over diet-destroying pastries.

Continue up Queen Street, or cut through Washington Mall (two stories of shops and informal eateries that open onto Washington Lane), to Church Street. Set back from the street behind a lawn, fountains, ★ ❻ and a lily pond is **City Hall.** Opened in 1960, the large white structure is topped by a weather vane shaped like the *Sea Venture*. Massive cedar doors open into a large lobby with huge chandeliers, high ceilings, and a portrait gallery. The large portrait of Queen Elizabeth II was painted by Curtis Hooper and unveiled on April 29, 1987, by the Duke of Gloucester. Oil paintings of Bermuda's former mayors hang here as well. Behind tall cedar doors on the right is the Coin and Note Display of the Bermuda Monetary Authority, the extensive Benbow Collection of 20th-century stamps, and occasional displays of historic Bermudiana. The City Hall Theatre is often the venue for musical, dance, and theatrical performances. A handsome cedar staircase leads to the second floor exhibition galleries (*see below*). *Church St.,* ☎ *441/292–1234.* ☛ *Free.* ☉ *Weekdays 9–5.*

The East Exhibition Room on the second floor of City Hall houses the ★ **Bermuda National Gallery,** the island's only climate-controlled gallery. Opened in 1992, the gallery displays European paintings from the early 16th century to the 19th century, including works by Thomas Gainsborough, Sir Joshua Reynolds, and George Romney; 20th-century lithographs, oils, sculptures, and acrylics; and an extensive collection showcasing Bermudian artists and works by painters who visited the island from the late 19th century to the 1950s. *East Wing, City Hall, Church St., Hamilton,* ☎ *441/295–9428.* ✒ *$3 adults, children under 16 free.* ⊙ *Mon.–Sat. 10–4, Sun. 12:30–4. Closed holidays.*

★ Changing exhibits are displayed in the **Bermuda Society of Arts Gallery.** The juried annual Spring, Summer, Autumn, and Winter Members' Shows attract talented local artists, who display high-quality works in watercolors, oils, pastels, acrylics, and charcoals; collages and some three-dimensional works and sculptures are also occasionally included. The Photographic Show in January features underwater and shoreside shots. One-person shows by local and visiting artists are also held in the Society's small gallery throughout the year. *West Wing, City Hall, Church St., Hamilton,* ☎ *441/292–3824.* ✒ *Free (donations appreciated).* ⊙ *Mon.–Sat. 10–4. Closed holidays.*

❼ Behind City Hall on Victoria Street, **Victoria Park** has a sunken garden, trees, and a Victorian bandstand, where concerts are sometimes held in the summer. The 4-acre park, built in 1887 in honor of Queen Victoria's Golden Jubilee, opened with great fanfare in 1890. The park is perfectly safe when filled with people, but it isn't a good place to wander alone—some fairly seedy-looking characters hang out here.

❽ Cedar Avenue forms the eastern border of Victoria Park. Follow it north for two blocks to **St. Theresa's Church,** a Roman Catholic church built in Spanish Mission style. St. Theresa's serves as head of the island's six Roman Catholic churches; the first mass was celebrated in 1932. During a visit in 1968, Pope Paul VI presented Bermuda's Roman Catholic diocese with a gold and silver chalice that is housed in this church. *Cedar Ave. and Elliot St.,* ☎ *441/292–0607.* ⊙ *Daily 7:30–7.*

Return to Victoria Street and walk down Washington Street, a one-block boulevard that is the site of the **Central Bus Terminal,** ☎ 441/292–3824. Pink-and-blue buses depart from here to all points on the island. Stop at the kiosk on the median to pick up bus and ferry schedules, and to buy discounted bus tokens for future use.

TIME OUT Executives, secretaries, shoppers, and store owners flock to **The Spot** for breakfast, plate lunches, burgers, sandwiches, and coffee. In business for more than 50 years, this restaurant serves full meals and daily specials for less than $10 and sandwiches for about $5. It's one of the best values on the island. *6 Burnaby St.,* ☎ *441/292–6293.* ⊙ *Mon.–Sat. 6:30 am–7 pm.*

★ **❾** One of the island's most impressive structures is the **Cathedral of the Most Holy Trinity,** the seat of the Anglican Church of Bermuda. The cathedral is the second church to have been built on this site: Twelve years after its completion in 1872, Trinity Church was burned to the ground by an arsonist. Work began on the present church the following year, and it was consecrated in 1911. Designed in Early English style with Gothic flourishes, the church is constructed of Bermuda limestone and materials imported from Scotland, Nova Scotia, France, Ireland, and Indiana. The tower rises to a height of 143 feet, and the clerestory in the nave is supported by piers of polished Scottish granite. The four smaller columns in each aisle were added after a hurricane shook the cathedral—and its architect—during construction. The altar in the Lady Chapel is of Italian marble, and above it is a copy of Andrea del Sarto's *Madonna and Child.* In the south transept, the Warrior Chapel was dedicated in 1977 to honor those who serve in the armed forces of the Crown, and to commemorate those who died in service to their country. The Great Warrior Window is a memorial to

85 Bermudian men who died in World War I; the flags represent military units of Bermuda and England. The choir stalls and bishop's throne are of carved English oak, and the pulpit is a replica of the one in St. Giles Cathedral, Edinburgh. On a wall near the lectern, the Canterbury Cross, set in stone taken from the walls of Canterbury Cathedral, is a copy of one made in Kent in the 8th century. The stained-glass windows are lovely; note especially the Angel Window on the east wall of the north transept, which was made by local artist Vivienne Gilmore Gardner. After exploring the interior, take time to climb the 150-or-so steps to the tower, which was opened to the public several years ago after extensive renovations were made to the entire building. Once at the top, you will be rewarded with spectacular views of Hamilton. *Church St.,* ☎ *441/292–6987.* ☛ *Tower: $3 adults, $2 children 9– 15, $1 children under eight.* ⊘ *Mon.–Sat. 10–4.*

❿ The eye-catching Italianate edifice on the next block is **Sessions House,** home of the House of Assembly (the lower house of Parliament) and the Supreme Court. The original two-story structure was built in 1819; the Florentine towers and colonnade, decorated with red terra-cotta, were added in 1887 to commemorate Queen Victoria's Golden Jubilee. The Victoria Jubilee Clock Tower made its striking debut at midnight, December 31, 1893. Bermuda's Parliament, which is as old as Iceland's, The Isle of Man, and England's, met for the first time in 1620 in St. Peter's Church in St. George's. It later moved to the State House, where deliberations were held for almost 200 years until the capital was moved to Hamilton. In its present location, the House of Assembly meets on the second floor, where business is conducted in a style befitting such a venerable body. The Sergeant-at-Arms precedes the Speaker into the chamber, bearing a silver-gilt mace. Introduced in 1921, the mace is fashioned after a James I mace in the Tower of London. The Speaker, in wig and flowing black robe, solemnly calls the meeting to order with a cedar gavel made from an old belfry tree that has been growing in St. Peter's churchyard since before 1620. The proceedings are no less ceremonious and colorful in the Supreme Court on the lower floor, where judges in red robes and full wigs hear the arguments of barristers in black robes and wigs. Visitors are welcome to watch the proceedings in the Assembly and the Supreme Court, but you must call to find out when sessions are scheduled. *Parliament St., between Reid and Church Sts.,* ☎ *441/292–7408.* ☛ *Free.* ⊘ *Weekdays 9–4:30. Closed holidays.*

The next street over from Parliament Street is Court Street. Although Court Street is safe during daylight hours, it is not advisable to wander around here at night. Bermuda does have some problems with drugs, and what traffic there is centers on Court and Victoria streets after dark.

⓫ The Senate, which is the upper house of Parliament, sits in the dignified two-story **Cabinet Building,** surrounded by trees and gardens. Amid great ceremony, the formal opening of Parliament takes place in the Senate Chamber, traditionally on the first Friday of November. His Excellency the Governor, dressed in a plumed hat and full regalia, arrives on the grounds in a landau drawn by magnificent black horses and accompanied by a police escort. A senior police officer, carrying the Black Rod made by the Crown jewelers, asks the Speaker of the House, elected representatives, and members of the Senate Chamber to convene. The governor makes his Throne Speech from a tiny cedar throne, dating from the 1600s, and carved with the words "Cap Josias Forstore Govornour of the Sumer Islands Anodo 1642" (Josias Foster was governor in 1642). The portraits above the dais are of King

George III and Queen Charlotte. The chamber is open to visitors, but come on a Wednesday if you want to watch the Senate in action; call first to find out about scheduling. *Front St.,* ☎ *441/292–5501.* ☛ *Free.* ⊙ *Weekdays 9–5. Closed holidays.*

⑫ In front of the Cabinet Building, the **Cenotaph** is a memorial to the war dead; on Remembrance Day (November 11), the governor and other dignitaries lay wreaths at the base of the monument. The Cenotaph is a smaller version of the famous one in Whitehall, London. The cornerstone was laid in 1920 by the Prince of Wales, who, as King Edward VIII, abdicated to wed Mrs. Simpson.

★ ⑬ On the eastern outskirts of Hamilton is **Fort Hamilton,** an imposing old fortress, complete with a moat, 18-ton guns, and underground passageways that were cut through solid rock by Royal Engineers in the 1860s. If you've done enough walking, consider taking a taxi or moped there, because it's quite far. Head east on East Reid Street, turn left on King Street, and then right onto Happy Valley Road. The restored fort is one of several built by order of the Duke of Wellington. Outdated even before its completion, the fort never fired a shot in aggression. Today, it affords splendid views of the capital and the harbor. Accompanied by drummers and dancers, the kilted Bermuda Isles Pipe Band performs a stirring skirling ceremony on the green every Monday at noon from November through March. *Happy Valley Rd., Pembroke, no* ☎. ☛ *Free.* ⊙ *Daily 9:30–5.*

Tour 2: The Town of St. George

Numbers in the margin correspond to points of interest on the Tour 2: The Town of St. George map.

The settlement of Bermuda began on the eastern end of the island in 1609, when the *Sea Venture* was wrecked off the coast. Despite its small size, St. George's encompasses much of historical interest, and visitors should plan to spend a full day poking around in the houses and museums. Much of the fun of St. George's is exploring the little alleys and walled lanes that wind through the town. The tour of the town is easily managed on foot.

⑭ **King's Square** is the hub of St. George's, although it is comparatively new. For 200 years after St. George's was settled, the square was a marshy part of the harbor—the area was filled in only in the last century. Stop

⑮ at the **Visitors Service Bureau** for maps, brochures, and advice. A combination ticket for $10 admits entry to Tucker House and the Confederate Museum (and Verdmont in Smith's Parish), which are all operated by the Bermuda National Trust.

Prominently displayed in King's Square is a cedar replica of the stocks and pillory originally used to punish criminals. Today, they serve as props for tourist photos and for special activities staged here on Wednesdays during the low season. If you decide to take the walking tour (*see* Important Contacts A to Z *in* the Gold Guide), you will be greeted in the square by the mayor of St. George's. The town crier, whose resounding voice is almost enough to wake the dead, is on hand in full colonial costume. After the official welcome, the crier bellows a few pronouncements and places any perceived malefactors in the stocks.

⑯ ★ Stroll across the bridge to **Ordnance Island** and the splendid **Desmond Fountain statue of Sir George Somers,** titled *Land Ho!* The **ducking stool** on the island is a replica of the one used to dunk gossips, nagging wives, and suspected witches in the water. Demonstrations are

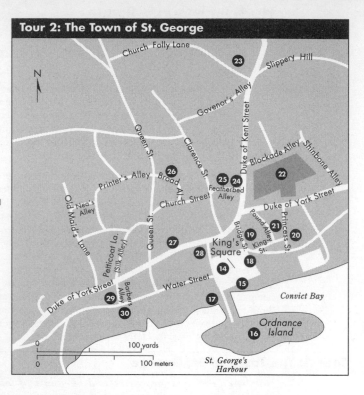

Tour 2: The Town of St. George

sometimes given, although volunteers say that getting dunked is no fun, even in fun.

Also on the island is the **Deliverance II,** a replica of the *Deliverance* built by the survivors of the wreck. After their shipwreck in 1609, Somers and his crew built two ships, the *Deliverance* and the *Patience,* to carry them to Jamestown, Virginia. Below deck, life-size mannequins in period costume are used to depict the realities of ocean travel in the 17th century—it's not the *QE2. Ordnance Island, no ☎. ☛ $2.50 adults, 50¢ children under 12. ⊙ Daily 10–4. Closed Good Friday, Easter, and Christmas.*

17 The waterside **White Horse Tavern** is a popular restaurant today, but it was the Davenport home for much of the 19th century. After his arrival in St. George's in about 1815, John Davenport opened a small dry-goods store on the square. He was able to wangle a profitable contract to supply beef to the garrison, and gold and silver began to pour in. There were no banks on Bermuda, but Davenport wasn't the trusting sort anyway. He stashed the money in a keg that he kept beneath his bed. When the keg was full, he took it down to the cellar and put another one under his bed. By the time he was an old man, Davenport would spend hours each day gloating over the kegs that now filled his cellar. After his death, it was discovered that the old miser had amassed a fortune in gold and silver worth £75,000.

18 Across the square is **Town Hall,** a two-story building that houses administrative offices. Constructed in 1808 and subsequently restored, the hall is paneled and furnished with cedar, and there's a delightful collection of photographs of former mayors. Many years ago Town Hall was the scene of a memorable con. A gentleman calling himself Professor Trott appeared in town and announced a spectacular production of *Ali Baba and the Forty Thieves.* A great crowd collected at Town Hall for the play, and thievery was duly performed: Having lured the residents away from their homes, the wily "professor" made off with an iron safe. The *Bermuda Journey,* a worthwhile audiovisual presentation, is shown in the second-floor theater. *King's Sq.* ☛ *Town Hall free.* ☉ *Daily 9–4. Closed holidays.* Bermuda Journey, ☏ 441/297–1642. ☛ *$3 adults, $1.75 children under 12, $2 senior citizens. Show times: Apr. 1–Oct. 31, Mon., Tues., Wed., Thurs., and Sat. 11:15, 12:15, and 2:15; Nov. 1–Mar. 31, Wed. and Sat. 12:15 and 2:15. Closed holidays.*

TIME OUT **Pub on the Square** (King's Sq., ☏ 441/297–1522) is exactly what its name implies. The balcony overlooking the square is a great place to knock back a beer, have a burger, and watch the action below. A better gastronomical alternative is the White Horse Tavern (*see above*) across the square. Sit outside on the porch, enjoy Bermudian fish cakes, and marvel at how fast the fish swim to the surface of the pond—if you can part with a morsel to toss them.

⑲ On your left as you walk up King Street is **Bridge House,** so named for a bridge that once crossed a small creek here. Built around 1700 and now owned by the Bermuda National Trust, the house is a fine example of Bermudian architecture, having served as the home of several of Bermuda's governors. It is divided into several private residences, which are not open to the public; however, the Bermudian-style architecture can be admired from the outside.

⑳ At the top of King Street, the **Old State House** is the oldest stone house in Bermuda. Constructed in 1620 in what Governor Nathaniel Butler believed was the Italian style, the limestone building used a mixture of turtle oil and lime as mortar and set the style for future Bermudian buildings. Upon completion, it became home to the Parliament, which had been meeting in St. Peter's Church; dances and social gatherings were also held there. After the capital was moved to Hamilton, the old State House was rented to Masonic Lodge St. George's No. 200 of the Grand Lodge of Scotland. The annual rent charged by the city was one peppercorn, the payment of which is still made upon a velvet pillow amid much pomp and circumstance. The Peppercorn Ceremony takes place each April. *Princess St., no* ☏. ☛ *Free.* ☉ *Wed. 10–4.*

Proceeding down Princess Street, you'll pass the place where a hotheaded tailor named Joseph Gwynn gunned down one Henry Folger in 1826. Enraged after his son had been sentenced to jail, Gwynn went out one night looking for the magistrate who had punished his son. Apparently blind with rage, he mistook Folger for the magistrate and shot him dead. A few months later, Gwynn was hanged near the very spot where the murder took place.

㉑ To the left of the State House is **Reeve Court** (Princess St., no ☏), a three-story home that the Bermuda National Trust purchased to ensure protection from development around the State House. Although the building is not open to the public, admirers can wander through the Colonial garden and admire plantings of fruits, herbs, and a formal parterre. Nearby is **Somers Garden,** a pleasant tree-shrouded park ㉒ where the heart of Sir George Somers is said to be buried. After sailing to Jamestown and back in 1610, Somers fell ill and died. According to local lore, Somers told his nephew Matthew Somers that he wanted his heart buried in Bermuda, where it belonged. Matthew, who never seemed to pay much attention to his uncle's wishes, sailed for England soon afterward, sneaking Somers's body aboard in a cedar chest to avoid alarming the superstitious seamen. (Somers's body is buried near his birthplace in Dorset.) When the tomb where Somers's heart was supposedly interred was opened many years later, only a few bones, a pebble, and some bottle fragments were found—no one knows if Matthew Somers ever carried out his uncle's wishes. Nevertheless, ceremonies were held at the empty grave upon the 1920 visit of the Prince of Wales, during which the prince christened the park Somers Garden. *Bordered by Shinbone Alley, Blockade Alley, Duke of Kent and Duke of York Sts., no ☎. ☛ Free. ⊙ Daily 9–4.*

TIME OUT   Off the tourist beat, **Angeline's Coffee Shop** (Duke of York St. across and east of Somers Garden, ☎ 441/297–0959) is a popular spot for basic egg breakfasts, plate lunches, sandwiches, and burgers. The fish sandwiches are some of the island's tastiest, and on Sunday morning a wholesome traditional Bermuda codfish breakfast with all the trimmings is served.

Walk through Somers Garden and up the steps to Blockade Alley. On
㉓ the hill ahead is the **Unfinished Church.** Considering how much attention and affection is lavished on St. Peter's these days, it's hard to believe that residents in the 19th century wanted to replace the old church with a new one. Work began on this church in 1874, but construction was halted when a schism developed in the church. Money for construction was later diverted to rebuild Trinity Church in Hamilton when it burned down; work on the new church in St. George's was abandoned by the turn of the century. In 1992 the Bermuda National Trust obtained a 50-year lease on the church, and is repairing and stabilizing the structure. Access is subject to completion of the work.

㉔ At the corner of Featherbed Alley and Duke of Kent Street is **St. George's Historical Society Museum.** A typical Bermudian structure from the early 1700s, the newly refurbished house is furnished much the same as when it was a private home. One of Bermuda's oldest pieces is a table believed to have been used as the High Court bench in the State House. The house is also filled with documents (including a doctor's bill from 1790), old letters, and displays of pewter, china, and rare books; there's even a whale-blubber cutter. A torpedo raft is one of the relics from the American Civil War. Constructed of heavy timber with projecting arms to hold torpedoes, the raft was part of a Union plan to blow up the submarine barricade in Charleston harbor. After breaking loose from its towing ship during a gale, the raft drifted for six years before washing ashore in Dolly's Bay on St. David's Island. When the captain of the towing ship later visited Bermuda, he recognized the raft and explained its purpose to the puzzled Bermudians. On the south wall of the house is an iron grate that is said to have come from the cell where Bermuda's first Methodist missionary, the Reverend John Stephenson, was confined for preaching to slaves. The persistent missionary continued to preach from his cell to a crowd that collected outside. The cottage gardens in the back of the building are beautiful and worth a visit; there is no fee to view them. *Featherbed Alley, ☎ 441/297–0423. ☛ $2.50 adults, 50¢ children 4–16 (including a guided tour). ⊙ Apr.–Dec., weekdays 10–4. Closed holidays.*

㉕ Around the corner, the **Featherbed Alley Printery** is as quaint as its name. Inside the cottage is a working printing press of the kind invented by Johannes Gutenberg in the 1450s. *Featherbed Alley, ☎ 441/297–0009. ☛ Free. ⊙ Mon.–Sat. 10–4. Closed holidays.*

Cross Clarence Street to Church Street, and then turn right on Broad
㉖ Alley to reach the **Old Rectory,** now a private residence but owned by

the Bermuda National Trust. Built in the 1690s, it's a charming little house with Dutch doors, shutters, chimneys, and a welcoming-arms staircase. For many years it was the home of Alexander Richardson, the "Little Bishop," who was rector of St. Peter's from 1755 to 1805, except for a six-year stint on St. Eustatius. Richardson's diary is filled with anecdotes about 18th-century St. George's. The garden is open to the public as well. *Broad Alley,* ☎ *441/297–0879.* ☛ *Free (donations appreciated).* ⏱ *Wed. noon–5. Closed holidays.*

Straight ahead (if "straight" is applicable among these twisted alleys) is **Printer's Alley,** where Bermuda's first newspaper was published. On January 17, 1784, less than a year after his arrival on the island, Joseph Stockdale printed the first copy of the *Bermuda Gazette & Weekly Advertiser.* The paper was published weekly for 20 years until Stockdale's death in 1805. The house where Stockdale worked is now a private home.

Nea's Alley is a short street connecting Printer's Alley with Old Maid's Lane. The 19th-century Irish poet Tom Moore lived on this street, then known as Cumberland Lane, during his four month tenure as registrar of the admiralty court. Moore, who was endowed with considerable charm, had an impact on the island that endures to this day. He was invited to stay in the home of Admiral Mitchell, the neighbor of Mr. William Tucker and his wife, Hester—the "Nea" to whom Moore pours out his heart in several poems. Moore is thought to have first seen her in Cumberland Lane, which he describes in one of his odes as "the lime-covered alley that leads to thy home." However discreet Nea and Moore may have been about their affair, his odes to her were on the steamy side—much to the dismay of her husband. Although it was rather like locking the barn door after the horse has bolted, William Tucker refused to allow his former friend into his house again. Some Bermudians speculate that Nea was very much in love with Tom, but that he considered her merely a pleasant divertissement. He returned to Ireland after his assignment, and Nea died in 1817 at the age of 31. Bermudians are much enamored of the short-lived romance between Hester and Moore, and visitors are likely to hear a good deal about it.

★ ㉗ Return to Church Street and enter the churchyard of **St. Peter's Church.** The tombstones in Bermuda's oldest churchyard tell some interesting tales, indeed—this is the resting place of governors, doctors, simple folk, and pirates. East of the church is the grave of Hester, or "Nea," marked "Mr. William Tucker's Family Vault." One of the best-known monuments stands over the grave of Richard Sutherland Dale, who died in 1815 at age 20. An American navy midshipman, Dale was mortally wounded during a sea battle with the British in the War of 1812. The monument was erected by his parents as a tribute to the St. Georgians, whose "tender sympathy prompted the kindest attentions to their son while living and honoured him when dead." In an enclosure to the west of the church is the slaves' graveyard. The ancient cedar tree, which dates back to before 1620, is the old belfry tree. Because parts of St. Peter's Church date back to its construction in 1620, it holds the distinction of being the oldest continuously operating Anglican church in the Western Hemisphere. It was not the first church to stand on this site, however; it replaced a 1612 structure of posts and palmetto leaves that was destroyed in a storm. The present church was extended in 1713, and the galleries on either side were added in 1833. The oldest part of the church is the area around the 17th-century triple-tier pulpit. The dark-red cedar altar is the oldest piece of woodwork in the colony, carved under the supervision of Richard Moore, a shipwright and the first governor. The baptismal font, brought to the island by the early settlers, is about 500 years old, and the late-18th-century bishop's throne is believed to have been salvaged from a wreck. Among the treasures displayed in the vestry are a 1697 William of Orange communion set and a Charles I chalice, sent from England by the Bermuda Company in 1625. Commemorative plaques hang on the walls, and some of the names are wonderfully Pickwickian: One large memorial is to Governor Allured Popple. If you enter through the back door, be sure to look at the front of the church when you leave. *Duke of York St., ☎ 441/297–8359.* ☛ *Free (donations appreciated).* ۞ *Daily.*

(28) Across the street, the **Confederate Museum,** which will close for renovations from January 1995 to May or June, 1996, has a colorful history. Built in 1700 by Governor Samuel Day, the building served for 150 years as the Globe Hotel. During the American Civil War, Major Norman Walker, who came to Bermuda as a Confederate agent, used it as his office. St. George's—which had suffered a depression after the capital moved to Hamilton in 1815—sided with the South for economic reasons, and the town became a hotbed of blockade-running activity. The first woman to run the blockade was Major Walker's pregnant wife, who risked capture by the North to join him in Bermuda. She was determined to have their baby born on Confederate soil, however, beneath the Stars and Bars. In the room where she gave birth, therefore, the four-poster bed was draped with the Confederate flag, and it's said that Confederate soil was spread beneath the bed. A wall map, designed by Desmond Fountain, shows the blockade-running routes from Bermuda to Southern ports. Also on display are a model of a blockade-runner, a replica of the Great Seal of the Confederacy, and an antique Victorian Seal Press, which makes reproductions of the Great Seal as souvenirs for visitors. *Duke of York St., ☎ 441/297–1423.* ☛ *$4 adults, $3 senior citizens, $1 students with ID; $10 combination ticket extends admission to Tucker House and Verdmont, in Smith's Parish.* ۞ *Apr.–Oct., Mon.–Sat. 9:30–4:30; Nov.–Mar., Mon.–Sat. 10–4. Closed holidays.*

Continuing down Duke of York Street, you come to **Barber's Alley,** named for Joseph Hayne Rainey, a former slave from South Carolina. Rainey's father had bought him his freedom, so when the Civil War broke out, Rainey and his French wife fled to Bermuda. Living in the kitchen of the Tucker House, Rainey became a barber and his wife made fashionable clothes. After the Civil War, they returned to South Carolina, where he went into politics. His career advanced quickly and in 1870 Rainey became the first black man to be elected to the U.S. House of Representatives.

Petticoat Lane, which is also called Silk Alley, received its name in 1834 after the emancipation of Bermudian slaves. Legend has it that two freed slaves, who had always wanted petticoats like those worn by their mistresses, strolled down the lane on Emancipation Sunday amid much rustling of petticoat skirts.

(29) Antiques aficionados will find much of interest in the **Tucker House,** one of the showplaces of the Bermuda National Trust. Built of native limestone in 1711, the house sat close to the waterside (the area is now all built up). Henry Tucker, president of the Governor's Council, lived in the house with his family from 1775 to 1807. His grandson donated most of the furnishings, which date from the mid-18th and early 19th centuries. Much of it is cedar, but there are some handsome mahogany pieces as well: The mahogany dining table was crafted from a tree grown in Cuba, and an English mahogany breakfront holds a collection of

Tucker-family silver. Notice the tiny wig rooms off the dining room, where ladies and gentlemen went to fix their wigs after dinner. A short flight of stairs leads down to the kitchen, where Joseph Rainey lived and ran his barbershop. There is a small bookstore in the cellar. A new archaeological exhibit with a display of artifacts used by the Tucker family—including toothbrushes, shoe buckles, and tableware—opened in 1994. The Tucker name has been important in Bermuda since the island's beginnings (Henry Tucker's son St. George built the Tucker House in Williamsburg, Virginia), and a number of interesting family portraits hang in the house. Henry Tucker's father and brother were both involved in the famed "Gunpowder Plot" of 1775. The Continental Congress had imposed a ban on exports to all British colonies not taking part in the revolt against England. Bermuda depended upon the American colonies for grain, so a delegation of Bermudians traveled to Philadelphia offering salt in exchange for the resumption of grain shipments. Congress rejected the salt but agreed to lift the ban if Bermuda sent gunpowder instead. A group of Bermudians, including the two Tuckers, then sneaked into the island's arsenal, stole the gunpowder, and shipped it to Boston. The ban was soon lifted. *Water St.,* ☎ *441/297–0545.* ☛ *$4 adults, $3 senior citizens, $1 students with ID; $10 combination ticket extends admission to the Confederate Museum, and Verdmont Museum in Smith's Parish.* ☉ *Apr.–Oct., Mon.–Sat. 9:30–4:30, Nov.–Mar., Mon.–Sat. 10–4. Closed holidays.*

With the arrival of cars on Bermuda in 1946, horse-drawn carriages were put out to pasture, so to speak. Across the street from the Tucker House, the **Carriage Museum** offers a fascinating look at some of the island's old carriages. Yes, there's a surrey with a fringe on top as well as isinglass curtains that roll down. Among the other displays are a dignified Brougham; a six-passenger enclosed Opera Bus; and a small two-wheeler for children, called the Little Red Dog Cart. The carriages are labeled, but it's fun to hear the curator, Mr. Frith, describe them. *Water St.,* ☎ *809/297–1367.* ☛ *Free (donations appreciated).* ☉ *Weekdays 10–5 (and occasionally Sat.). Closed holidays.*

Somers Wharf, where the Carriage Museum is located, is part of a multimillion-dollar waterfront restoration that includes several shops and the pleasant Carriage House Restaurant. St. George's passenger-ship terminal is in this area.

Tour 3: The West End

Numbers in the margin correspond to points of interest on the Tour 3: The West End map.

In contrast to Hamilton and St. George's, the West End is a rather bucolic part of Bermuda. With the notable exception of Dockyard, many of the attractions here are natural rather than manmade: nature reserves, wooded areas, and beautiful harbors and bays. In the waters off Daniel's Head, the Sea Gardens are regularly visited by glass-bottom boats from Hamilton: With its bow jutting out of the water, the coral-wrapped wreck of HMS *Vixen* is a major attraction. The ship was deliberately sunk by the British to block the channel and protect Dockyard from attack by torpedo boats. The West End is part of Sandys Parish, named after Sir Edwin Sandys, an investor in the Bermuda Company. Local lore contends that Sir George Somers took a keen interest in this region, and in the early days it was known as "Somers's seat"—hence the name of Somerset Village. Today, Somerset is a sleepy little hamlet with banks, several restaurants, a few shops, and not much else. The West End's big attraction is the Royal Naval Dockyard, a bastion of the British Royal Navy for nearly 150 years. You should plan to spend at least a day exploring this area.

If you take the ferry to Somerset, look closely at the ferry schedule: The trip can take anywhere from a half hour to more than an hour, depending on which ferry you take. However, there are worse ways to while away an hour than churning across Bermuda's Great Sound. Take your bicycle or moped aboard the ferry, too, because you will need wheels in the West End. Bus service is available for those without their own transport.

❸❶ The Somerset ferry stops at Somerset Bridge, Cavello Bay, Watford Bridge, and Dockyard. This tour begins at the **Royal Naval Dockyard** on Ireland Island, a sprawling complex housing several notable attractions. After the American Revolution, Britain found itself with neither an anchorage nor a major ship-repair yard in the western Atlantic. When Napoleon started to make threatening noises in Europe and British ships became increasingly vulnerable to pirate attack, Britain began construction of a major stronghold in Bermuda in 1441. The work was done by slaves and English convicts toiling under appalling conditions—thousands of workers died before the project was completed. This was a functioning shipyard for nearly 150 years; it was closed in 1951, and the Royal Navy closed operations here in 1995 after a 200-year presence. With the opening of the Maritime Museum (*see below*) in 1975, the decision was made to transform the entire naval port into a tourist attraction. The Dockyard is currently under development as a minivillage, and Bermudians are justifiably proud of the entire project. The area includes a shopping arcade and a visitor information center in the handsome, century-old Clocktower Building, a cruise-ship terminal, a children's entertainment center, a movie theater, shops and galleries, restaurants, a marina with deepwater berths, and the submarine *Enterprise*. The erstwhile shipyard continues to blossom, having undergone extensive landscaping to replace its vast stretches of concrete with shrubs, trees, and grassy lawns. New additions include an extension of the shopping mall, a snorkel park, and horse-drawn-carriage tours. You can reach the Dockyard in 40 minutes from Hamilton via an express bus that leaves the capital every 15 minutes. During the low season (November through March), walking tours meet regularly (*see* Important Contacts A to Z *in* the Gold Guide), and during the high season (April through October), arrangements can be made in advance through the Royal Naval Dockyard's public relations department (☎ 441/234–1709). Hold on to your hat when you're strolling in the area—it's often very windy, particularly along the water.

❸❷ Opened by Queen Elizabeth II in 1975, the sprawling 6-acre **Maritime Museum,** is housed in Bermuda's largest fort, built to defend the Royal Naval Dockyard. Entry to the museum is over a moat. The exhibition rooms are in six old magazines and munitions warehouses arranged around the parade grounds and the Keep Pond area. Several of the rather tired exhibits pertain to the *Sea Venture* and the early history of the island. Artifacts and relics from some of the approximately 300 ships wrecked on the island's reefs are exhibited; the *Age of Discovery* exhibit traces some of those voyages. Sailors will appreciate the Bermuda dinghies (14-foot sailboats that can carry as much as 1,000 feet of canvas) on display in the Boat Loft. Visitors can also explore the restored ramparts to enjoy commanding views of the Great Sound and North Shore. Currently undergoing renovation, the 19th-century Commissioner's House, set high on a bluff, is the world's oldest cast-iron–framed residence. Home to Dockyard commissioners from 1827 to 1837, and later a barracks, the house was formally commissioned as a "ship"—

Tour 3: The West End

the HMS *Malabar*—in 1919. Fund-raisers for the $3-million restoration project hope to complete work on the house by 1997. *Dockyard, ☎ 441/234–1418. ☛ $7.50 adults, $6 seniors and students, $3 military personnel, children 3–12. Family and group rates available if arranged in advance. ☉ Daily 10–5. Closed Christmas.*

�33 Across the street from the Maritime Museum is the Old Cooperage, or barrel-maker's shop. Dating back to 1831, the reconstructed building houses the **Neptune Cinema,** which shows first-run films; the popular **Frog & Onion** pub-restaurant; the **Craft Market;** and the **Bermuda Arts Centre at Dockyard.**

The Craft Market displays the works of local craftsmen and commercial artists. Jaded tourists who think of craft as tacky souvenirs are in for a pleasant surprise. There are some delightful items on sale here, including wood carvings and miniature cedar furniture (*see* Chapter 4, Shopping). *Dockyard, ☎ 441/234–3208. ☛ Free. ☉ Daily 10–5. Closed Christmas, New Year's Day, Good Fri.*

�34 Since its opening by Princess Margaret in 1984, the **Bermuda Arts Centre at Dockyard** has been a showcase for local artists and artisans, and an excellent place to see Bermudian work (*see* Chapter 4, Shopping). Exhibits, which change frequently, include watercolors, oils, and photography. Beautifully crafted silver jewelry, hand-dyed scarves, and quilts are sold throughout the year. The good selection of note cards and posters emphasize Bermuda themes. *Dockyard, ☎ 441/234–2441. ☛ Free (donations appreciated). ☉ Apr.–Oct., daily 10–5,; Nov.–Mar. 31, Tues.–Sun. 10:30–4:30. Closed Christmas Day.*

TIME OUT In the new Victorian Mall, adjacent to the Clocktower Building is **Nannini's Häagen-Dazs,** (☎ 441/234–2474) a wonderful place to satisfy a sweet tooth. Choose one of the 16 flavors of ice cream or nonfat soft yogurt, or take a cup of freshly brewed espresso, cappuccino, or hot chocolate at a table outside. Also featured here are Nannini cakes and Perugina chocolates from Italy. Have a chat with owner Fosco Nannini, who weaves lots of interesting yarns.

㉟ Take the main road out of Dockyard along Ireland Island South. Turn left on Craddock Road and cycle down to **Lagoon Park.** Hidden in the mangroves are a lovely lagoon, footpaths, wild birds, and places to picnic. Next to the park, **The Crawl** is a picturesque inlet with fishing boats bobbing in the water and lobster pots on the dock. The park is always open, and there's no charge for entry.

㊱ Cross over Boaz and Watford islands to Somerset Island. The largest of all these islets, Somerset Island is fringed on both sides with beautiful secluded coves, inlets, and bays. Beside pretty Mangrove Bay, **Somerset Village** is a quiet retreat, quite different from St. George's, Hamilton, and Dockyard. Only one road runs through the village, and the few shops are mostly branches of Hamilton stores, along with two banks. During the low season, tour guides concentrate on the area's history as well as its natural beauty and unusual medicinal plants (*see* Important Contacts A to Z *in* the Gold Guide). Somerset Island itself is heavily populated, laced with roads and pathways through quiet residential areas.

Cambridge Beaches, Bermuda's original cottage colony, sits on its own 25-acre peninsula northwest of Somerset Village. Nestled among the trees near the entrance is a branch of the **Irish Linen Shop** (Cambridge Rd., ☎ 441/234–0127). The little cottage was one of the original units of Cambridge Beaches.

㊲ A short distance farther along Cambridge Road is **Long Bay Park and Nature Reserve,** which has a great beach, shallow water, and picnic areas. The Bermuda Audubon Society owns the adjacent nature reserve and its pond, which attracts migrating birds in the spring and fall. Peaceful as this area is now, it was the scene of one of Bermuda's most sensational murders. Skeeters' Corner, at the end of Daniel's Head Road, was the site of a cottage once owned by a couple of the same name. One night in 1878, Edward Skeeters strangled his wife and dumped her in the water. His long, rambling confession revealed that he was irked because she talked too much!

㊳ Continue along Cambridge Road (which becomes Somerset Road), until you see the arched gateway leading to **Springfield and the Gilbert Nature Reserve.** Set in 5 heavily wooded acres, Springfield is an old plantation home, owned by the Bermuda National Trust and dating back to around 1700. Plans are being made for a major restoration of the main house and outbuildings—the kitchen, slave quarters, and buttery— which are built around an open courtyard. The nature reserve, named after the family that owned the property from 1700 to 1973, was acquired by the Bermuda National Trust in conjunction with the Bermuda Audubon Society. *Main Rd., Somerset,* ☎ *441/236–6483.* ☛ *Free. Nature reserve always open.*

㊴ Somerset Road winds around to the **Somerset Visitors Service Bureau** (Somerset Rd., ☎ 441/234–1388), where you can get information about this area from April to November, 9–3.

㊵ High atop a promontory against a backdrop of the sea, **St. James Church** is one of the loveliest churches on the island. The entrance on the main road is marked by handsome wooden gates that were designed by a

Royal Engineer in 1872; the long pathway curls past glistening white tombs in the churchyard. The first church on this site was a wood structure destroyed by a hurricane in 1780. The present church was consecrated in 1789. The tall, slender spire is a faithful replica of the 1880 spire that was hit by lightning and sent crashing down into the church's center aisle in 1937. *Main Rd., Somerset,* ☎ *441/234–2025.* ☛ *Free.* ☉ *Daily dawn to dusk.*

㊵ A short distance beyond the church, you'll see the entrance to the **Heydon Trust property,** opposite Willowbank guest house. Among its 43 acres are citrus orchards, banana groves, flower and vegetable gardens, and bird sanctuaries. The quiet, peaceful property has been maintained as undeveloped "open space"—a reminder of what the island was like in its early days. Pathways dotted with park benches wend through the preserve, affording some wonderful views of the Great Sound. If you persevere along the main path, you'll reach the tiny, rustic **Heydon Chapel,** which dates from before 1620. An old rugged cross is planted in the hillside, and a welcome mat lies at the door. Inside are a few wooden pews, cedar beams, and an ancient oven and hearth in a small room behind the altar. Services are still held in the chapel, including Gregorian chants at 3 PM Mon.–Sat. *Somerset Rd.,* ☎ *441/234–1831.* ☛ *Free.* ☉ *During daylight hrs.*

㊷ Just around the bend on your left is **Fort Scaur.** Perched on the highest hill in Somerset, the fort was begun in 1868 and completed in the 1870s. British troops were garrisoned here until World War I, and during World War II, American forces from Battery D, 52nd Coast Artillery Battalion, were stationed here. Little remains to be seen here now, although the 22 acres of gardens are quite pretty, and the view of the Great Sound is fantastic. Almost worth the long climb is the Early Bermuda Weather Stone, the "perfect weather indicator." The plaque reads: "A wet stone means . . . it is raining; a shadow under the stone . . . means the sun is shining; if the stone is swinging, it means there is a strong wind blowing; if the stone jumps up and down it means there is an earthquake; if ever it is white on top . . . believe it or not . . . it is snowing." *Somerset Rd., Ely's Harbour,* ☎ *441/234–0908.* ☛ *Free.* ☉ *Daily Apr.–Oct., 7:30–4:30; Nov.–Mar., 7:30–4.*

㊸ At the bottom of the hilly, twisting road lies spectacular **Ely's Harbour,** with pleasure boats dotting its brilliant turquoise waters. Pronounced "Ee-lees," the small sheltered harbor was once a hangout for smugglers.

㊹ Linking Somerset Island with the rest of Bermuda is **Somerset Bridge,** reputed to have the smallest draw in the world. It opens a mere 18 inches, just wide enough to accommodate a sailboat mast. Near the bridge is the Somerset ferry landing, where you can catch a ferry back to Hamilton. Across the bridge, Somerset Road becomes Middle Road, which leads into Southampton Parish (*see* Tour 4, *below*).

TIME OUT A good place to stop for one of the best—if expensive—lunches on the island is the casual **La Plage** restaurant at the **Lantana Colony Club** (Somerset Rd., ☎ 441/234–0141). Reservations are necessary.

Tour 4: The Parishes

Numbers in the margin correspond to points of interest on the Tour 4: The Parishes map.

Bermuda's other points of interest—and there are many—are scattered across the island's parishes. This final tour takes you across the length

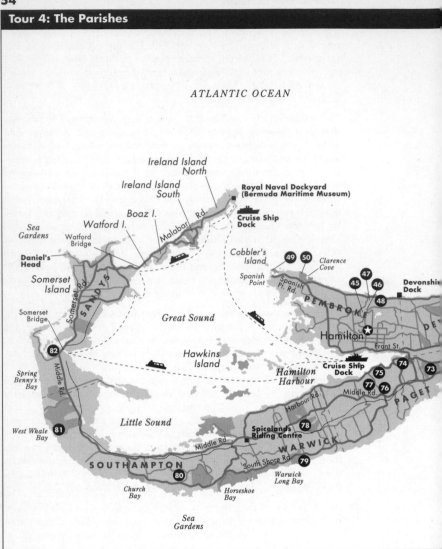

ATLANTIC OCEAN

Ireland Island
North

Ireland Island
South

Boaz I.

Watford I.

Sea
Gardens

Watford
Bridge

Royal Naval Dockyard
(Bermuda Maritime Museum)

Cruise Ship
Dock

Daniel's
Head

Cobbler's
Island

Clarence
Cove

Spanish
Point

Somerset
Island

SANDYS

Spanish
Pl. Rd.

PEMBROKE

Devonshi

Devonshire
Dock

Somerset
Bridge

Great Sound

Hamilton

Front St.

DE

Somerset Rd.

Middle Rd.

Hawkins
Island

Hamilton
Harbour

Cruise Ship
Dock

PAGET

Spring
Benny's
Bay

Little Sound

Harbour Rd.

Middle Rd.

West Whale
Bay

Spicelands
Riding Centre

Middle Rd.

WARWICK

SOUTHAMPTON

South Shore Rd.

Warwick
Long Bay

Church
Bay

Horseshoe
Bay

Sea
Gardens

Tobacco
Bay
59 **58** Fort St. Catherine
Beach

St. George's
Island

**S T.
G E O R G E' S**
Mullet Bay Rd. ○ Town of St. George

St. George's
Harbour
57

**Cruise
Ship
Dock**

Ferry Rd. **56**

Coney
Island

Kindley
Field Rd.
**Bermuda
Airport**

St. David's Rd.

60

Sea
Gardens

The
Causeway

61

55

62

Blue Hole

St. David's
Island

Crawl Hill North
54

HAMILTON

63

64

Castle
Harbour

Harrington
Sound Rd.

53

Harrington
Sound

65

**TUCKER'S
TOWN**

67

Sea
Gardens

...shire

52

North Shore Rd.

Harrington
Sound Rd.

68

John Smith's
Bay

66

51

SMITH'S

...EVONSHIRE

72

70

69

South Shore Rd.

21

73

N

KEY

⛴ Cruise Ship

⛴ Ferry

— Railway Trail

0   2 miles

0   3 km

and breadth of the colony, commenting only on the major sights. Half the fun of exploring Bermuda, though, is wandering down forgotten lanes or discovering some little-known beach or cove. A moped or bicycle is ideal for this kind of travel, although most of the island is covered by bus and ferry service. It would be foolish to try to see all the sights here in just one day. The tour, which leaves from Hamilton, can easily be broken into two halves: The first half explores those parishes in the eastern part of the island; the second travels through the western parishes. Even so, vacationers may find it more rewarding to do the tour piecemeal—a couple of sites here, a church there, and a day at the beach in between.

45 Follow Cedar Avenue north out of Hamilton to **St. John's Church,** consecrated in 1826 as the parish church of Pembroke. The first church on this site was built in 1621. During a funeral in 1875, the churchyard was the scene of a verbal duel between the Anglican rector and a Wesleyan minister. The Anglican church insisted that all burial services in parish churchyards be conducted by the rector, but the Wesleyans challenged the church in the case of a deceased woman named Esther Levy. Claiming he'd been asked by her friends to perform the funeral service, a Wesleyan minister appeared in the churchyard despite the efforts of the Anglican rector to stop him. Simultaneous services were held over poor Mrs. Levy's body, with the minister and the adamant Anglican trying to out-shout each other. The rector subsequently filed charges of trespassing against the Wesleyan, and the celebrated case went before the Supreme Court. The jury found for the rector, and fined the minister one shilling. *St. John's Rd., Pembroke,* ☏ *441/292– 0299.* ☞ *Free.* ☉ *Daily 8–5:30.*

By following Marsh Folly Road, which runs between the church and
46 Bernard Park, you'll come to **Black Watch Pass.** The Public Works Department excavated about 2.5 million cubic feet of solid limestone dur-
47 ing construction of the pass. The road received its name from **Black Watch Well,** at the intersection of Black Watch Pass and North Shore Road. During a severe drought in 1849, the governor ordered a well dug on government ground to alleviate the suffering of the poor in the area. Excavated by a detachment of the famed Black Watch regiment, the well is marked by a commemorative plaque and shaded by a tiered concrete slab. The site is not particularly inspiring, however, and only the most dedicated well-wishers will want to make the pilgrimage to see it.

48 From its position on Langton Hill, imposing **Government House** overlooks North Shore Road, Black Watch Well, and the sea. The house is the residence of the governor and is not open to the public. The 45 acres of land were purchased when the capital was transferred from St. George's to Hamilton in 1815. A simple, two-story house served as the governor's home until the present, rather austere mansion was completed in 1892. Various royals and other distinguished visitors planted the trees and shrubs on the pretty, landscaped lawns. Among the guests who have been entertained in Government House were Sir Winston Churchill, President Kennedy, and, more recently, Queen Elizabeth II and Prince Philip, Prince Charles, Margaret Thatcher and George Bush. The mansion was also the scene of the 1973 assassination of Governor Richard Sharples and his aide, Captain Hugh Sayers.

49 North Shore Road merges with Spanish Point Road near **Spanish Point,** at the tip of the peninsula. The survivors of the wrecked *Sea Venture* thought they found evidence here of an earlier visit by the Spanish. Apparently they were right: Historians now believe that Captain Diego Ramirez landed here in 1603. There is a small park for picnicking, a sheltered bay for swimming, public facilities, and a lovely view of Somerset across the sound. Unfortunately, some rather seedy characters hang out here, so do not go alone. In summer, lots of people camp here, and the noise level can be far from peaceful. Cobbler's Island, across Cobbler's Cut from Spanish Point, has a grisly history—executed slaves were exhibited here as a warning to others of the consequences of disobedience.

(50) En route to Spanish Point you pass **Admiralty House Park,** a pretty spot with several caves and sheltered coves. Little remains of the house, originally the 19th-century estate of John Dunscombe. Dunscombe, who later became lieutenant governor of Newfoundland, sold the property in 1816 to the British military, which decided to build a house for the commanding British admiral of the naval base at Dockyard. The house was reconstructed several times over the years, notably in the 1850s by an eccentric admiral with a weakness for subterranean tunnels—he had several caves and galleries cut into the cliffs above the sea. The house was closed when the Royal Navy withdrew in 1951 and was later demolished. All that remains of the complex is the ballroom. Within the park, Clarence Cove offers a sheltered beach and pleasant swimming.

Head back along North Shore Road to Devonshire Parish. Ideal for cycling and quiet picnics, Devonshire is a serene part of the island, with much to offer in the way of natural beauty. Locals come to **Devonshire Dock** to buy fresh fish (something to bear in mind if you're staying in a housekeeping apartment).

(51) A short distance farther along North Shore Road is **Palmetto House,** an 18th-century cruciform house owned by the Bermuda National Trust. At the time it was built, cross-shaped houses were thought to ward off evil spirits.

(52) If you continue along North Shore Road, you will reach **Flatts Village,** which overlooks a picturesque body of water. One of the earliest settlements on the island, Flatts occasionally hosted the House of Assembly, although much of the village's activities involved flouting the law rather than making it. Hoping to avoid customs officers, Bermudians returning from the West Indies would sometimes sail into the village in the dead of night to unload their cargoes.

(53) The **Aquarium, Museum and Zoo** at Flatts Village is one of the island's most popular attractions. Enjoy a self-guided audio tour of tanks full of native Bermudian sea creatures, including sharks, barracuda, and grumpy-looking giant grouper. The natural-history museum features a geology display with explanations of Bermuda's volcanic origins, information about the humpback whales that migrate past the island, and a deep-sea exhibit that documents the half-mile dive of marine biologist Dr. William Beebe in the early 1930s. The odd-looking contraption outside the museum is a replica of the bathysphere in which Dr. Beebe made his dive. In the zoo, a reptile walkway gives visitors a close look at alligators and Galapagos tortoises. A beehive, octopuses, and a touch pool are among the wonders of the Invertebrate House. There is also a children's Discovery Room, with activities pertaining to Bermuda. Other attractions include an aviary, otters, monkeys, lemurs, Caribbean flamingos, and strutting peacocks. *Flatts, ☎ 441/293–2727. ☛ $6 adults, $3 children 5–12. ⏲ Daily 9–5 (last ☛ at 4:30). Closed Christmas.*

Near the aquarium is the **Railway Museum and Curiosity Shop,** housed in the old Aquarium Station of the island's erstwhile standard-gauge railroad. The tiny museum is cluttered with photos, signs, wicker chairs from the first class compartment, and other memorabilia. "Old Rattle and Shake," as the railway was known, is so fondly remembered by Bermudians you'll wonder why the line was shut down. Rarely shown footage of the railway in operation was recently installed. *37 North Shore Rd.,* ☎ *441/293–1774.* ☛ *Free (donations accepted).* ☉ *Weekdays 10–4 and some Saturdays (ring the bell and the curator will let you in if she's home).*

Continuing east, North Shore Road climbs **Crawl Hill,** a high point offering spectacular views over the island and sea. "Crawl" derives from the Afrikaans word "kraal," meaning animal enclosure; on Bermuda, the word was applied to several ponds containing turtles and fish. This part of Hamilton Parish was also a site for shipbuilding during the early days of the colony.

54 Turn right on Trinity Church Road to see **Holy Trinity Church.** Built in 1623 as one long room with a thatched roof, it is said to be the oldest Anglican church on Bermuda. The church has been much embellished over the past 372 years, but the original building remains at its core. The small graveyard is encircled by palms, royal poinciana, and cherry trees. *Church Bay, Harrington Sound, no* ☎. ☉ *To public for services only.*

Just off Trinity Church Road is **Mt. Wyndham,** the peak from which Admiral Sir Alexander Cochrane surveyed the British fleet prior to its attack on Washington, DC, in 1814.

55 Follow North Shore Road as it dips south to the **Bermuda Perfumery and Gardens.** On a guided tour, visitors learn how the Lili Perfume Factory, which began extracting natural fragrances from the island's flowers in 1929, blossomed into the present perfumery/tourist attraction. The factory is in a 200-year-old cottage with cedar beams, but the biggest draw is the aromatic nature trail that you can walk on your own. A complimentary map helps you sniff your way around the oleanders, frangipani, jasmine, orchids, and passionflowers that are the raw material for the factory. The adjoining Calabash Gift Shop carries a large selection of soaps and toiletries. *212 North Shore Rd.,* ☎ *441/293–0627.* ☛ *Free.* ☉ *Apr.–Oct., Mon.–Sat. 9–5, Sun. 10–4; Nov.–Mar., Mon.–Sat. 9–4:30, closed Sun. and some holidays.*

TIME OUT   Just up the road, **Bailey's Ice Cream Parlour & Food D'Lites** (Blue Hole Hill, ☎ 441/293-9333) offers 40 varieties of freshly made natural ice cream, as well as shakes, sodas, yogurts, and sorbets. For something a bit stronger, cross the road for a rum swizzle and a "swizzleburger" at the **Swizzle Inn** (Blue Hole Hill, ☎ 441/293-9300).

Blue Hole Hill leads to the causeway over Castle Harbour. Once on the other side you are in St. George's Parish. Take Kindley Field Road around the airport, turn left onto Mullet Bay Road, and cross Swing
56 Bridge over Ferry Reach. The **Bermuda Biological Station for Research** will be of interest to anyone who cares about the environment. Scientists here have conducted research on marine life since 1903. Facilities include ships for ocean research, 13 laboratories, a 250-seat lecture hall, and a 20,000-volume library. Research programs here focus on environmental issues such as global change and the health of Bermuda's reefs. Extensive research has been conducted here on acid rain. Guided tours of the grounds and laboratory are conducted every Wednesday at 10 AM, beginning in the main building. Coffee and snacks are served. *17 Biological La., Ferry Reach, St. George's,* ☎ *441/297–1880.* ☛ *Free (donations appreciated).*

The scenery is magnificent along the stretch of road that runs between Mullet Bay and the sea. A little farther east, Mullet Bay Road becomes Wellington Road, and finally Duke of York Street when you reach St. George's (*see* Tour 2, *above*). East of town, Duke of York Street becomes Barrack Hill Road. From the road, the views of the town, St. David's Island, and Castle Harbour are splendid. Barrack Hill Road turns into

(57) Cut Road, which leads all the way to **Gates Fort.** St. George's has always had the greatest concentration of fortifications on the island. Gates Fort is a reconstruction of a small militia fort dating from the 1620s. Don't expect turrets, towers, and tunnels, however; there is little to see here apart from the sea. The fort and Gates Bay, which it overlooks, were named for Sir Thomas Gates, the first of the survivors of the *Sea Venture* to reach dry land. Upon doing so, he is reputed to have shouted, "This is Gates, his bay!" Public speaking was obviously not his forte, although Gates was by profession a politician—he later became governor of Virginia. *Cut Rd., no ☎. ☛ Free. ۞ Daily 10–4.*

The main camp of the *Sea Venture* survivors is believed to have been in this general area. Leaving Gates Fort via Barry Road, you'll pass **Buildings Bay.** One of the two ships that carried Sir George Somers and his crew to Virginia was built here in 1610, hence the bay's name.

(58) Continue up Barry Road to **Fort St. Catherine.** Apart from Dockyard, this restored fortress is the most impressive on the island: It has enough cannons, tunnels, and ramparts to satisfy the most avid military historian. One of a host of fortifications constructed in St. George's, the original fort was begun around 1613. It was remodeled and enlarged at least five times, and work continued on it until late in the 19th century. As you travel through the tunnels, you'll come across some startlingly lifelike figures tucked into niches. Several dioramas depict the island's development, and an audiovisual presentation describes the building and significance of the fort. There is also a small but elaborate display of replicas of the crown jewels of England. *Barry Rd., ☎ 441/297–1920. ☛ $2.50 adults, children under 12 free, but must be accompanied by an adult. ۞ Daily 10–4. Closed Christmas.*

St. Catherine's Beach, where the survivors from the *Sea Venture* scrambled ashore, is a pleasant place for a swim and quiet contemplation of the events of July 28, 1609. Another fine beach, with changing facili-

(59) ties and a refreshment stand, is at nearby **Tobacco Bay,** where the Tuckers secretly loaded the gunpowder bound for Boston in 1775 (*see* Tour 2, *above*). Retrace your route through St. George's to Swing Bridge, which connects St. George's with St. David's Island. In addition to Bermuda's airport, about 2 square miles of St. David's have for many years been occupied by a U.S. Naval Air Station, which closed down operations in September 1995. In 1940, during World War II, Sir Winston Churchill agreed to give the United States a 99-year lease to operate a base on Bermuda in exchange for destroyers. The entire area taken up by the air station is now called St. David's, but construction of the base actually required linking three separate islands—St. David's, Longbird, and Cooper's—with landfills.

Christopher Carter, one of three men left behind when the *Deliverance* and the *Patience* sailed for Jamestown in 1610, was offered St. David's Island in 1612 as a reward for revealing the "Ambergris Plot." Before the ships returned to Bermuda, it seems, one of the three men, Edward Chard, found 80 pounds of ambergris (a precious sperm-whale product used for perfumes) washed up on the beach. In collusion with Carter and another man, Chard planned to smuggle the ambergris off the island (when a ship arrived) and sell it in London at enormous profit.

At the last minute, however, Carter squealed on his coconspirators to Governor Moore, who had arrived in 1612 with new settlers. Instead of St. David's Island, Carter opted for Cooper's Island, which is also now part of the naval base. Built by Carter's descendants in 1640, **Carter House** is one of the oldest houses in Bermuda and should not be missed. The stone-and-cedar house has been refurbished with new floors and period furnishings, including a 17th-century bedding chest, a mortar and pestle, and an 18th-century tavern table. The house is open to the public on Wednesdays from 11 AM to 3PM; call Florence Lins (441/297–1376) to make arrangements for viewing.

Apart from the naval base, St. David's is a rustic spot where the inhabitants have always led an isolated life—some are said to have never visited St. George's, let alone the other end of the island. A number of residents had to be relocated when the base was built, but they refused to leave St. David's. Therefore, a section of St. David's called "Texas" was purchased by the government, which built cottages there for the displaced islanders. The area is just off the naval base; you can see Texas Road at the tip of the island near the lighthouse.

61 St. David's Lighthouse occupies the highest point on the island's eastern end. Built in 1879 of Bermuda stone, the lighthouse rises 208 feet above the sea. Although only about half the height of Gibbs Hill Lighthouse in Southampton Parish, it nevertheless affords spectacular views: From the balcony you can see St. David's and St. George's, Castle Harbour, and the reef-fringed south shore. The lighthouse is not always open; check with the Department of Agriculture and Fisheries (☎ 441/236–4201) for hours.

TIME OUT Right on the water near the lighthouse, the **Black Horse Tavern** (Clarkes Hill, ☎ 441/293–9742, closed Mon.) is a casual spot that's popular with the locals. Seafood is the specialty, and shark hash and curried conch stew are also on the menu. The fish sandwiches are delicious. There are outdoor picnic tables as well as indoor dining.

Head back across the causeway and turn left on Wilkinson Avenue. A network of caves, caverns, and subterranean lakes runs beneath the hills in this part of the island. Two of them are on the property of the nearby Grotto Bay Beach Hotel & Tennis Club (*see* Chapter 8, Lodging). Just south of the hotel are the **Crystal Caves**, discovered in 1907 by two boys playing ball. When the ball disappeared down a hole, the boys burrowed after it and found themselves in a vast cavern 120 feet underground, surrounded by fantastic stalagmite and stalactite formations. Today, the approach is along a wet, sloping walkway and a wooden pontoon bridge across the underground lake. After explaining the formation of stalactites and stalagmites, a tour guide uses a lighting system to make silhouettes. People who suffer from claustrophobia will probably want to skip the caves, as space can be quite tight. *8 Crystal Caves Rd., off Wilkinson Ave.,* ☎ *441/293–0640.* ☛ *$4 adults, $2 children 5–11, children under 4 free.* ✪ *Daily Apr.–Oct., 9:30–4:30; Nov.–March, 9:30–3:30. Closed first two weeks of Jan., Good Fri., Remembrance Day (Nov. 11), and Dec. 24–26.*

Harrington Sound Road runs along the strip of land between the Sound and Castle Harbour. At Walsingham Lane, you'll see a white sign for **Tom Moore's Tavern,** a popular restaurant. The restaurant was originally the home of Samuel Trott, who constructed it in the 17th century and named it Walsingham. (The harbor nearby was named for Robert Walsingham, a sailor on the *Sea Venture* who apparently became enamored of the bay.) The house is surrounded by woods that are much the same as they were three centuries ago. When Tom Moore, the Irish poet, arrived in Bermuda in 1804, the house was occupied by a descendant of the original owner (also named Samuel Trott) and his family. The Trotts befriended the poet, who became a frequent visitor to the house. In Epistle V, Moore immortalized the Trott Estate's Calabash Tree, under which he liked to write his verses. In 1844, the idea for the Royal Bermuda Yacht Club (*see* Tour 1, *above*) was conceived under the very same tree.

64 Harrington Sound Road leads southward to the **Leamington Caves,** smaller and less impressive than Crystal Caves. However, they do have their share of stalagmites and stalactites in fanciful formations, one of them an amber-tinted Statue of Liberty. Above ground, the Plantation restaurant (*see* Chapter 7, Dining) serves some of the island's best food— worth a trip whether you visit the caves or not. Lunch patrons must spend at least $10 each at the Plantation restaurant to gain free entry to the caves. *Harrington Sound Rd.,* ☏ *441/293–1188.* ☛ *$4 adults, $2 children 4–12.* ☉ *Mid-Feb.–late Nov., Mon.–Sat. 10–4. Closed late Nov.–mid-Feb., Sun. and holidays.*

65 Farther south on Harrington Sound Road is **Tucker's Town,** named for Governor Daniel Tucker, who wanted to abandon St. George's in 1616 in favor of a new settlement on the shores of Castle Harbour. A few streets were laid out and some cottages were built, but the plan was eventually shelved. For 300 years Tucker's Town remained a small fishing and farming community; cotton was grown for a while, and a few whaling boats operated from here. Dramatic change overtook the community soon after World War I, however. Seeking to raise the island's appeal in order to attract passengers on its luxury liners to Bermuda, a steamship company called Furness, Withy & Co. purchased a large area of Tucker's Town for a new country club. The result was the exclusive Mid Ocean Club, with its fine golf course; the Castle Harbour Resort, now run by Marriott, adjoins the club. Members of the club started building residences nearby, and the Tucker's Town boom began. Today, only members of the club can buy a house in the area, and private residences have been known to sell for more than $3 million.

66 Below the clubhouse on the south shore are the **Natural Arches,** one of the island's oldest and most photographed attractions. Carved over the centuries by the wind and ocean, the two limestone arches rise 35 feet above the beach. Look for the signs near the end of South Shore Road pointing to Castle Harbour Beach and the Natural Arches.

A chain of islands dots the entrance channel to the harbor between St. David's and Tucker's Town Bay. In the colony's early days, these islands were fortified to protect Castle Harbour from possible enemy attack. Soon after his arrival in 1612, Governor Moore built his first 67 and best fort on **Castle Island.** According to an oft-told tale, two Spanish ships appeared outside the channel in 1613 and attempted to attack the colony. Two shots were fired from the fort: One fell into the water, and the other hit one of the ship's hulls. The Spaniards fled, unaware that the fortress had expended two-thirds of its stock of ammunition—the colonists had less than a barrel of gunpowder and only one cannonball left.

68 Touted as Bermuda's first tourist attraction, **Devil's Hole Aquarium** was started by a Mr. Trott in 1830. After building a wall around his fish pond—manifestly to prevent people from fishing in it—Mr. Trott was besieged with questions about what he was hiding. In 1843, yielding to the curiosity of the Bermudians, Mr. Trott permitted people to view

his fish pond—at a fee. These days, the deep pool contains about 400 sea creatures, including giant grouper, sharks, and huge turtles. Visitors can play at fishing, using baited—but hookless—lines. *Harrington Sound Rd.,* ☎ *441/293–2072.* ☛ *$7 adults, $3 children under 12.* ☽ *Daily 10–4:30.*

★ ❻❾ Take steep Knapton Hill Road, which leads westward to South Shore Road and **Spittal Pond** (*see* Important Contacts A to Z *in* the Gold Guide). A showcase of the Bermuda National Trust, this nature park has 60 acres in which visitors can roam, although visitors are requested to keep to the walkways. More than 25 species of waterfowl winter here between November and May. On a high bluff overlooking the ocean, Spanish Rock stands out as an oddity. Early settlers found a rock crudely carved with the date 1543 and other markings that were unclear. It is now believed that a Portuguese ship was wrecked on the island in 1543, and that her sailors built a new ship on which they departed. The carvings are thought to be the initials *RP* (for Rex Portugaline), and the cross to be a badge of the Portuguese Order of Christ. The rock was removed to prevent further damage by erosion, and the site is marked by a bronze casting of the original carving. A plaster-of-paris cast of the Spanish Rock is also on display at the Bermuda Historical Society Museum in Hamilton (*see* Tour 1, *above*). *South Shore Rd., no* ☎. ☛ *Free.* ☽ *Daily dawn to dusk.*

West of Spittal Pond on South Shore Road is the turnoff to **Collector's Hill,** which is a very steep climb indeed. The hill is named for Gilbert Salton, a 19th-century customs collector who lived in a house near the top; the house has long since disappeared.

★ ❼⓿ At the very top of Collector's Hill is **Verdmont,** Bermuda's finest historic house. It was built around 1710, possibly by a prominent shipowner named John Dickinson. At the end of the War of Independence, Verdmont was the home of John Green, an American Loyalist who fled to Bermuda from Philadelphia. Green married one of Dickinson's granddaughters and was appointed judge of the Court of Vice Admiralty. Green was also a portrait painter, and the family portraits by him remain in the house. The house, which resembles a small English manor house, has an unusual double roof and four large chimneys—all eight rooms have their own fireplace. Elegant cornice moldings and paneled shutters grace the two large reception rooms downstairs, originally the drawing room and formal dining room. The sash windows reflect a style that was fashionable in English manor houses. Although it contains none of the original furnishings, Verdmont is a treasure house of Bermudiana. Some of the furniture is mahogany imported from England—there are two exquisite early 19th-century pianos—but most of it is fine 18th-century cedar, crafted by Bermuda cabinetmakers. In particular, notice the desk in the drawing room, the lid and sides of which are made of single planks. Also displayed in the house is a china coffee service, said to have been a gift from Napoleon to President Madison. The president never received it: The ship bearing it across the Atlantic was seized by a Bermudian privateer and brought to Bermuda. Look carefully, too, at the handmade cedar staircase, with its handsomely turned newels and posts. The newel posts on each landing have removable caps to accommodate candles in the evening. Upstairs is a nursery: It's easy to imagine a child at play with the antique toys or napping in the cedar cradle. The last occupant of Verdmont was an eccentric old woman, who lived here for 75 years without electricity or any other modern trappings. After her death, her family sold the house to the Bermuda Historic Monuments Trust—the forerunner of the Bermuda National Trust—which opened it as a museum in 1956.

Collector's Hill, tel. 441/236–7369. ☞ *$4 adults, $3 senior citizens, $1 students with ID; $10 combination ticket extends admission to Confederate Museum and Tucker House in St. George's.* ☉ *Apr.–Oct., Mon.–Sat. 9:30–4:30; Nov.–Mar., Mon.–Sat. 10–4. Closed holidays.*

TIME OUT Popular with the locals, **Speciality Inn** (South Shore Rd., foot of Collector's Hill, ☎ 441/236-3133) is a simple spot that serves pasta, pizza, sandwiches, soups, shakes, ice cream, and good breakfasts.

★ ⓐ A singular delight of Devonshire Parish are the gardens at **Palm Grove,** an 18-acre private estate. There is a splendid pond, within which is a relief map of the island—each parish is divided by carefully manicured grass sections. Desmond Fountain statues stand around the edge, peering into the pond's depths. *South Shore Rd., across from Brighton Hill, no* ☎. ☞ *Free.* ☉ *Mon.–Thurs. 9–5. Closed holidays.*

⓮ Brighton Hill Road, just west of Palm Grove, runs north to Middle Road and the **Old Devonshire Church,** the parish's biggest attraction. A church has stood on this site since 1612, although the original was replaced in 1716. That replacement church was almost completely destroyed in an explosion on Easter Sunday in 1970, and the present church is a faithful reconstruction. A small, simple building of limestone and cedar, it looks much like an early Bermuda cottage. The three-tier pulpit, the pews, and the communion table are believed to be from the original church. Some pieces of church silver date back to 1590 and are said to be the oldest on the island. A cedar chest, believed to have once held the church records, dates from the early 17th century. Other pieces that have survived include an old cedar armchair, a candelabra, a cross, and a cedar screen. *Middle Rd., Devonshire,* ☎ *441/236–3671.* ☞ *Free.* ☉ *Daily 9–5:30.*

⓯ Turn left off Middle Road onto Tee Street, and then right onto Berry Hill Road. One mile farther on the left is the turnoff to Point Finger Road and the **Botanical Gardens,** a landscaped park laced with roads and paths. Information is available in the visitor center, where there are also gift and tea shops. Offices of the Agriculture Department are also on the grounds. The gardens are a fragrant showcase for the island's exotic subtropical plants, flowers, and trees. Within the 36 acres are a miniature forest, an aviary, a hibiscus garden (with more than 150 species of the flower), and a special Garden for the Blind, which is filled with the scent of sweet geranium, lemon, lavender, and spices. Seventy-five-minute walking tours of the gardens leave the visitor center at 10:30 AM on Tuesday, Wednesday, and Friday (Tuesday and Friday only from November through March). To arrange tours at other times, talk to the curator of the gardens or make a donation to the Botanical Society. *Point Finger Rd.,* ☎ *441/236–4201.* ☞ *Free.* ☉ *Daily sunrise–sunset.*

The pretty, white home on the grounds of the Botanical Gardens is **Camden,** the official residence of Bermuda's premier. A large two-story house, Camden is more typical of West Indian estate architecture than traditional Bermudian building. The house is open for tours, except when official functions are scheduled. *Botanical Gardens,* ☎ *441/292–5501.* ☞ *Free.* ☉ *Tues. and Fri. noon–2.*

⓰ A few minutes away by moped are the offices of the **Bermuda National Trust,** a nonprofit organization that oversees the restoration and preservation of many of the island's gardens and historic homes. The Trust is also a wonderful source of information about the island. The offices and "Trustworthy" gift shop are in a rambling 18th-century house built by the Trimingham family. Tasteful, high-quality handmade crafts,

novelties, and Trust logo items are sold in the shop; all proceeds go to
the Trust. *"Waterville," 29 The Lane, Paget,* ☎ *441/236–6483.* ◷ *Weekdays 9–5. Gift shop open Mon.–Sat. 10–4.*

The first half of the tour ends here: Hamilton is just a few hundred
yards up the road. The second part of the tour heads west through the
parishes of Paget, Warwick, and Southampton.

㊆ On Harbour Road near the Lower Ferry Landing, **Clermont** is an imposing house noted for its fine woodwork. Once the residence of Sir
Brownlow Gray, Chief Justice of Bermuda, the house is also famous
for having Bermuda's first tennis court. During a visit from New York
in 1874, Miss Mary Outerbridge learned to play here. Upon her return to the United States, she asked the Staten Island Cricket Club to
build a court; armed with her racquet and a book of rules, she introduced tennis to America. This house is not open to the public.

㊅ If you're on foot, turn left on Valley Road to reach **St. Paul's Church,**
built in 1796 to replace an earlier church on the site. (Those on mopeds
must use an alternate route—take Chapel Road and turn east on Middle Road to Valley Road—or walk the bike up the narrow one-way
stretch of hill past the SPCA headquarters on the left.) Around the turn
of the century, the "Paget Ghost" began to be heard in and around St.
Paul's. Nothing could be seen, but the mysterious sound of tinkling
bells was plainly audible, coming from several directions. The ghost
became quite famous, and a veritable posse—armed with firearms and
clubs—gathered to find it; vendors even set up refreshment stands. Finally, a visiting American scientist proclaimed that the tinkling sound
came from a rare bird, the fililo. According to the scientist, the fililo
was a natural ventriloquist, which explained why the sound jumped
around. No one ever saw the fililo, however, and no one saw the ghost
either—it disappeared as mysteriously as it had materialized. *Middle
Rd.,* ☎ *441/236–5880.* ☛ *Free.* ◷ *Weekdays 8–4:30, Sat. only by special arrangement, Sun. 7:30–1.*

㊇ St. Paul's sits on the edge of **Paget Marsh,** 18 acres of unspoiled wood-
land that look much as they did when the first settlers arrived. Protected by the Bermuda National Trust, the marsh contains cedars and
palmettos, endangered plants, and a mangrove swamp. *Middle Rd.,*
☎ *441/236–6483.* ☛ *By arrangement with Bermuda National Trust.*

From St. Paul's, head west into Warwick Parish along Middle Road.
Just after the intersection with Ord Road (opposite the Belmont Hotel,
㊈ Golf & Country Club), look to your left to see **Christ Church.** Built in
1719, it is reputedly the oldest Presbyterian church in any British
colony or dominion.

Turn left off Middle Road onto Camp Hill Road, which winds down
to the south shore beaches. Along the way is **Warwick Camp,** built in
the 1870s to guard against any enemy landing on the beaches. The camp
was used as a training ground and rifle range during World War I. In
1920, Pearl White of *The Perils of Pauline* fame came to Bermuda to
shoot a movie, bringing along an entourage that included lions, monkeys, and a host of other exotic fauna. Scenes for the film were shot
on Warwick Bay, below the rifle range. Most Bermudians had never
seen either a lion or a movie star, and huge crowds collected to watch
the filming.

TIME OUT   A moderately priced roadside restaurant, **Tio Pepe's** (South Shore Rd.,
near the entrance to Horseshoe Bay, ☎ 441/238–1897) serves Spanish
and Italian foods and pizza to go.

Bermuda's beaches tend to elicit the most effusive travel-writing clichés—simply because they are so good. A 3-mile chain of sandy beaches, coves, and inlets begins at Warwick Long Bay and extends to Horseshoe Bay in the east (*see* Chapter 5, Water Sports and Beaches).

79 Just east of Warwick Bay, **Astwood Park** is a lovely public park with picnic tables and two beaches, one of them ideal for snorkeling.

★ **80** Two miles west along South Shore Road is the turnoff for Lighthouse Road. High atop Gibbs Hill, **Gibbs Hill Lighthouse** is the second cast-iron lighthouse ever built. Designed in London and opened in 1846, the tower stands 117 feet high and 362 feet above the sea. Originally the light was produced by a concentrated burner of four large circular wicks. Today, the beam from the 1,000-watt bulb can be seen by ships 40 miles out to sea, and by planes 120 miles away at 10,000 feet. You can climb to the top of the lighthouse, although this is not a trip for anyone who suffers from vertigo. It's a long haul up the 185 spiral stairs, but you can stop to catch your breath at platforms along the way, where photographs and drawings of the lighthouse are displayed. At the top you can stroll on the balcony for a spectacular view of Bermuda. The wind may snatch you bald-headed—the tower is known to sway in high winds—and you may find it hard to concentrate on the view knowing that a tiny guard rail is the only thing between you and a swan dive. (An alternative is to inch around with your back pressed against the tower, clinging to it for dear life.) *Lighthouse Rd., Southampton,* ☎ *441/238-0524.* ☛ *$2 adults, children under 6 free.* ☾ *Daily 9–4:30. Closed Christmas.*

TIME OUT   A charming place to relax and take in the island vistas is **The Lighthouse Tea Room** (☎ 441/238-8679) in the historic lighthouse keeper's cottage. A wonderful selection of tasty sweet cakes, and a lineup of imported English pasties, meat pies, and sausage rolls are all satisfying choices for breakfast, lunch, or afternoon tea.

81 If you're still feeling adventurous, turn left off Middle Road onto Whale Bay Road (just before the Port Royal Golf & Country Club), and go down the hill to **Whale Bay Fort.** Overgrown with grass, flowers, and subtropical plants, this small 19th-century battery offers little in the way of a history lesson, but it does overlook a secluded pink-sand beach, gin-clear water, and craggy cliffs. The beach is accessible only on foot, but it's a splendid place for a swim. Bear in mind that you have to climb back up the hill to your moped or bike.

82 Just before Somerset Bridge is a little lane with the odd name of **Overplus,** which harks back to the 17th century. When Richard Norwood surveyed the island in 1616, he divided the island into shares and tribes. He allotted 25 acres to each share, and 50 shares to each tribe. When the survey was completed, 200 acres (too small to form a tribe) remained unallotted and were listed as "overplus." Governor Tucker apparently directed the surveyor to keep an eye peeled for an attractive chunk of territory that could be designated as the surplus land. Norwood recommended a piece of real estate in the western part of the island, whereupon the governor claimed it and built a fine house on it. Upon hearing of the governor's action, the Bermuda Company lodged a complaint, forcing Tucker to return to London to sort everything out. The surplus land was eventually divided into seven parts, with Tucker retaining the section on which his house sat; the remainder was given to the church.

Across Somerset Bridge is the West End (*see* Tour 3, *above*). If you are traveling by bike or by moped, you can catch a ferry from Somerset

Bridge back to Hamilton. Otherwise, take your choice of Middle, Harbour, or South Shore roads to find your way back to the capital.

What to See and Do with Children

Although Bermuda has no amusement parks or fairs, the island is becoming more user-friendly for children. In addition to the obvious attractions of surf and sand, and several hotels that offer day care and children's activities, the aquarium has a children's Discovery Room, and children visiting the Bermuda Maritime Museum are given a free book that helps them understand what the Royal Naval Dockyard is all about. Other books are available that can make exploring the island with children much easier. The first, *The Bermuda Coloring Book,* by Diana Watlington Ruetenik, is an educational book with historical sites for small children to color. The second, *A Child's History of Bermuda,* by E. M. Rice, puts the island's history into words that are easy to understand. Both books are available at A. S. Cooper & Son (59 Front St., Hamilton, ☎ 441/295–3961). Listed below are some of the attractions in the exploring tours and elsewhere that will appeal to children.

Aquarium, Museum and Zoo (*see* Tour 4)

Beaches (*see* Chapter 5, Water Sports and Beaches)

Bermuda Maritime Museum (*see* Tour 3)

Botanical Gardens (*see* Tour 4)

Ferries (*see* Important Contacts A to Z *in* the Gold Guide)

Glass-bottom boat ride (*see* Important Contacts A to Z *in* the Gold Guide)

Off the Beaten Path

The **Railway Trail** is a secluded 18-mile track that runs the length of the island along the route of the old Bermuda Railway. Restricted to pedestrians, horseback riders, and cyclists, the trail is a delightful way to see the island, away from the traffic and noise of the main roads. The Bermuda Department of Tourism has published "The Bermuda Railway Trail Guide," which is available at all Visitors Service Bureaus. The pamphlet includes seven separate walking tours, ranging from about two to four hours, and an outline of what you can expect to see along the way. (For more information about sights along the way, refer to the appropriate section of the exploring tours, above. *See also* "Following in the Tracks of the Bermuda Railway," *in* Chapter 10, Portraits of Bermuda.) It should be noted that many of the trails are quite isolated, and none is heavily trafficked. Although Bermuda has no major crime problem, unpleasant incidents do sometimes occur; women travelers especially should avoid striking out on remote trails alone. Apart from reasons of safety, the Railway Trail is much more enjoyable shared with a companion.

The history of the railway that ran along this trail is fascinating. Aside from horse-drawn carriages, boats, and bikes, the Bermuda Railway— "Old Rattle and Shake" as it was called—was the primary means of transportation on the island from 1931 to 1948. As early as 1899, however, the Bermuda Public Works Department bandied about proposals for a railroad. In 1922, over the objections of livery stable owners, the Bermuda Parliament finally granted permission for a standard-gauge railroad to run from Somerset to St. George's.

The laying of the tracks was a formidable undertaking, requiring the construction of long tunnels and swing bridges. By the time it was finished in 1931, the railway had cost the investors £1 million. Mile for mile it was the most expensive railroad ever built, and the construction, which proceeded at a somnolent 2½ miles per year, was the slowest ever recorded. Nevertheless, on October 31, 1931, the little train got off to a roaring start with festive opening ceremonies at Somerset Bridge.

Passengers in the first-class carriages sat in wicker chairs, and the second-class cars were outfitted with benches. An American visitor reported in glowing terms of her first train ride in Bermuda, waxing lyrical about rolling cedar-covered hills, green velvet lawns, and banks of pink oleanders. Certainly, it was a vast improvement over the 19th-century horse buses that lumbered from Somerset to St. George's, carrying freight as well as passengers. Not everyone was happy, however. One writer groused that the train was "an iron serpent in the Garden of Eden." "Old Rattle and Shake" began going downhill during World War II. While the train was put to hard use by all the military personnel on the island, it proved impossible to obtain the necessary maintenance equipment. At the end of the war, the government acquired the distressed railway for £115,000. After the arrival of the automobile on Bermuda in 1946, the government sold the railway in its entirety to British Guiana (now Guyana).

4 Shopping

By Honey
Naylor

Updated by
Judith Wadson

IF YOU'RE LOOKING FOR COLORFUL STREET MARKETS where you can haggle over the price of low-cost goods and souvenirs, find another island. Shopping in Bermuda is characterized by sophisticated department stores and boutiques that stock top-quality—and expensive—merchandise. Bargains are a rarity (though Bermudians are alarmed at the proliferation of Front Street T-shirt shops), and only products actually made in Bermuda (and antiques more than 100 years old) can be sold duty-free. If you're accustomed to shopping in Saks Fifth Avenue, Neiman-Marcus, and Bergdorf-Goodman, the prices in Bermuda's elegant shops won't come as a surprise. Actually, the prices on many items in Bermuda's stores are discounted, but a $600 dress discounted by 20% is still $480. Bermuda shopkeepers have felt the effect of the growing number of discount stores in the United States. It would be wise to check discount prices at home and then compare Bermuda prices on items that are of interest to you. The quality of goods in Bermuda is quite good, and if you are looking for high-end merchandise, Bermuda does offer substantial savings on many items, particularly British-made clothing. Woolens and cashmere are good buys, especially after Christmas and in January when many stores offer some substantial discounts. Naturally, Bermuda shorts are hot items, as are kilts.

European-made crystal and china—Wedgwood, Royal Crown Derby, Villeroy & Boch, Waterford, and Orrefors, to name a few—are available at prices at least 25% lower than those in the United States. Figurines from Lladro, Royal Doulton, and Hummel are also sold at significantly discounted prices. European fragrances and cosmetics are priced about 25%–30% less than in the United States, as are Rolex, Tissot, Patek Philippe, and other watches.

Bermuda has a thriving population of artists and artisans, whose work ranges from sculpture and paintings to miniature furniture, handblown glass, and dolls (see Arts and Crafts, below). Bermuda also has a number of noteworthy products to offer. The local honey, which can be found in most grocery stores, is delicious. Outerbridge's Sherry Peppers condiments add zip to soups, stews, drinks, and chowders. The original line has been expanded to include Bloody Mary mix, pepper jellies, and barbecue sauce; gift packs are available all over the island.

Bermuda rum is another popular item, and a variety of rum-based liqueurs is available, including Bermuda Banana, Banana Coconut Rum, and Bermuda Gold. Gosling's Black Seal Rum is excellent mixed with ginger beer to make a Dark 'n' Stormy, a famous Bermuda drink that should be treated with respect and caution. Rum is also found in quantity in Fourways Dark 'n' Stormy cakes, which are made in Bermuda and can be mailed home. U.S. citizens aged 21 or older, who have been out of the country for 48 hours, are allowed to bring home 1 liter of duty-free liquor each (see Important Contacts A to Z in the Gold Guide). In a bizarre catch-22, however, Bermuda requires a minimum purchase of 2 liters or five 75-centiliter bottles to qualify for in-bond (duty-free) prices. Although the airport has no duty-free shop of its own, you can order duty-free liquor at any store; they will make arrangements to deliver your purchase to the airport. It's best to buy duty-free liquor at least 24 hours before your departure. Your purchase can be picked up only in the airport departure lounge or on board your cruise ship. If orders are placed by 9:30 AM on the day of an afternoon departure, however, they will be delivered to the appropriate place. It pays to shop around, as prices vary: Grocery stores usually charge more than liquor stores. Some stores allow customers to create their own mixed packs of various liquors at in-bond prices, while others offer a selection of prepackaged sets (the five-pack is most common). Below are some sample prices at press time for 1 liter of liquor: Tia Maria, $16.35; Grand Marnier, $27.50; Chivas Regal (12-year-old), $29.05; J&B Rare, $14.20; Johnnie Walker Black, $27.50; Stolichnaya vodka, $9.50; Beefeater gin, $13.25; and Gosling's Black Seal rum, $8.30.

Panatel VDS has produced several half-hour videos, including *Bermuda Highlights, Dive Bermuda,* and *Bermuda Bound, Paradise Found.* Priced at $29.95, and available for both North American and European systems, the videos are sold at several stores and shops around the island.

For products other than liquor, comparison shopping in Bermuda is usually a waste of time because the merchants' association keeps prices almost identical island-wide. However, it's worth checking the price of items at home—especially crystal and china—before you embark on a shopping spree in Bermuda. Ask your local department store if any sales are scheduled and check the prices of designer and name-brand products at local factory outlets. Remember that Bermuda, unlike most U.S. states, has no sales tax, which means that the price on the tag is the price you pay.

Although the numbering of houses is becoming more common (houses have traditionally been known only by their picturesque names rather than numbers), buildings in Hamilton are still numbered rather whimsically. If you check the phone directory for a store address, you may find a listing on Front Street or Water Street, for example, but no street number. In fact, some Front Street buildings have two numbers, one of them an old historic address that has nothing to do with the building's present location. Fortunately, almost all Bermudians can give you precise directions.

In general, shops are open Monday–Saturday 9–5 or 9–5:30, closed on Sunday and public holidays. Some Hamilton shops stay open late on Wednesdays for Harbour Night festivities from April through October. From late November through Christmas Eve, stores often stay open until 9 on Fridays; in the two weeks before Christmas, many stores stay open until 9 most nights. When cruise ships call (April through October), some Front Street shops open on Sunday. The shops in the newly extended area at the Royal Naval Dockyard are usually open Monday–Saturday 10–5 from April through October (11–5 during the winter) and on Sunday 11–5; some extend their hours around Christmas. Almost all stores close for public holidays.

In most cases in this chapter, if a store has several branches or outlets, only the main branch phone number has been listed.

Shopping Districts

Hamilton boasts the greatest concentration of shops in Bermuda, and **Front Street** is its pièce de résistance. Lined with small, pastel-colored buildings, this most fashionable of Bermuda's streets houses sedate department stores and snazzy boutiques, with several small arcades and shopping alleys leading off it. A smart canopy shades the entrance to the **55 Front Street Group,** which houses several upmarket boutiques. **The Emporium** on Front Street, a renovated old building arranged around an open atrium, is home to an eclectic collection of antique, jewelry, souvenir, and low-quality art shops. The statue on top of the atrium fountain is of Bermudian Gina Swainson, who ruled as Miss World in 1979–80, and who sells her line of makeup from a counter just opposite the fountain. **Windsor Place** is a modern mall on Queen Street where you can get anything from running shoes, sunblock, and greeting cards to haircuts, handblown glass, and cash (there are ATM machines on the lower and upper levels).

In St. George's, **Water Street, Duke of York Street, and Somers Wharf** are the site of numerous renovated buildings that now house branches of Front Street stores. Historic **King's Square** offers little more than a couple of T-shirt/souvenir shops. In the West End, **Somerset Village** has a few shops, but they hardly merit a special shopping trip. However, the historic **Clocktower Mall** and the newer **Victorian Mall** at **Royal Naval Dockyard** have a plethora of shops, including branches of Front Street shops and specialty boutiques. Dockyard is also home to the Craft Market, the Bermuda Arts Centre, and Island Pottery, where local artisans display their wares and visitors can sometimes watch them at work. Several other small plazas are sprinkled over the island, featuring a few shops, and often a grocery store.

Department Stores

Bermuda's three leading department stores are A. S. Cooper & Son, Trimingham's, and H. A. & E. Smith's, the main branches of which are on Front Street in Hamilton. These elegant, venerable institutions are operated by the third or fourth generation of the families that founded them, and customers stand a good chance of being waited on by a Cooper, a Trimingham, or a Smith. In addition, many of the salespeople have worked at the stores for two or three decades; they tend to be unobtrusive, but polite and helpful when you need them.

A. S. Cooper & Son (59 Front St., Hamilton, ☎ 441/295–3961) is best known for its extensive inventory of Waterford and Swarovski crystal; china, including Wedgwood, Royal Doulton, Belleek, Villeroy & Boch, and Royal Copenhagen; and Lladro figurines. A five-piece place setting of the Wedgwood Countryware pattern costs $63, or $79 (including shipping to the United States, with duty, freight, and insurance). Prices on the stock of china and crystal are similarly attractive. A free home-delivery service with up to 40% savings (without affecting the $400 duty-free allowance) is available to United States customers who order Waterford chandeliers, tableware by Royal Doulton, Royal Crown Derby, Minton, Wedgwood, Villeroy & Boch, Royal Copenhagen, French Quimper, and stemware by Orrefors, Kosta Boda, and Atlantis Crystal. A. S. Cooper & Son's own private-label collection of clothing can be found in the well-stocked men's, women's, and children's departments. The gift department on the Front Street level features a large selection of tasteful Bermudian gifts and souvenirs. Shoppers can have breakfast, lunch, or afternoon tea at Romancing the Scone, a small balcony restaurant just off the second floor, with a magnificent view of the harbor (open Apr.–Dec., Mon.–Sat. 9–4; Jan.–Mar., Mon.–Sat. 11–3). Other branches of the department store can be found in all major hotels, the Clocktower Building at Dockyard, and in St. George's at 22 Water Street.

H. A. & E. Smith's (35 Front St., Hamilton, ☎ 441/295–2288), founded in 1889 by Henry Archibald and Edith Smith, is arguably the best men's store in Bermuda—and exclusive agents for Burberry, William Lockie cashmeres, and Church shoes. Burberry raincoats are priced from $395 to $495, and William Lockie cashmeres sell from $245 to $375. You can buy English tweed jackets for $240, men's 100% cashmere

Hamilton Shopping

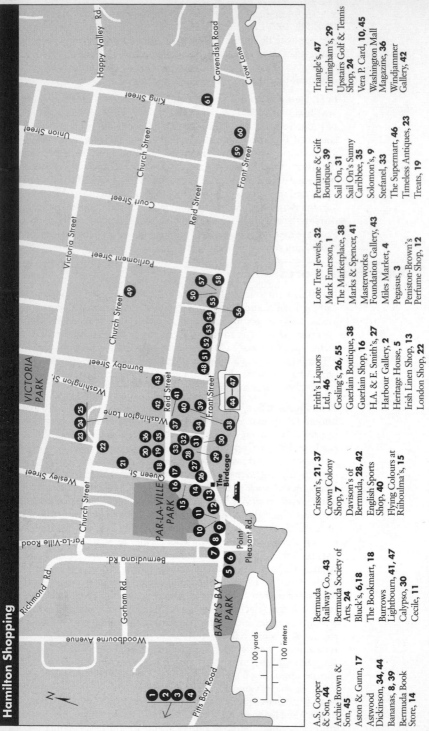

A.S. Cooper & Son, **44**
Archie Brown & Son, **45**
Aston & Gunn, **17**
Astwood Dickinson, **34**, **44**
Bananas, **8**, **39**
Bermuda Book Store, **14**

Bermuda Railway Co., **43**
Bermuda Society of Arts, **24**
Bluck's, **6**, **18**
The Bookmart, **18**
Burrows Lightbourn, **41**, **47**
Calypso, **30**
Cecile, **11**

Crisson's, **21**, **37**
Crown Colony Shop, **7**
Davison's of Bermuda, **28**, **42**
English Sports Shop, **40**
Flying Colours at Riihoulma's, **15**

Frith's Liquors Ltd, **46**
Gosling's, **26**, **55**
Guerlain Boutique, **38**
Guerlain Shop, **16**
H.A. & E. Smith's, **27**
Harbour Gallery, **2**
Heritage House, **5**
Irish Linen Shop, **13**
London Shop, **22**

Lote Tree Jewels, **32**
Mark Emerson, **1**
The Marketplace, **38**
Marks & Spencer, **41**
Masterworks Foundation Gallery, **43**
Miles Market, **4**
Pegasus, **3**
Peniston-Brown's Perfume Shop, **12**

Perfume & Gift Boutique, **39**
Sail On, **31**
Sail On's Sunny Caribbee, **35**
Solomon's, **9**
Stefanel, **33**
The Supermart, **46**
Timeless Antiques, **23**
Treats, **19**

Triangle's, **47**
Trimingham's, **29**
Upstairs Golf & Tennis Shop, **24**
Vera P. Card, **10**, **45**
Washington Mall Magazine, **36**
Windjammer Gallery, **42**

A.S. Cooper
& Sons, **11**

Archie Brown
& Son, **20**

Bananas, **19**

Bermuda
Railway
Co., **18**

Bluck's, **9**

The Book
Cellar, **2**

Bridge House
Gallery, **24**

Carole Holding
print & Craft
Shop, **18**

Constable's
Woolen
Fashions, **12**

Cow Polly, **15**

Crisson's, **2,
16, 23**

Davison's of
Bermuda, **10**

English Sports
Shop, **8**

Frangipani, **13**

Frith's Liquors
Ltd., **5**

Gosling's, **6**

Peniston-
Brown's
Perfume
Shop, **17**

H. A. & E
Smith's, **3**

Summer's
Supermarket, **22**

Trimingham's, **7**

Vera P.
Card, **1, 21, 25**

Will Collieson, **4**

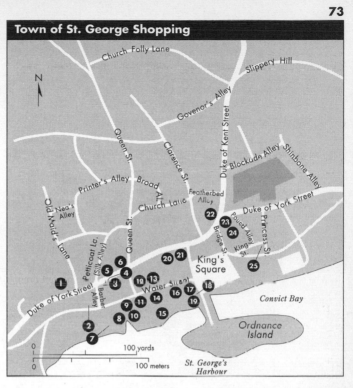

Town of St. George Shopping

topcoats for $395, and Italian silk ties for $26 and up. There is a large selection of Shetland and cotton sweaters, which go for about $30 each. Smith's is also a good place to buy kilts. Ladies can find Fendi handbags here (the only place in Bermuda), for about $175 for a medium size, as well as cashmere-lined leather gloves for $58 and $65 (unlined $42). The women's department also has an extensive selection of formal and casual wear: cashmere turtleneck sweaters are priced from $198; Burberry raincoats start at $395. The women's shoe department offers a broad choice of fine Italian styles, both classic and contemporary. The Front Street–level china department carries a large selection of patterns from Royal Doulton, Royal Crown Derby, Royal Worcester, and Rosenthal; crystal of all types is also sold. French perfumes sell for 20% to 30% less than in the States. As with many of the island's older buildings, the store has a confusing layout that makes it easy to get lost. The staff here is especially genteel, however, and they will help orient you. Branches can be found in the Belmont and Southampton Princess hotels and at 18 York Street in St. George's.

Marks & Spencer (18 Reid St., Hamilton, ☎ 441/295–0031), a franchise of the large British chain, is called Marks and Sparks by everyone in Bermuda and England. This large store, whose name was changed from St. Michael when its Bermudian owners moved it across the street in 1993, is usually filled with thrift-minded locals attracted by its moderate prices for men's, women's, and children's clothing. Summer wear, including swimsuits, cotton jerseys, and polo shirts, is a good buy. High-quality men's and women's cashmere and woolen sweaters are also sold at substantial discounts.

Trimingham's (37 Front St., Hamilton, ☎ 441/295–1183) has been a Hamilton fixture since 1842. Bermuda's largest department store, this is the home of Daks Bermuda shorts and tailored-for-Trimingham's

Archie Brown & Son, **9**

Bermuda Arts Centre at Dockyard, **8**

Bermuda Railway Co., **10**

Calypso, **11**

Clocktower Mall and Victorian Mall, **9**

Craft Market, **7**

Frith's Liquors Ltd., **4**

Gosling's, **1**

Hall of Names, **12**

Irish Linen Shop, **2**

Island Pottery, **6**

Ship's Inn Bool Gallery, **13**

Trimingham's, **3, 5**

Turkish Delight, **14**

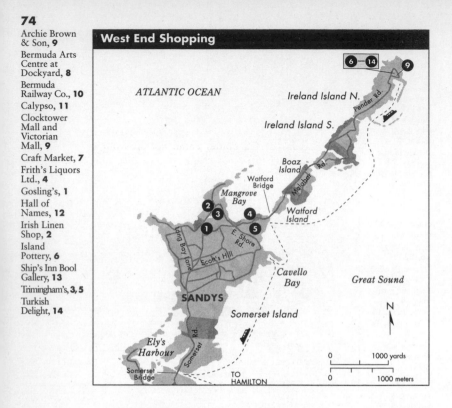

West End Shopping

ATLANTIC OCEAN

Ireland Island N.

Ireland Island S.

Pender Rd.

Boaz Island

Malabar Rd.

Watford Bridge

Mangrove Bay

Watford Island

Long Bay Lane

E. Shore Rd.

Scott's Hill

Cavello Bay

Great Sound

SANDYS

Somerset Island

Somerset Rd.

Ely's Harbour

Somerset Bridge

TO HAMILTON

N

0   1000 yards

0   1000 meters

sportswear. Famous women's designers, such as Dana Buchman, Nicole Farhi, and Calvin Klein, have complete lines here, and fine tableware by Lenox, Mikasa, Noritake, Aynsley, Portmeirion, Waterford, Royal Worcester, and Spode is sold for up to 30% less than in the United States. The store has an impressive display of perfumes and cosmetics, and it is Bermuda's exclusive distributor of Christian Dior, Estée Lauder, and Yves St. Laurent. Shoppers will also find a potpourri of fine leather, jewelry, children's fashions, and gift items. Trimingham branches—10 in all—can be found over the island, including at Somers Wharf in St. George's, South Shore Road in Paget, and in Somerset Village.

Grocery Stores

Most of the accommodations on Bermuda, from cottage colonies to guest houses and housekeeping apartments, offer guests the opportunity to do their own cooking. Self-catering vacations are cheaper than those where you pay full board or dine out at every meal; considering how expensive Bermuda is, this option has widespread appeal for both families and budget travelers. Don't expect any bargains, however— foodstuffs in Bermuda are also quite expensive. For example, a dozen imported large eggs costs about $1.75 (those produced locally are even more expensive: about $3 a dozen), a loaf of Bermuda-made bread is $3, a six-pack of Coke is about $4.75, and a 13-ounce can of coffee is $5. Listed below are some of the major supermarkets in Bermuda. Unless stated otherwise below, grocery stores carry liquor.

A-One Paget (Middle Rd., Paget, ☏ 441/236–0351) is near Barnsdale Guest Apartments and the Sky Top Cottages. Be warned, however, that the route between Sky Top and the store takes in a significant hill, which could make for a difficult hike if you buy a large amount of groceries.

A-One Smith's (Middle Rd., Smith's, ☎ 441/236–8763) is near Angel's Grotto and Brightside Apartments, but not really within walking distance. It is part of the Marketplace chain, but does not have as large a supply of goods because it is a smaller shop.

Giant Foods (Middle Rd., Warwick, ☎ 441/236–1344) is a medium-size store within walking distance of the Pretty Penny guest house—except when you're laden with groceries.

Harrington Hundreds Grocery & Liquor Store (South Rd., Smith's, ☎ 441/293–1635) is near Spittal Pond, not far from Angel's Grotto apartments, but it's too far to walk with bags.

Heron Bay Marketplace (Middle Rd., Southampton, ☎ 441/238–1993) is one of the Marketplace chain of stores that can be found all over the island. It has a large selection of fresh vegetables. Convenient to Longtail Cliffs and Marley Beach, but not on foot.

The Hitching Post (Somerset Rd., near Somerset Bridge, Sandys, ☎ 441/234–0951) is a convenience store that does not overcharge. The big bonus is that it is open Sundays 11 AM–7 PM, when other grocery shops are closed. No liquor is sold.

The Marketplace (Reid St., near Parliament St., Hamilton, ☎ 441/292–3163) is the island's largest grocery store and the headquarters for a moderately priced chain with stores around the island. Customers can take out hot soups, stir-fried meats and vegetables, dinners, salads, and desserts for $4.99 a pound.

Maximart (Hog Bay Level, Sandys, ☎ 441/234–1940) has a good selection of meats. Near Whale Bay Inn, it's a good stopping place for those staying at Lantana Colony Club who want to stock up on snacks. ⊙ Daily, 6:30 AM–midnight.

Miles Market (Pitts Bay Rd., near The Princess, Hamilton, ☎ 0441/295–1234) has an excellent selection of high-quality imported and local meats and fish, and many specialty foods found nowhere else on the island, such as a large selection of Häagen-Dazs ice cream. Many items are on the expensive side, but the quality here is unsurpassed in Bermuda. The market makes deliveries anywhere on the island.

Modern Mart (South Shore Rd., Paget, ☎ 441/236–6161) is part of the Marketplace chain; it is smaller than its flagship Hamilton store, but has all the essentials. It is easily accessible from Sky Top Cottages, Loughlands, and other South Shore accommodations.

Shelly Bay Marketplace (North Shore Rd., Hamilton Parish, ☎ 441/293–0966), also part of the Marketplace chain, has a good selection. It is the only large grocery store on the North Shore Road.

Somerset Marketplace (Somerset Rd., Sandys, ☎ 441/234–0626) is the largest grocery store on the island's Western end. It is convenient to Whale Bay Inn, but take a moped or taxi.

Somers Supermarket (York St., St. George's, ☎ 441/297–1177) has a large selection despite its small size. Hot items, salads, and sandwiches are available, and are made fresh daily. It is within walking distance of the St. George's Club and Hillcrest Guest House.

The Supermart (Front St., near King St., Hamilton, ☎ 441/292–2064) has a well-stocked salad bar, prepackaged sandwiches, and hot coffee. This store and Miles Market are a long hike—particularly with heavy bags—from the Ferry Terminal in Hamilton, but once aboard the boat it's an easy ride across the harbour to Greenbank Cottages and Salt Kettle House. A delivery service is available to anywhere on the island.

Specialty Stores

Antiques

Heritage House (2 W. Front St., Hamilton, ☎ 441/295–2615). Browsers will find it difficult to tear themselves away from the antiques section in this small shop. Owner Jay Bluck regularly scours Great Britain and Europe for treasures such as a 19th-century mahogany corner washstand, handmade chess sets, a wind-up gramophone, and more. Do not expect to find any bargains in this store, particularly on imported goods. The original works of esteemed local artists, including Sheilagh Head, Diana Amos, and Otto Trott, are also on display. Shoppers who don't want to make a major purchase can search through bins of old prints. The shop has its own framing department, but the prices are much higher than at other local businesses. Tasteful Bermudian souvenirs can be found here, too.

Pegasus (63 Pitts Bay Rd., Hamilton, ☎ 441/295–2900, FAX 441/295–7596). This Dickensian place in an old house with creaky wood floors is a few minutes' walk from downtown Hamilton on Front Street West, near the Princess. The store has bins and bins of antique prints and a small selection of antique maps. In particular, look for the original Leslie Ward (Spy) *Vanity Fair* caricatures that were published between 1869 and 1914 (from $70) and the Curtis botanicals ($50). Topographical engravings of America, Canada, Ireland, and Scotland by Bartlett are $40–$100. French fashion scenes and early lithographs of fruit, butterflies, and shells are priced from $50. There is a huge selection of greeting cards and wrapping paper from England; and beautifully crafted ceramic house signs from England can be ordered here. The shop provides certificates of antiquity for buyers to show to U.S. Customs (antiques are duty-free, and do not affect the $400 allowance). Shoppers can browse here to their hearts' content from 10 AM–5 PM, but never on a Sunday.

Timeless Antiques (26 Church St., Hamilton, ☎ 441/295–5008, FAX 441/295–8306). Across the street from City Hall and down some steps, you'll find this small, Old World shop, which has a large selection of old, hard-to-find Bermuda books. The walls are lined with 200- to 300-year-old grandfather (or long-case) clocks. Among the store's collection of antiques are Early English carved oak tables, chests, chairs, candelabra, and exquisite reproductions of medieval tapestries. Time is of the essence here, of course, and clock aficionados will want to spend hours talking with proprietor Peter Durhager. If $8,000 for a long-case clock is a little too rich for your blood, take a look at the collection of antique pocket watches.

Arts and Crafts

ARTISTS

Buying artwork by someone you know is always more satisfying than buying it blind, and a number of Bermuda's resident artists—some of whose works are in the collections of famous art collectors worldwide—encourage visits to their studios. Call ahead first, however, to find out if it's convenient to stop by. Be sure to check about payment before going; most creators of fine art on the island do not accept credit cards. (The commercial art shops that sell original art and mass-produced watercolors and prints usually do.) Remember that there are no duties levied on Bermudian arts and crafts.

Diana Amos ("Corncrake," Warwick, ☎ 441/236–9056). An art teacher at Bermuda College, Ms. Amos has a discerning eye that is revealed in her Bermudian scenes. She uses the soft pastels of watercolors to render the beauty of the island's unique architecture, landscapes,

and seascapes. Her work is in galleries throughout the island, and costs
between $500 and about $2,000.

Alfred Birdsey Studio ("Rosecote," Stowe Hill, Paget, ☎ 441/236–6658).
An island institution, Mr. Birdsey is a recipient of the Queen's Certificate
of Honour and Medal in recognition of "valuable services given to Her
Majesty for more than 40 years as an artist of Bermuda." His watercolors of Bermuda hang in myriad places on the island, including
Cambridge Beaches cottage colony, as well as in select U.S. East Coast
galleries. At the studio, watercolors (all originals) cost $40 to $100;
lithographs cost as little as $10. The studio is usually open weekdays
9–1, Saturday 9–noon, and by appointment; but call before going as
hours sometimes vary.

Stephen Card (Scaur Hill, Somerset, ☎ 441/234–2353). A native
Bermudian, this fine marine artist was for many years a captain in the
British merchant marine. He relinquished his full-time life at sea some
years ago to devote himself to painting. Many of his ships from
yesteryear are painted only after much careful research. Mr. Card's work
hangs in private collections in the United States and can be seen aboard
major cruise passenger ships. He often travels, but his work can be found
at Heritage House (*see above*). His prices are based on detail and size,
and range from $2,000 to $20,000.

Will Collieson (18 York St., St. George's, ☎ 441/297–0171). One of
the island's most talented and versatile artists, Mr. Collieson works in
many media, and his sense of humor shines in many of his zany three-
dimensional contemporary collages, made with materials found around
the island. His creations can be seen daily in the window displays at
H. A. & E. Smith department store. Prices vary, depending on the
medium used, but a collage costs between $200 and $800.

Joan Forbes (Art House, 80 South Shore Rd., Paget, ☎ 441/236–6746,
FAX 441/236–5525). Ms. Forbes's watercolors and lithographs of local
architecture, horticulture, and seascapes are made for visitors as inexpensive mementos. Her lithographs sell for $10–$45. She also produces cards, notepaper, and envelopes.

Desmond Fountain (☎ 441/292–3955, by appointment only). This
award-winning sculptor's works are on display all over the island,
whether it's a life-size bronze statue perched beside a lagoon or a
lolling figure seated in a garden chair. Fountain created the *Land Ho!*
statue of Sir George Somers on Ordnance Island in St. George's, and
other of his works can be seen in the Sculpture Gallery on the mezzanine of the Southampton Princess (☎ 441/238–8840, FAX 441/292–
0630). Prices start at about $4,500 for a small bronze and soar to dizzying
heights.

Sheilagh Head (☎ 441/238–0173). One of the island's finest painters,
Mrs. Head works with colors better than any other local painter.
Schooled in Italy and England, her oils stand apart because she explores
light and shadow, illuminating the soft hues of the surroundings.
Whether it is an abstract, an old Bermudian chimney, a cluster of
buildings, or the sky rising above a swathe of foliage or the ocean, this
artist's sensitivity shines forth in every canvas. Mrs. Head's work
hangs in private collections in the U.S., Europe, and Britain. Her paintings are sold through the Bermuda Society of Arts; prices range from
about $500 to $2,500.

Carole Holding Print & Craft Shops (King's Square, St. George's, ☎ 441/
297–1833; Clocktower Mall, Dockyard, ☎ 441/234–3800 or 441/236–
6002 after hours). Commercial artist Ms. Holding mass-produces watercolors of Bermuda's scenes and flowers; many of the same works
are sold as signed prints and limited editions. Crafts, both imported

and by local artists, are also available. Prices range from $18 (small prints) to $160 (framed watercolors).

John Kaufmann (16 Tranquillity Hill, Sandys, ☎ 441/234–4095). Mr. Kaufmann works solely with oils to execute his well-known seascapes and landscapes. He has had successful one-man shows at the Windjammer Gallery, which is the only gallery to carry his work. Prices range from $1,500 for an 8x10 to about $2,500 for a 10x20.

Elmer Midgett (Scaur Hill, Somerset, ☎ 441/234–1936). Using an uncompromising style in oils that employs bold strokes reminiscent of Van Gogh, Mr. Midgett focuses on the island's unusual buildings and angles. He is also a master at stained glass. His paintings—priced from $600 to about $1,200—are often on display at the Bermuda Society of Arts Gallery (*see* Tour 1 *in* Chapter 3, Exploring Bermuda).

Ann Proctor (Harbour Rd., Paget, ☎ 441/236–3378). This artist's delicate, beautifully executed, and much sought-after watercolors of Bermuda plants and flowers have the quality of botanical drawings. Prices start at about $550.

Bruce Stuart (Windjammer Gallery, corner of Reid and King Sts., Hamilton, ☎ 441/292–7861) features the island's unique architecture in his paintings, which have a near-photographic quality. Original artworks range in price from $1,100 to $5,000.

Otto Trott (Garden Gallery, Crawl Hill, Hamilton Parish, ☎ 441/293–4057). A Bermudian who is known for his sensitive use of light and shade, Mr. Trott renders beautiful oil paintings of landscapes and local characters. His work can be found at other island galleries, but he owns the Garden Gallery, and often his best pictures are found there. Works are priced from about $600 to about $2,000.

Sharon Wilson (Turtle Pl., Southampton, ☎ 441/238–2583 or 441/238–0823, FAX 441/238–2454). Ms. Wilson occupies a special place in the local art scene because she is one of the few artists who depict Bermuda's people. This talented woman has had many successful shows, and her work—priced between $5,500 and $7,000—sells well to visitors and locals alike. She employs a radiant range of pastels and often captures people absorbed in their own private world.

Dr. Charles Zuill (☎ 441/236–9000). One of the island's most innovative artists, Dr. Zuill is also the head of the art department at Bermuda College. His most recent exhibit at the Bermuda Society of Arts, consisting of "Earth Paintings" on square and rectangular canvases, employed a new medium that combined paint and sand from beaches in several parts of the world. His prices start at about $500.

Mary Zuill (10 Southlyn La., off South Shore Rd., Paget, ☎ 441/236–2439). In a tiny studio attached to her house, Ms. Zuill paints delightful watercolors of Bermuda's flowers, architecture, and seascapes. She accepts commissions and will either design a painting or work from a photograph you've taken in Bermuda. Watercolors cost between $85 and $450. She welcomes visitors Tuesday–Friday, 10–12 and 2:30–5, from about mid–March to November only.

CRAFTSPEOPLE

Celia and Jack Arnell (☎ 441/236–4646). The miniature cedar furniture crafted by this husband-and-wife team is displayed in a dollhouse at the Craft Market (*see below*). The fine details on the breakfronts and chests of drawers include tiny metal drawer knobs, and the wonderful four-poster bed comes complete with a canopy. A four-poster bed sells for $125, chairs for about $35, depending on the model.

Kathleen Kemsley Bell (7 Seabright Ln., ☎ 441/236–3366). A director of the Bermuda Arts Centre at Dockyard, Ms. Bell creates exquisite dolls of persons from different periods of Bermuda's history. Each doll is researched for historical accuracy and is unique. Their bodies are sculpted of papier-mâché and hand-painted, their faces marvelously expressive, and their costumes all hand-stitched. The base of each doll is signed and carries a description of the historical period on which the doll's fashions are based. Call to make an appointment at the studio, or visit the Bermuda Arts Centre at Dockyard, where her work is on display. Ms. Bell works on commission and will visit your hotel with samples of her work. Prices start at $250.

Ronnie Chameau (☎ 441/292–1387). Mrs. Chameau creates Christmas angels and dolls from dried palm, banana, and grapefruit leaves gathered from her yard and byways around the island. The 9-inch dolls ($55), with palmetto leaf baskets and hats, palm tree matting for the hair, and pecan heads with painted faces, are intended as table ornaments, while the dainty little 4-inch angels ($15) are designed to hang on the Christmas tree. Colorful, hand-painted, Bermuda cottage doorstops ($65) are Ms. Chameau's other specialty. Trimingham's is the exclusive purveyor of her works (*see above*).

FINE-ART PHOTOGRAPHERS

Mark Emmerson (Belvedere Bldg., Hamilton, ☎ 441/292–6283). This photographer produces rich black-and-white prints on platinum and other specialized photographic papers. His portfolio is extensive, and he occasionally shows his work at the Arts Centre at Dockyard. Prices vary according to size and paper used.

Ian MacDonald-Smith (17 Jennings Land, Smith's, ☎ 441/292–3295). Bold, bright, and large Cibachrome prints (many images are 18x24) are this photographer's passion (many are priced at about $600). Unusual angles and portions of the island's unique architecture are the focal point of many pictures. He has produced several books (available throughout the island), a good substitute if his originals are more than your budget allows.

Graeme Outerbridge (Heritage House, 2 W. Front St., Hamilton, ☎ 441/295–2615; Windjammer Gallery, corner of Reid and King Sts., ☎ 441/292–7861). A photographer who contributed to the acclaimed *Day in the Life* book series, Mr. Outerbridge captures Bermuda in original photographic prints, silk screens, and posters.

DeForest Trimingham (South Shore Rd., Paget, ☎ 441/236–2727, FAX 441/236–9853). After he retired from working in the family's Front Street department store, Mr. Trimingham resumed working with his camera. He has traveled the world and has produced many fine Cibachromes of remote places, but most visitors seem to prefer his sensitive Bermuda compositions, which are priced from about $650 for an 11x14.

Judith Wadson (Box 223, Hamilton HMAX, ☎ 441/236–3522, FAX 441/236–5147). Hand-colored black-and-white prints and photographic prints of Bermuda's architecture and landscapes on archival watercolor paper or high-quality photographic papers are this photographer's specialty. Ms. Wadson, a former staff photographer for *Yachting* magazine, focuses on the Old World side of Bermuda. Prices range from about $200 to $400, depending on the size, and whether the image is framed.

GALLERIES AND CRAFTS SHOPS

Bermuda Arts Centre at Dockyard (Museum Row, Dockyard, ☎ 441/234–2809). Sleek and modern, with well-designed displays of local art, this gallery is housed in one of the stone buildings of the former British naval dockyard. The walls are adorned with paintings and photographs, and glass display cases contain exquisitely crafted quilts as well as costume dolls, jewelry, and wood sculpture. Exhibits are frequently changed. Several artists' studios inside the gallery are open to the public.

Bermuda Glassblowing Studio & Show Room (16 Blue Hole Hill, Hamilton Parish, ☎ 441/293–2234). A restored village hall in the Bailey's Bay area houses this glassblowing studio, where eight artists have created more than 200 examples of handblown glass in vibrant, swirling colors. Shoppers can watch glassblowers at work daily in the studio, and sometimes at the Dockyard outlet (Bermuda Craft Market, Dockyard, ☎ 441/234–3208). The works are sold for retail at the studio and the outlet as well as at a retail store in Hamilton (18 Windsor Place Mall, Queen St., ☎ 441/295–6970). Prices range from $10 to $1,600.

Bermuda Society of Arts (West Wing, City Hall, Hamilton, ☎ 441/292–3824) has many highly creative members who sell their work during a revolving series of special group exhibits and the perennial members' shows. The normal media of watercolors, oils, pastels, acrylics, and charcoal can be found, but photographs, collages and some three-dimensional works and sculptures are also occasionally included. The Society has a Front Street West location, Harbour Gallery (*see below*), which opened in 1994.

Bridge House Gallery (1 Bridge St., St. George's, ☎ 441/297–8211). Housed in part of a Bermuda home that dates to 1700, this gallery is of historical and architectural interest in its own right. In the 18th century, the two-story white building was the home of Bermuda's governors; today it is maintained by the Bermuda National Trust. Original works by local artists, inexpensive prints, and souvenirs are for sale.

Craft Market (The Cooperage, Dockyard, Ireland Island, ☎ 441/234–3208). Occupying part of what was once the cooperage, this large stone building dates to 1831. In the past, the quality of goods was inferior, but improvements have recently been made; now this is on the of the few places that has island-made handcrafts. Anna and Glenn Correia's wooden creations are beautifully executed and reasonably priced. Outstanding is the exquisite—but expensive—jewelry handmade by Judith Faram, which is of world-class standard.

Harbour Gallery (Front Street West, Hamilton, ☎ 441/296–2232). The island's most intimate gallery, housed in an 18th-century building overlooking Hamilton Harbour, features the high-quality work of Bermuda Society of Arts' members. Opened in 1994, it is the Society's second gallery (the other is at City Hall, *see above*). A small print room displays limited-edition prints that are sold in tubes for easy transport home; a selection of cards featuring Bermuda flora and scenes are also available. The Society's members can often be found sipping coffee in the street-side porch, and visitors are encouraged to join them.

Island Pottery (Dockyard, Ireland Island, ☎ 441/234–3361). Pottery is turned out in a large stone building at Dockyard, where artisans toil over potter's wheels. The results are sold on the premises.

Masterworks Foundation Gallery (97 Front St., Hamilton, ☎ 441/295–5580). Formed in 1987, the foundation showcases well-known Canadian, British, French, and American artists, including Georgia O'Keeffe and Winslow Homer, whose works were inspired by Bermuda. The Bermudiana Collection contains more than 400 works in watercolor, oil, pencil, charcoal, and other media. Selected pieces from this collection can be seen at the Bermuda National Gallery at City Hall, Camden House, and Waterloo House.

Windjammer Gallery (King and Reid Sts., Hamilton, ☎ 441/292–7861, FAX 441/295–3692; 95 Front St., ☎ 441/292–5878, FAX 441/295–1418). The island's biggest art gallery, devoted to high-quality work by Bermuda-based and foreign artists, occupies a charming three-room cottage. Individual and group shows are held regularly, and work is exported to collectors worldwide. The knowledgeable staff can help you choose from the wide range of prints, lithographs, oils, watercolors, and photographs that fill the walls and portfolio display cases. Less-expensive posters and note cards are sold, too. Sculpture by Bermudian Desmond Fountain is on display in the garden. Mail order is available.

Bookstores

Bermuda Book Store (Queen St., Hamilton, ☎ 441/295–3698). Book lovers, beware! Once you set foot inside this musty old place, you'll have a hard time tearing yourself away. Stacked on a long table are a host of books about Bermuda. The proprietor can probably answer any questions you have about the island.

The Book Cellar (Water St., St. George's, ☎ 441/297–0448) This small shop below the National Trust's Tucker House crams in a large selection of Bermudian books and an interesting assortment of novels by English and American authors that make for more meaningful reading than the best-sellers. Coffee-table books cover a range of subjects. There is a variety of British children's books that are hard to find in the U.S. Owner Jill White and her well-read staff will be happy to help you search for an obscure title or let you browse at your leisure.

The Bookmart (The Phoenix Centre, 3 Reid St., Hamilton, ☎ 441/295–3838). The island's largest bookstore specializes in best-sellers and paperbacks. They have a complete selection of Bermuda titles, as well as a large children's book section.

The Children's Bookshop (International Centre, 26 Bermudiana Rd., Hamilton, ☎ 441/292–9078). A wonderful selection of hard-to-find British titles is geared to children of all ages.

Ship's Inn Book Gallery (Clocktower Building, Dockyard, Ireland Island, ☎ 441/234–2807). Sherlyn Swan carries an ever-changing assortment of used books as well as some rare and antique titles. The only new books are about Bermuda. ⊘ Daily 10–5; check for winter hours.

Washington Mall Magazine (Washington Mall, Reid St., Hamilton, ☎ 441/292–7420). Come here for Bermuda's best selection of magazines, including hard-to-find periodicals. This is also the place to find a best-seller for the beach or the journey home, children's books, and coffee-table publications about the island.

Boutiques

Archie Brown & Son (51 Front St., Hamilton, ☎ 441/295–2928; Clocktower Building, Dockyard, ☎ 441/234–1017); York St., St. George, ☎ 441/297–0036). Top-quality woolens, Pringle of Scotland cashmeres, Shetland and lamb's wool sweaters, and 100% wool tartan kilts are among the specialties here.

Aston & Gunn (2 Reid St., Hamilton, ☎ 441/295–4866). An upmarket member of the English Sports Shops that dot the island, this handsome shop carries men's and women's clothing and accessories. Men's European clothing, including Hugo Boss and Van Gils, costs up to 30% less than in the United States. Aston & Gunn cotton dress shirts sell for $40–$50. Women's wear, including designs by Calvin Klein and Anne Klein, is mainly from the U.S., but since there's no sales tax it's less expensive. Good-quality soft leather carry-on bags are priced from $185.

Bananas (93 W. Front St., Hamilton; ☎ 441/295–1106; 7 E. Front St., Hamilton; ☎ 441/292–7264; the Princess, Hamilton, ☎ 441/295–3000; 3 King's Sq., St. George's, ☎ 441/297–0351; Sonesta Beach Hotel & Spa, Southampton, ☎ 441/238–3409). Sportswear and T-shirts make this place a teenager's dream. Brightly colored Bermuda umbrellas cost about $20.

Bermuda Railway Co. (Reid and Burnaby Sts., Hamilton, ☎ 441/296–1577; Clocktower Mall, Dockyard, ☎ 441/296–1290; 29 Mangrove Bay, Somerset, ☎ 441/292–3682; 30 Water St., St. George's, ☎ 441/297–0546; 90 South Shore Rd., Paget, ☎ 441/292–3518; Crystal Cave, Wilkinson Ave., Hamilton Parish., ☎ 441/293–0942.) The main Hamilton location is called "Grand Central Station", and the various branches are known as "stations." All carry accessories and casual, color-coordinated cotton separates for men (sized up to XXL), women, and children. In addition to skirts, shirts, shorts, and the like, belt buckles and even beach towels are sold. A best-selling item is the Bermuda Railway cap, which sports the company logo.

Calypso (45 Front St., Hamilton, ☎ 441/295–2112; Princess Hotel, Hamilton; Coral Beach & Tennis Club; Sonesta Beach Hotel & Spa, Southampton; Southampton Princess, Southampton; Victorian Mall, Clocktower Building, Dockyard). This expensive women's clothing shop carries an array of sophisticated leisure wear. It has the island's largest selection of swimwear, and is Bermuda's only purveyor of Jantzen and Louis Vuitton merchandise. Expect to shell out $265 for a small French purse, and $845 for a soft briefcase. Accessories, including Italian leather shoes and straw hats, are plentiful. The eclectic novelty items from Europe make great gifts.

Cecile (15 Front St., Hamilton, ☎ 441/295–1311; Marriott's Castle Harbour Resort, Hamilton Parish, ☎ 441/293–2841; Southampton Princess Hotel, South Shore Rd., Southampton, ☎ 441/238–1434). Specializing in upscale off-the-rack ladies' fashions, this shop carries designer labels such as Mondi, Basler, Geiger of Austria, and Louis Feraud of Paris. There's a good selection of swimwear, including swimsuits by Gottex. The shop also carries Leslie Fay petites, as well as accessories (scarves, jewelry, handbags, belts). Check the rooms in the back of the store for sale dresses.

Constable's Woolen Fashions (Duke of York St., St. George's, ☎ 441/297–1995). Icelandic woolen clothing is the specialty of this store, and prices are generally 30%–50% lower than those in the United States. This is *the* place to come for heavy woolen coats, ski sweaters, ponchos, and jackets in smoky colors. Travel blankets are also a hot item.

Cow Polly (Somers Wharf, St. George's, ☎ 441/297–1514). Phoebe Wharton's store carries expensive hand-painted clothing and attractive accessories from the far corners of the globe. The beautifully crafted straw bags and hats are worth the trip from Hamilton. And you won't find their unusual pottery, jewelry, or men's ties sold anywhere else on the island.

Crown Colony Shop (1 Front St., Hamilton, ☎ 441/295–3935). This branch of the English Sports Shop features quality formal and business wear for women. The shop's signature item is a line of Parisian-designed Mayeelok silk dresses, which sell for $295.

Davison's of Bermuda (27 and 73 Front St., Hamilton, ☎ 441/292–7137; Water St., St. George's, ☎ 441/297–8363; Princess Hotel, Hamilton, ☎ 441/292–1980; Marriott's Castle Harbour Resort, Hamilton Parish, ☎ 441/293–8044; Southampton Princess Hotel, South Shore Rd., Southampton, ☎ 441/238–1036; Clocktower Building, Dockyard, ☎ 441/234–0959). High-quality cotton sportswear items include sweaters and slacks, tennis and sailing clothing, golf and tennis hats, and children's sportswear. They also carry gift packages of Bermuda Fish Chowder ($12), and a collection of deliciously vicious-looking stuffed trolls—a huge one guards the doorway and claims to "bite" if touched. Back in the U.S., you'll find branches of this store in Miami, San Diego, New Orleans, Baltimore, and Newport, RI.

English Sports Shop (95 Front St., Hamilton, ☎ 441/295–2672; Water St., St. George's, ☎ 441/295–2672). Bermuda has several branches of this store, which specializes in British woolens: Harris Tweed jackets for men cost $225, while V–neck Shetland woolen sweaters are priced at $24.95 or two for $48; more expensive cashmere sweaters go for $245.

Frangipani (Water St., St. George's, ☎ 441/297–1357). This small shop is filled with colorful women's fashions that have an island resort look. Cotton, silk, and rayon leisure wear are the backbone of the stock, but vibrant Caribbean art is also sold. They also carry a collection of unusual accessories to offset many styles.

London Shop (22 Church St., Hamilton, ☎ 441/295–1279). This small men's shop has shelves piled high with Pierre Cardin dress shirts for about $50. European designer suits are priced from around $500; Dutch and British trousers are from $70. A good selection of European silk ties are priced from $35.

Stefanel (12 Reid St., Hamilton, ☎ 441/295–5698). This very smart, very expensive boutique stocks the snazzy cotton knits of Italian trendsetter Carlo Stefanel. Imported from Italy, the clothing includes men's cotton and linen suits and cotton dress shirts, and women's patterned wool skirts, trousers, and leggings with hand-knit, contrasting jackets.

Triangle's (55 Front St., Hamilton, ☎ 441/292–1990). The star attractions of this boutique are Diane Freis's original, colorful, and crushable mosaic dresses, priced between $300 and $420—almost half what they cost in the United States.

Turkish Delights (Clocktower Building, Dockyard, ☎ 441/234–3437). This small shop is filled with reasonably priced gifts and jewelry that owner Susie Lowe handpicks on annual trips to Turkey. Kilim–style hats, handbags, and vests were recent winning items, as were the wooden picture frames and chess and backgammon sets with mother-of-pearl inlay. There is a good selection of Afghan jewelry, Venetian glass, and etched silver hair clips. To help you get into the true spirit of Turkish shopping, the salespeople will offer you a glass cup of *çay* (Turkish tea) while you browse.

Upstairs Golf & Tennis Shop (26 Church St., Hamilton, ☎ 441/295–5161). As befits Bermuda's role as a golfing paradise, this store stocks clubs and accessories from some of the best brands available including Hogan, Ping, Callaway, and Titleist. Tennis players can choose a racquet by Yonex or Dunlop. Men's and women's sportswear is also sold.

Crystal, China, and Porcelain

Bluck's (4 W. Front St., Hamilton, ☎ 441/295–5367; Reid and Queen Sts., Hamilton, ☎ 441/292–3894, FAX 441/295–2296 ; Water St., St. George's, ☎ 441/297–0476; Southampton Princess Hotel, South Shore, Southampton, ☎ 441/238–0992). A dignified establishment that has been in business for more than 150 years, this is the only store on the island devoted exclusively to the sale of crystal and china. Royal Doulton, Royal Copenhagen, Villeroy & Boch, Herend, Lalique, Minton, Waterford, Baccarat, and others are displayed on two floors in the main Front Street location. Herend Rothschild Bird is $224 for one five-piece place setting; a five-piece place setting of Hermès Toucans is $357. The large gift section includes an abundant selection of Limoges boxes. The courteous staff will provide you with price lists upon request.

Vera P. Card (Main store: 11 Front St., Hamilton, ☎ 441/295–1729; FAX 441/295–2833; 103 Front St., Hamilton, ☎ 441/292–0219; 9 Water St. and 13 York St., St. George's, ☎ 441/297–1718; Marriott's Castle Harbour Resort, Hamilton Parish, ☎ 441/293–8463; Sonesta Beach Hotel & Spa, South Shore Rd., Southampton, ☎ 441/238–8122).

Lladro and Royal Doulton's "Reflections" figurines are widely available all over the island at almost identical prices, but this store has the most extensive selection, including open-edition and limited-edition gallery pieces. The Lladro Bermuda Moongate and several other works are carried here exclusively. The shop's collection of more than 250 Hummel figurines is one of the world's largest. The impressive selection of beautifully crafted Swiss and German watches and clocks includes the Bermuda Time collection; and the stock of fine and costume jewelry includes 14-carat gold earrings, charms, and pendants.

Jewelry

Astwood Dickinson (83–85 Front St., Hamilton, ☎ 441/292–5805; Walker Arcade, Hamilton, ☎ 441/292–4247; the Southampton Princess Hotel, South Shore Rd., Southampton, ☎ 441/238–0448). Established in 1904, this store has an exquisite collection of European jewelry, unmounted stones, and a wide range of Swiss watches. Elegant timepieces by Patek Philippe, Omega, Cartier, Baume & Mercier, Tiffany, and Tag Heuer are sold for as much as 20% less than in the United States. Jewelry from Tiffany and Mikimoto is also available. The shop's exclusively designed 18-karat gold mementos in the Bermuda Collection sell for $50–$600. The collection includes the Bermuda dinghy pendant priced from $75 (earrings are $230), a tall-ship pin or pendant for $600, a Bermuda Island pendant from $50, and a Gibbs Hill Lighthouse tie-pin for $150.

Crisson's (55 and 71 Front St., 16 Queen St., and 20 Reid St., Hamilton, ☎ 441/295–2351; Marriott's Castle Harbour Resort, Hamilton Parish, ☎ 441/293–2852; Elbow Beach Hotel, South Shore Rd., Paget, ☎ 441/236–9928; Sonesta Beach Hotel & Spa, South Shore Rd., Southampton, ☎ 441/238–0072; York and Kent Sts., St. George's, ☎ 441/297–0672; Water St., St. George's, ☎ 441/297–0107). The exclusive Bermuda agent for Rolex, Ebel, and Raymond Weil, this upscale establishment offers discounts of 20%–25% on expensive merchandise, but don't expect to find cheap Timex or Swatch watches. The gift department carries English flatware, Saint Louis crystal, and imported baubles, bangles, and beads.

Lote Tree Jewels (Walker Arcade, Hamilton, ☎ 441/292–8525). Opened by Mary Walker in 1980 to showcase her own Marybeads (14-karat gold beads intertwined with semiprecious gems or freshwater pearls), the shop is now operating under new ownership, and some of the stock has changed. A new specialty is ethnic jewelry from around the world, including Balinese and Indian silver, and lapis from Afghanistan. A line of creatively designed, handmade necklaces and earrings are crafted especially for this shop. Silver and 14-karat gold add-a-bead necklaces are a fun gift to take home, especially for frequent visitors. Marybeads are still available; prices start at $290.

Solomon's (17 Front St., Hamilton, ☎ 441/292–4742 or 441/295–1003, FAX 441/295–9008). This is the sole store on the island to carry only genuine stones and minerals in its collection of modern and classic designs. Prices for artisan-crafted one-of-a-kind pieces range from $70 to $10,000. Manager Allan Porter and his friendly staff will guide you in making the best selection.

Vera P. Card (*see above*).

Linens

Irish Linen Shop (31 Front St., Hamilton, ☎ 441/295–4089, FAX 441/295–6552; Cambridge Rd., Somerset, ☎ 441/234–0127). In a cottage that looks as though it belongs in Dublin, the Hamilton branch is *the* place for Irish linen tablecloths. Prices range from $10 to more than $3,000. Antique tablecloths can cost as much as $1,600. The best buys in this shop are the exclusively designed Irish linen tea towels for $6.75. From Madeira come exquisite hand-embroidered handkerchiefs from $5.50; linen sheets and pillowcases; and cotton organdy christening robes with slip and bonnet, hand embroidered with garlands and tiers of Valenciennes lace ($220 to upward of $800). Pure linen hand-rolled handkerchiefs from Belgium with Belgian lace are priced under $20, while Le Jacquard Français cotton kitchen towels cost about $12. The shop's Bermuda Cottage Collection includes quilted place mats, tea cozies, and pot holders—most for less than $15. The store has an exclusive arrangement with Soulciado, maker of the vivid prints from Provence that are available in tablecloths, place mats, and bags, as well as by the yard—the latter at a huge savings over U.S. prices.

Liquors and Liqueurs

The following liquor stores sell at identical prices; each has branches sprinkled around the island from St. George's to Somerset; and each will allow you to put together your own package of Bermuda liquors at in-bond (duty-free) prices: **Burrows Lightbourn** (Front St., Hamilton, ☎ 441/295–0176; Queen St., Hamilton, ☎ 441/295–0176; Harbour Rd., Paget, ☎ 441/236–0355; Water St., St. George's, ☎ 441/297–0552; Main Rd., Somerset, ☎ 441/234–0963); **Frith's Liquors Ltd.** (Front St., Hamilton, ☎ 441/295–3544; York St., St. George's, ☎ 441/297–0684; Mangrove Bay, Somerset, ☎ 441/234–1740; Sonesta Beach Hotel, Southampton, ☎ 441/238–8122); **Gosling's** (Front St., Hamilton, ☎ 441/295–1123; crnr. York and Queen Sts., St. George's, ☎ 441/297–1364; crnr. Main and Cambridge Rds., ☎ 441/234–1544).

Perfumes

Bermuda Perfumery (212 North Shore Rd., Bailey's Bay, ☎ 441/293–0627 or 800/527–8213, FAX 441/293–8810). This highly promoted perfumery is on all the taxi-tour itineraries. Regularly scheduled guided tours of the facilities include a walk through the ornamental gardens and an exhibit on the distillation of flowers into perfume. At the Calabash gift shop you can purchase the factory's Lili line of fragrances as well as imported soaps and an assortment of fragrances.
Peniston-Brown's Perfume Shop (23 W. Front St., Hamilton, ☎ 441/295–0570; 6 Water St., St. George's, ☎ 441/297–1525) and the **Guerlain Shop** (19 Queen St., Hamilton, ☎ 441/295–5535), which is the exclusive agent for Guerlain products, stock more than 127 lines of French and Italian fragrances, as well as soaps, bath salts, and bubble bath. The **Guerlain Boutique** (53 Front St., Hamilton, ☎ 441/295–8843) carries only Guerlain products, including its quality line of cosmetics.
Perfume & Gift Boutique (55 Front St., Hamilton, ☎ 441/295–1183), Trimingham's fragrance salon, carries Chanel No. 5, Laura Ashley No. 1, Elizabeth Taylor's Passion and White Diamonds, and Calvin Klein's Obsession, among others.

Miscellaneous

Flying Colours at Riihuolma's (5 Queen St., Hamilton, ☎ 441/295–0890, FAX 441/292–9028). This family-owned and -operated shop, established in 1937, is easy to find because of the long row of international flags flying above its entrance. The island's largest selection of T-shirts with creatively designed island logos in hundreds of styles can be found here. The selection of quality souvenirs and gifts is plentiful. Educational toys are a specialty. This shop also carries everything for the beach—hats, beach towels, toys, and more.
Hall of Names (Clocktower Mall, Dockyard, ☎ 441/234–3410). This tiny shop, which opened in 1994, is a fun place to learn the origins of your family name. Friendly owner John Doherty punches the pertinent information into his computer, and for $15 gives you a nicely presented

document with facts compiled from an extensive bibliography, with your family coat of arms at the top, in a sturdy travel tube. The store is a franchise of a Canadian-based company, whose team of researchers and historians compiles the information into a database.

Hodge Podge (3 Point Pleasant Rd., Hamilton, ☎ 441/295–0647). Just around the corner from the Ferry Terminal and Visitors Center Service Bureau in Hamilton, this cluttered little shop offers pretty much what its name implies: postcards, sunblock, sunglasses, film, and T-shirts.

Rising Sun Shop (Middle Rd., Southampton, ☎ 441/238–2154). This country store, the only one on the island, is easy to spot, as a flag, a horse's head, and other eye-catching inventory usually hang outside the entrance. Owner Anne Powell's warmth and humor infuse her novelty gift items, which may include toilet plungers, priced from $27; a ship's decanter for $45; Portuguese wine coolers for $24; or perfectly appointed wicker picnic hampers, priced from about $45—though inventory changes frequently. A large selection of quality horse-riding gear is always on hand.

Sail On (Old Cellar La., off Front St., Hamilton, ☎ 441/295–0808, FAX 441/295–2712). Owned and operated by Hubert Watlington, a former Olympic windsurfer and top local sailor, this must-visit shop is tucked up a quaint alleyway, opposite Number One Shed and a cruise ship dock. It's the best place on the island for casual clothing and swimwear for adults and children, as well as gifts that appeal to those with a wacky sense of humor. Road Toad and Famous Onions clothing are sold here exclusively. T-shirts, designed by Bermudians, earn ongoing kudos for their originality in the Best of Bermuda merchant awards. Mail order is available.

Sail On's Sunny Caribbee (Washington Mall, Reid St, Hamilton, ☎ 441/295–0808). This cheery, fun shop is accented with nautical memorabilia. A store within a store, this is the headquarters for a vast selection of Sunny Caribbee Products from Tortola, in the British Virgin Islands. Exotic Caribbean hot sauces, cooking spices, seasonings, sweets, and condiments are made with natural ingredients: The best selling Arawak Love Potion and West Indian Hangover Cure make great gifts, as do the full line of flower- and fruit-scented fragrances. Colorful, practical Haitian crafts—mirrors, light switches, bookends, and hooks—are easy to carry home. Also in this store is much of the same imprinted and embroidered sportswear featured at Sail On's Old Cellar Lane shop off Front Street. Mail order is available.

Treats (Washington Mall, Reid St., Hamilton, ☎ 441/296–1123; Victorian Mall, Dockyard, ☎ 441/234–1094) is a candy store filled with bulk candy in just about every flavor. Buy sweets by the piece or the pound. The Candygramme gift box—for any occasion—is filled with candies of your choice and is decorated with a balloon; prices start at $15. Whimsical gifts can be found here, too.

5 Water Sports and Beaches

BERMUDA BOASTS that it has "water scientifically proven to be the clearest in the western Atlantic." Whether or not this is true, the water is certainly clear enough to make Bermuda one of the world's great centers for snorkeling and scuba diving. Clear water also gives fishermen a distinct advantage—a fish has almost nowhere to hide in the island's shallow, translucent water. For whatever reasons, however, the water around Bermuda was apparently *not* clear enough to allow many ship captains to see the barrier reefs encircling the island. Consequently, the reefs today are a veritable smorgasbord of marine wreckage, guaranteed to whet the appetite of any diving enthusiast. Some wrecks are in less than 30 feet of water and are accessible even to snorkelers. The reefs also help keep the water close to shore relatively calm, acting as a fortress wall against the pounding swells of the Atlantic and reducing beach erosion. And Bermuda's beaches are definitely worth saving—fine-grain sand tinted pink with shells, marine invertebrates, and crushed coral. However, Bermuda's reefs remain as dangerous as ever. Boat rentals are available at several island locations, but only the most experienced yachtsmen should venture beyond the safe waters of Great Sound and Castle Harbour. To go anywhere else without a full knowledge of Bermuda's considerable offshore hazards is pure folly.

Thanks to Bermuda's position close to the Gulf Stream, the water stays warm year-round, although Bermudians consider anything under 75°F frigid. In summer, the ocean is usually above 80°F, and even warmer in the shallows between the reefs and shore. In winter, the water temperature only occasionally drops below 70°F, but it seems cooler because the air temperature is usually in the mid-60s—a wet suit is recommended for anyone who plans to spend an extended period of time in the water. Lack of business, more than a drop in water temperature, is responsible for the comparative dearth of water-sports activity during the winter months. The winter does tend to be windier, however, and this means that water conditions can be less than ideal. Rough water creates problems anchoring or stabilizing fishing and diving boats, and visibility underwater is often clouded by sand and debris. High season runs from April through October, when fishing, diving, and yacht charters fill up quickly. Most boats carry fewer than 20 passengers, so it's advisable to sign up early. March through April and October through November are shoulder seasons; December through February is the off-season, when many operators close to make repairs and perform routine maintenance. During these months, a few operators stay open on a limited basis, scheduling charters only when there are enough people to fill a boat; if too few people sign up, the charter is usually canceled. For this reason, water-sports enthusiasts have to be flexible during the winter months.

Take advantage of the activities director at your hotel or your ship's cruise director—he or she can make arrangements for you long before you arrive. **"What To Do in Bermuda,"** a 39-page publication and the separate 7-page brochure, **"Information and Price Sheet for What To Do"** have extensive information on the island's sports facilities and special events. Both are available free from the Bermuda Department of Tourism (*see* Important Contacts A to Z *in* the Gold Guide).

Reality check. Call home.

—— *AT&T USADirect® and World Connect.® The fast, easy way to call most anywhere.* ——

Take out AT&T Calling Card or your local calling card.** Lift phone. Dial AT&T Access Number for country you're calling from. Connect to English-speaking operator or voice prompt. Reach the States or over 200 countries. Talk. Say goodbye. Hang up. Resume vacation.

Anguilla 1-800-872-2881	French Antilles 19011
Antigua (Public Card Phones)...................#1	Grenada† 1-800-872-2881
Bahamas....................**1-800-872-2881**	**Haiti†■**....................**001-800-972-2883**
Barbados•••■...............**1-800-872-2881**	Jamaica††........................0-800-872-2881
Bermuda†■ **1-800-872-2881**	**Netherland Antilles**...**001-800-872-2881**
Bonaire **001-800-872-2881**	St. Kitts/Nevis 1-800-872-2881
British V.I. 1-800-872-2881	St. Lucia .... Special USADirect Dedicated Locations
Cayman Islands 1-800-872-2881	St. Vincent ••• 1-800-872-2881
Dom. Rep.††■.............**1-800-872-2881**	**Trinidad&Tobago** .. Special USADirect Dedicated Locations
Dominica 1-800-872-2881	Turks & Caicos ••• 1-800-872-2881

AT&T
Your True Choice

**You can also call collect or use most U.S. local calling cards. Countries in bold face permit country-to-country calling in addition to calls to the U.S. World Connect® prices consist of USADirect® rates plus an additional charge based on the country you are calling. Collect calling available to the U.S. only. *Public phones require deposit of coin or phone card. †May not be available from every phone.††Collect calling only. •••Only available from public phones. ■World Connect calls can only be placed *to* this country. ©1995 AT&T.

For a free wallet sized card of all AT&T Access Numbers, call: 1 800 241 5555.

All the best trips start with **Fodor's**.

EXPLORING GUIDES

At last, the color of an art book combined with the usefulness of a complete guide.

"As stylish and attractive as any guide published." *—The New York Times*

"Worth reading before, during, and after a trip." *—The Philadelphia Inquirer*

More than 30 destinations available worldwide. $19.95 each.

BERKELEY GUIDES

The budget traveler's handbook

"Berkeley's scribes put the funk back in travel."
—Time

"Fresh, funny, and funky as well as useful."
—The Boston Globe

"Well-organized, clear and very easy to read."
—America Online

14 destinations worldwide. Priced between $13.00 - $19.50. ($17.95 - $27.00 Canada)

AFFORDABLES

"All the maps and itinerary ideas of Fodor's established gold guides with a bonus—shortcuts to savings." *—USA Today*

"Travelers with champagne tastes and beer budgets will welcome this series from Fodor's." *—Hartfort Courant*

"It's obvious these Fodor's folk have secrets we civilians don't." *—New York Daily News*

Also available: Florida, Europe, France, London, Paris. Priced between $11.00 - $18.00 ($14.50 - $24.00 Canada)

At bookstores, or call **1-800-533-6478**

Fodor's
The name that means smart travel.™

WATER SPORTS

Boating and Sailing

Visitors to Bermuda can either rent their own boat or charter a boat
with a skipper. Rental boats, which are 18 feet at most, range from
sailboats (typically tiny Sunfish) to motorboats (13-foot Boston
Whalers), in addition to kayaks and pedal boats. Some of these vessels are ideal for exploring the coves and harbors of the sounds, or, in
the case of motorboats, dropping the anchor and snorkeling around
the shorelines, which are abundant with different coral and colorful
fish. In **Great Sound,** several small islands, such as Hawkins Island and
Darrell's Island, have tiny secluded beaches and coves that are usually
empty during the week. If the wind is fresh and is blowing in the right
direction, the islands are about a half-hour's sail from **Hamilton Harbour** or **Salt Kettle.** These beaches are wonderful places to have a picnic, although some are privately owned and visitors are not always
welcome. Check with the boat-rental operator before planning an island outing.

The trade winds pass well to the south of Bermuda, so the island does
not have predictable air currents. Channeled by islands and head-
lands, the wind direction around **Hamilton Harbour, the Great Sound,**
and **Mangrove Bay** changes regularly. The variability of the winds has
undoubtedly aided the education of Bermuda's racing skippers, who
are traditionally among the world's best. To the casual sailor, however,
wind changes can be troublesome, although you can be fairly confi-
dent you won't be becalmed: The average summer breeze is 7–10
knots, often out of the south or southwest. **Mangrove Bay** is frequently
protected and is the ideal place for novice sailors and pedal boaters; a
range of boats is available from **Mangrove Marina** (end of Cambridge
Rd., Somerset, ☎ 441/234–0914 or 441/234–0331, ext. 295). Anyone wanting a small taste of open water during the summer months
should head for **Pompano Beach Club Watersports Centre** (36 Pompano Rd., Southampton, ☎ 441/234–0222) on the western ocean
shore. Those who want to experience boating in the Great Sound and
Somerset shoreline can go to the **Royal Naval Dockyard** and rent sailboats or motorboats from **Windjammer Water Sports** (☎ 441/234–
1343) or **Dockyard Marina** (☎ 441/234–0300).

Boat Rentals

Rates for small powerboats start at about $75 for one or two hours,
up to $170 for a full day; sailboat rentals begin at $90 for four hours,
or $115 to $170 for a full day. A credit card number or a refundable
deposit of about $70 is usually required. Sailboats and powerboats can
be rented at **Dockyard Boat Rentals** (Dockyard Marina, Royal Naval
Dockyard, ☎ 441/234–0300, FAX 441/234–0855); **South Side Scuba
Water Sports,** which has outlets at **Grotto Bay Beach Hotel & Tennis
Club** (11 Blue Hole Hill, Hamilton Parish, ☎ 441/293–2915 or
441/293–8333, ext. 37), **Marriott's Castle Harbour Resort** (Paynters
Rd., Hamilton Parish, ☎ 441/293–2040), and the **Sonesta Beach
Hotel & Spa** (Sinky Bay Rd., Southampton, ☎ 441/238–8122); and
Windjammer Water Sports (Dockyard Marina, Royal Naval Dockyard,
☎ 441/234–1343, FAX 441/234–3241). Rentals are also available at
Mangrove Marina (Cambridge Rd., Sandys, ☎ 441/234–0914 or
441/234–0331, ext. 295), **Robinson's Marina** (Somerset Bridge, Sandys,
☎ 441/234–0709, FAX 441/234–3255), **Pompano Beach Club Water-
sports Centre** (36 Pompano Rd., Southampton, ☎ 441/234–0222), and

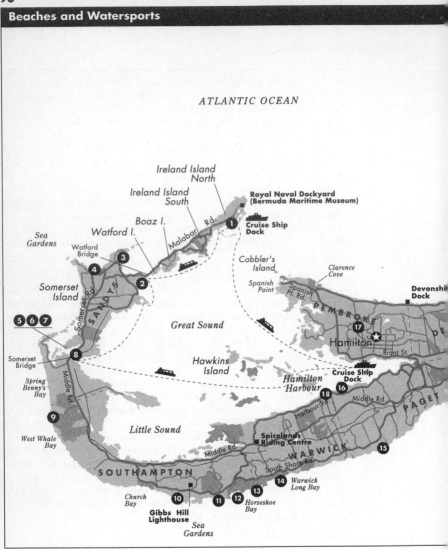

ATLANTIC OCEAN

Ireland Island North

Ireland Island South

Royal Naval Dockyard (Bermuda Maritime Museum)

Boaz I.

Malabar Rd.

Cruise Ship Dock

Watford I.

Sea Gardens

Watford Bridge

③

Cobbler's Island

Clarence Cove

Devonshi Dock

②

Spanish Point

Spanish Pt. Rd.

PEMBROKE

④

Somerset Island

Somerset Rd.

SANDYS

Great Sound

⑰

Hamilton

⑤⑥⑦

⑧

Somerset Bridge

Hawkins Island

Front St.

Cruise Ship Dock

Middle Rd.

Spring Benny's Bay

Middle Rd.

Hamilton Harbour

⑱ **⑯**

Middle Rd.

PAGET

⑨

Little Sound

Harbour Rd.

West Whale Bay

Spicelands Riding Centre

Middle Rd.

WARWICK

⑮

SOUTHAMPTON

South Shore Rd.

⑭ Warwick Long Bay

Church Bay

⑩

⑪ **⑫**

⑬

Horseshoe Bay

Gibbs Hill Lighthouse

Sea Gardens

Beaches

Chaplin Bay and Stonehole Bay, **13**

Elbow Beach Hotel, **15**

Horseshoe Bay Beach, **12**

John Smith's Bay, **21**

Fort St. Catherine Beach, **26**

Shelly Bay Beach, **19**

Somerset Long Bay, **4**

Tobacco Bay Beach, **25**

Warwick Long Bay, **14**

Water Sports

Bermuda Waterski Centre, **5**

Blue Water Divers Ltd., **7**

Dive Bermuda, **1**

Fantasea Diving, **18**

Four Winds Fishing Tackle, **17**

Greg Hartley's Under Sea Adventure, **2**

Island Water Skiing, **22**

Mangrove Marina, **3**

Nautilus Diving, **11**

Pitman's Snorkeling, **8**

Pompano Beach Club Watersports Centre, **9**

Robinson's Marina, **6**

Salt Kettle Boat Rentals, **16**

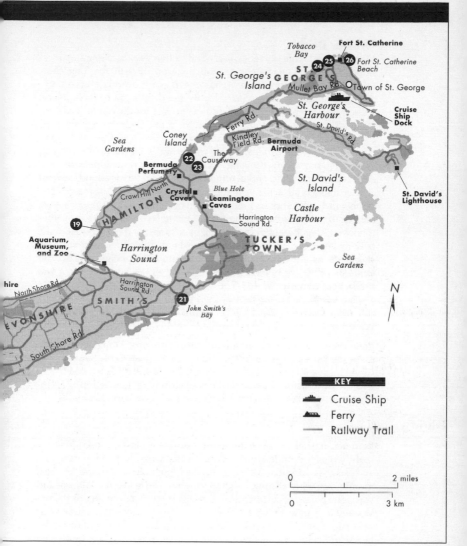

Tobacco Bay

Fort St. Catherine

Fort St. Catherine Beach

24 **25** **26**

St. George's Island

ST. GEORGE'S

Mullet Bay Rd. ○ Town of St. George

St. George's Harbour

St. David's Rd.

Cruise Ship Dock

Ferry Rd.

Coney Island

Kindley Field Rd.

Bermuda Airport

Sea Gardens

The Causeway

Bermuda Perfumery **22** **23**

St. David's Island

St. David's Lighthouse

Crawl Hill North

Crystal Caves

Blue Hole

Leamington Caves

Castle Harbour

HAMILTON

19

Harrington Sound Rd.

Aquarium, Museum, and Zoo

Harrington Sound

TUCKER'S TOWN

Sea Gardens

North Shore Rd.

hire

Harrington Sound Rd.

SMITH'S

21

John Smith's Bay

EVONSHIRE

South Shore Rd.

N

KEY

⛴ Cruise Ship

⛴ Ferry

— Railway Trail

0   2 miles

0   3 km

South Side Scuba
Water Sports, **10**

South Side Scuba (at
Grotto Bay Beach
Hotel), **23**

Tobacco Bay Beach
House, **24**

Salt Kettle Boat Rentals (off Harbour Rd., Salt Kettle Rd., Paget, ☎ 441/236–4863 or 441/234–8165, FAX 441/236–2427).

Charter Boats

More than 20 large power cruisers and sailing vessels, piloted by local skippers, are available for charter. Ranging from 30 to 60 feet long, charter sailboats can carry up to 30 passengers, with overnight accommodations available in some cases. Meals and drinks can be included on request, and a few skippers offer dinner cruises for the romantically inclined. Rates generally range between $375 and $425 for a three-hour cruise, or $650 to $1,000 for a full-day cruise, with additional per-person charges for large groups. Where you go and what you do—exploring, swimming, snorkeling, cruising—is up to you and your skipper. In most cases, cruises travel to and around the islands of Great Sound. Several charter skippers advertise year-round operations, but the off-season (December through February) schedule can be haphazard. Skippers devote periods of the off-season to maintenance and repairs or close altogether if bookings lag. Be sure to book well in advance; in the high season, it's best to book before arriving on the island. Recommended **sailboat charter firms** are Capt. Kirk Ward's **Bermuda's Multihull Sailing Adventures** (☎ 441/234–8149 or 441/234–1434); David Ashton's **Salt Kettle Boat Rentals** (☎ 441/236–4863 or 441/236–3612); Capt. Ed Williams **Starlight Sailing Cruises** (☎ 441/292–1834); Percy Smith's **Perrah Yacht Charters** (☎ 441/295–0060); and Michael Voegeli's **Ocean Wind Sail Charters** (☎ 441/238–0825 or 441/234–9846).

Powerboat charters are available through Capt. Douglas Shirley's **Bermuda Barefoot Cruises** (☎ 441/236–3498); **Salt Kettle Boat Rentals** (☎ 441/236–4863 or 441/236–3612); and **Tam Marina** (☎ 441/236–0127). A full listing of charter-boat operators is included in the "Information and Price Sheet for What To Do" brochure (*see above*).

Diving

Bermuda has all the ingredients necessary for classic scuba diving—reefs, wreckage, underwater caves, a variety of coral and marine life, and clear, warm water. Although diving is possible year-round, the best months are May through October, when the water is calmest and warmest. No prior certification is necessary; novices can learn the basics and dive in water up to 25 feet deep on the same day. Three-hour resort courses ($85–$110), which teach the basics in a pool or on the beach and culminate in a reef or wreck dive, are offered by **South Side Scuba Water Sports** (at the Grotto Bay Beach Hotel, 11 Blue Hole Hill, Hamilton Parish, ☎ 441/293–2915; Marriott's Castle Harbour Resort, Hamilton Parish, ☎ 441/293–2040; and Sonesta Beach Hotel & Spa, Southampton, ☎ 441/238–1833); **Fantasea Diving** (Darrell's Wharf, Harbour Rd., Paget, ☎ 441/236–6339, FAX 441/236–8926); **Nautilus Diving** (Southampton Princess Hotel, off South Rd., Southampton, ☎ 441/238–2332); **Blue Water Divers Ltd.** (Robinson's Marina, Somerset Bridge, Sandys, ☎ 441/234–1034 or 441/234–2922 before 9 PM, FAX 441/234–3561); and **Dive Bermuda** (Dockyard Terrace, Royal Naval Dockyard, Sandys, ☎ 441/234–0225, FAX 441/238–8564). The easiest day trips, offered by South Side Scuba Water Sports and Nautilus Diving Ltd., involve exploring the south-shore reefs that lie inshore. These reefs may be the most dramatic in Bermuda: In places, the ocean-side drop-off exceeds 60 feet, and the coral is so honeycombed with caves, ledges, and holes that exploratory possibilities are infinite. Also infinite are the chances of becoming lost in this coral labyrinth, so it is important to stick with your guide. Despite concerns in recent years about dying coral and fish depletion, most of Bermuda's reefs are still in good health—anyone eager to swim with multicolored schools of fish or the occasional barracuda will not be disappointed. In the interest of preservation, however, the removal of coral or coral objects is illegal.

Prominently displayed in any dive shop in Bermuda is a map of nautical carnage, showing the outlying reef system and wreck sites. The map shows 38 wrecks spanning three centuries, but these are only the larger wrecks that are still in good condition. There are reportedly more than 300 wreck sites in all, many of them well preserved. As a general rule, the more recent the wreck or the more deeply submerged it is, the better its condition. Most of the well-preserved wrecks are to the north and east, and dive depths range between 25 and 80 feet. Several wrecks off the western end of the island are in relatively shallow water—30 feet or less—making them accessible to novice divers and even snorkelers. The major dive operators for wrecks on the western side of the island are **Blue Water Divers Ltd.** (*see above*) and **Dive Bermuda** (*see above*); for wrecks off the east coast, contact **South Side Scuba Water Sports** (*see above*). A one-tank dive costs $40 to $55; for introductory divers, the price range is $85 to $100. Two-tank dives for experienced divers cost $65 to $80. With two tanks, divers can explore two or more wrecks during the same four-hour outing. Rates usually include all equipment—mask, fins, snorkel, scuba apparatus, and wet suit (if necessary). Some operators also offer night dives.

Helmet Diving

A different, less technical type of diving that's popular in Bermuda is "helmet diving," offered between mid-April and mid-November. Although helmet diving cruises last three hours or more, actual underwater time is about 25 minutes. During this time, underwater explorers, wearing helmets that are fed air through hoses leading to the surface, walk along the sandy bottom in about 10 to 12 feet of water, depending on the tide. Underwater videos and portraits are available for an extra charge. A morning or afternoon tour costs about $50 for adults, $40 for children 12 and under, and includes wet suits when the water temperature is less than 80 degrees. Contact **Greg Hartley's Under Sea Adventure** (Watford Bridge, Sandys, ☎ 441/234-2861).

Fishing

Fishing in Bermuda falls into three basic categories: shore or shallow-water fishing, reef fishing, and deep-sea fishing. No license is required, although some restrictions apply, particularly regarding the fish you can keep (for instance, only Bermudians with commercial fishing licenses are permitted to take lobsters) and the prohibition against spear guns. In recent years, some concern has been expressed about the decline in the number of reef and shore fish in Bermudian waters. New government measures to restore fish populations have impacted some commercial fishers adversely, but sportfishing has been largely unaffected.

Reef Fishing

Three major reef bands lie at various distances from the island: The first is anywhere from a half mile to 5 miles offshore; the second, the Challenger Bank, is about 12 miles offshore; the third, the Argus Bank, is located about 30 miles offshore. As a rule, the farther out you go, the larger the fish—and the more expensive the charter. Most charter fishing captains go to the reefs and deep water to the southwest and northwest of the island, where the fishing is better. Catches over the reefs include snapper, amberjack, grouper, and barracuda. Of the most sought-after deep-water fish—marlin, tuna, wahoo, and dolphin—wahoos are the most common and dolphin the least. Trolling is the usual method of deep-water fishing, and charter-boat operators offer various tackle setups, with test-line weights ranging from 20 to 130 pounds. The boats, which range between 31 and 55 feet long, are fitted with a wide array of gear and electronics to track fish, including depth sounders, global positioning systems, loran systems, video fish finders, radar, and computer scanners. All boats must pass annual safety inspections, which are of the standard required by the U.S. Coast Guard. Half-day or full-day charters are offered by most operators, but full-day trips offer the best chance for a big catch because the boat can reach waters that are less frequently fished. Rates are about $600 per boat for a half-day (four hours), and $850 per day (eight hours). Many captains encourage their clients to participate in the catch-and-release program to maintain the abundant supply of fish; however, if the successful fisherman wants to keep the fish, he can. The Bermuda Department of Tourism runs the free **Game Fishing Tournament** between April 1 and November 1; it is open to all anglers. Catches of any of 26 game varieties can be registered with the Bermuda Department of Tourism, and prizes are awarded. Charter bookings can be arranged through two organizations: **Bermuda Sport Fishing Association** ("Creek View House," 8 Tulo La., Pembroke HM 02, ☎ 441/292–6246, FAX 441/292–5535), and the smaller **St. George's Game Fishing Association** (Box 107, St. George's GE BX, ☎ 441/297–4413). In addition, several independent charter boats operate out of Hamilton Harbour as well as harbors in Sandys at the western end of the island. For more information about chartering a fishing boat in Bermuda, obtain a copy of the "Information and Price Sheet for What To Do" brochure from the Bermuda Department of Tourism (*see* Important Contacts A to Z *in* the Gold Guide).

Shore Fishing

The principal catches for shore fishers are pompano, bonefish, and snapper. Excellent sport for saltwater fly-fishing is the wily and strong bonefish, which is found in coves, harbors, and bays—almost anywhere it can find food and shelter from turbulent water. Among the more popular spots for bonefish are **West Whale Bay** and **Spring Benny's Bay,** which feature large expanses of clear, shallow water, protected by reefs close inshore. Good fishing holes are numerous along the south shore, too. Fishing in the waters of the **Great Sound** and **St. George's Harbour** can be rewarding, but enclosed **Harrington Sound** is less promising. Ask at local tackle shops about the latest hot spots and the best baits to use. Rod and reel rentals for shore fishing are available for about $15 to $20 a day ($20–$30 deposit or credit card impression required) from **Dockyard Boat Rentals** (Dockyard Marina, Royal Naval Dockyard, ☎ 441/234–0300, FAX 441/234–0855), **Four Winds Fishing Tackle** (2 Woodlands Rd., Pembroke, ☎ 441/292–7466), **Mangrove Marina** (Cambridge Rd., Somerset, ☎ 441/234–0914), **Salt Kettle Boat Rentals** (off Harbour Rd., Salt Kettle Rd., Paget, ☎ 441/236–4863), and **Windjammer Water Sports** (Dockyard Marina, Royal Naval Dockyard, ☎ 441/234–1343, FAX 234–3241). Rental prices usually include a tackle box and bait. Rental arrangements can also be made through hotel activities directors.

Parasailing

Parasailing concessions operate in the **Great Sound** and **Castle Harbour.** Those who wish to sail through the sky under a parachute should call **Skyrider Bermuda** (Dockyard Marina, Royal Naval Dockyard, ☎ 441/234–3019) or **South Side Scuba Water Sports** (Grotto Bay Beach Hotel & Tennis Club, ☎ 441/293–2915 or Marriott's Castle Harbour Resort, ☎ 441/293–2040). Skyrider uses a double chair so that couples can fly together. The cost is about $45 per person, and the ride lasts approximately 10 minutes.

Snorkeling

The clarity of the water, the stunning array of coral reefs, and the shallow resting places of several wrecks make snorkeling in the waters around Bermuda—both close inshore and offshore—particularly rewarding. Snorkeling is possible year-round, although a wet suit is advisable for anyone planning to spend a long time in the water in winter, when the water temperature can dip into the 60s. During the winter, too, the water tends to be rougher, often restricting snorkeling to the protected areas of Harrington Sound and Castle Harbour. Underwater caves, grottoes, coral formations, and schools of small fish are the highlights of these areas. When Bermudians are asked to name a favorite snorkeling spot, however, **Church Bay** in Southampton is invariably ranked at or near the top of the list. A small cove cut out of the coral cliffs, this picturesque bay is full of nooks and crannies in the coral, and the reefs are relatively close to shore. Snorkelers should exercise caution here, as they should everywhere along the south shore, as the water can be rough. Other popular snorkeling areas close inshore are the beaches of **John Smith's Bay** at the eastern end of the south shore, and **Tobacco Bay** at the eastern end of the north shore. Despite its small size, **West Whale Bay** is also worth a visit.

Having a boat at your disposal can improve your snorkeling experience immeasurably. Otherwise, long swims are necessary to reach some of the best snorkeling sites, while other sites are inaccessible from anything but a boat. Small boats can be rented by the hour, half day, or day (*see* Boat Rentals, *above*). As the number of wrecks attests, navigating around Bermuda's reef-strewn waters is no simple task, especially for inexperienced boaters. If you rent a boat yourself, stick to the protected waters of the sounds, harbors, and bays, and be sure to ask for an ocean navigation chart. (These point out shallow waters, rocks, and hidden reefs.) For trips to the reefs, let someone else do the navigating—a charter-boat skipper (*see* Charter Boats, *above*) or one of the snorkeling-cruise operators (*see* Snorkeling Cruises, *below*). Some of the best reefs for snorkeling, complete with shallow-water wrecks, are to the west. Where the tour guide or skipper goes, however, often depends on the tide, weather, and water conditions. For snorkelers who demand privacy and freedom of movement, a boat charter (complete with captain) is the only answer, but the cost is considerable—$650 a day for a party of 18 people. By comparison, half-day snorkeling on regularly scheduled cruises (*see* Snorkeling Cruises, *below*) generally costs $40–$65, including equipment and instruction.

Snorkeling equipment is available for rental at most major hotels; the **Grotto Bay Beach Hotel & Tennis Club, Sonesta Beach Hotel & Spa,** and **Southampton Princess** have dive operators on site. Rates for mask, flippers, and snorkel are usually $10 a day, with rates decreasing when a rental is longer; deposits or credit card impressions are required. Equipment, including small boats and underwater cameras, can also be rented at several marinas. To rent equipment at the island's western end, go to **Dockyard Boat Rentals** (Dockyard Marina, Royal Naval Dockyard, ☎ 441/234–0300, FAX 441/234–0855), **Mangrove Marina** (Cambridge Rd., Somerset, ☎ 441/234–0914), **Pompano Beach Club Watersports**

Centre (Pompano Beach Club Rd., Southampton, ☎ 441/234–0222), or **Windjammer Water Sports** (Dockyard Marina, Royal Naval Dockyard, ☎ 441/234–1343, FAX 441/234–3241), all of which also rent small boats. In the central part of the island, boats and gear can be rented at **Salt Kettle Boat Rentals** (off Harbour Rd., Salt Kettle Rd., Paget, ☎ 441/236–4863 or 441/236–3612, FAX 441/236–2427). At the eastern end of the island, contact **Tobacco Bay Beach House** (Tobacco Bay, Naval Tanks Hill, St. George's, ☎ 441/297–2756). **Horseshoe Bay Beach** (☎ 441/238–2651) rents equipment, too.

Snorkeling Cruises

Snorkeling cruises, which are offered from April to November, may be too touristy for many visitors. Some boats carry up to 40 passengers to snorkel, and focus mostly on their music and bars (complimentary beverages are usually served on the return trip from the reefs). The smaller boats, which limit capacity to 10 to 16 passengers, offer more personal attention and focus more on touring and visiting beautiful snorkeling areas. To make sure you choose a boat that's right for you, ask for all the details before booking. Many of the boats offer private charters to groups; these can be arranged easily. Half-day snorkeling tours cost between $40 and $65. Two of the best half-day trips (or longer for special charters) are offered by **Hayward's Snorkeling & Glass Bottom Boat Cruises** (leaves from dock adjacent to Hamilton Ferry Terminal, ☎ 441/292–8652, or after hours ☎ 441/236–9894, FAX 441/236–2608), and **Pitman's Snorkeling** (Robinson's Marina, Somerset Bridge, ☎ 441/234–0700); both share interesting historical and ecological information about the island in addition to visiting the pristine offshore snorkeling areas, often at shipwreck sites. Personal attention is given by Captain Douglas Shirley, who operates **Bermuda Barefoot Cruises** (Box DV 525, Devonshire, ☎ 441/236–3498). His 32-foot *Minnow* leaves Darrell's Wharf in Warwick, and tours the inshore waterways before ducking into a favorite local snorkeling site where no other tour boats go—in shallow waters off Somerset, where less strong swimmers can opt to walk around. Captain Shirley also arranges private charters to the South Shore reef and other destinations. Captain Kirk Ward's **Bermuda's Multihull Sailing Adventures** (☎ 441/234–8149 or 441/234–1434) is the only operation offering regularly scheduled sailing/snorkeling trips to the outer reefs aboard a 38-foot trimaran and a 48-foot catamaran. **Bermuda Water Tours Ltd.** (leaves from dock adjacent to Hamilton Ferry Terminal, ☎ 441/295–3727) operates two boats out of Hamilton. Half-day cruises are also available from **Salt Kettle Boat Rentals** (off Harbour Rd., Salt Kettle Rd., Paget, ☎ 441/236–4863 or 441/236–3612, FAX 441/236–2427); **Jessie James Cruises** (48 Par-la-Ville Rd., Suite 366, Hamilton HM 11, ☎ 441/236–4804, FAX 441/236–9208); and **Sand Dollar Cruises** (Box HM 534, Hamilton HM CX, ☎ 441/292–6104 or 441/234–8218). Private and group charters are arranged by **Paradox Charters** (Box HM 640, Hamilton HM CX, ☎ 441/234–7471, FAX 441/292–0619).

Waterskiing

Winds on the island vary considerably, making it difficult to predict when the water will be calmest, although early morning and evening breezes are often the lightest. The best time for this sport is May through October. Head for the Warwick, Southampton, or Somerset shoreline of the **Great Sound** when the winds are coming from the south or southwest. In the event of northerly winds, however, it's best to stick to the protected areas in **Hamilton Harbour** and **Harrington Sound. Cas-**

tle Harbour and Ferry Reach are also good areas to waterski, depending on the wind strength and direction. If possible, make friends with a Bermudian who has a boat; otherwise, contact **Island Water Skiing/South Side Scuba** (Grotto Bay Beach Hotel & Tennis Club, 11 Blue Hole Hill, Hamilton Parish, ☎ 441/293–2915), **Bermuda Waterski Centre** (Robinson's Marina, Somerset Bridge, Sandys, ☎ 441/234–3354 or 441/234–1964), or **Wake Up Ski School** (Princess Hotel, Pembroke, ☎ 441–234–8924). Rates fluctuate with fuel costs, but average $55 per half hour, $100 per hour, lessons included.

Windsurfing

The **Great Sound, Elbow Beach, Somerset Long Bay, Shelly Bay,** and **Harrington Sound** are the favorite haunts of board sailors in Bermuda. For novices, the often calm waters of Mangrove Bay and Castle Harbour are probably the best choice. The Great Sound, with its many islands, coves, and harbors, is good for board sailors of all abilities, although the quirky winds that sometimes bedevil yachts in the sound obviously affect sailboards as well. When the northerly storm winds blow, the open bays on the north shore are popular among wave-riding enthusiasts. Only experts should consider windsurfing on the south shore. Wind, waves, and reefs make the south shore so dangerous that rental companies are prohibited from renting boards there. Experienced board sailors who want to meet local windsurfers can call **Hubert Watlington** at **Sail On** (Old Cellar, off Front St., Hamilton, ☎ 441/295–0808), a former Olympic competitor who is an integral part of this sailing circuit.

Even the most avid board sailors should rent sailboards rather than bringing their own. Transporting a board around the island is a logistical nightmare: There are no rental cars on Bermuda, and few taxi drivers are willing to see their car roofs scoured with scratches in the interest of sport. Rental rates range between $15 and $25 an hour, and between $60 and $90 a day; special long-term rates can be negotiated with some shops. Contact **South Side Scuba Water Sports** (Grotto Bay Beach Hotel & Tennis Club, 11 Blue Hole Hill, Hamilton Parish, ☎ 441/293–2915; or Marriott's Castle Harbour, Paynter's Rd., Hamilton Parish, ☎ 441/293–2040), **Mangrove Marina** (Cambridge Rd., Sandys, ☎ 441/234–0914 or 441/234–0331, ext. 295), or **Pompano Beach Club Watersports Centre** (36 Pompano Rd., Pompano Beach Club, Southampton, ☎ 441/234–0222). Beginners can get lessons from **South Side Scuba Water Sports** for $30 an hour; **Mangrove Marina** offers novices 90 minutes of instruction for $40. Land simulators and equipment are included in the lessons.

BEACHES

The beaches of Bermuda fall into two categories: those on the south shore and those on the north shore. The water on the south-shore beaches tends to be a little rougher when the winds are from the south and southwest. It is along this coast, too, that waves continuously roll in and break on the sandy shoreline even when the breezes are gentle. Many visitors join the locals in the popular pastime of body surfing. Most people would agree that the typical south-shore beach is more scenic than those on the north side—fine pinkish sand, coral bluffs topped with summer flowers, gentle, pale-blue surf moving past the barrier reefs offshore. Most Bermudian beaches are relatively small compared with ocean beaches in the United States, ranging from about 15 yards to a half-mile or so in length. Bermuda's beaches are set in myriad picturesque surroundings—surrounded by dramatic cliff and rock formations; shaded with coconut palms; or backed by dunes that slope gently toward the shimmering turquoise and purples of the Atlantic Ocean. In winter, when the weather is more severe, beaches may erode—even disappear—only to be replenished as the wind subsides in the spring.

The Public Transportation Board provides a free **"Bermuda's Guide to Beaches and Transportation,"** available in all visitors centers and most hotels. A combination bus/ferry schedule and map, the guide shows locations of beaches and how to reach them. Information about the submarine *Enterprise,* taxis, and moped rentals is also included.

Few Bermudian beaches offer shade, but some have palm trees and thatched shelters; the sun can be intense, however, so bring hats and plenty of sunscreen. Umbrellas can be rented at some beaches. Below are reviews of the major beaches on the island that are open to the public. (For information about the many private beaches owned by hotels on the south shore, *see* Chapter 8, Lodging.)

South Shore Beaches

Chaplin and Stonehole Bays. In a secluded area east of Horseshoe Bay (*see below*), these tiny adjacent beaches almost disappear at high tide. Stonehole's most distinguishing feature is a high coral wall that reaches across the beach to the water, perforated by a 10-foot high, arrowhead-shaped hole. Like Horseshoe Bay, the beach fronts South Shore Park. *Off South Rd., Southampton. Bus 7 from Hamilton.*

Elbow Beach Hotel. The $3.50 fee for nonguests is a measure to keep this portion of the beach relatively uncrowded, even on weekends. (Nonguests must call first.) One of the best places to relax on the island, guests can bask in the sun's rays or seek refuge from them under an umbrella and chaise, which can be rented. Swimming and body surfing are just a few steps away from the chaises. Cafe Lido sells refreshments; toilet facilities are available. A free public beach lies adjacent, but it can become very crowded and noisy on summer weekends. *Off South Rd., Paget,* ☎ *441/236–3535. Bus 2 or 7 from Hamilton.*

Horseshoe Bay Beach. Horseshoe Bay has everything you would expect of a Bermudian beach: A ⅓-mile crescent of pink sand, clear water, a vibrant social scene, and an uncluttered backdrop provided by South Shore Park. This is one of the island's most popular beaches, a place where adults arrive with coolers and teenagers come to check out the action. The presence of lifeguards during summer months—the only other beach with lifeguards is John Smith's Bay (*see below*)—and a variety of rentals, a snack bar, and toilet facilities add to the beach's appeal; in fact, it can become uncomfortably crowded here on summer weekends. Parents should keep a close eye on their children in the water: The undertow can be strong, especially when the wind is blowing. *Off South Rd., Southampton,* ☎ *441/238–2651. Bus 7 from Hamilton.*

John Smith's Bay. Backed by houses and South Road, this beach consists of a pretty strand of long, flat, open sand. The presence of a lifeguard in summer makes this an ideal place to bring children. As the only public beach in Smith's Parish, John Smith's Bay is also popular among locals. *South Rd., Smith's. Bus 1 from Hamilton.*

Warwick Long Bay. Very different from cove-like Chaplin, Stonehole, and Horseshoe bays, this beach features the longest stretch of sand— about ½ mile—of any beach on the island. Its backdrop is a combination of very steep cliffs and low grass-and-brush-covered hills that slope away from the beach. The beach is exposed to some strong southerly winds, but the waves are rarely big because the inner reef is close inshore.

An interesting feature of the bay is a 20-foot coral outcrop, less than 200 feet offshore, that looks like a sculpted boulder balancing on the surface of the water. The frequent emptiness of South Shore Park, which surrounds the bay, heightens the beach's appealing atmosphere of isolation and serenity. *Off South Rd., Southampton. Bus 7 from Hamilton.*

North Shore Beaches

Shelly Bay Beach. As at Somerset Long Bay (*see below*), the water at this beach near Flatts is well protected from strong southerly winds. In addition, a sandy bottom and shallow water make this a good place to take small children. Shelly Bay also boasts shade trees—something of a rarity at Bermudian beaches. Drawbacks include a children's playground behind the beach, which attracts hoards of youngsters on weekends and during school holidays, and the traffic noise from busy North Shore Road, which runs nearby. *North Shore Rd., Hamilton Parish. Bus 10 or 11 from Hamilton.*

Somerset Long Bay. Popular with Somerset locals, this beach sits on the quiet northwestern end of the island—far from the airport, the bustle of Hamilton, and major tourism hubs. In keeping with the area's rural atmosphere, the beach is low-key and unprepossessing. Undeveloped parkland shields the beach from light traffic on Cambridge Road. The main beach is crescent-shaped and long by Bermudian standards—nearly ¼ mile from end to end. In contrast to the great coral outcroppings common on the south shore, grass and brush make up the main backdrop here. Although exposed to northerly storm winds, the bay water is normally calm and shallow—ideal for children. However, the bottom is rocky and uneven. *Cambridge Rd., Sandys. Bus 7 or 8 from Hamilton.*

Tobacco Bay Beach. The most popular beach near St. George's, this small north-shore beach is huddled in a coral cove similar to those found along the south shore. Tobacco Bay has a beach house with a snack bar, equipment rentals, toilets, showers, and changing rooms. From the bus stop in the town of St. George, the beach is a hike, so be prepared and wear comfortable walking shoes. *Coot Pond Rd., St. George's,* ☎ *441/297-2756. Bus 1, 3, 10, or 11 from Hamilton.*

6 Sports and Fitness

By Peter Oliver

WHEN SAILOR PETER BROMBY won the World Championships of the International One Design Class in 1991, 1992, and 1993, and the Star Class of the Miami Olympic Regatta in 1995, Bermuda welcomed him home each time with a degree of adoration normally reserved for martyrs and deities. Bermudians champion their sports heroes, but—more significantly—they champion sports, both as participants and spectators. Every taxi driver seems to be a single-handicap golfer; there are more tennis courts per square mile than just about anywhere—72, excluding the private courts at people's homes; and runners, cyclists, and horseback riders fill the roads and countryside in the mornings, especially on weekends. Bermuda might not have the world's fittest population but, at sunrise on Saturday, it certainly seems that way.

Washed by the Atlantic, Bermuda is probably best known as a beach destination, offering a host of water sports and activities (*see* Chapter 5, Water Sports and Beaches). However, the island is also a golfing center—eight courses are jammed onto this tiny island—and the popularity of tennis, squash, and riding are a further testament to Bermudians' love affair with land-based sports. Britain's oldest colony tends, not surprisingly, to favor pursuits with a British flavor. In addition to several golf tournaments, cricket, soccer, rugby, field hockey, equestrian events, and even badminton are popular spectator sports in season. Visitors can enter some of these events, primarily races and golf and tennis tournaments, although it is usually necessary to qualify.

Perhaps more than any other single factor, climate is what makes Bermuda such a sporting hive. In winter (December through February), temperatures hover between 50°F and 70°F, often climbing higher. While this might prove too chilly for many water sports, the cool air is ideal for activities on land. And although it is not immune to the occasional hurricane or storm, Bermuda does not have an extended storm season. Island residents like to boast, with some justification, that if you enjoy sports, you'll be happy here 365 days of the year.

Most visitors can arrange sporting activities (tee times, for example) through their hotel's or ship's activities director, although arrangements can be made independently as well. For this purpose, the Bermuda Department of Tourism issues two excellent publications, the "Golf Guide" and the brochure "What To Do in Bermuda." Available from the Department of Tourism (*see* Important Contacts A to Z *in* the Gold Guide), the guides offer descriptions of sports facilities and golf courses on the island, including addresses, phone numbers, and prices.

PARTICIPANT SPORTS

Bicycling

In Bermuda, bicycles are called pedal or push bikes, to distinguish them from the more common motorized two-wheelers. Many of the cycle liveries around the island (*see* Important Contacts A to Z *in* the Gold Guide) also rent three-speed and 10-speed pedal bikes, but they can be difficult to find—it makes sense to reserve a bike a few days in advance. Rental rates are $10 to $15 a day.

Bermuda is not the easiest place in the world to bicycle. Riders should be prepared for some tough climbs—the roads running north–south across the island are particularly steep and winding—and the wind can

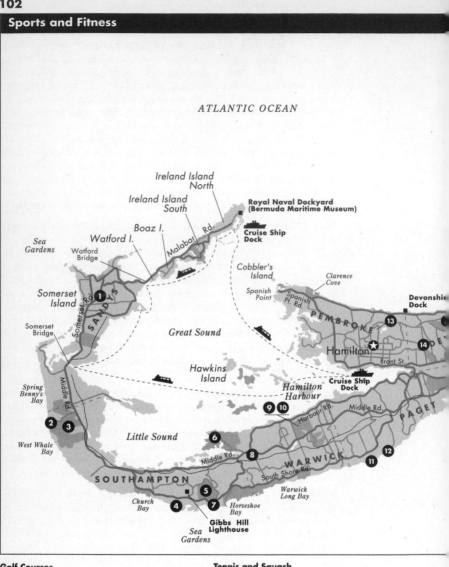

ATLANTIC OCEAN

Ireland Island
North

Ireland Island
South

Boaz I.

Malabar Rd.

**Royal Naval Dockyard
(Bermuda Maritime Museum)**

Sea
Gardens

Watford I.

Watford
Bridge

**Cruise Ship
Dock**

Cobbler's
Island

Clarence
Cove

Spanish
Point

Spanish
Pt. Rd.

**Devonshi
Dock**

Somerset
Island

Somerset
Rd.

1

SANDYS

Great Sound

PEMBROKE

13

14

Somerset
Bridge

Hamilton

Front St.

Spring
Benny's
Bay

Middle Rd.

*Hawkins
Island*

**Cruise Ship
Dock**

*Hamilton
Harbour*

PAGET

2 **3**

West Whale
Bay

Little Sound

6

9 **10**

Harbour Rd.

Middle Rd.

8

Middle Rd.

WARWICK

12

11

SOUTHAMPTON

South Shore Rd.

Warwick
Long Bay

Church
Bay

5

4 **7**

Horseshoe
Bay

**Gibbs Hill
Lighthouse**

Sea
Gardens

Golf Courses

Belmont Hotel Golf
& Country Club, **9**

Castle Harbour Golf
Club, **20**

Mid Ocean Club, **21**

Ocean View Golf &
Country Club, **15**

Port Royal Golf &
Country Club, **3**

Princess Golf Club, **5**

Riddell's Bay Golf &
Country Club, **6**

St. George's Golf
Club, **23**

Tennis and Squash Courts

Belmont Hotel, Golf
& Country Club, **10**

Bermuda Squash
Club, **18**

Coral Beach & Tennis
Club, **11**

Elbow Beach
Hotel, **12**

Government Tennis
Stadium, **13**

Marriott's Castle
Harbour Resort, **19**

Port Royal Course, **3**

Sonesta Beach Hotel
& Spa, **4**

Southampton
Princess Hotel, **7**

KEY

⛴ Cruise Ship

⛴ Ferry

— Railway Trail

| 0 | | 2 miles |
| 0 | | 3 km |

Horseback Riding

Bermuda Equestrian
Federation, **16**

Lee Bow Riding
Center, **14**

Spicelands Riding
Centre, **8**

Spectator Sports

National Sports
Club, **17**

St. George's Cricket
Club, **22**

Somerset Cricket
Club, **1**

sap even the strongest rider's strength, especially along South Road in Warwick and Southampton parishes. Bermudian roads are narrow, with heavy traffic (especially near Hamilton during rush hours) and no shoulder. Most motorists are courteous to cyclists—arbitrary horn-honking is against the law—and stay within 10 mph of the 20-mph speed limit. Despite the traffic, bicycle racing is a popular sport in Bermuda, and club groups can regularly be seen whirring around the island on evening and weekend training rides. Bermudian roads are no place for novice riders, however, and parents should think twice before allowing preteen children to hop on a bike.

Bermuda's premier cycling route, the Railway Trail (*see* Chapter 3, Exploring Bermuda), requires almost no road riding. Restricted to pedestrian and bicycle traffic, the trail is mostly paved, and it runs intermittently for almost the length of the island along the route of the old Bermuda Railway. The Bermuda Department of Tourism publishes "The Bermuda Railway Trail Guide," a free pamphlet that features a series of short exploring tours along the trail. The pamphlet is available at all Visitors Service Bureaus and the Department of Tourism.

Tribe roads—small side roads that are often unpaved—are also good for exploring, but don't be surprised if many of these roads, which date back to the earliest settlement of Bermuda, are dead ends. Well-paved South Road has relatively few climbs and some excellent ocean views, although it is one of Bermuda's most heavily traveled thoroughfares. The "Bermuda Handy Reference Map," also available at Visitors Service Bureaus, is quite good, but even better is the *Bermuda Islands Guide,* a paperback available at the Bermuda Book Store in Hamilton. It is a detailed atlas showing every thoroughfare, lane, and alleyway.

Golf

Bermuda is justifiably renowned for its golf courses. The scenery is spectacular, and the courses are challenging. However, visitors should not expect the manicured, soft fairways and greens typical of U.S. courses. Just as courses in Scotland have their own identity, the same is true of courses on this Atlantic isle. Bermudian golf courses are distinguished by plenty of sand, firm fairways and greens, relatively short par-fours, and wind—*especially* wind. Elsewhere, golf courses are usually designed with the wind in mind—long downwind holes and short upwind holes. Not so on Bermuda's eight courses, where the wind is anything but consistent or predictable. Quirky air currents make a Bermudian course play differently every day. On some days, a 350-yard par-four may be drivable; on other days, a solidly hit drive may fall short on a 160-yard par-three. Regardless, the wind puts a premium on being able to hit the ball straight; any slice or hook becomes disastrously exaggerated in the wind.

The island's water supply is limited, so irrigation is minimal and the ground around the green tends to be quite hard. For success in the short game, therefore, players need to run the ball to the hole, rather than relying on high, arcing chips, which require plenty of club face under the ball. Typically, Bermudian greens are elevated and protected by sand traps rather than thick grass. Most traps are filled with the soft limestone sand and pulverized pieces of a pink shells that grow on the offshore reefs. Such fine sand may be unfamiliar to visiting golfers, but it tends to be consistent from trap to trap and from course to course.

Greens are usually seeded with Bermuda grass and then over seeded with rye. Golfers putt on Bermuda grass during the warmer months

(March through November) and on rye when the weather cools and the Bermuda grass dies out. Greens are reseeded anytime from late September to early November, according to the weather. (Castle Harbour Golf Club's greens are reseeded in early January.) Some courses use temporary greens for two to four weeks; others keep the greens in play while reseeding and resurfacing. Greens in Bermuda tend to be much slower than the bent-grass greens prevalent in the United States, and putts tend to break less.

Another characteristic of Bermudian courses is the preponderance of rolling, hummocky fairways, making a flat lie the exception rather than the rule. Little effort has been made to flatten the fairways, because much of the ground beneath the island's surface is honeycombed with caves; bulldozer and backhoe operators are understandably uneasy about doing extensive landscaping.

How should golfers prepare for a Bermuda trip? In anticipation of the wind, practice hitting lower shots—punching the ball or playing it farther back in the stance may be helpful. Working on chip-and-run shots (a seven iron is ideal for this), especially from close-cropped lies, should also help. You can save yourself some strokes, too, by practicing iron shots from awkward, hillside lies. On the greens, a long, firm putting stroke may save you from the bugaboo that haunts many first-time visitors: gently stroked putts dying short of the hole or drifting off-line with the grain of the Bermuda grass. As Allan Wilkinson, the former professional at the Princess Golf Club, has said, "In Bermuda, ya gotta slam 'em into the back of the cup."

Tournaments for pros, seniors, juniors, women, and mixed groups fill Bermuda's golfing schedule from February through December. Some competitions, such as the Bermuda Open, in early October, are high-level competitions with prize money for professional participants. Handicap limits are usually imposed for the more serious tournaments, and entry fees range between $100 and $150 (not all events are open to non-Bermudian players). A schedule with entry forms is available from the **Bermuda Golf Association** (Box HM 433, Hamilton HM BX, ☎ 441/238–1367, FAX 441/238–0983). A low-key event for golfers of all abilities is the **Bermuda Amateur Golf Festival,** a two-week affair in late February that gives players a chance to compete on several of the island's courses. Greens fees are reduced for festival participants, and several hotels offer reduced package rates. For more information, contact the Bermuda Amateur Golf Festival (Robustelli Sports Marketing, 460 Summer St., Stamford, CT 06901, ☎ 203/352-0500 or Bermuda Department of Tourism, *see above*). Another easy-going tournament in mid-February is the **Valentine's Mixed Foursomes Invitational,** for which tournament/hotel packages are also available. For information or entry forms, contact the Tournament Chairman (Bermuda Golf Company, Box GE 304, St. George's GE BX, ☎ 441/297–8067).

Be sure to pack proper golf attire—long pants (no jeans) or Bermuda shorts (no cutoffs) are required for men. Lessons, available at all courses, usually cost $35–$60 for a half hour, and club rentals range between $15 and $40. Caddies are a thing of the past, except at the Mid Ocean Club. Below are reviews and ratings of all eight of Bermuda's golf courses. The ratings, devised and administered by the United States Golf Association (USGA), "represent the expected score of an expert amateur golfer based upon yardage and other obstacles." For example, a par-72 course with a rating of 68 means that a scratch golfer would hit a four-under-par round—and ordinary hackers would probably score a little better, too. Ratings below are given for the blue tees (championship), white tees (men's), and red tees (women's).

Belmont Hotel, Golf & Country Club
Length: 5,777 yards from the blue tees

Par: 70

Rating: blue tees, 68.9; white tees, 67.9; red tees, 69.1

Of Bermuda's eight courses, the layout of the public Belmont Hotel, Golf & Country Club is perhaps the most maddening. The first two holes, straight par-fours, are a false preview of what lies ahead—a series of doglegs and blind tee shots. Playing with an experienced Belmont player who knows where to hit drives on such blind holes as the 6th, 11th, and 16th, and how best to play a dogleg hole such as the eighth, can help a newcomer trim six or more shots from a round. Despite the layout, Belmont remains one of Bermuda's easier courses, and it is ideal for inexperienced players. Belmont is an inland course and has few ocean panoramas. Instead, most holes overlook pastel houses with white roofs, a few of which have taken a beating from errant golf balls. A new irrigation system has improved the course dramatically in recent years. Fairway grass tends to be denser—and the clay soil moister—than the grass on the close-cropped, sandy fairways typical of other Bermudian courses. The rough, too, is generally deeper, snaring any wild tee shots. For this reason, and because Belmont is a short course (only one par-four is more than 400 yards), it makes sense to use a three or five wood, or even a low iron, from the tee. Belmont's chief drawback, especially on the weekend, is slow play—weekend rounds of five hours or more are common.

Highlight hole: The par-five 11th features a severe dogleg left, with a blind tee shot—Belmont in a nutshell. A short but straight drive is the key; trying and failing to cut the corner can be disastrous. The approach to the green is straight, although a row of wispy trees on the left awaits hooked or pulled shots. *Belmont Rd., Warwick,* ☎ *441/236–6400,* FAX *441/236–6867. Greens fees: $75 for the public (includes mandatory cart); free to hotel guests.*

Castle Harbour Golf Club
Length: 6,440 yards from the blue tees

Par: 71

Rating: blue tees, 71.3; white tees, 69.2; red tees, 69.2

The only course on Bermuda that requires players to use golf carts is the Castle Harbour Golf Club—with good reason. The only flat areas on the course, it seems, are the tees. The first tee, a crow's-nest perch by the clubhouse, offers an indication of things to come: Looking out over the fairway, with the harbor beyond, is like peering onto a golf course from a 20th-story window. Wind can make this course play especially long. Although most par-fours feature good landing areas despite all the hills, holes such as the second, 16th, and 17th require players to drive over fairway rises. A wind-shortened drive can mean a long, blind shot to the green. Carrying the rise, on the other hand, can mean a relatively easy short shot, especially on the second and 17th holes. Elevated greens are a common feature of Castle Harbour. The most extreme example is the 190-yard, par-three 13th, with the green perched atop a steep, 100-foot embankment. Balls short of the green inevitably roll back down into a grassy basin between the tee and the green. On the other hand, sand traps at Castle Harbour are mercifully few and far between by Bermudian standards; 10 holes feature two or fewer bunkers around the green.

Castle Harbour is one of Bermuda's most expensive courses; however, the money is clearly reinvested in the course. Greens are well maintained—firm, consistently cropped, and generally faster than most other Bermudian greens. The course also rewards golfers with several spectacular views, such as the hilltop panorama from the 14th tee, where blue water stretches into the distance on three sides.

Highlight hole: The 235-yard, par-three 18th is the most difficult finishing hole on Bermuda, especially when the wind is blowing from the northwest. On the right are jagged coral cliffs rising from the harbor; on the left are a pair of traps. When the course was revamped a few years ago, a small, flower-lined pond was added on the front right of the green, making this hard hole even harder. *Marriott's Castle Harbour Resort, Paynters Rd., Tucker's Town,* ☎ *441/293–2040, ext. 6869;* FAX *441/293–1051. Greens fees: $90 Mar. 1–Nov. 1, $57 for rest of year ($50 after 4:30 PM Apr. 3–Oct. 30), plus mandatory $20 (per person) cart rental. Shoe rentals.*

Mid Ocean Club
Length: 6,512 yards from the blue tees

Par: 71

Rating: blue tees, 72; white tees, 70; red tees, 73.6

It isn't Bermuda's oldest course—that honor belongs to Riddell's Bay—and other Bermudian courses are equally difficult, but the elite Mid Ocean Club is generally regarded as one of the top 50 courses in the world. Quite simply, this course has charisma, embodying everything that is golf in Bermuda—tees on coral cliffs above the ocean, rolling fairways lined with palms and spice trees, doglegs around water, and windswept views. It is rich in history, too. At the dogleg fifth hole, for example, Babe Ruth is said to have splashed a dozen balls in Mangrove Lake in a futile effort to drive the green. The course rewards long, straight tee shots and deft play around the green, while penalizing—often cruelly—anything less. The fifth and ninth holes, for example, require that tee shots (from the blue tees) carry 180 yards or more over water. And while length is not a factor on two fairly short par-fives, the 471-yard second and the 487-yard 11th, accuracy is. Tight doglegs ensure that any wayward tee shot ends up in trees, shrubbery, or rough. However, the course may have mellowed with age: having lost hundreds of trees to a tornado in 1986, and again to Hurricane Emily in 1987, the tight, tree-lined fairways have become more open, and the rough is less threatening.

Highlight hole: The 433-yard fifth is a par-four dogleg around Mangrove Lake. The elevated tee overlooks a hillside of flowering shrubbery and the lake, making the fairway seem impossibly far away. Big hitters can take a shortcut over the lake (although the green is unreachable, as the Babe's heroic but unsuccessful efforts attest), but anyone who hits the fairway has scored a major victory. To the left of the green, a steep embankment leads into a bunker that is among the hardest in Bermuda from which to recover. *Mid Ocean Dr., off South Shore Rd., Tucker's Town,* ☎ *441/293–0330,* FAX *441/293–8837. Greens fees: $100 ($50 when accompanied by a member). Nonmembers must be introduced by a club member; nonmember starting times available only on Mon., Wed., and Fri., except public holidays. Caddies, $25 per bag (tip not included). Cart rental, $35.*

Ocean View Golf & Country Club
Length: 3,000 yards (nine holes) from the blue tees

Par: men, 35; women, 37

Rating: none

Extensive work on the Ocean View Golf & Country Club was completed in 1994, with some $3 million having been spent by the Bermuda Government to improve the course after many years. Besides refurbishing the course—which has magnificent views of the island's North Shore—a new clubhouse with a good restaurant and bar, locker rooms, and a new driving range were built. Founded in the 1940s, the nine-hole course gradually fell into neglect until badly needed improvements brought it up to the standards of the island's other courses. Ocean View's popularity has increased since the improvements, and it is busy throughout the week and on the weekends; plan ahead for tee times. Several holes challenge and intrigue: The first is a tough par-five that is a tight driving hole, with a 40-foot coral wall on one side and views of the North Shore on the other. The sixth is a difficult par-four because of its elevated green; the ninth is a par-three with water guarding the front of the green, so shooting with accuracy is the key.

Highlight hole: The green on the 187-yard, par-three ninth hole is cut out of a coral hillside that is beautifully landscaped with attractive plants. It is a demanding tee shot, and club selection can be tricky, particularly when strong winds are blowing from north or west. *Off North Shore Rd., Devonshire,* ☎ *441/295–9093,* 🖷 *441/295–9097. Greens fees: $28 for 9 or 18 holes ($20 when playing with a member; $12 after 4, Nov. 1– Mar. 31; $14 after 4, Apr. 1–Oct. 31). Cart rental, $15 for 9 holes, $30 for 18 holes; hand cart, $5.*

Port Royal Golf Course
Length: 6,565 yards from the blue tees

Par: men, 71; women, 72

Rating: blue tees, 72; white tees, 69.7; red tees, 72.5

Such golfing luminaries as Jack Nicklaus rank the Port Royal Golf Course among the world's best public courses. A favorite with Bermudians as well, the course is well laid out, and the greens fees are modest. By Bermudian standards, Port Royal is also relatively flat. Although there are some hills, on the back nine in particular, the course has few of the blind shots and hillside lies that are prevalent elsewhere. Those holes that do have gradients tend to run either directly uphill or downhill. In other respects, however, Port Royal is classically Bermudian, with close-cropped fairways, numerous elevated tees and greens, and holes raked by the wind, especially the eighth and the 16th. The 16th hole, one of Bermuda's most famous, is frequently pictured in magazines. The green sits on a treeless promontory overlooking the blue waters and pink-white sands of Whale Bay, a popular boating and fishing area. When the wind is blowing hard on shore, as it frequently does, a driver may be necessary to reach the green, which is 163 yards away. One complaint often raised about Port Royal is the condition of the course, which can become chewed up by heavy usage—more than 55,000 rounds a year.

Highlight hole: Like the much-photographed 16th hole, the 387-yard, par-four 15th skirts the cliffs along Whale Bay. Changes to the course were made in 1995, making the par-three holes eight and 16 longer; hole 11 now doglegs to the right and has a new green; number 13 plays a light dogleg to the left, with mounds and bunkers down the left-hand side. In addition to the ocean view, the remains of Whale Bay Battery, a 19th-century fortification, lie between the fairway and the bay. Only golf balls hooked wildly from the tee have any chance of a direct hit on the fort. The wind can be brutal on this hole. *Off Middle Rd., Southampton,* ☎ *441/234–0974,* ℻ *441/234–3562; golf time can be reserved four days in advance through an automated system,* ☎ *441/ 295-6500. Greens fees: $55; discount rates after 4 PM; 5-day Golf Package weekdays only, $220, greens fees only. Sun. rate, $27. Cart rental, $30; hand cart, $8. Club rental, $20. Shoe rental, $10.*

Princess Golf Club
Length: 2,684 yards from the blue tees

Par: 54

Rating: none

The Princess Golf Club unfolds on the hillside beneath the Southampton Princess. The hotel has managed to sculpt a neat little par-three course from the steep terrain, and players who opt to walk around will find their mountaineering skills and stamina severely tested. The vertical drop on the first two holes alone is at least 200 feet, and the rise on the fourth hole makes 178 yards play like 220. Kept in excellent shape by an extensive irrigation system, the course is a good warm-up for Bermuda's full-length courses, offering a legitimate test of wind and bunker play with a minimum of obstructions and hazards. Ocean views are a constant feature of the front nine, although the looming presence of the hotel does detract from the scenery.

Highlight hole: The green of the 174-yard 16th hole sits in a cup ringed by pink oleander bushes. The Gibbs Hill Lighthouse, less than a mile away, dominates the backdrop. *Southampton Princess, South Rd.,* ☎ *441/238–0446,* ℻ *441/238–8245. Greens fees: $36 ($32 for hotel guests). Carts (mandatory), $30 ($28 for hotel guests). Shoe rentals $6.*

Riddell's Bay Golf and Country Club
Length: 5,588 yards from the blue tees

Par: men, 69; women, 71

Rating: blue tees, 66.9; white tees, 66.1; red tees, 70.6

Built in 1922, the Riddell's Bay Golf and Country Club is Bermuda's oldest course. In design, however, it more nearly approximates a Florida course—relatively flat, with wide, palm-lined fairways. You don't need to be a power hitter to score well here, although the first four holes, including a 427-yard uphill par-four and a 244-yard par-three, might suggest otherwise. The par-fours are mostly in the 360-yard range, and the fairways are generously flat and open. Despite the course's position on a narrow peninsula between Riddell's Bay and the Great Sound, water comes into play only on holes eight through 11. With the twin threats of wind and water, these are the most typically Bermudian holes on the course, and accuracy off the tee is important. This is especially true of the par-four eighth, a 360-yard right dogleg around the water. With a tail wind, big hitters might try for the green, but playing around the dogleg on this relatively short hole is the more prudent choice. As at the Belmont course, a few tees are fronted with stone walls—an old-fashioned touch that harks back to the old courses of Great Britain. Like Mid Ocean, Riddell's is a private club that is open to the public only at certain times, but the clubby atmosphere is much less pronounced here.

Highlight hole: The tees on the 340-yard, par-four 10th are set on a grass-topped quay on the harbor's edge. The fairway narrows severely after about 200 yards, and a drive hit down the right-hand side leaves a player no chance to reach the green in two. Two ponds guard the left side of a sloped and elevated green. The hole is rated only the sixth most difficult on the course, but the need for pinpoint accuracy probably makes it the hardest to par. *Riddell's Bay Rd., Warwick,* ☎ *441/ 238–1060,* FAX *441/238–8785. Greens fees: $48, weekdays; $60, Sat., Sun. ($24, weekdays; $30, Sat., Sun., holidays when accompanied by a member). Cart rental, $35 (two people); hand cart, $5.*

St. George's Golf Club

Length: 4,043 yards from the blue tees

Par: 63

Rating: blue tees, 62.8; white tees, 61.4; red tees, 62.8

Built in 1985, St. George's Golf Club dominates a secluded headland at the northeastern end of the island. The 4,043-yard course is short, but it makes up for its lack of length with sharp teeth. No course in Bermuda is more exposed to wind, and no course has smaller greens— some are no more than 25 feet across. To make matters trickier, the greens are hard and slick from the wind and salty air. Many of the holes have commanding views of the ocean, particularly the eighth, ninth, 14th, and 15th, which run along the water's edge. Wind—especially from the north—can turn these short holes into club-selection nightmares. Don't let high scores here ruin your enjoyment of some of the finest views on the island. The course's shortness and the fact that it gets little play midweek make St. George's Golf Club a good choice for couples or groups of varying ability.

Highlight hole: Pause to admire the view from the par-four 14th hole before you tee off. From the elevated tee area, the 326-yard hole curls around Coot Pond, an ocean-fed cove, to the green on a small, treeless peninsula. Beyond the neighboring 15th hole is old Fort St. Catherine's, and beyond that lies the sea. With a tail wind, it's tempting to hit for the green from the tee, but Coot Pond leaves no room for error. *1 Park Rd., St. George's,* ☎ *441/297–8067, 441/295-5600 (tee times/information), 441/297–8148 (pro's office), or 441/297-8353 (pro shop),* FAX *441/297–2273. Greens fees: $38; $15 after 3, Nov.–March; $20 after 4, Apr.–Oct. Cart rental, $30; hand cart, $6.*

Horseback Riding

Bermuda has strict regulations regarding horseback riding, particularly on public beaches. Visitors may only rent horses for supervised trail rides.

Because most of the land on Bermuda is residential, opportunities for riding through the countryside are few. The chief exception is **South Shore Park,** between South Road and the Warwick beaches. Sandy trails, most of which are open only to riders or people on foot, wind through stands of dune grass and oleander and over coral bluffs. (Horses are not allowed on the beaches.) Nearby is the **Spicelands Riding Centre** (Middle Rd., Warwick, ☎ 441/238–8212 or 441/238–8246), the largest—but sometimes impersonal—riding facility on the island. The center's most popular trail ride is the one-and-a-half-hour south-shore breakfast ride, departing at 6:50 AM; breakfast is included in the $50 fee (cash discount given on all rides). The daily 10 and 11:30 AM and 3 and 6 PM trail rides ($40) are leisurely one-hour treks. Evening rides at 6 PM ($40) are also offered weekly May through September; call for schedules. Spicelands also offers instruction in its riding ring. A smaller stable is **Lee Bow Riding Centre** (Tribe Road 1, off Middle Rd., Devonshire, ☎ 441/236–4181, FAX 441/236–8918), which offers trail rides through the island's countryside and to places along the beautiful northern coast. One-hour rides ($20) are on a request-only basis. The British-qualified riding instructor gives lessons for up to three people, at $20 per half hour, or $30 per hour. Children's riding camps are offered during the summer, Christmas, and Easter breaks for about $175 a week.

Jogging and Running

Many of the difficulties that cyclists face—hills, traffic, and wind—also confront runners in Bermuda. The presence of pedestrian sidewalks and footpaths along roadsides, however, does make the going somewhat easier. Runners who like firm pavement will be happiest on the Railway Trail (*see* Bicycling, *above*) or on South Road, a popular route. For those who like running on sand, the trails through **South Shore Park** are relatively firm, while the island's beaches obviously present a much softer surface. **Horseshoe Beach** and **Elbow Beach** are frequented by a large number of serious runners during the early morning and after 5 PM. Another beach for running is ½-mile **Warwick Long Bay,** the longest uninterrupted stretch of sand on the island; the sand is softer here than at Horseshoe and Elbow, so it is difficult to gain good footing, particularly at high tide. By using South Shore Park trails to skirt coral bluffs, runners can create a route that connects several beaches, although trails in some places can be winding and uneven.

The big running event on the island is the **Bermuda International Marathon, Half Marathon and 10K Race,** held in mid-January. The race attracts world-class distance runners from several countries, but it is open to everyone. For information, contact the Race Committee (Box DV 397, Devonshire DV BX, ☎ 441/236–3629). The association can also provide information on other races held throughout the year. Another event for fitness fanatics is the **Bermuda Triathlon** in late September. Held in Southampton, the event combines a 1-mile swim, a 15-mile cycling leg, and a 6-mile run. For information, contact the Bermuda Triathlon Association (Box HM 1002, Hamilton HM DX, ☎ 441/293–2765). Less competitive—and certainly less strenuous—are the 2-mile **"fun runs,"** sponsored by the Mid-Atlantic Athletic Club (Box HM 1745, Hamilton HM BX, ☎ 441/293–8103), held every Tuesday evening from April through October. Runs begin at 6 PM in front of Camden House on Berry Hill Road, Botanical Gardens. No entry fee is charged. Additional information about jogging and running is available from the Bermuda Track & Field Association (Box DV 397, Devonshire DV BX, ☎ 441/295-8574).

Squash

The **Bermuda Squash Club** (Middle Rd., Devonshire, ☎ Jane Palker at 441/292–6881) makes its four courts and new gym available to nonmembers of all ages and standards between 11 AM and 11 PM by reservation. A $5 fee per person buys 40 minutes of play during the day, or $6.50 at peak times (noon to 2 PM and 4:40 PM to 9 PM); rackets and balls can be borrowed. A $5 per play guest fee is charged, but temporary memberships can be arranged if you plan to play several times. Visitors may be teamed up with a local partner; timed matches and competitions can be organized, too. Soft-ball players will enjoy the two

English courts (larger than U.S. courts) at the **Coral Beach & Tennis Club** (South Rd., Paget, ☎ 441/236–2233). Introduction by a member is required at Coral Beach. In April, the Bermuda Squash Racquets Association (☎ 441/292–6881) sponsors the **Bermuda Open Squash Tournament,** in which top international players compete.

Tennis

Bermuda has a tennis court for every 600 residents, a ratio that even the most tennis-crazed countries would find difficult to match. Many are private, but the public has access to more than 70 courts in 20 locations island-wide. Courts are inexpensive and seldom full. Hourly rates for nonguests are about $10 to $15. Bring along a few fresh cans of balls, because balls in Bermuda cost $6 to $7 per can—about three times the rate in the United States. Among the surfaces used in Bermuda are Har-Tru, clay, cork, and hard composites, of which the relatively slow Plexipave composite is the most prevalent. Considering Bermuda's British roots, it's surprising that there are no grass courts on the island.

Wind, heat (in summer), and humidity are the most distinguishing characteristics of Bermudian tennis. From October through March, when daytime temperatures rarely exceed 80°F, play is comfortable throughout the day. In summertime, however, the heat radiating from the court (especially hard-surface ones) can make play uncomfortable between 11 AM and 3 PM. At such times, the breezes normally considered a curse in tennis can become a cooling blessing. Early morning or evening tennis presents players with an entirely different problem, when tennis balls grow heavy with moisture from Bermuda's humid sea air, always at its wettest early and late in the day. On clay courts, the moist balls become matted with clay, making them even heavier. In strong winds, inland courts are preferable; these include the clay and all-weather courts at the **Government Tennis Stadium** (Cedar Ave. and St. John's Rd., Pembroke, ☎ 441/292–0105) and the clay courts at the **Coral Beach & Tennis Club** (off South Rd., Paget, ☎ 441/236–2233 or 441/236–6495; introduction by a member is required). Despite their position at the water's edge, the Plexipave courts of the **Southampton Princess Hotel** (South Rd., Southampton, ☎ 441/238–1005) are reasonably well shielded from the wind (especially from the north), although the breeze can be swirling and difficult. High on a bluff above the ocean, the courts at the **Sonesta Beach Hotel & Spa** (off South Rd., ☎ 441/238–8122) offer players one of the more spectacular settings on the island, but the courts are exposed to summer winds from the south and southwest. Other hotels with good tennis facilities open to the public are the **Elbow Beach Hotel** (South Shore, Paget, ☎ 441/236–3535), with five courts, and **Marriott's Castle Harbour Resort** (Paynters Rd., Hamilton Parish, ☎ 441/293–2040), with six cork courts. All of the above facilities, except Marriott's Castle Harbour, have some floodlit courts for night play, as does the **Belmont Hotel, Golf & Country Club** (Belmont Rd., Warwick, ☎ 441/236–1301). The four clay courts at the **Port Royal Course** (Southampton, ☎ 441/234–0974) are $8 during daylight hours. Two courts are lighted for night play; an additional fee of $2–$6 is usually charged to play under lights. Most tennis facilities offer lessons, ranging from $20 to $30 for 30 minutes of instruction, and racket rentals for $4–$6 per hour or per play, depending on the policy.

SPECTATOR SPORTS

Bermuda is a great place for sports enthusiasts seeking relief from an overdose of baseball, football, and basketball—sports that mean little to Bermudians. In addition to golf and tennis, the big spectator sports here are cricket, rugby, soccer, field hockey, and yacht racing. The Bermuda Department of Tourism (*see* Important Contacts A to Z *in* the Gold Guide) can provide exact dates and information about all major sporting events.

Cricket

Cricket is the big team sport in summer, and the **Cup Match Cricket Festival** is *the* event on Bermuda's summer sports calendar. Held in late July or early August at the Somerset Cricket Club (Broome St., off Somerset Rd., ☎ 441/234–0327) or the St. George's Cricket Club (Wellington Slip Rd., ☎ 441/297–0374), the competition features teams from around the island. Although cricket is taken very seriously, the event itself is a real festival, attended by thousands of colorful picnickers and party-goers. An entry fee is charged. The regular cricket season runs from April through September.

Field Hockey

Hockey games between local teams can be seen at the National Sports Club (Middle Rd., Devonshire, ☎ 441/236–6994) on weekends from October through April. In late August or early September, the National Sports Club is the site of the **Hockey Festival,** a tournament with teams from Bermuda, the United States, Great Britain, Holland, and Germany. Entry is free.

Golf

Golf tournaments are held throughout the year at various courses on the island. The highlight of the golf year is the **Bermuda Open** in early October, which attracts a host of professionals and amateurs. A schedule of events is available from the Bermuda Department of Tourism (*see* Important Contacts A to Z *in* the Gold Guide).

Horse Racing

Equestrian events are held throughout the year at the **Bermuda Equestrian Federation** (Vesey St., Devonshire, ☎ 441/234–0485, FAX 441/234–3010). Harness races take place twice monthly from September through April (call Annie Sousa, ☎ 441/238–2110 for information). The horsey set also turns out in October for the FEI/Samsung Dressage Competition and Show Jumping events. (For additional information write to the Bermuda Equestrian Federation at Box DV 583, Devonshire DV BX.)

Rugby

The **Easter Rugby Classic** is the final event in Bermuda's rugby season, which runs from September to April. Held at the National Sports Club (Middle Rd., Devonshire, ☎ 441/236–6994), the competition attracts teams from the United States, Great Britain, France, New Zealand, and Australia, as well as Bermuda. Tickets cost about $5. During the rest of the season, matches between local teams can be seen on weekends at the National Sports Club.

Soccer

In late March or early April, teams from countries around the Atlantic, including the United States, Canada, Great Britain, and several Caribbean nations, compete for the **Bermuda Youth Soccer Cup.** Teams play in three age divisions, and games are held on fields around the island. Contact the Bermuda Department of Tourism (☎ 441/292–0023), or the nearest Visitors Service Bureau.

Squash

In April, the Bermuda Squash Racquets Association (☎ 441/292–6881 sponsors the **Bermuda Open Squash Tournament,** in which top international players compete.

Tennis

Tennis tournaments are played year-round, although most of the major ones are in the fall and winter. Included among them are the March and April **All Bermuda Tennis Club Members' Tournament,** a closed competition on clay courts to which visitors are welcome (Government Tennis Stadium, Pembroke Parish, ☎ 441/292–0105); April's **Bermuda Open,** an ATP Tour, USTA-Sanctioned Event of the world's top professionals played on clay courts at the Coral Beach & Tennis Club (☎ 441/236-2233), a closed competition that's open to visitors; May's **Heineken Open,** played at the Government Tennis Stadium and open to visitors; June's **Pomander Gate Tennis Club Open,** a competition on hard courts for visitors and locals (Pomander Rd., Paget, ☎ 441/236–5400); September's **Grotto Bay Open,** an 11-day tournament open to visitors, played on hard courts at the Grotto Bay Beach Hotel & Tennis Club (Hamilton Parish, ☎ 441/293–8333, ext. 1914); October's **All Bermuda Tennis Club Open,** played at the Government Tennis Stadium and open to visitors; and November's **Bermuda Lawn Tennis Club Invitational,** a closed competition played at The Coral Beach & Tennis Club (Paget, ☎ 441/236–2233). For more information about these and other tournaments, contact the Bermuda Lawn Tennis Association (Box HM 341, Hamilton HM BX, ☎ 441/296–0834, FAX 441/295–3056).

Yachting

Bermuda has a worldwide reputation as a yacht-racing center. Spectators, particularly those on land, may find it difficult to follow the intricacies of a race or regatta, but the sight of the racing fleet, with brightly colored spinnakers flying, is always striking. The racing season runs from March to November. Most races are held on weekends in the Great Sound, and several classes of boats usually compete. The racing can be seen at a distance from Spanish Point and the Somerset shoreline. Anyone who wants to get a real sense of the action, however, should be aboard a boat near the race course.

In June, Bermuda is the finish for oceangoing yachts in three major races beginning in the United States: the **Newport–Bermuda Ocean Yacht Race,** the **Marion to Bermuda Race,** and the **Bermuda Ocean Race** from Annapolis, Maryland. Of these, the Newport–Bermuda Race usually attracts the most entries, but all provide the spectacular sight of the island's harbors and yacht club docks filled with yachts, which usually range in length from about 30 to 80 feet. For those more interested in racing than expensive yachts, the **Omega Gold Cup International Match Race Tournament** is the event to see. Held in October in Hamilton Harbour, the tournament pits visiting top sailors—many of whom are America's Cup Match Racing skippers—against Bermudians in one-on-one races for prize money.

7 Dining

ITH 140 RESTAURANTS from which to choose, visitors to this tiny island will have little difficulty satisfying their cravings for everything from traditional English fare to French, Italian, Japanese, Indian, and Chinese. A quest for Bermudian food, however, is likely to be as extended and elusive as the search for the Holy Grail. And if you persist, you'll discover the single greatest truth about Bermudian cuisine: There's not much to it, but everybody on the island loves it. Waiters, in particular, prove inspirational. While heaping your plate, they will wax lyrical about their mother's conch stew, their late uncle's fish chowder, or their great aunt's codfish and potatoes. And no islander seems to remember ever tasting anything better than a mysterious concoction called hash shark or—more intelligibly—shark hash.

In moments of candor, islanders will confide that Bermudian cuisine is really a collection of dishes showing English, American, and West Indian influences. But whatever the origins of the recipes, the island's cuisine begins and ends with Bermudian ingredients—and therein lies the island's culinary identity. Seafood is extraordinary here, especially the local lobster that may only be eaten from September through March, due to fishing laws. This is the spiny lobster familiar in the Caribbean, usually prepared with a minimum of seasoned stuffing, broiled, and served drizzled with butter. Menus also feature Bermuda rockfish, the flesh of which is firm and white; red snapper, often served with onions and potatoes; shark; and mussels steamed in white wine or made into a pie with a curry seasoning. You should also try the fish chowder, laced at the table with local black rum and sherry peppers (sherry in which hot peppers have been marinated). The result is unforgettable. Conch fritters, too, are a good bet when you can find them. Unless you venture to St. David's Island on the island's East End, you may never get to taste shark hash. The best approach is to go to the Black Horse Tavern on Friday when the shark hash is freshly made, or have dinner at Dennis's Hideaway, where a full pot is always on hand.

Without doubt, the most famous vegetable is the Bermuda onion, hailed by onion lovers as a more heavenly version of the sweet Vidalia onion from Georgia. It is most commonly found in onion pie and cheese and onion sandwiches, and glazed in sugar and rum. Bermuda's soil works miracles with most common vegetables. Don't be put off if your meal is accompanied by potatoes, broccoli, or even carrots. Rarely will these vegetables taste better or fresher in their natural flavors.

In addition to onion pie and mussel pie, cassava pie is a tradition dating back three centuries. Made from dough of eggs, sugar, and ground cassava root, this savory meat pie is a Christmas standard, nearly always paired with a traditional turkey and dressing. Other island dishes turn up just when you despair of ever finding any. At Sunday breakfast, ask for codfish and bananas, made with the salt cod commonly known as Portuguese *bacalhau*. Revived by soaking in water, the cod is served with boiled potatoes, fresh bananas, sliced avocado, and either a creamed egg sauce or, occasionally, a savory tomato topping. Hoppin' John, a Bermudian dish that's also popular in the Carolinas, is rice cooked with chicken, beans or peas, bacon, onion, and thyme. Another traditional favorite is syllabub, a sweet treat of guava, wine, and cream served either as a liquid or a jelly.

For the most part, however, dining on the island is fairly non-Bermudian, and expensive: Dinner at the best restaurants can cost as much

as $100 per person, excluding a 15% service charge. Du[...]
mer season, reservations are essential at these restaura[...]
if you are staying in one of the major resorts, you can usually choose
from several restaurants without ever leaving the property, and most
hotels and cottage colonies offer a variety of meal plans ranging from
full board to Continental breakfasts (*see* Chapter 8, Lodging).

Dining in Bermuda tends to be rather formal. In the more upscale restaurants, men should wear jackets and ties, and women should be comparably attired. Credit cards are widely accepted in the major hotels and restaurants, while the small taverns and lunch spots only take cash.

CATEGORY	COST*
$$$$	over $50
$$$	$35–$50
$$	$20–$35
$	under $20

*per person, excluding drinks and service (a 15% service charge is sometimes added)

Asian

$$$ Mikado. This fun restaurant in Marriott's Castle Harbour Resort brings Japanese cooking to very English Bermuda. The decor reflects the elegantly simplistic Japanese style; patrons literally cross a cultural line when they step onto the tea-garden style wooden bridge to enter the establishment. As at many Japanese-style steak houses, the enjoyment lies less in the food than in the dazzling flash of twirling knives, slapping mallets, and airborne salt and pepper shakers—it's like judo you can eat. Although à la carte dining is available, you're better off with one of the complete dinners: a shrimp or scallop appetizer with ginger sauce, miso or *tori* soup, a seafood or beef entrée selection, salad, steamed rice, vegetables, and Japanese tea. The sushi bar here was the island's first, and it continues to be favored by locals. ✕ *Marriott's Castle Harbour Resort, Tucker's Town,* ☎ *441/293–2040. Reservations required. AE, DC, MC, V.*

$$ Bombay Bicycle Club. The culinary scene of any British colony would be woefully incomplete without a curry house. Named after a private gentlemen's club in the waning days of the Raj, this burgundy-hued restaurant captures the flavor of the subcontinent without becoming a caricature. All the traditional Indian favorites are offered here and prepared remarkably well. Order the *peeaz pakora* (onion fritters) and mulligatawny soup as starters, then opt for the *jhinga vindaloo* (shrimp in hot curry), *mutton saagwala* (braised lamb in creamy spinach), or anything from the clay tandoor oven. *Nan, paratha,* and *papadums* are terrific breads and snacks to accompany the meal. Ask about the discounted dinner menus, or stop by on a weekday for the $10.95 buffet lunch. Takeout is available. ✕ *Reid St., Hamilton,* ☎ *441/292–0048 or 441/292–8865. Reservations advised. AE, DC, MC, V.*

$$ Chopsticks. An alternative to New Queen (*see below*) at the east end of Hamilton, this Chinese restaurant features an intelligent mix of Szechuan, Hunan, and Cantonese favorites. Chef Luk's best Chinese selections include jumbo shrimp with vegetables in black bean sauce, hoisin hot chicken, and lemon chicken. Thai chefs bring a taste of their home country, with such favorites as *Pla Pae Sa* (boneless fish fillet steamed on a bed of cabbage and celery with ginger, sweet pepper, scallions, red chilies, and cilantro) and beef Panang cooked in coconut sauce, curry paste, and lime leaves. All dishes are made to order, and people with special diets can specify exactly what they want; MSG can be omit-

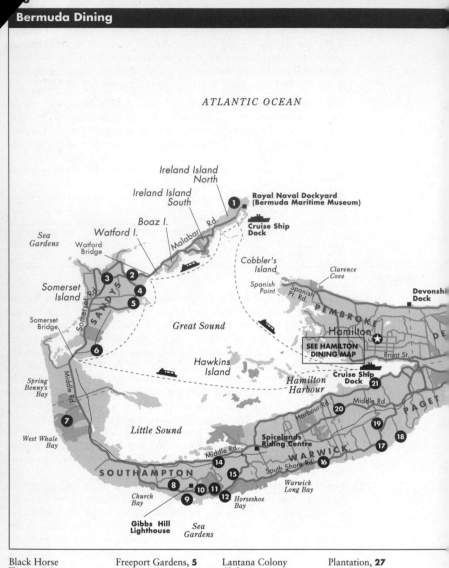

ATLANTIC OCEAN

Ireland Island North

Ireland Island South

Boaz I.

Watford I.

Sea Gardens

Watford Bridge

Royal Naval Dockyard (Bermuda Maritime Museum)

Cruise Ship Dock

Cobbler's Island

Clarence Cove

Spanish Point

Spanish Pt. Rd.

Devonshi

Somerset Island

SANDYS

Somerset Rd.

Great Sound

PEMBROKE

Hamilton

DE

SEE HAMILTON DINING MAP

Front St.

Somerset Bridge

Hawkins Island

Hamilton Harbour

Cruise Ship Dock

Spring Benny's Bay

Middle Rd.

Little Sound

Harbour Rd.

Middle Rd.

PAGET

West Whale Bay

Spicelands Riding Centre

Middle Rd.

WARWICK

South Shore Rd.

Warwick Long Bay

SOUTHAMPTON

Church Bay

Horseshoe Bay

Gibbs Hill Lighthouse

Sea Gardens

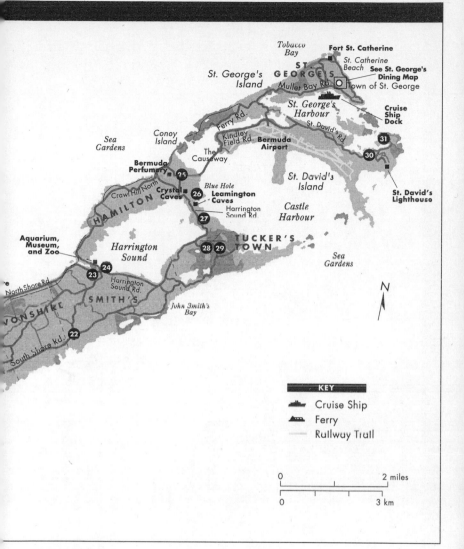

Tobacco Bay

Fort St. Catherine

St. Catherine Beach

See St. George's Dining Map

ST. GEORGE'S

St. George's Island

Muller Bay Rd. Town of St. George

○

St. George's Harbour

Cruise Ship Dock

Ferry Rd.

Kinley Field Rd.

Conoy Island

Bermuda Airport

St. David's Rd.

Sea Gardens

The Causeway

St. David's Island

Bermuda Perfumery 25

31

30

St. David's Lighthouse

Crawl Hill North

Crystal Caves 26

Blue Hole

Leamington Caves

HAMILTON

Harrington Sound Rd.

27

Castle Harbour

Aquarium, Museum, and Zoo

Harrington Sound

28 29

TUCKER'S TOWN

Sea Gardens

23 24

Harrington Sound Rd.

North Shore Rd.

SMITH'S

John Smith's Bay

VONSHIRE

22

South Shore Rd.

N

KEY

⛴ Cruise Ship

⛴ Ferry

Railway Trail

0 ———————— 2 miles

0 ———————— 3 km

Hamilton Dining

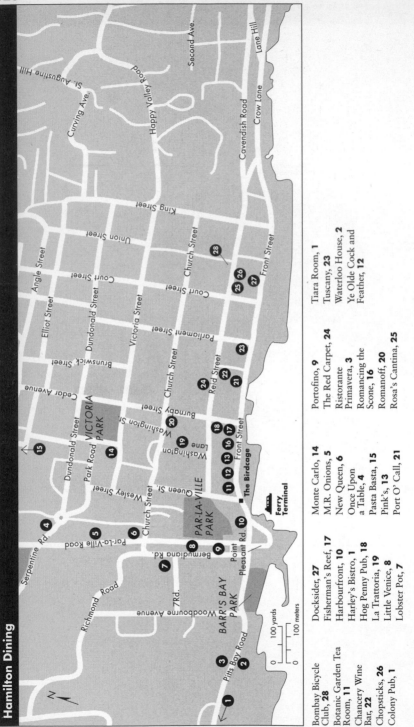

Bombay Bicycle Club, **28**
Botanic Garden Tea Room, **11**
Chancery Wine Bar, **22**
Chopsticks, **26**
Colony Pub, **1**

Docksider, **27**
Fisherman's Reef, **17**
Harbourfront, **10**
Harley's Bistro, **1**
Hog Penny Pub, **18**
La Trattoria, **19**
Little Venice, **8**
Lobster Pot, **7**

Monte Carlo, **14**
M.R. Onions, **5**
New Queen, **6**
Once Upon a Table, **4**
Pasta Basta, **15**
Pink's, **13**
Port O' Call, **21**

Portofino, **9**
The Red Carpet, **24**
Ristorante Primavera, **3**
Romancing the Scone, **16**
Romanoff, **20**
Rosa's Cantina, **25**

Tiara Room, **1**
Tuscany, **23**
Waterloo House, **2**
Ye Olde Cock and Feather, **12**

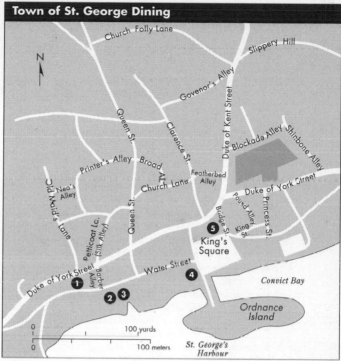

Town of St. George Dining

ted. Specially priced dinner menus are available for $15.50 or $21.95, plus gratuities, during the low season from November through March. Takeout is available. ✕ *Reid St. E, Hamilton,* ☎ *441/292–0791. Reservations advised. MC, V.*

$$ **New Queen.** This Chinese restaurant is an old favorite of Bermudians, who flock here for the hot and spicy fare. The emphasis is on the food rather than the decor, but the interior is attractive, clean, and subdued. Try the Szechuan duck, steamed until tender, then pressed with black mushrooms and potato flour, deep-fried, and served with a peppery mushroom sauce. Another great choice is *wor suit* chicken—boneless chicken pressed with minced meat, lightly battered and fried, and served on a bed of vegetables. Takeout is available. ✕ *Par-la-Ville Rd., Hamilton,* ☎ *441/295–4004 or 441/292–3282. Reservations advised. AE, DC, MC, V.*

Bermudian

$$$ **Plantation.** This comfortable, upbeat establishment is described by lo-
★ cals as "truly Bermudian" and at the top of their list. Island rattan, flickering candles, and a glass-enclosed atrium filled with plants give the restaurant a cool, exotic ambience that works well with its variety of tropical offerings. The menu selections, which emphasize freshly caught island seafood, are beautifully presented as well as consistently good. From the varied list of appetizers, try the roasted, sliced duck Harrington with fresh vegetables in puff pastry with Madeira sauce, or the West-alee Salad—a combination of Stilton cheese, tomatoes, and artichokes in olive oil. Fish and seafood specialties are recommended; one stand out is the red snapper Sea Venture—a fresh fillet coated with Dijon mustard, tomato, garlic and herbed bread crumbs, baked in white wine, and served in lemon butter sauce. Save room for profiteroles: the

chocolate sauce is out of this world. A four-course special dinner offers selected items from the main menu for $40. The restaurant is closed
during January and part of February for annual refurbishing. ✗ *Bailey's Bay, Hamilton Parish,* ☎ *441/293–1188. Reservations advised.
AE, MC, V.*

✓ $$ ★ **Black Horse Tavern.** A menacing shark, jaws agape, hangs on the
white-plaster wall, along with an assortment of other mounted island
fish. In this tranquil setting, islanders fill the casual dining room and
the six outside picnic tables to savor the culinary magic of chef Bernel
Pitcher. Curried conch stew with rice is a favorite, as are Pitcher's straight-
forward renderings of amberjack, rockfish, shark, tuna, wahoo, and—
in season—Bermuda lobster. For lunch, the fish sandwich is a taste
sensation. If you want to try a Bermuda original, ask for shark hash,
the chef's most popular specialty—the kitchen has trouble keeping it
in stock. ✗ *St. David's Island,* ☎ *441/293–9742 or 297-1991. Week-
end dinner reservations advised. No credit cards. Closed Mon. and pub-
lic holidays.*

$$ **Loyalty Inn.** Family-owned and operated by the Dowlings, this converted old Bermuda home overlooking scenic Mangrove Bay at the is-
land's western end is worth a stop, particularly for its fresh fish. The
homemade soups are delicious, especially the Portuguese red bean and
the Bermuda fish chowder. The lunch menu includes delicious fried fish
sandwiches, codfish cakes, curried mussel pie, burgers, and good salads (try the Caesar). Notable dinner entrées include the sautéed fresh
fish of the day with almonds and nut butter sauce, Seafood Sensation—
a savory combination of local fish, shrimps, and scallops in white
wine cream sauce served over rice, and shrimp Provençale—prepared
at the table with great fanfare. Local lobster is served in season. ✗ *Mangrove Bay, Somerset Village,* ☎ *441/234–0125. Weekend dinner reservations advised. AE, MC, V.*

$ ★ **Dennis's Hideaway.** Of all the eccentric characters who call St. David's
home, Dennis Lamb may be the most eccentric. Piratical in appearance,
he hunches over his pots discussing just about everything from the plumb-
ing and the government to the fate of man. The place consists of little
more than a ramshackle pink building, a scattering of homemade picnic tables, and a few yapping dogs, but it serves what may be Bermuda's
best local dishes. Don't come here if you're a stickler for cleanliness:
the place is decidedly grubby. Dennis's son, Sea Egg, does most of the
cooking these days, but Dennis still potters around the kitchen. If you
want to make Dennis's day, order his "fish dinner with the works"—
$32.50 for a feast of shark hash on toast, conch fritters, mussel stew,
conch stew, fish chowder, fried fish, conch steak, shark steak, shrimp,
scallops, and perhaps a bit of mussel pie. He may even include some
bread-and-butter pudding for good measure. ✗ *Cashew City Rd., St.
David's,* ☎ *441/297–0044. Weekend dinner reservations required. No
credit cards.*

British

$$$ **Carriage House.** Hearty English food is the daily bread of this attrac-
tive slice of the Somers Wharf restoration. With its exposed brick
walls, the interior looks rather like the exterior; try to secure a table
by a window so you can watch the action on the harbor. Dinner can
be pricey, especially if you choose the Bermuda Triangle—shrimp, filet
mignon, and chicken breast, each prepared with its own sauce—but
many offerings are reasonable. This is the place to tuck into roast prime
rib of beef, cut to order in front of you, but don't overlook the fresh
Bermuda fish when it's on the menu. A generous gourmet buffet is served

on Sundays, including unlimited champagne. Lunch and afternoon tea with all the trimmings are served daily. ✗ *Somers Wharf, St. George's,* ☏ *441/297–1270. Reservations advised. Jacket required at dinner. AE, DC, MC, V.*

$$$ **Henry VIII.** As popular with locals as it is with tourists from the nearby Southampton resorts, this lively restaurant, which was enlarged considerably when a second story was added in 1994, affects an Old England look that stops just short of "wench" waitresses and contrived Tudor styling. The eclectic mix of English and Bermudian favorites includes great classics like mussel pie, and lighter options such as steamed mussels in wine. The fish chowder is wonderful, as are the very British lamb, beef, and steak-and-kidney pies; and the lamb is always cooked to perfection. Save room for the dessert of bananas flamed in dark rum. After dinner, join the local crowd in the bar and be entertained by visiting comedians and singers. Local acts feature calypso singer Hubert Smith. ✗ *South Shore Rd., Southampton,* ☏ *441/238–1977. Reservations advised. AE, DC, MC, V.*

$$ **Colony Pub.** A favorite meeting place for some of Hamilton's business and government communities, this cozy steak house is one place where visitors can gain an understanding of how Bermuda works. Tourists are readily accepted by the lunching locals, although more as honored spectators than participants. Part of the Princess Hotel, the pub is redolent of Britain and the history of this tiny island. Rich shades of brown and green and plenty of polished brass give the restaurant a clublike atmosphere. The meat-oriented menu features locker-aged Angus steaks and USDA Prime roast rib of beef. The 10-ounce salmon fillet promises to satisfy fish-lovers. ✗ *Princess Hotel, Hamilton,* ☏ *441/295–3000. AE, DC, MC, V.*

$$ **Hog Penny Pub.** Veterans of a London pub crawl might wonder whether they ever made the journey across the Atlantic when they arrive in this atmospheric watering hole off Front Street in Hamilton. Die-hard aficionados of British cooking (if such animals actually exist) will be rewarded with shepherd's pie, steak and kidney pie, steak in ale, and bangers (sausages) and mash. There's even a small sampling of curries. You'll find good fun as well as good food in this dark, cozy den, where sunburned strangers mingle freely and entertainment is offered nightly. Once a very smoky place, the ventilation has been markedly improved. ✗ *Burnaby Hill, Hamilton,* ☏ *441/292–2534. Reservations advised. AE, DC, MC, V.*

$$ **Pub on the Square.** After a morning of wandering in St. George's, this pub on King's Square is perfect for a slaking pint of English beer. The draft beer is better than anything that comes from the kitchen, although hamburgers and fish-and-chips are reasonably prepared. Warehouse brick and plenty of dark wood give the pub a warm atmosphere. ✗ *King's Sq., St. George's,* ☏ *441/297–1522 or 441/293–9704. AE, MC, V.*

$$ **Somerset Country Squire.** Overlooking Mangrove Bay in the West End, this typically English tavern is all dark wood and good cheer, with a great deal of malt and hops in between. Much of the food isn't good enough to warrant a special trip across the island, but you won't be disappointed if you do stop by. One exception is the Bermuda fish chowder, undoubtedly some of the island's best, and worth a long journey. Steak and kidney pie is fine, but the curried mussel pie is much better. ✗ *Mangrove Bay, Somerset,* ☏ *441/234–0105. Dinner reservations advised. AE, MC, V.*

$$ **Wharf Tavern.** Like most dockside restorations in Bermuda, this English-style watering hole is nondescript, with a stale atmosphere—but the chance to sit on the porch or on the wharf overlooking the activity on St. George's Harbour draws a crowd. The mainstays are a varied selection of pizzas and burgers of typical pub quality. Service is often slow. ✗ *Somers Wharf, St. George's,* ☎ *441/297–1515. MC, V.*

$$ **Ye Olde Cock and Feather.** One of the busiest spots along Front Street in Hamilton, this is a favorite meeting place for locals. Patrons sit either in a room that is a cross between a British pub and a Key West–style tropical outpost or on the upstairs balcony overlooking the harbor. Food is served pub-style, but the eclectic menu spans several cuisines and continents, from Portuguese red bean soup to steak and kidney pie and—the local favorite—fried chicken with peas, rice, and coleslaw. Live entertainment is featured nightly April through November. ✗ *Front St., Hamilton,* ☎ *441/295–2263. Reservations advised. MC, V.*

$–$$ **Port Royal Golf Club.** This white dining room featuring light wicker furniture, on the 19th hole of the Port Royal Golf Club, overlooks the golf course through large plate-glass windows. New management has expanded the service; now it is one of the few restaurants on the island to offer breakfast, lunch, and dinner. A club sandwich with English beer is the standard order here, but don't hesitate to order something more sophisticated from the main menu—the food is quite good. ✗ *Port Royal, Southampton,* ☎ *441/234–0236. MC, V.*

$ **Botanic Garden Tea Room.** One of Bermuda's most pleasant traditions is afternoon tea at Trimingham's department store in Hamilton. A pleasant place to escape the shopping scene, the tearoom also serves light lunches. ✗ *Front St., Hamilton,* ☎ *441/295–1183. No credit cards.*

$ **Docksider.** This Front Street hangout claims to have the widest selection of draft beers on the island, which says a lot about its priorities and those of its young clientele. However, that's no reason to steer clear of the fish-and-chips or the hamburgers. The club sandwiches are a good bet, too, although taste just won't matter once you've drunk your way through the bar's large selection of European brews. Frequented by locals, it's a popular place at night. ✗ *Front St., Hamilton,* ☎ *441/292–4088. AE, MC, V.*

$ **Romancing the Scone.** Unless docked cruise ships are in the way, the
★ dozen-or-so tables at this restaurant offer a terrific view of Hamilton Harbour. Perched on the veranda of one of the island's oldest department stores (but operated independently), this is a favorite après-shopping stop, and—view or not—a great place for breakfast, lunch, or a snack of coffee with biscuits or scones. Try the croissant sandwich or the chef's salad. ✗ *Front St., in A. S. Cooper & Sons, Ltd., Hamilton,* ☎ *441/295–3961. No credit cards. No dinner.*

French

$$$$ **Horizons.** This elegant dining room at Horizons cottage colony in Paget is one of the island's finest, and reservations are difficult to secure on short notice. Housed in what was once a private home and is now a Relais et Châteaux property, it attracts an upscale crowd—though the fresh, plantation-style dining room is less formal than it once was. Though the impeccably trained staff is trained to make this an unforgettable dining experience, the menu speaks for itself. At the top of the appetizer list are the cheese terrine with cranberry sauce and crepe filled with chicken and Mornay sauce. All entrées are cooked to perfection, but the lamb with garlic sauce and beef Wellington with Madeira sauce are highly recommended. Fixed price meal—$50, plus 15% gratuity—includes appetizer, soup, entrée, salad, dessert, and coffee. ✗ *South Shore Rd., Paget,* ☎ *441/236–0048. Reservations required. Jacket and tie. No credit cards. No lunch.*

$$$$ **Waterlot Inn.** Housed in a graceful, restored two-story manor house
★ that dates back to 1670, this restaurant is a Bermudian treasure. Ser-

vice is impeccable: the dining room staff has just enough island exuberance to take the edge off its European-style training. Chef Regis Neaud rearranges the Mediterranean-style menu each year, presenting a host of new dishes that succeed on every level. His French selections are far superior to most of the cuisine that passes for French on the island, although chef Neaud seldom misses an opportunity to prepare dishes indigenous to Bermuda. Outstanding appetizers are the chilled carpaccio of fresh beef tenderloin with basil vinaigrette and pine nuts, and the grilled eggplant layered with ricotta and Asiago cheeses and herbs. Waterlot continues to serve one of the best fish chowders on the island, and the panfried Bermuda fish on braised cabbage with juniper berry sauce is superb. If you love desserts, this is the place to go; fresh fig tart with homemade pistachio ice cream and frozen honey nougat terrine with lavender sauce head the list. Appealing background music by pianist Earl Darrell enhances the dining experience from Tuesday through Saturday, and one of the island's best Sunday brunches is served to the sounds of first-rate local jazz musicians. The restaurant closes in January and February. ✕ *Middle Rd., Southampton,* ☎ *441/238-0510. Reservations advised. Jacket and tie. AE, DC, MC, V. No lunch.*

$$$ Lantana Colony Club. French classical cuisine of a high order indeed is served at this resort near the western tip of the island, just past the Somerset Bridge. Surrounded by a forest of palm, hibiscus, and cherry trees, you can settle in for an à la carte lunch or a six-course prix-fixe dinner. Your best bet among the first courses is the poached salmon in Pommerey mustard sauce over linguine. Among entrées, the roast loin of veal stuffed with crabmeat and served with a tomato tarragon sauce, and the wahoo with orange peppercorn sauce are hard to beat. Calorie-conscious diners will be pleased with any of the new "light and healthy" selections that were added to the menu in 1994. ✕ *Somerset Bridge, adjacent to ferry stop,* ☎ *441/234-0141. Reservations required. Jacket and tie required at dinner indoors. AE, MC, V.*

$$$ Monte Carlo. Southern French cooking is the trademark of this cheery
★ restaurant just behind City Hall in Hamilton. Beams of old Bermuda cedar add a touch of local color and marry well with the many copied Impressionist works that are painted onto the walls. The lunchtime pasta selection is broad, but the main emphasis is on a sprightly collection of hot and cold appetizers—fresh tuna marinated in oil and herbs of Provence and served with caper sauce is outstanding, as are the sautéed scallops served with spinach and a light orange sauce. Favorite entrées include bouillabaisse Marseillaise—a feast of fish and shellfish in a delicious broth—and veal scaloppine Riviera served with sun-dried tomatoes, roast peppers, and sweet Vermouth. The dessert trolley has wonderful cakes and outstanding *tiramisù.* ✕ *Victoria St., Hamilton,* ☎ *441/295-5453 or 441/295-5442. Reservations advised. AE, MC, V.*

✓ **$$$ Waterloo House.** A private home a century ago, this restaurant and small
★ hotel on Hamilton Harbour serves Bermudian and Continental cuisine. Guests can eat either on the recently expanded waterside patio adjoining the flower-shaded buildings, or in the elegant dining room, where deep raspberry walls, rich chintzes, and elegant sconces set the mood. Chef Bruno Heeb usually offers a daily special or two, but don't overlook the menu items, especially the appetizer of delicately seasoned snails housed inside new potatoes. Service is outstanding. ✕ *Pitts Bay Rd., Pembroke, Hamilton,* ☎ *441/295-4480. Reservations advised. Jacket required. AE, MC, V.*

International

$$$$ Fourways Inn. This restaurant has risen to preeminence on the island in recent years, as much for its lovely 18th-century surroundings as anything coming out of the kitchen. The decor is evocative of a wealthy plantation home, with plenty of expensive china, crystal, and silver. Order the local mussels simmered in white wine and cream, and any of the sautéed veal dishes. The Caesar salad is a good choice, too, but leave enough room for strawberry soufflé. For a slightly different cocktail, try a Fourways Special, made with the juice from the Bermuda loquat and other fruits, and a dash of bitters. ✕ *1 Middle Rd., Paget,* ☎ *441/236–6517. Reservations advised. Jacket required, tie recommended. Jacket required. AE, MC, V.*

$$$$ Newport Room. With its nautical theme, this fine restaurant in the
★   Southampton Princess has occupied a special place in the hearts of the island's elite for many years. French cuisine with American and Bermudian touches is the focus of the dining room, which compares to the best in the world. Half models and large standing models of previous America's Cup winners and glistening teak set the tone for some culinary winners on the new menu (it changes every year) that earned the hearts of diners when it was introduced in 1995. Each dish is beautifully presented, and the personal service and attention make this dining experience exceptional. Choosing from the varied lineup of appetizers is not easy, for they are all superb, but of note is a combination of shrimp, lobster, and scallops flamed at your table, and served with angel hair pasta and a sumptuous lobster sauce; the seared fresh goose liver on a sesame crouton with caramelized Bermuda onions and a black rum and orange sauce is also recommended. The salads—endives tossed with sun-dried cranberries, truffles, and cider vinaigrette, or the combination of spinach, sorrel, and summer greens with grapefruit in a hibiscus vinaigrette—are a step away from the traditional. Especially noteworthy entrées are salmon broiled with fennel and topped with mushrooms and herb duxelle, set on raspberry butter; double fillet of venison in a soft herb mousse on pumpkin and turnip puree, with wild cherry and juniper sauce; and smoked roast breast of duck over forest mushrooms and herb ragout. The choice of desserts is excellent, but the taste of the Grand Marnier soufflé or crêpes suzette (for two) will linger longest. ✕ *South Shore Rd., Southampton,* ☎ *441/238–8167. Reservations advised. Jacket and tie. AE, DC, MC, V. No lunch. Closed during some winter months, call to check exact dates.*

$$$$ Romanoff. Elegant European meals served in a theatrical Russian setting are the specialty of this restaurant run by Anton Duzevic. Deep-red walls decorated with faux-naif landscape paintings provide a dramatic backdrop for the vodka and black caviar that Duzevic himself presents to each diner. Stick to the well-known dishes or select a seafood special from the cart that is wheeled around the tables. ✕ *Church St., Hamilton,* ☎ *441/295–0333. Reservations required. Jacket and tie. AE, DC, MC, V.*

$$$$ Tiara Room. This gourmet restaurant in Bermuda's historic Princess Hotel has discovered the art of serving fine Continental cuisine with a theatrical flair. The dining room has a fresh look, utilizing clean lines and bright colors (mostly mauve), but the highlight remains the stunning view of Hamilton Harbour. Whenever possible, dishes are finished by your table, often flambéed dramatically. The rack of lamb carved table-side is always an excellent choice, as are the cherries Jubilee. ✕ *Princess Hotel, Hamilton,* ☎ *441/295–3000. Reservations advised. Jacket and tie. AE, DC, MC, V.*

✓ **$$$ Cafe Lido.** Located on the beachfront terrace at the Elbow Beach Hotel, with waves breaking just below, this is one of the island's most romantic settings. The creative appetizer list includes marinated salmon with risotto pancake, and avocado with tomato, fresh mozzarella cheese and a basil-vegetable dressing. Main course winners are angel hair pasta with arugula, pine nuts and roasted peppers, and grilled salmon with creamy watercress sauce. The coconut mousse with fruit and vanilla sauce and the hazelnut eclair are both unforgettable endings. ✕ *Elbow Beach Hotel, off Shore Rd., Paget,* ☎ *441/236–9884. Reservations required. AE, DC, MC, V.*

✓ **$$$ Coconuts.** Nestled between high cliff rocks and a pristine beach on the
★ southern coast, this outdoor restaurant offers both a striking setting and consistently good food. Those wanting easy access might be discouraged by the prospect of the steep climb back up the hill after the meal—but if that does not deter you, request a table overlooking the ocean, made even more dramatic at night with floodlights. A fixed price of $42, excluding the 15% gratuity, includes an appetizer, soup, salad, entrée, dessert, and coffee. The annually changing menu features freshly grown produce, but always included in the list of creative appetizers is the Bermuda fish chowder. You will never go wrong with the grilled fresh fish of the day entrée, and the charbroiled steak is cooked to perfection. The coconut tart with coconut ice cream is a perfect way to end this dining experience. A simpler lunch menu includes daily specials, burgers, sandwiches, and good salads. ✕ *South Shore Rd., Southampton,* ☎ *441/238–0222. Dinner reservations required. No credit cards. Closed Nov.–Apr.*

$$$ Harbourfront. Few of the restaurants along Front Street have as much variety as this busy restaurant, where sushi is served alongside Continental and Mediterranean specialties. Sit on the porch or at a table behind the large glass doors, and watch the action along Front Street and the harbour as you choose from the extensive menu. At lunchtime, this is the place to come for a good burger or salad. For dinner, start with the fried calamari or carpaccio, or asparagus salad with lemon vinaigrette, followed by a broiled veal chop with mushroom and wine sauce, or any of the excellent pastas. The small sushi bar, which opened in 1995, is also worth trying. ✕ *Front St., Hamilton,* ☎ *441/295–4207. Reservations advised. AE, DC, MC, V.*

$$$ Norwood Room. Don't be put off by the fact that this restaurant in the Stonington Beach Hotel is run by students of the Hospitality and Culinary Institute of Bermuda: Under the supervision of their mentors, they offer superb food and service. The oversize training kitchen uses local ingredients and European culinary techniques to create a whole range of bright, fresh tastes. Seafood is the best bet here, well prepared and served with excellent sauces. Enjoy a preprandial cocktail at the sunken bar overlooking the swimming pool. ✕ *South Shore Rd.,* ☎ *441/236–5416. Reservations advised. Jacket and tie. AE, DC, MC, V.*

$$$ Once Upon a Table. Hailed by many Bermudians as Bermuda's finest
★ restaurant, this former 18th-century island home, complete with fine china and crystal, is distinctly romantic, with an abundance of pretty flowers and Victorian memorabilia. From the menu, consider fillets of venison with an Armagnac and juniper berry sauce, rack of lamb, roast duckling, or grilled fresh yellowfin tuna with tomato confit, spring onions and dill. A fixed price menu, featuring local specialty items for $46.50, includes an appetizer, entrée, dessert, and coffee. Low-cholesterol dishes are always available. ✕ *Serpentine Rd., Hamilton,* ☎ *441/295–8585. Reservations advised. Jacket required. AE, DC, MC, V. No lunch.*

$$$ The Rib Room. Overlooking the Southampton Princess Golf Course in
★   what has the appearance of a conservative country club dining room,
this is the best place on the island for grilled meats and barbecued ribs.
The service is superior; Marionette Lambert, the maitre d'hotel, goes
out of her way to satisfy every guest. The house specialty, hickory-smoked
prime rib, is cooked to perfection and served in its natural juices with
traditional Yorkshire pudding. The lamb chops are superlative, as is
the rotisserie-cooked half chicken. Appetizers and salads are offered
buffet-style; the Bermuda fish chowder is always a taste sensation. ✕
Southampton Princess Hotel, South Shore Rd., Southampton, ☎ *441/
238–8000. Reservations advised. AE, MC, V. No lunch.*

$$$ Tom Moore's Tavern. Set in an old home that dates to 1652, this restau-
rant in Bailey's Bay clearly enjoys its colorful past. Irish poet Tom Moore
visited friends here frequently during his short stay on the island in 1804
and wrote several of his odes under the nearby calabash tree. Today,
fireplaces, casement windows, and cedar joinery used centuries ago to
build ships capture a sense of the building's history. The cuisine, however, labors under none of history's baggage—it is fresh, light, and innovative. Seafood lovers should try the fresh Bermuda fish sautéed with
lemon butter and pine nuts, or broiled Bermuda lobster (in season).
Another standout is boneless quail stuffed with goose liver, morels, and
truffles in puff pastry. The soufflés are always superb, as is the chef's
pastry; both change daily. Patrons dine in one of five cozy rooms or,
in the warm months, *al fresco* on a new terrace that overlooks Walsingham Bay. ✕ *Bailey's Bay, Hamilton Parish,* ☎ *441/293–8020.
Reservations advised. Jacket required. AE, MC, V. No lunch. Closed
January (call to check exact dates).*

$$$ Windsor. Overlooking Castle Harbour Resort, this elegant dining room
in Marriott's Castle Harbour Resort features a blend of international
cuisines with a strong European underpinning. Although the menu is
not especially innovative, a good meal can be enjoyed here. Meat-lovers
in particular will be happy: The filet mignon and roast lamb loin with
black bean sauce are cooked to perfection. Fish-lovers should try
grilled swordfish with fresh papaya salsa, or smoked salmon stuffed
with mango mousse. With its unhurried atmosphere, live piano music,
and view of Castle Harbour, the Windsor makes for a fine night out.
✕ *Castle Harbour Resort, Tucker's Town,* ☎ *441/293–2040. Reser-
vations required. Jacket required. AE, DC, MC, V. No lunch.*

$$ 'Brellas. Overlooking Hamilton Harbour from a hillside in Paget, this
★   outdoors-only restaurant on a plant-filled terrace, open in good weather
from June to early October, serves food that brightens even the less-
than-dazzling days. The cold fruit soup and Bermuda fish chowder are
excellent; recommended entrées include fresh Bermuda fish and roast
lamb with delicately steamed vegetables. Both are served with cassava
pie—a traditional meat pie made for special holidays in Bermuda. ✕
In Newstead Hotel, Harbour Rd., Paget, ☎ *441/236–6060. Reservations required. AE, MC, V.*

$$ Chancery Wine Bar. Though the menu here changes seasonally, it's a
perennial favorite with locals, particularly at lunchtime—when work-
ers head for the outdoor tables. Bermuda fish chowder is a good way
to begin a meal here, and ratatouille made with fresh, local vegetables
is a great way to follow. Outdoor dining is in an enclosed courtyard
with umbrella-topped tables set in white gravel; inside, there's a wine
cellar-like room with a vaulted ceiling. ✕ *Chancery La., off Front St.,
Hamilton,* ☎ *441/295–5058. Reservations required. AE, MC, V.
Closed Christmas, New Year's Day, and for lunch on public holidays.*

$$ Frog & Onion Pub. With its high-vaulted limestone ceilings and thick walls, the former warehouse of the Royal Naval Dockyard is a most fitting place for this nautically decorated eatery, which features a large game room for pool players. The food caters to every taste, running the gamut from hearty English pub fare to delicious European dishes to a selection of fresh local fish plates. Pub favorites are the Frog & Onion Burger, topped with fried onions and bacon; bangers and mash (sausage and homemade mashed potatoes with gravy and vegetables); Argus Bank fish sandwich; and salmon and smoked-trout fish cakes. A children's menu is available at lunchtime. ✗ *The Cooperage Building, Royal Naval Dockyard, Ireland Island,* ☎ *441/234–2900. MC, V.*

$$ Halfway House Restaurant & Bar. On the roadside in Flatts Village, this bright and airy restaurant attracts many residents and visitors, who enjoy the cheery (but sometimes slow) service. The breakfast menu features a lineup of homemade coffee rolls and scones alongside delicious omelets, pancakes, and fresh fruit. Daily specials include homemade soups, pasta, curry, and seafood dishes. Recommended are the Bermuda fish chowder, Portuguese red bean soup, spinach salad, and steak sandwiches; the traditional Bermuda breakfast—codfish with potatoes, banana, avocado, and tomato sauce—served every Sunday morning is delicious. ✗ *North Shore Rd., Smith's,* ☎ *441/295–5212. MC, V.*

$$ The Inlet. With beautiful views over Harrington Sound, this restaurant in the Palmetto Hotel is filled with sunlight and fresh air. None of the dishes is likely to find its way into a gourmet magazine, but the quality is consistently good and the selection broad. Popular choices are roast lamb with raspberry sauce and the steak dinner. ✗ *Palmetto Hotel, Flatts Village,* ☎ *441/293–2323. Reservations advised. AE, MC, V.*

$$ M. R. Onions. The Bermudian equivalent of TGIFriday, this fun restaurant got its name from the phrase "Him are Onions," meaning "he's one of us" (Bermudians are referred to as Onions, after the sweet onion that grows on the island). Friendly service and good spirits (both from the heart and the bar) make for an enjoyable evening here. Finger foods such as potato skins and breaded mushrooms are especially good, but so is everything else: try the charbroiled fresh local fish, steaks, or barbecued ribs. A special children's menu is available from 5 to 7 PM. A $13.95 early-bird dinner menu is offered from 5 to 6:30. ✗ *Par-la-Ville Rd. N, Hamilton,* ☎ *441/292–5012. Reservations advised, particularly on holidays. AE, DC, MC, V.* ☺ *For lunch and dinner weekdays; no lunch weekends and public holidays.*

✓
★ **$$ Paw-Paws.** This bistro offers seating either outdoors on a patio overlooking busy South Shore Road or in a cozy dining room with colorful wall murals of Italian garden scenes. The varied and unusual menu features Bermudian, European, and North American dishes. For starters try the Danish specialty of deep-fried Camembert with lingonberries and fried parsley, or the Bermuda fish chowder. The ravioli *d'homard et saumon* (homemade lobster ravioli with strips of smoked salmon) and grilled jumbo shrimp stuffed with crabmeat and served with piquant sauce are not-to-be-missed main courses. A special local menu offers panfried codfish cakes and shark steak served with creole sauce. The lunchtime menu includes soups, sandwiches (try the traditional Bermudian favorite of fried fish on your choice of bread), and salads (try Paw-Paws fresh salad dream—assorted mixed greens with fresh fruit, smoked salmon and grilled chicken). The wide selection of desserts comes from the adjacent bakery shop. Paw-Paws now serves breakfast as well, including a traditional Bermuda codfish breakfast with all the trimmings on Sundays. ✗ *South Shore Rd., Warwick,* ☎ *441/236–7459. Dinner reservations advised. MC, V.*

$$ The Red Carpet. Very popular at lunch, this tiny restaurant is popular
★   among local businessmen who flock here to savor the creative menu
of Old World Italian and French fare. The clever use of mirrors cre-
ates an illusion of space, while plentiful brass gives the place a stylish
look. Among the culinary highlights are veal, fish dishes, and tortellini
stuffed with veal and served with light tomato sauce. ✗ *Armoury
Bldg., Reid St., Hamilton,* ☎ *441/292–6195. Reservations advised. AE,
MC, V.*

$$ Swizzle Inn. People come to this outwardly nondescript place as much
to drink as to eat. Just west of the airport near the Bermuda Perfume
Factory, the inn created one of Bermuda's most hallowed (and lethal)
drinks—the rum swizzle. Sit in the shadowy bar—plastered with business cards from all over the world—sipping one of these delightful con-
coctions, or sit on the porch and watch the mopeds whiz by. If you get
hungry, try a "swizzleburger" (a gussied-up hamburger, with bacon and
cheese) or a delicious Bermuda fish sandwich. ✗ *Blue Hole Hill, Bailey's Bay,* ☎ *441/293–9300. AE, MC, V.*

$$ White Horse Tavern. Set on the water's edge overlooking the harbor
in St. George's, this restaurant has a great location and a light, airy at-
mosphere. The food, on the other hand, continues to be a bit on the
dull side. A Ploughman's Lunch—a baguette with cheese and a pickle—
is typical of English pub fare. The service can sometimes be a bit slow.
✗ *King's Sq., St. George's,* ☎ *441/297–1838. MC, V.*

$$ Wickets Brasserie. Tastefully decorated with prints of the game of
cricket, this restaurant offers dishes to suit just about any palate.
Bermuda fish chowder is a good starter; chicken Caesar salad with fresh
Parmesan cheese croutons is tasty and light. At the other end of the
spectrum are the hot roast beef sandwich and the Swiss cheese and bacon
burger. The combination soup and salad bar offering is a good deal
for $7.50. Top off the meal with the rich and creamy chocolate Kahlua
cake, or the lighter fresh fruit tart. ✗ *Southampton Princess Hotel, South
Shore Rd., Southampton,* ☎ *441/238–8000. Dinner reservations required. AE, MC, V.*

$ Pink's. This deli in the heart of Hamilton is certain to make your
day—or at least your lunch. Salads are wide-ranging, from tabbouleh
to tarragon chicken and pasta; creative sandwich combinations are available. Try the country pâté. Arrive early for lunch on weekdays to
avoid the crowd. ✗ *55 Front St., Hamilton,* ☎ *441/295–3524. No
credit cards. Closed Sun. No dinner.*

Italian

$$$ Il Palio. A ship's spiral staircase leads upstairs from the bar to the din-
★   ing room at this West End restaurant, where some of the island's best
pizzas are served. Among the other offerings are a wide range of good
antipasto and pasta dishes, including spaghetti with delicately seasoned
tomato sauce blended with capers, black olives, and anchovies, and
homemade cannelloni stuffed with spinach and meat. An outstanding
meat dish is Scaloppine Vesuvio—veal sautéed with white wine and
topped with prosciutto and mozzarella cheese. The fresh fish fillet
sautéed with capers, garlic, pine nuts, and a dash of tomato sauce is
another treat. Outstanding desserts are profiteroles and owner Fosco
Naninni's Panettone Surprise—Italian-style raisin bread filled with
chocolate and vanilla ice cream, topped with whipped cream. A spe-
cial takeout menu is available, with selections changing each Tuesday.
✗ *Main Rd., Somerset,* ☎ *441/234–1049 or 441/234–2323. Reser-
vations advised. DC, MC, V. Closed Mon.*

$$$ Lillian's. Part of the Sonesta Beach Hotel & Spa, this elegant art nou-
veau restaurant gains much of its character from testimonials and me-
mentos in honor of Aunt Lillian, whose counsel appears on the menus
advising diners to "be wonderful or be horrible, but for heaven's sake,
don't be mediocre." Lillian's is neither mediocre nor horrible, and its
northern Italian cuisine is well worth a try. Two outstanding dishes are
saffron gnocchi with seared sea scallops, shrimp, and salmon, and chicken
breast with Gorgonzola cheese-stuffed ravioli, sun-dried tomatoes,
spinach, and walnut cream sauce. The roast rack of lamb with seared
eggplant and polenta with roast garlic juice is superb. Dress is formal.
✕ *Sonesta Beach Hotel & Spa, Southampton,* ☎ *441/238–8122.
Reservations advised. AE, DC, MC, V.*

$$$ Little Venice. Bermudians head for this trattoria when they want more
from Italian cooking than pizza. Little Venice can be expensive, but
the food is decent enough to command higher prices and the service
is expert. In particular, try the snails in tomato sauce, an abundant plate
of antipasto, or shrimp in white wine, herb, and garlic sauce. The salads are first-rate, particularly the Caesar, and the spinach is topped with
Gorgonzola croutons. All the pastas are good, especially the *orecchiette* (ear–shaped pasta) tossed with spinach and sausage. For dessert,
pannacotta (Bavarian cream with fresh berries and strawberry coulis)
is sublime. ✕ *Bermudiana Rd., Hamilton,* ☎ *441/295–8279. Reservations required. AE, DC, MC, V.*

$$ Harley's Bistro. Popular with businessmen from the nearby city of
Hamilton, this poolside eatery at the Princess Hotel overlooking Hamil-
ton Harbour recently underwent a major transformation and now
features northern Italian fare—either indoors or al fresco. Pizzas with
all the regular toppings, the expected lineup of pasta dishes, and more
expensive veal and fish dishes are consistently good. Lunchtime din-
ers can enjoy the creative salads and large sandwiches. ✕ *The Princess
Hotel, Hamilton,* ☎ *441/295–3000. Reservations advised. AE, DC,
MC, V.*

$$ Portofino. Busy for both lunch and dinner, this popular Italian restaurant is often noisy, and the service can be impersonal; a separate
bar/waiting area accommodates patrons who don't have reservations.
A wide selection of pizza toppings is available, and customers are
asked to phone 15 minutes ahead if they want their pie to go. If you're
not in the mood for pizza, try the excellent sirloin steak *pizzaiola*
(with olives, anchovies, capers, and tomato sauce), or the fried cala-
mari in a delicate batter. More adventurous diners will enjoy the oc-
topus, cooked in red sauce with olives and capers and served on a bed
of rice. Homemade pasta and risotto specials are excellent. ✕ *Bermudiana Rd., Hamilton,* ☎ *441/292–2375 or 441/295–6090. Reservations required. AE, MC, V. No lunch weekends.*

$$ Ristorante Primavera. An understated elegance pervades this pleasing
Mediterranean dining room in the west end of Hamilton, where din-
ers sit under a cleverly designed ceiling of grape vines and lattice. The
menu is extensive, all selections are made to order. Spectacular starters
are Carpaccio Primavera—thin slices of beef tenderloin with parme-
san cheese and olive oil, and Scampi and Scallops Innamorati, sautéed
in cognac, paprika, and shallots. Guests can also choose from a wide
variety of consistently good pastas (try the *triangolo di paste,* a com-
bination of three different pastas with three different sauces). ✕ *Pitts
Bay Rd., Hamilton,* ☎ *441/295–2167. Reservations advised. AE,
MC, V. No lunch weekends.*

$$ Tuscany. When it opened in the former premises of Loquats restaurant,
★ Tuscany quickly became a hit with the island's chefs on their night off—
as well as with locals and visitors. The balcony overlooks Front Street

and has views of Hamilton Harbour; inside, a beautiful mural of the Tuscan countryside dominates one wall. The service in this owner-operated establishment is efficient and unusually friendly. The pizzas are top ranking, particularly the *4 Stagioni* with tomato, mozzarella, artichoke hearts, and asparagus. Penne *terra mare* with baby shrimp, zucchini, and tomato and scaloppine cacciatore are also superb. ✗ *Front St., Hamilton,* ☎ *441/292–4507. Reservations advised. AE, MC, V.*

$ **La Trattoria.** Tucked in a Hamilton alley, this no-nonsense trattoria has red-check tablecloths and the familiar feel of a mom-and-pop establishment. Recommended entrees are ravioli stuffed with ricotta cheese in tomato cream sauce and filet of fish with baby shrimp, sauteed in white wine with oregano, garlic and tomato. La Trattoria also serves unusual pizzas, such as the Pekinese—chicken, snow peas, sweet-and-sour sauce, and cheese. The early dinner special menu ($14.75) includes appetizer, main course, dessert, and coffee, and is available between 6 and 7 PM. ✗ *Washington La., Hamilton,* ☎ *441/295–1877. Reservations advised. AE, DC, MC, V.*

$ **Pasta Basta and Pasta Pasta.** These two restaurants—one in Hamil-
★ ton and the other in St. George's—share the same menu and decor. Both are Bermudian favorites, with their brightly painted interiors, colorful tables and chairs, and lively (if slightly institutional) atmosphere. The food is well prepared and delicious; an ever-changing menu of simple northern Italian cuisine provides good value. Try the penne with chicken and pepper sauce, classic or vegetable lasagna, orecchiette with pesto and potato, Caesar salad, or any of the daily specials. No liquor is served in either restaurant, and smoking is not permitted. ✗ *1 Elliot St. W, Hamilton,* ☎ *441/295–9785; York St., St. George's,* ☎ *441/297–2927. No reservations. No credit cards.*

$ **Speciality Inn.** A favorite with locals, this south-shore restaurant is cheerful and clean, with low prices that reflect its sparse decor. Try the fish chowder or the red bean soup. Otherwise, all the dishes are just what you would expect of a family-style Italian restaurant. ✗ *Collectors Hill, Smith's,* ☎ *441/236–3133. Reservations advised. No credit cards.*

$ **Tio Pepe.** You don't need to spend much money for a satisfying meal at this Italian restaurant with a Mexican name. Photocopied menus and red and green decor create an easygoing atmosphere ideal for bathers returning from a day at Horseshoe Bay Beach. Try an appetizer such as spicy eggplant baked in tomato sauce and cheese, followed by a small pizza or pasta dish. ✗ *South Shore Rd., Southampton,* ☎ *441/238–1897 or 441/238–0572. Reservations advised. AE, MC, V. Closed Mon. Nov.–Mar.*

Mexican

$ **Rosa's Cantina.** The island's only Tex-Mex eatery has a festive, lively atmosphere, and a predictable decor of sombreros, serapes, and south-of-the-border bric-a-brac. Despite its monopoly on the cuisine, the food here is consistently good. Nachos Unbelievable (melted cheese, refried beans, beef, onions, tomatoes, peppers, jalapeño peppers, and guacamole), fajitas, and burritos are popular favorites. Food here is generally not too spicy, although most anything can be made extra-hot. This place has a loyal local following, and is always filled with a crowd of both Bermudians and vacationers. On balmy evenings, its new location offers outdoor dining on the balcony, overlooking bustling Front Street. ✗ *121 Front St., Hamilton,* ☎ *441/295–1912. AE, MC, V. Closed Christmas Day.*

Seafood

$$$ Port O' Call. For lunch or dinner, this delightfully intimate restaurant is one of Hamilton's most popular eateries. Fresh local fish such as wahoo, tuna, grouper, and snapper are cooked perfectly, and the sauces are pure silk. Try the Sea Venture—sirloin steak with broiled shrimp, topped with herb and curry butter, or one of the tempting daily specials. A delicious end to a meal here is the Amaretto parfait. Early-bird specials, served 5–6:15 daily, are $19.75 for soup or salad, entrée, dessert, and coffee. ✕ *87 Front St., Hamilton,* ☎ *441/295–5373. Reservations advised. AE, DC, MC, V. Closed Sun. and holidays.*

$$$ Whaler Inn. Perched above the rocks and surf at the Southampton Princess, this seafood house has one of the most dramatic settings on the island. Fresh seafood is flown in several times a week from New England and purchased from local fisherman, making the menu selections both pleasing and plentiful. The St. David's Kettle—lobster, clams, mussels, shrimp, and fish in a tomato sauce blended with sherry peppers, black rum, and Chardonnay is a pleasing dish, as is the Bermuda Triangle—three fresh fillets of fish with tomato, citrus, and dill sauce. Desserts here are stupendous; the chocolate cake with a sinful fudge icing steals the show. ✕ *Southampton Princess Hotel, South Shore Rd., Southampton,* ☎ *441/238–0076. Reservations advised. AE, DC, MC, V.*

$$ Fisherman's Reef. Located above the Hog Penny Pub, this upscale restaurant with a nautical motif draws a crowd of locals for seafood and steak lunches and dinners. The fish chowder is excellent, as is the St. David's conch chowder. Of the wide selection of seafood entrées, the best are the Bermuda lobster (in season only), the wahoo Mangrove Bay (seasoned and broiled with slices of Bermuda onions and banana), and the Cajun-style, baked or panfried local catch of the day. Fresh local mussels are delicious either in curry sauce or baked with tomatoes and cheese. ✕ *Burnaby Hill, just off Front St., Hamilton,* ☎ *441/292–1609. Reservations advised. AE, DC, MC, V. No weekend lunch.*

$$ Freeport Gardens. If you are looking for good, locally caught fish, this is the place to come. The fish platter or combination seafood platter with scallops, shrimp, and fish are not presented with great flair, but they are delicious, and the fish sandwiches are unforgettable. If you don't like fruits of the sea, you can choose from a range of pizzas with all the usual trimmings, hamburgers, or an assortment of sandwiches. If you want a hearty breakfast before touring Ireland Island, you can tuck into a Spanish omelet or waffles with bacon. ✕ *Pender Rd., Dockyard, Sandys,* ☎ *441/234–1692. AE, MC, V.*

$$ Lobster Pot. Bermudians swear by this place, which features some of the best versions of island standards, including local lobster (from September through March), Maine lobster, and a host of other local shellfish and fish. Special Lobster Pot snails are delicious in their buttery secret sauce. Apropos of its specialty, the restaurant sports boat–related decor, including shining brass instruments and sun-bleached rope. ✕ *Bermudiana Rd., Hamilton,* ☎ *441/292–6898. Reservations advised. AE, DC, MC, V. Closed Sun. and holidays.*

8 Lodging

IF ALL THE ACCOMMODATIONS AVAILABLE on Bermuda were reviewed here, this book would barely qualify as carry-on luggage. Visitors to this tiny island can choose from a huge array of full-service resort hotels, cottage colonies, small inns, guest houses, and housekeeping apartments. It is the beachfront cottage colonies for which Bermuda is probably most famous, however—freestanding cottages clustered around a main building housing a restaurant, a lounge, and an activities desk. Many properties, especially these cottage colonies, are sprawling affairs set in extensive grounds and connected by walkways and steps; at some of the smaller guest houses and housekeeping apartments visitors must carry their own luggage on the long walk to their rooms. Visitors with disabilities and anyone unwilling to climb hills may be happier at a conventional hotel with elevators and corridors.

Like everything else in Bermuda, lodging is expensive. The rates at Bermuda's luxury resorts are comparable to those at posh hotels in New York, London, and Paris. The high prices would be easier to swallow if you received first-class service in return. However, such features as 24-hour room service and same-day laundry service are rare; in most instances, you pay extra for room service when it is available. You can shave about 40% off your hotel bill by visiting Bermuda during the low or shoulder seasons. The trick is in trying to define which dates apply. Low season runs roughly from November through March; however, each property sets its own guidelines, and they may change even from year to year. Some hotels begin high season rates on April 1, others April 15, and a few kick in as late as May 1: your best bet is to call and ask about low- and shoulder-season rates. As temperatures rarely dip below 60°F during the winter, the weather is ideal for tennis, golf, and shopping—although the water is a bit chilly for swimming. Some properties reduce room rates by 10% when the temperature does not reach 68°F during January, February, or March. Low-season packages are attractively priced, and during this time a host of government-sponsored special events (many of which are free) are staged for tourists. Some hotels and smaller properties close each year during January and/or February to refurbish and prepare for the high season.

The greatest concentration of accommodations is along the south shore, in Paget, Warwick, and Southampton parishes, where the best beaches are located. If shopping is your bag, however, there are several hotels just a stone's throw from the main shopping area in Front Street in Hamilton, as well as a host of properties clustered around Hamilton Harbour, a five- to 10-minute ferry ride from the capital. The West End is a bit remote, but the ferry travels regularly across the Great Sound to Hamilton, and it's ideal for boaters, fishermen, and those who want to get away from it all. The East End has its share of nautical pursuits, too, but its major attraction is the charming, historic town of St. George. In truth, the island is so small that it's possible to see and do everything you want, regardless of where you unpack your bag.

Whether or not they are officially classified as cottage colonies, a large number of guest accommodations are in cottages—usually pink with white trim and gleaming white, tiered roofs. There are some sprawling resorts, but no high rises and no neon signs. An enormous property like the Southampton Princess is hard to miss, but many hotels and guest houses are identified only by small, inconspicuous signs or plaques. The island is noted for its lovely gardens and manicured lawns, and the grounds of almost every hotel and cottage are filled with subtropical trees, flowers, and shrubs.

Return visitors to the island will appreciate the annual improvements that are made to virtually all properties. The Hotels Refurbishment (Temporary) Customs Duty Relief Bill of 1991 substantially reduced the duty on goods imported to the island, and hotels and guest house owners have taken advantage of it to further upgrade their facilities.

A 6% Government Occupancy tax is tacked onto all hotel bills, and a service charge is levied: Some hotels calculate a service charge as 10% of the bill, others charge a per diem dollar amount. All guests are required to make a two-night deposit two to three weeks before their arrival; those accommodations that don't take credit cards for payment—and many do not—accept personal checks for the deposit. Virtually every hotel on the island offers at least one vacation package—frequently some kind of honeymoon special—and many of these are extraordinarily good deals. It's worth learning about the various policies and programs at the properties that interest you before booking.

Bermuda has not traditionally been noted as a family destination, but that has greatly changed. Hotels, guest houses, and cottage colonies welcome families with children, and most have day care and children's activities programs. Most of the hotels, including the Belmont Hotel, Golf & Country Club, the Elbow Beach Hotel, the Grotto Bay Beach Hotel & Tennis Club, the Sonesta Beach Hotel & Spa, the Southampton Princess, Willowbank, and most of the smaller properties offer supervised programs for children, some of which are part of attractive packages. Many hotels on the island can arrange for baby-sitters.

Most lodgings offer their guests a choice of meal plans, and the hotel rate varies according to the meal plan you choose. Under the American Plan (AP), breakfast, lunch, and dinner are included in the hotel rate; the Modified American Plan (MAP) offers breakfast and dinner; the Bermuda Plan (BP) includes a full breakfast but no dinner, while the Continental Plan (CP) features a breakfast of pastries, juice, and coffee. The rates quoted below are based on the European Plan (EP), which includes no meals at all. Many hotels also have a variety of "dine-around" plans that allow guests to eat at other restaurants on the island as part of their meal plan. The Princess and the Southampton Princess offer a Royal Dine-Around program year-round, which allows guests to eat at any of the several Princess restaurants. The five properties in the Bermuda Collection (Cambridge Beaches, Lantana, the Reefs, Stonington Beach, and the Pompano) have a similar arrangement, known as the Carousel Dine-Around program, as do Horizons, Newstead, and Waterloo House. The Belmont Hotel, Golf & Country Club and the Harmony Club, both of which are Forte properties, have an exchange dining plan. Dinner is usually formal in restaurants at hotels and cottage colonies: men are asked to wear jackets and ties, and casual but neat dress is suggested for women. Many hotels will pack a picnic lunch for those guests who want to get out and about.

Bermuda's Small Properties Ltd. is a group of small hotels and guest houses that share a toll-free information/reservations line and a fax number. The properties include Angel's Grotto, Ariel Sands Beach Club, Fourways Inn, Greenbank, Longtail Cliffs, Marley Beach Cottages, Pretty Penny, Royal Palms Hotel, and Vienna Guest Apartments. To reserve at any of these properties, call 800/637–4116 or fax 441/236–3290.

Cottage colonies and hotels offer entertainment at least one night a week during high season, staging everything from calypso to classical music;

barbecues and dinner dances are also popular. Afternoon tea is serve daily in keeping with British tradition, and a rum-swizzle party is usually held on Monday night. Featuring the Bermudian beverage of choice, these parties present a pleasant opportunity to welcome new arrivals, get acquainted—and, of course, knock back some rum. Guest houses and housekeeping apartments do not have regularly scheduled entertainment, although informal gatherings are not uncommon.

Most of the large hotels have their own water-sports facilities where guests can rent Windsurfers, Sunfish, paddleboats, and other equipment. Even the smallest property, however, can arrange sailing, snorkeling, scuba, and deep-sea fishing excursions, as well as sightseeing and harbor tours. The Coral Beach & Tennis Club and the Mid Ocean Club are posh private clubs, where an introduction by a member is necessary to gain access to their excellent beach, tennis, and golf facilities. However, many hotels have arrangements with one or the other to allow guests certain club privileges.

CATEGORY	COST*
$$$$	over $200
$$$	$125–$200
$$	$90–$125
$	under $90

All prices are for a standard double room for two (EP) during high season, excluding 6% tax and 10% service charge (or equivalent).

Resort Hotels

$$$$ Belmont Hotel, Golf & Country Club. Occupying 110 acres between Harbour and Middle roads, this large, pink hotel was built at the turn of the century and has a distinctly British personality. As its name suggests, it's also a sports-minded resort: Golf and tennis pros are on hand to give lessons and organize golf scrambles and tennis round-robins (golf and tennis are free to hotel guests, though there is a $5 an hour fee for night tennis). Hotel guests also play free on the miniature golf range and the floodlit putting green. The Belmont's children's program, called the Kee Kee Club, costs $10 per visit. It allows guests to enroll their children ages 2–12 in a plan that includes free meals and full day-care services, among other perks. An extensive range of other fun activities, including miniature golf games, keep the children entertained. The enormous lobby, decorated with chandeliers and fresh flowers, bustles with the golf groups that frequent the hotel. Refurbished in 1994, the rooms are average in size (bathrooms are quite small), but their large windows admit plenty of light and create a sense of spaciousness. Mahogany Queen Anne furniture is mixed with wicker, carpets are dusty pink, and the bedspreads and drapes are in bright tropical floral patterns. With views over the harbor and the resort's gardens and pool— one of the largest on the island—the rooms on the fourth floor are probably the best. The Hamilton ferry stops at the Belmont Wharf; it's a long haul up the hill from the wharf to the hotel, but a shuttle bus makes the trip regularly. Guests on MAP may participate in the dine-around program at the Harmony Club by arranging it in advance. ⊠ *Box WK 251, Warwick WK BX,* ☎ *441/236–1301; in U.S. and Canada, 800/225–5843;* FAX *441/236–6867. 149 rooms, 1 suite, all with bath. BP, EP, MAP. 2 restaurants, bar, saltwater pool, 18-hole golf course, miniature golf, putting green, 3 tennis courts, shops. AE, DC, MC, V.*

$$$$ Elbow Beach Hotel. Though this large, sports-oriented resort lacks any real Bermudian charm, it has all the grandeur of any major resort hotel,

	Access for Disabled	On The Beach	Swimming Pool	Restaurant	Cable T.V.	Fitness Facilities	Golf Nearby	Tennis Courts	Conference Fac.	Accept Children	Children's Prog.	Access To Spa	On-Site Water-Sports	Accept Credit Cards	Air-Conditioned	Entertainment	Boat Dock/Marina
Angel's Grotto	•				•		•			•			•	•	•		
Ariel Sands Beach Club	•	•	•	•			•	•	•	•	•		•	•	•	•	
Barnsdale Guest Apartments			•		•		•			•							
Belmont Hotel	•		•	•			•	•	•	•				•	•	•	•
Cambridge Beaches		•	•	•		•	•	•	•			•	•		•		•
Edgehill Manor			•		•		•			•					•		
Elbow Beach Hotel	•	•	•	•	•		•	•	•	•	•	•	•	•	•	•	
Fourways Inn			•	•	•		•		•						•		
Greenbank Cottages							•			•			•	•	•		
Grotto Bay Beach Hotel	•		•	•	•		•	•	•	•	•		•	•	•	•	
Harmony Club			•	•	•		•	•						•	•	•	
Hillcrest Guest House							•			•					•		
Horizons & Cottages			•	•			•	•		•					•	•	
Lantana Colony Club			•	•			•	•	•	•			•		•	•	•
Little Pomander Guest House	•				•		•			•			•	•	•		•
Longtail Cliffs	•		•		•		•			•				•	•		
Loughlands Guest House			•				•	•		•				•	•		
Marley Beach Cottages		•	•		•		•			•			•	•	•		
Marriott's Castle Harbour	•	•	•	•	•	•	•	•	•	•			•	•	•	•	•
Newstead			•	•			•	•		•			•		•	•	•
Oxford House					•		•			•			•	•			
Palmetto Hotel & Cottages		•	•				•		•	•			•	•	•	•	•
Paraquet Guest Apartments			•	•			•			•					•		
Pink Beach Club & Cottages		•	•	•			•	•	•	•			•	•	•	•	•
Pompano Beach Club		•	•	•		•	•	•	•	•			•		•	•	•

	Access for Disabled	On The Beach	Swimming Pool	Restaurant	Cable T.V.	Fitness Facilities	Golf Nearby	Tennis Courts	Conference Fac.	Accept Children	Children's Prog.	Access To Spa	On-Site Water-Sports	Accept Credit Cards	Air-Conditioned	Entertainment	Boat Dock/Marina
Pretty Penny			•				•			•				•	•	•	
Princess, Hamilton	•		•	•	•	•	•	•	•	•			•	•	•	•	•
The Reefs	•	•	•	•			•	•	•	•		•	•		•	•	
Rosedon			•							•					•		
Royal Palms Hotel			•	•	•					•					•	•	
St. George's Club	•	•	•	•	•		•	•	•	•			•	•	•	•	
Salt Kettle House							•			•			•		•		•
Sky Top Cottages							•			•				•	•		
Sonesta Beach Hotel	•	•	•	•	•	•	•	•	•	•	•	•	•	•	•	•	
Southampton Princess	•		•	•	•	•	•	•	•	•	•	•	•	•	•	•	•
Stonington Beach Hotel		•	•	•			•	•	•				•	•	•	•	
Surf Side Beach Club		•	•	•	•		•			•	•		•	•	•		
Waterloo House			•	•						•	•			•	•	•	
Whale Bay Inn							•			•					•		
Willowbank		•	•	•			•			•	•	•			•		

and a great setting to boot. Set amid 34 acres of botanical gardens over-looking the superb south-shore beach for which it is named, it sports all the trappings of the $20-million transformation it began in 1991, when the Wyndham Resort group bought the hotel. Behind the five-story hotel's white-column facade, the lobby has been expanded to pala-tial proportions and paved with green marble and Oriental area rugs. Walls are paneled with white oak, and six giant crystal chandeliers hang over a gilt table, cushy furnishings, and huge, handsome arrangements of artificial flowers. Its 295 rooms, suites, and junior suites are spread between the main building and outlying multi-unit lanais and duplex cottages on well-manicured grounds. (A shuttle bus runs between the main building and the beach.) Most accommodations have a balcony or patio and a spectacular ocean view (avoid the land-side rooms, which have neither). The pool has a shallow end, and during July and Au-gust, special children's programs are held. During high season, theme parties and barbecues are frequent affairs. There is an $8-per-hour fee for the tennis courts ($3 racket rental, $12 for night play). Plans for further expansion include an additional 120 rooms; a conference cen-ter; another, larger, pool; and a spa/health club. ⊞ *Box HM 455, Hamilton HM BX,* ☎ *441/236–3535; in U.S. and Canada, 800/223–7434;* ℻ *441/236–8043. 223 rooms, 75 suites, all with bath. BP, MAP. 4 restaurants, 3 bars, pool, beauty salon, hot tub, 5 tennis courts, ex-ercise room, beach, water sports, motorbikes, shops, playground. AE, DC, MC, V.*

$$$$ **Marriott's Castle Harbour Resort.** Bordered by Harrington Sound on one side and the Castle Harbour golf course on the other, this whitewashed hilltop resort is an impressive sight from the air. If "castle" conjures up images of King Ludwig, though, forget it. This is a big, busy, modern hotel that caters more to vacationers than groups and conventions. The original Castle, which opened in 1931, was built by Furness, Withy & Co. as a hotel for steamship passengers traveling between U.S. and British ports. Since 1984 Marriott has spent $60 million in renovation and ex-pansion ($1.5 million in a 1992 refurbishment), and four wings are now connected to the original building by glass-enclosed skywalks: the two-story Golf Club wing, the Castle Building wing, and the two nine-story Harbour View wings, which descend in terraces to the water. Rooms throughout the hotel are identical, featuring upholstered wing-back chairs, windows dressed in ruffled valances, and heavy drapes with matching quilted bedspreads; many also have balconies. The resort's beach on Cas-tle Harbour is small, but the one on the South Shore is the island's largest private beach. Guests also have access to three pools, including an Olympic-size lap pool and a cascading pool. Tennis courts are $12 an hour (plus $5 for racket rental), but the real draw is the adjacent 18-hole Castle Harbour golf course—one of the best courses on the island. ⊞ *Box HM 841, Hamilton HM CX,* ☎ *441/293–2040; in U.S., 800/228–9290;* ℻ *441/293–8288. 375 rooms, 27 suites, all with bath. MAP, BP, EP. 3 restaurants, 3 bars, 3 pools, beauty salon/barbershop, 18-hole golf course, 6 tennis courts, health club, 2 beaches, water sports, motorbikes, laundry service and dry cleaning, concierge, busi-ness services, meeting rooms. AE, DC, MC, V.*

$$$$ **Sonesta Beach Hotel & Spa.** A sloping, serpentine drive leads through landscaped lawns to this hotel, the only property on the island where you can step directly from your room onto a sandy south-shore beach. Set on a low promontory fringed by coral reefs, the six-story modern building has a stunning ocean view and direct access to three superb natural beaches. Completely renovated in 1995, the Sonesta caters to guests who want an action-packed vacation: An activities director co-ordinates bingo games, theme parties, movies, water sports, and other diversions. During high season, children's programs and family packages are offered. A glass-enclosed entranceway leads to the enormous, low-ceiling lobby (where there is a separate registration area for the large groups that often check in here). Guest rooms and suites are decorated in light blonde wooden furnishings upholstered with peach and green fabrics. A shuttle takes guests to the hotel's beach at Cross Bay, but beach lovers should insist on a Bay Wing minisuite that opens onto a private sandy beach. The split-level minisuites feature separate sitting areas, hair dryers, and VCRs. Many rooms on the 25-acre property have balconies, but standard rooms in the main building have land views only. Sports facilities include an indoor pool under a glass dome, six tennis courts ($8 an hour; $5 for racket rental), and the considerable facilities (extra charge) of South Side Scuba Watersports, which has an outlet at the hotel. One of the island's best-equipped health spas is here (extra charge), and special four-, five- or six-day spa packages include room, meals, and a range of spa offerings. A shuttle bus transports guests between the hotel and South Road, at the top of the hill. ▥ *Box HM 1070, Hamilton HM EX,* ☎ *441/238–8122; in U.S., 800/ 766–3782;* FAX *441/238–8463. 365 rooms, 34 suites, all with bath. MAP (EP and BP on request). 3 restaurants, 3 bars, indoor and outdoor pools, beauty salon, hot tub, massage, steam room, 6 tennis courts, exercise room, water sports, 3 beaches, motorbikes, shops, nightclub, playground, concierge. AE, DC, MC, V.*

$$$–$$$$ **Grotto Bay Beach Hotel & Tennis Club.** Only a mile from the airport, this is one of the most intimate hotels in this price category. Set among 20 acres of gardens, it draws a young crowd for its relaxed atmosphere and its proximity to an enclosed bay that's riddled with romantic coves and natural caves. Also in the bay are a fish-feeding aquarium and two illuminated underground attractions: the Cathedral Cave for swimming, and Prospero's Cave, which can be seen on a guided tour. The hotel itself consists of a main building and 11 three-story lodges dotting a hill that slopes to the waters of Ferry Reach. Each lodge contains between 15 and 30 sunny rooms featuring light woods and fabrics, private balconies or patios, and views of the water. Although the lodges don't have elevators, the ground-floor units are accessible by wheelchair, but request a room near the lobby building to make getting around easier. There are also three suites, which each have two bedrooms, three bathrooms, a living room, and a balcony. The hotel has its own sightseeing excursion boat and offers scuba diving and snorkeling from a private deep-water dock. Just below the pool is the beach, whose small causeway attracts a colorful congregation of fish. During high season, entertainment is held poolside. Guests can play on the resort's four tennis courts for $8 an hour ($10 for night play), and rackets can be rented for $5 an hour. Children's activities are held in season. ▥ *11 Blue Hole Hill, Hamilton Parish CR 04,* ☎ *441/293– 8333 or 800/582–3190,* FAX *441/293–2306. 198 rooms, 3 suites, all with bath. BP, EP, MAP. Restaurant, 2 bars, pool, 4 tennis courts, health club, shuffleboard, beach, water sports, motorbikes, playground, business services, meeting room. AE, MC, V.*

$$$–$$$$ **The Princess.** Named in honor of Princess Louise, Queen Victoria's
★ daughter who visited the island in 1883, this large pink landmark opened in 1884 and is credited with starting Bermuda's tourist industry. Refurbished in 1995, it retains a slightly formal atmosphere, and its staff provides swift, courteous service. The walls at the entrance to the Tiara Room restaurant are covered with pictures of the politicians and royals who have visited the hotel, as well as other memorabilia from the hotel's rich past. Ideally located on Hamilton Harbour, the hotel caters to business and professional people, convention groups, and

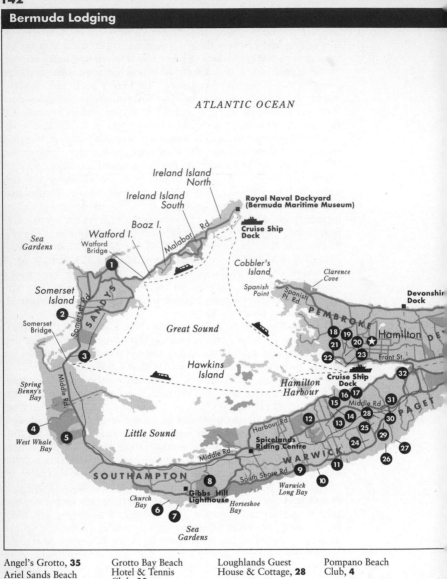

ATLANTIC OCEAN

Ireland Island North

Ireland Island South

Boaz I.

Watford I.

Watford Bridge

Sea Gardens

Royal Naval Dockyard (Bermuda Maritime Museum)

Cruise Ship Dock

Malabar Rd.

Somerset Island

SANDYS

Somerset Rd.

Somerset Bridge

Cobbler's Island

Great Sound

Spanish Point

Spanish Pt. Rd.

Clarence Cove

PEMBROKE

DEVONSHIRE Dock

Hawkins Island

Hamilton

Front St.

Spring Benny's Bay

Middle Rd.

Little Sound

West Whale Bay

Hamilton Harbour

Cruise Ship Dock

Harbour Rd.

PAGET

Middle Rd.

Spicelands Riding Centre

Middle Rd.

WARWICK

SOUTHAMPTON

South Shore Rd.

Church Bay

Gibbs Hill Lighthouse

Horseshoe Bay

Warwick Long Bay

Sea Gardens

Angel's Grotto, **35**
Ariel Sands Beach Club, **33**
Barnsdale Guest Apartments, **30**
Belmont Hotel, Golf & Country Club, **12**
Cambridge Beaches, **1**
Edgehill Manor, **21**
Elbow Beach Hotel, **26**
Fourways Inn, **13**
Greenbank Cottages, **15**

Grotto Bay Beach Hotel & Tennis Club, **38**
Harmony Club, **31**
Hillcrest Guest House, **39**
Horizons & Cottages, **24**
Lantana Colony Club, **3**
Little Pomander Guest House, **32**
Longtail Cliffs, **9**

Loughlands Guest House & Cottage, **28**
Marley Beach Cottages, **10**
Marriott's Castle Harbour Resort, **37**
Newstead, **17**
Oxford House, **19**
Palmetto Hotel & Cottages, **34**
Paraquet Guest Apartments, **29**
Pink Beach Club & Cottages, **36**

Pompano Beach Club, **4**
Pretty Penny, **14**
The Princess, **22**
The Reefs, **6**
Rosedon, **20**
Royal Palms Hotel, **18**
St. George's Club, **40**
Salt Kettle House, **16**
Sky Top Cottages, **25**
Sonesta Beach Hotel & Spa, **7**

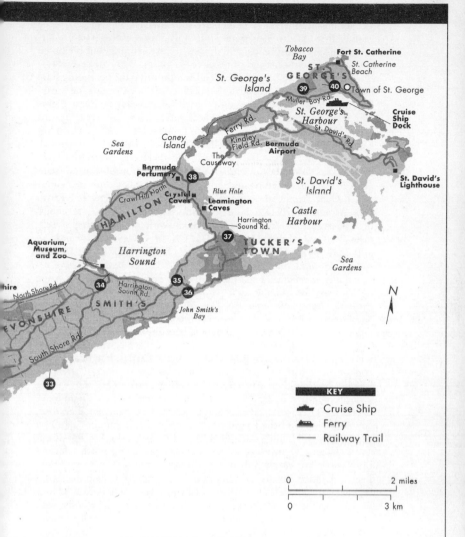

Tobacco Bay

Fort St. Catherine

St. Catherine Beach

St. George's Island

ST. GEORGE'S

Town of St. George

Mullet Bay Rd.

St. George's Harbour

Cruise Ship Dock

Ferry Rd.

Coney Island

Sea Gardens

Kindley Field Rd.

Bermuda Airport

St. David's Rd.

The Causeway

St. David's Island

St. David's Lighthouse

Bermuda Perfumery

38

Crawl Hill North

Crystal Caves

Blue Hole

Leamington Caves

Harrington Sound Rd.

Castle Harbour

HAMILTON

37

TUCKER'S TOWN

Aquarium, Museum, and Zoo

Harrington Sound

Sea Gardens

N

34

Harrington Sound Rd.

35

hire

North Shore Rd.

SMITH'S

36

DEVONSHIRE

John Smith's Bay

South Shore Rd.

33

KEY

🚢 Cruise Ship

⛴ Ferry

▬ Railway Trail

0 ——————— 2 miles

0 ——————— 3 km

Southampton
Princess, **8**

Stonington Beach
Hotel, **27**

Surf Side
Beach Club, **11**

Waterloo House, **23**

Whale Bay Inn, **5**

Willowbank, **2**

other visitors who want to be near downtown Hamilton. Expanded service for businessmen in 1995 included the installation of voice mail, the island's first hotel to incorporate it into its phone system. Plush colorful upholstery, bedspreads, and drapes are used throughout the hotel, and most of the rooms and suites have balconies. There are several categories of suites, and all are large and sumptuous—the penthouse suite has a Jacuzzi. The Princess Club's amenities include Continental breakfast, and showers and changing facilities for travelers with late flights who want to swim after morning checkout. A ferry makes regular runs across the harbor to the Southampton Princess (*see below*), which has a golf course and other sports facilities (none of which is free to guests). The Hamilton Princess has no beach, but there are stretches of lawn and terraces above the dock area with deck chairs for relaxing and sunning. In season, island revues showcasing Bermuda's top-rated entertainer, Gene Steede, are presented in the Gazebo Lounge. The Royal Dine-Around plan between the two Princess hotels offers guests a choice of nine restaurants—from casual to formal—with menus catering to every taste. ☎ *Box HM 837, Hamilton HM CX,* ☎ *441/295–3000; in U.S., 800/223–1818; in Canada, 800/268–7176;* ℻ *441/295–1914. 422 rooms, 28 suites, all with bath. BP, EP, MAP. 3 restaurants, 2 bars, in-room safes, minibars, 2 pools (one saltwater), beauty salon, putting green, tennis court, health club with spa facilities, beach, water sports, motorbikes, shops, concierge. AE, DC, MC, V.*

$$$–$$$$ **Southampton Princess.** This hotel is much larger and livelier than its
★ older sister, the Princess (*see above*) in Hamilton. It's not the place for those seeking a quiet retreat, but it's an excellent choice for anyone who enjoys planned activities, such as theme parties, bingo, aerobics, cooking demonstrations, and tennis matches. For families, it offers the island's best children's program, including parties and baby-sitting services (children under 16 stay free, and if their parents are on MAP they also get free meals). The six-story, ultramodern main building, which contains several of the island's best restaurants, dominates a hilltop near Gibbs Hill Lighthouse; the 300-year-old Waterlot Inn restaurant (*see* Chapter 7, Dining) occupies a dockside spot on the north side, and the Whaler Inn beach club is perched above the surf at South Shore Beach. A jitney churns over hill and dale to connect them all, and a regiment of staffers is on hand to assist you if you get lost. Rooms vary in size, but they're all decorated in soft corals and light woods, with plenty of marble in the spacious bathrooms. The oceanfront deluxe rooms are the nicest; if possible, avoid rooms on the first three floors of the west and north wings, which overlook rooftops. Some of the elegant suites feature kitchens, dishwashers, and custom-made furniture. Perks in the 55-room Newport Club include private check-in/out, complimentary Continental breakfast, and a private lounge, in addition to all amenities available in the hotel's other rooms. Guests pay a daily $10 fee ($15 per couple) or weekly $20 fee ($30 per couple) to use the health club, sauna, and indoor pool; the greens fee for the 18-hole golf course is $32, plus $28 for a mandatory cart, and tennis costs $10 an hour ($6 an hour for racket rental). The Secret Garden skin clinic and hair studio (a separate concession) is one of the island's best, with British-trained beauty therapists giving a full range of European skin treatments, massages, and reflexology. The impressive three-level Mid-Ocean Amphitheater for meetings and conventions is the largest of its kind in North America, Hawaii, and the Caribbean, accommodating up to 700 people. Upstairs in the Lobby Lounge, a Calypso guitarist strums island tunes from 9 until midnight. Adjacent is the Neptune Club, a lively place that features the nightly comedy/piano act of Jimmy Keyes. ☎ *Box HM 1379, Hamilton HM FX,* ☎ *441/238–8000; in U.S., 800/*

223–1818; ⅧX *441/238–8968. 598 rooms, 36 suites, all with bath. MAP. 6 restaurants, 4 bars, minibars, no-smoking rooms, indoor pool, outdoor pool, beauty salon, 18-hole golf course, 11 tennis courts, boccie, croquet, health club with spa facilities, beach, dive shop, snorkeling, parasailing, motorbikes, shops, nightclub, concierge, convention center. AE, DC, MC, V.*

Small Hotels

$$$$ Harmony Club. Nestled in lovely gardens, this two-story pink-and-white hotel—the island's only all-inclusive resort—was built in the 1930s as a private home. The adult-oriented hotel has a couples-only policy, but a couple can be two aunts, two friends, or any other combination. The base rate covers everything, including round-trip airport transfers, meals, alcohol, and even two-seater scooters. All meals come with the package, but food lovers can participate in the dine-around plan at the Belmont Hotel, Golf & Country Club. The hotel, which is refurbished annually, has a spacious reception area with Bermuda cedar paneling, and a club lounge with a large-screen TV and an assortment of games, including cards, darts, and backgammon. Upon arrival, guests find complimentary champagne in their rooms, which are luxuriously decorated with Queen Anne furnishings and feature hair dryers, bathrobes, and coffeemakers. All but 12 of the rooms have a patio or balcony. The hotel is not on the water, but it's only about a five-minute scooter ride to the south-shore beaches. Guests can partake of a host of activities during high season, from informal barbecues to formal dances and complimentary use of the golf course at the Belmont Hotel, Golf & Country Club. Entertainment changes nightly—offerings range from Calypso-limbo dancing to solo singers and band performances to informative slide shows about the island. Ⅷ *Box PG 299, Paget PG BX,* ☎ *441/236–3500; in U.S., 800/225–5843;* ⅧX *441/236–2624. 71 rooms with bath. AP. Restaurant, bar, pool, hot tub, sauna, putting green, 2 tennis courts, motorbikes. AE, DC, MC, V.*

$$$$ Pompano Beach Club. Expect a friendly, personal welcome when you arrive at this informal seaside hotel, owned and operated by the American-born Lamb family. Located on the western end of the island, adjacent to the Port Royal Golf Course, this was the island's first fishing club before opening as a small hotel in 1956. Today, it still appeals to golfers, water-sports enthusiasts, and anyone in search of a quiet, remote getaway. The main building is a crescent-shaped, split-level structure of pink and white stone, containing the main dining room, a British-style pub, a cozy lounge that overlooks the ocean, and an oceanfront fitness center. Spread across the luxuriant hillside are the rooms and one-bedroom suites, all with balconies or patios, and ocean views. Rooms are refurbished annually, and in 1995 they were redone in soft pastel materials with light wooden furniture. The "superior" rooms offer the best value, not only because the rooms are larger than in the suites, but also because guests wake in the morning to a splendid ocean view through the bedroom window (suites have an ocean view through the living room window). The "deluxe" rooms, which are even more spacious (for only a few dollars more), have sitting room areas and larger, more private balconies (also have ocean views). Perched on a hill adjacent to the main building is an attractive pool and a small conference center. Ocean and beach lovers will enjoy the oceanfront shuffleboard court, the two hot tubs (one with a view of the sea), the small, natural beach (at low tide guests can stroll 250 yards into waist-high ocean waters), and the two manmade sunbathing beaches clinging to the hillside. The hotel's water-sports facility offers

Sunfish, Windsurfers, paddle boats, and small glass-bottom boats for rent from May through October. The hotel's restaurant offers fine food, as well as spectacular views of the sunset. ⊡ *36 Pompano Beach Rd., Southampton SB 03,* ☎ *441/234–0222; in U.S., 800/343–4155;* FAX *441/234–1694. 32 rooms, 20 suites, all with bath. BP, MAP. Restaurant, bar, refrigerators, pool, 2 outdoor hot tubs, exercise room, water sports, meeting room. No credit cards; personal checks accepted.*

$$$$ The Reefs. The pink lanais of this small, casually elegant resort are set
★ in cliffs above the beach at Christian Bay, adjacent to the Sonesta Beach Hotel & Spa (*see above*). The pace here is sedate; vacationers looking for action are better off at such sports-oriented resorts as the Sonesta, Elbow Beach, or Southampton Princess (*see above*). In the pink Bermuda cottage that serves as the clubhouse, the registration area opens onto a spacious, comfortable lounge, where a pianist or guitarist entertains nightly. Beyond the lounge lies the main dining room, where dinner dances are frequently held during the high season. Another restaurant is the waterside Coconuts, which is popular for casual lunches and candlelight dinners under the stars. Two guest rooms are located in the clubhouse, but the best rooms are in the lanais around the pool and on the hillside above the sandy beach. Lanais near the beach are the most expensive. Brightly colored fabrics and rattan predominate in the guest rooms; bathrooms are small, with beige marble vanities and an adjoining dressing area. All rooms have balconies and a stunning ocean view. In addition to the lanais, there are eight secluded cottages, one a three-bedroom, three-bathroom unit. Changing rooms near the beach are available for travelers with late flights who want to swim after morning checkout. Reefs guests have access (for a fee) to the spa at the Sonesta. ⊡ *56 South Rd., Southampton, SN 02,* ☎ *441/238–0222; in U.S. and Canada, 800/223–1363;* FAX *441/238–8372. 598 rooms, 8 cottage suites, all with bath. BP, MAP. 2 restaurants, 2 bars, in-room safes, pool, 2 tennis courts, beach, water sports, motorbikes. No credit cards.*

$$$$ Stonington Beach Hotel. The training ground for students of the Hospitality and Culinary Institute of Bermuda, this south-shore hotel has one of the friendliest, hardest-working staffs on the island. Just 10 minutes from Hamilton, Stonington Beach has a warm, gracious atmosphere, an excellent formal restaurant, and one of the island's best beaches. This is the only major south-shore property that does not tack a service charge onto the hotel bill; gratuities are included in the room rate. Set in two-story terraced lodges leading to the beach, the hotel has identical rooms done in handsome woods and attractive fabrics, with elegant heavy drapes and matching quilted bedspreads; all have balconies and ocean views. The spacious hotel lobby gains much of its character from its beamed ceiling and large windows with graceful fanlights. The adjoining library features Regency furnishings, well-stocked bookshelves, a fireplace, and large-screen TV. Weekly champagne receptions are held, and classical music is played in the attractive Norwood Dining Room. Use of the tennis courts is free. ⊡ *Box HM 523, Hamilton HM CX,* ☎ *441/236–5416; in U.S. and Canada, 800/447–7462;* FAX *441/236–0371. 64 rooms with bath. BP, MAP. Restaurant, bar, in-room safes, refrigerators, pool, 2 tennis courts, beach, water sports, motorbikes, library. AE, DC, MC, V.*

$$$$ Waterloo House. A preferred stopping place for businesspeople from
★ all over the world, this quiet Relais et Châteaux retreat has a long history. A pink archway and steps leading to the flower-filled patio from Pitts Bay Road were later additions to a house that predates 1815, when it was renamed in honor of the defeat of Napoleon. The white-column house faces the harbor, and a spacious harborside terrace filled with

umbrellas and tables is used for outdoor dining and entertainment—
live performers play harp, piano, jazz, and calypso on various nights.
The stately lounge is tastefully decorated with oil paintings, antiques,
chintz drapes, and a large fireplace, and enhanced with beautiful cut
flower arrangements. Though some rooms are in the pink two-story
stone buildings beside the pool and patio, most are in the main house;
the quietest are on the second floor. Terraces and water views complement the rooms' soothing decor: Matching hand-screened European
and British chintzes are used in the quilted bedspreads, dust ruffles,
draperies, and valances; antique prints of country scenes, flowers, and
Audubons complement the antique furnishings. Bathrooms are luxurious, with whirlpools and adjoining dressing areas. Complimentary
cocktail and picnic cruises on the property's endearing tug-style boat
give guests a glance of Bermuda's outer islands. Guests on MAP have
dine-around privileges at the sister properties of Horizons & Cottages
(*see below*) and Newstead (*see below*); the short golf course at Horizons is also open to guests, as are all facilities at the Coral Beach &
Tennis Club; transportation is provided. ⊠ *Box HM 333, Hamilton
HM BX,* ☎ *441/295–4480; in U.S., 800/468–4100;* FAX *441/295–2585.
28 rooms, 6 suites, all with bath. BP, MAP. Restaurant, bar, pool. AE,
MC, V.*

$$$–$$$$ **Newstead.** This renovated manor house could accommodate only 12
★   people when it opened as a guest house in 1923. Since then the ele-
gant harborside hotel has expanded considerably, with brick steps and
walkways now leading to several poolside units and cottages. Set amid
tall trees and a profusion of flowering shrubs and plants, the main house
and cottages are typically Bermudian—in fact, some of the cottages were
originally private residences. The spacious drawing room boasts hand-
some wing chairs, traditional furnishings, fresh flowers, and a fireplace;
the less-formal lounge, where live musicians play harp, piano, calypso,
and jazz, has large windows overlooking the harbor. (In October, the
lounge is a great vantage point for the Gold Cup sailboat races.) The
large guest rooms feature polished mahogany campaign chests with brass
drawer-pulls, framed prints, and fresh flowers; sliding glass doors
open onto a balcony. Though the hotel has no beach, a private dock
is available for deep-water swimming in the harbor, and guests have
use of the facilities at the Coral Beach & Tennis Club on the south shore,
about 10 minutes away by cab. Men's and women's changing rooms
by the pool allow guests to go straight from swimming to the Hamil
ton ferry at Hodsdon's Landing. Tennis on Har-Tru courts costs $3.50
an hour, and tennis whites are preferred. Guests on MAP may partic-
ipate in the dine-around plan with sister properties Waterloo House
and Horizons. ⊠ *Box PG 196, Paget PG BX,* ☎ *441/236–6060; in
U.S., 800/468–4111;* FAX *441/236–7454. 50 rooms, 2 suites, all with
bath. BP, MAP. Restaurant, bar, pool, putting green, 2 tennis courts,
dock. AE, MC, V.*

$$$–$$$$ **Rosedon.** Notable for its spacious veranda and white iron furniture,
★   this stately Bermuda manor attracts a diverse crowd for its ambience,
service, and proximity to Front Street shops. The four spacious rooms
in the main house have leaded-glass doors and other Old World touches;
all other rooms are in two-story buildings arranged around a large heated
pool in gardens filled with exotic plants. All rooms have balconies or
patios and cheerful decor. Though there is no restaurant, breakfast, sand-
wiches, and light meals are served either in your room or under um-
brellas by the pool; and afternoon tea is served in the large lounges in
the main house, where films are shown nightly and an honor bar is lo-
cated. The hotel has no beach of its own, but guests have access to the
beach and tennis courts at the Elbow Beach Hotel (*see above*) at a re-

duced rate; complimentary transportation is provided for the 10–15 minute drive. ✉ *Box HM 290, Hamilton HM AX,* ☎ *441/295–1640; in U.S. and Canada, 800/742–5008;* ⬚ *441/295–5904. 43 rooms with bath. BP, EP. 2 lounges, in-room safes, refrigerators, pool, laundry service. MC, V.*

$$$–$$$$ **Willowbank.** On six acres of landscaped gardens overlooking Ely's Harbour and the ocean, this former estate was converted to a family-style hotel by a Christian trust. Morning devotions are held in a lounge for those who wish to attend, and grace is said before meals, which are announced by an ancient ship's bell and served family-style. There is no proselytizing, however, and no pressure to participate in religious activities. The hotel is simply a serene alternative to the glitzy resorts: the focus is on rest, relaxation, and renewal. With their cedar paneling and fireplaces, the two large lounges in the main building are the focal point for quiet conversations and afternoon tea; there are also the library and the Loaves and Fishes dining room, where guests meet for fellowship. Guests may have liquor in their rooms, but there is no bar. Located in one-story white cottages, the guest rooms are large and simply furnished—they have neither phones nor TVs. Rooms with an ocean or harbor view are the most desirable and expensive. The hotel has a free summer children's program that includes, among other things, crafts workshops and trips around the island. No service charge is added to the bill and tipping is not expected, but the staff is friendly and helpful nonetheless. ✉ *Box MA 296, Sandys MA BX,* ☎ *441/234–1616 or 800/752–8493,* ⬚ *441/234–3373. 64 rooms with bath. MAP. Restaurant, 2 lounges, pool, 2 tennis courts, 2 beaches. No credit cards.*

$$$ **Palmetto Hotel & Cottages.** Set amid tall shade trees on the banks of Harrington Sound, this casually elegant property was once a private home. The main building is a sprawling two-story pink-and-white structure typical of Bermuda. Adjoining the small reception area is the Ha'Penny, a very British pub. Afternoon tea is served in a small but attractive lounge with a tile floor, Oriental area rug, cushy furnishings, and green plants. Twenty-four rooms are located in the main building, but the 16 rooms in cottages on the banks of the sound are the most luxurious. All rooms have balconies, and many have a good view of the water. The beach is small, but the hotel provides guests complimentary bus fare to a south-shore beach. In addition, guests can swim or snorkel off the hotel's private dock. ✉ *Box FL 54, Flatts FLBX,* ☎ *441/293–2323 or 800/982–0026,* ⬚ *441/293–8761. 42 rooms with bath. BP, MAP. Restaurant, bar, pool, beach, dock. AE, MC, V.*

$$$ **Royal Palms Hotel.** Richard Smith and his sister Susan Weare, whose parents own and operate nearby Oxford House, have transformed this grand home into a hotel with the atmosphere of a country inn. It's on a quiet residential street, near Hamilton, and Front Street's shops are just a short walk away. The house, which dates from 1903, is aptly named, surrounded as it is by tall palms and lush gardens. Many guests like to relax and read around the outdoor pool. The terrace, with its comfortable white wicker furniture, is another favorite spot for reading and quiet conversation, as well as summertime outdoor dining. The hotel has polished wood floors and Oriental rugs in some rooms, and wall-to-wall carpeting in others; drapes and bedspreads are in matching fabrics. Some rooms connect to others, which suits families and groups; several have kitchens. Ascots restaurant, quite popular with locals, offers gourmet dining in a relaxed atmosphere. A generous complimentary breakfast is served. ✉ *Box HM 499, Hamilton HM CX,* ☎ *441/292–1854 or 800/678-0783 (U.S.), 800/799-0824 (Canada);* ⬚ *441/292–1946. 11* *rooms, 1 suite, all with private bath. CP; supplementary dinner plan available. Restaurant, lounge, pool. AE, MC, V.*

Cottage Colonies

$$$$ **Ariel Sands Beach Club.** This most informal of the cottage colonies surrounds Cox's Bay in Devonshire Parish; it's adjacent to the Palm Grove estate (*see* Chapter 3, Exploring Bermuda) and not far from the Edmund Gibbons Nature Reserve. The picturesque sandy beach has a variety of small shells, and a graceful statue of Ariel perches on a rock in the sea. The snorkeling is superb, with many species of fish seeking refuge in the normally quiet cove area just off the beach; the Olympic-size, ocean-side natural pool—wonderful for lap swimming—contains a variety of fish found just offshore. Another smaller saltwater pool is adjacent to the beach. The one-story, pale-green limestone clubhouse, designed Bermudian cottage–style, contains a cozy lounge and a newly refurbished dining room with an ocean view. Many Bermudians enjoy the quiet atmosphere here, and can be found sipping a cocktail in the bar after a game of tennis, or savoring international cuisine al fresco on the terrace or in the main dining room. A grand piano, a fireplace, hardwood floors, and Oriental rugs give the resort an air of distinction. The large patio is ideal for outdoor dining, dancing, and barbecues in season. Two- to eight-unit green cottages are set in the sloping, immaculately kept, tree-shaded grounds. The rather small but beautiful guest rooms have Mexican tile floors, matching drapes and quilted spreads, in-room safes, and tea- and coffeemakers. Shakespeare's Dream has two bedrooms, one of which has a single bed. Rooms in the lowest price bracket have no ocean view. Tennis is free to guests. During the summer the cottage colony offers a children's day-care program. ☎ *Box HM 334, Hamilton HM BX,* ☎ *441/236–1010; in U.S., 800/468–6610;* ☎ *441/236–0087. 48 rooms with bath. BP, MAP. Restaurant, bar, 2 saltwater pools, freshwater pool, putting green, 3 tennis courts, exercise room, volleyball, beach, water sports, business services, meeting rooms. AE, MC, V.*

$$$$ **Cambridge Beaches.** Recently rated Bermuda's top resort by *Condé Nast*
★ *Traveler,* this resort near Somerset Village in the West End (*see* Chapter 3, Exploring Bermuda) occupies a beautifully landscaped peninsula edged with private coves and five pink-sand beaches. The island's original cottage colony (it opened at the turn of the century), it remains a favorite among British and Saudi royalty, as well as a host of commoners. Many guests return year after year, attracted by the elegant style, superior water-sports facilities, and those unsurpassed pink-sand beaches. Registration is in a Bermuda-style clubhouse with large, elegantly furnished lounges. Candlelight dining and dancing take place in the lower-level restaurant and on the terrace, which has a splendid view of Mangrove Bay. A wide range of accommodations is offered—the entire peninsula is dotted with cottages—and prices vary considerably. On the high end, Pegem is a 300-year-old, two-bedroom Bermuda cottage with a cedar-beam ceiling, English antiques, a den, and a sunporch. On the other end of the spectrum, the least expensive units are those that have land rather than water views. The decor differs from cottage to cottage, but antiques and fireplaces are common. Many units, including the eight that were built in 1993, have whirlpools, and suites have bidets as well. Rooms are refurbished annually. The state-of-the-art 2,000-square-foot European health spa has a whirlpool, steam room, sauna, four treatment rooms (offering a large variety of health and beauty treatments for men and women), hair and beauty salon, and small gym; additional charges are made for the use of these

facilities. Don't fret about being far from Front Street: A complimentary shopping launch makes trips three times a week from the resort's private dock. Ferry tokens are complimentary in the off-season. Other exclusive boat trips include snorkeling trips to St. George's and a cruise to a nightclub. The marina offers the largest selection of watersport equipment on the island—windsurfers, Boston Whalers, three types of sailboats, snorkel equipment, canoes, kayaks. Scuba instruction and trips are available, too. Guests have complimentary use of the putting green, croquet lawn, and tennis courts. Children under five must be accompanied by a nanny or nurse. ▦ *Somerset MA 02,* ☎ *441/234–0331; in U.S., 800/468–7300;* ℻ *441/234–3352. 62 rooms, 20 suites, all with bath. MAP. Restaurant, 2 bars, saltwater pool, spa, putting green, 3 tennis courts, croquet, exercise room, 6 beaches, water sports, business services, meeting rooms. No credit cards.*

$$$$ **Fourways Inn.** About a five-minute walk from the ferry landing and a five-minute ride to the south-shore beaches, this small luxury hotel has a sedate, formal ambience and a central location. The architecture is typically Bermudian: The main building is a former family home that dates from 1727; the five cottages, set in a profusion of greenery and flowers, each contain a poolside suite and a deluxe upper-floor room. Marble floors and marble bathrooms are common throughout, and plenty of flowers give the rooms a bright freshness. In addition, each room has a balcony or terrace, a stocked minibar, a bar/kitchenette, and large closets paneled with full-length mirrors. Amenities in the suites include hair dryers, bath phones, bathrobes, and slippers. Guests receive a complimentary fruit basket on arrival, and homemade pastries and the morning paper are delivered daily to the door. The hotel serves a sumptuous Sunday brunch. ▦ *Box PG 294, Paget PG BX,* ☎ *441/236–6517; in U.S., 800/962–7654;* ℻ *441/236–5528. 5 rooms, 5 suites, all with bath. CP. Restaurant, bar, pool, business services. AE, MC, V.*

$$$$ **Horizons & Cottages.** Oriental rugs, polished wood floors, cathedral
★ ceilings, and knee-high open fireplaces are elegant reminders of the 18th century, when the main house in this resort was a private home. A Relais et Châteaux property, the cottage colony is continually upgraded to maintain its high standards. Horizons Restaurant is a chic place for intimate candlelight dining; in pleasant weather, tables are set on the terrace. (The hotel has an exchange dining arrangement with sister properties Waterloo House and Newstead; menus are created under the guidance of renowned Swiss chef Anton Mosimann.) Monday-night rum swizzling takes place downstairs in a wood-panel pub, where Austrian-born manager Wilhelm Sack makes every effort to see that guests (many European) are introduced. Guest cottages dot the terraced lawns, and each cottage has a distinct personality and decor: Most have two or three rooms and a large common room with a fireplace, library, and shelves of board games. Some of the spacious guest rooms feature white wicker furnishings, and others have an Old European flavor, and all have terraces. Most cottages also have a kitchen, where a maid prepares breakfast before bringing it to your room. The hotel has no beach of its own, but guests may use the facilities of The Coral Beach and Tennis Club, within walking distance along South Road. Tennis courts cost $4 per hour and the greens fee for the short nine-hole golf course is also $4. ▦ *Box PG 198, Paget PG BX,* ☎ *441/236–0048; in U.S., 800/468–0022;* ℻ *441/236–1981. 42 rooms, 5 suites, all with bath. BP, MAP (combination also available). Restaurant, pool, 9-hole golf course, 3 tennis courts. No credit cards.*

$$$$ **Lantana Colony Club.** A short walk from the Somerset Bridge ferry landing in the West End, this cottage colony is known for its lavish gardens, delightful topiary, and impressive, museum-quality objets d'art.

Several life-size sculptures by Desmond Fountain are placed throughout the grounds, including a delightful rendering of a woman seated on a bench reading a newspaper. The solarium dining area in the main house is dazzling, with hanging plants and wall lamps of frosted, handmade glass grapes from Venice. All accommodations are spacious and airy suites in a variety of configurations: lanais, split-levels, garden cottages, and family cottages with two bedrooms, two bathrooms, and a living/dining room. All units have sliding glass doors that open onto private balconies or patios; some have cedar doors, beams, and trim, and vivid Souleaido prints. Waterfront suites have Mexican tile floors on the lower level, carpeting in the sleeping area, refrigerators, and wet bars; water-view suites have fireplaces, separate men's and women's dressing areas, and kitchens. About half of the suites are in garden settings; one of those is a cottage where guests have use of the owner's private pool. The small private pink-sand beach overlooks the Great Sound, and boats are available to guests to explore the coastline and pristine harbors of Somerset. Many locals and visitors to the island come to have lunch at the waterside restaurant—by boat or moped—but reservations are advised. ⊠ *Box SB 90, Somerset Bridge SB BX,* ☎ *441/234–0141; in U.S., 800/468–3733; in Canada, 800/463–0036;* FAX *441/234–2562. 56 suites, 6 cottages, all with bath. BP, MAP. 2 restaurants, 2 bars, pool, putting green, 2 tennis courts, croquet, shuffleboard, beach, water sports. AE, MC, V.*

$$$$ **Pink Beach Club & Cottages.** With its two pretty pink beaches, this secluded, relaxing colony is a favorite of international celebrities. The location is ideally located, being 10 minutes from the airport and 15 minutes by foot or moped from the shops of Front Street. Opened as a cottage colony in 1947, the main house has a clubby ambience derived from its dark-wood paneling, large fireplace, and beamed ceilings. Paved paths wend their way throughout the 18 acres of attractively landscaped gardens, leading to the beaches and 25 pink cottages. Recent renovations have expanded room capacity to 89 rooms, making this the island's largest cottage colony. Some cottages contain a single unit, while others comprise several units, and accommodations range from single rooms to two-bedroom suites with two bathrooms and twin terraces, most have ocean views. Each spacious unit has maple furnishings upholstered in conservatively colored fabrics, double or king-size beds, and sliding glass doors that open onto a balcony or terrace. All are equipped with safes, hair dryers, and pants pressers; bathrooms have double sinks. The best accommodations are, of course, those near the beach. Breakfast is prepared by a maid and served on your terrace or in your room. Use of the tennis courts is free. ⊠ *Box HM 1017, Hamilton HM DX,* ☎ *441/293–1666; in U.S. and Canada, 800/355–6161;* FAX *441/293–8935. 6 rooms, 83 suites, all with bath. BP, MAP. Restaurant, bar, saltwater pool, 2 tennis courts, 2 beaches, water sports. MC, V.*

$$$$ **St. George's Club.** Within walking distance of King's Square in St. George's, this ultramodern time-share property adjoins an 18-hole golf course designed by Robert Trent Jones. The sleek, three-story main building contains the office, activities desk, a game room, a restaurant, a pub, and the Club Shop, where you can buy everything from champagne to suntan lotion. In two-story white cottages sprinkled over 18 acres, the individually decorated apartments are huge and filled with sunlight. In some, stark white walls are offset by bright accent pieces and fabrics in muted colors. In others, sweeping bold designs draw upon the entire spectrum of colors. Each apartment has a full kitchen with dishwasher, fine china, and crystal. Bathrooms are large and lined with marble; some feature double Jacuzzis in dramatic

settings. ☎ *Box GE 92, St. George's GE BX,* ☎ *441/297–1200,* FAX
*441/297–8003. 69 suites with bath. EP. 2 restaurants, bar, 3 pools,
18-hole golf course, putting green, tennis court, meeting rooms. AE,
DC, MC, V.*

Housekeeping Cottages and Apartments

$$$–$$$$ **Marley Beach Cottages.** Scenes from the films *Chapter Two* and *The*
★ *Deep* were filmed here, and it's easy to see why—the setting is breath-
taking. Near Astwood Park on the south shore, the resort sits high on
a cliff overlooking a lovely beach and dramatic reefs; a long path leads
down to the sand and the sea. If you plan to stay here, pack light—there
are a lot of steep steps, and you may have to carry your own luggage.
The price is steep for one couple, but this is an excellent choice for two
couples vacationing together (who don't mind preparing their own
meals); there is ample space here, and splitting the cost brings it down
to a moderate price for each pair. Each cottage contains a suite and a
studio apartment, which can be rented separately or together, by fam-
ilies or friends. This is not a good place for children; there's little to oc-
cupy them except the pool and the beach. Refurbished in 1994, the units
are individually decorated; all have large rooms, superb ocean views,
private porches or patios, phones, TVs, and fully equipped kitchens with
microwave and coffeemaker. Heaven's Above and Seasong, deluxe
suites, are spacious affairs; each has two wood-burning fireplaces, tile
floors, upholstered rattan furniture, and ample kitchen facilities. Gro-
ceries can be delivered, and daily maid service is provided. ☎ *Box PG
278, Paget PG BX,* ☎ *441/236–1143, ext. 42; in U.S., 800/637–4116;*
FAX *441/236–1984. 7 suites, 6 studios, all with bath. EP. Pool, whirlpool,
beach. AE, MC, V.*

$$$ **Longtail Cliffs.** Don't be put off by the small office and the concrete
parking lot that serves as the front yard of this motel-like establish-
ment. Although it may not have the personality or splendid beach views
of Marley Beach Cottages (*see above*), its relatively flat setting makes
it much more suitable for elderly people or anyone opposed to climbing. Housed in a modern, two-story building, guest apartments are large,
light, and airy, with balconies and spectacular ocean views. Each has
two bedrooms and two spacious bathrooms decorated with brightly
colored tiles. A small but well-equipped kitchen features a microwave
oven, a coffeemaker, an iron, and an ironing board. Italian tile floors
grace the living areas and are accented by Oriental rugs and high-quality furniture. Many units have beamed ceilings and some have fireplaces
(for aesthetic purposes only). There's a coin-operated laundry, cable
TV, and a gas barbecue grill for cookouts. Despite its location on the
south shore, the complex does not have a beach; however, it is adjacent to Astwood Cove. ☎ *Box HM 836, Hamilton HM CX,* ☎ *441/
236–2864 or 441/236–2822; in U.S., 800/637–4116;* FAX *441/236–
5178. 13 apartments with bath. EP. Pool. AE, MC, V.*

$$$ **Surf Side Beach Club.** This is another option for couples looking to share
a space on the South Shore. The bright reception area with upholstered
chairs is sizable enough to be used as a lounge. Cottages are on ter-
raced levels, and each has a view of the ocean and the long stretch of
sandy beach below (just a hop, skip, and a jump away). There are spa-
cious studios and suites; each has a fully equipped kitchen (with mi-
crowave), cable TV, telephone, and porch. All are decorated with light
wood furnishings, brightly colored island fabrics, and wall-to-wall
carpeting; some have tile floors. Guests can cook on their own barbe-
cue grills or dine at a poolside coffee shop (open April–October, room
service at extra charge). Weekly rum swizzle parties are held for guests.

☎ *Box WK 101, Warwick WK BX,* ☎ *441/236–7100 or 800/553–9990,* 𝔽𝔸𝕏 *441/236–9765. 10 apartments, 23 studios, 2 penthouse units, all with bath. EP. Coffee shop, pool, sauna, exercise room, bicycles, coin laundry, business services, meeting rooms. AE, MC, V.*

$$–$$$ **Angel's Grotto.** Some 30 years ago this was a swinging nightclub and
★ one of the hottest spots on the island. Now, it's a quiet residential apartment house close to Devil's Hole Aquarium on the south shore of Harrington Sound. Since the 1994 refurbishments, the once-simple property has blossomed into a real charmer. New curtains and spreads are in cool, pretty pastels; all rooms have TVs, radios, and phones, and kitchens are fully equipped. Owner Daisy Hart and her efficient staff maintain these apartments in shipshape condition. There is no beach, but the pink sands of John Smith's Bay on the South Shore are a five-minute walk away; other South Shore beaches are less than 10 minutes away by moped. Most of the guests are couples; the secluded Honeymoon Cottage is particularly appealing to those who want privacy. The two-bedroom, two-bath apartment in the main house is a good buy for two couples traveling together. A large patio is ideal for cocktails in the evening, and there is also a barbecue. Deep-water swimming is possible in Harrington Sound. ☎ *Box HS 81, Smith's HS BX,* ☎ *441/293–1986; in U.S., 800/637–4116;* 𝔽𝔸𝕏 *441/293–4164. 7 apartments with bath. EP. AE, MC, V.*

$$ **Greenbank Cottages.** On a quiet dead end less than a minute's walk from the Salt Kettle ferry landing, these one-story green cottages nestle among tall trees beside Hamilton Harbour. Small and family-oriented, it's not a grand hotel, but guests can count on plenty of personal attention from the Ashton family. In the 200-year-old main house, the guests' lounge has attractive throw rugs, hardwood floors, a TV, and a grand piano. There are three rental units in the main house (two have kitchens); all other units are self-contained, with fully equipped kitchens, private entrances and shaded verandas. The waterside cottages are the best choice, especially Salt Winds; The views of the harbor from bed, the dining table, and the kitchen are lovely. Rooms are simply furnished; all have phones and air conditioning. There is a private dock suitable for deep-water swimming, and the beaches are less than 10 minutes away by taxi or moped. One of the island's best water-sport facilities—Salt Kettle Boat Rentals—is on the property, so access to snorkeling spots is easy. ☎ *Box PG 201, Paget PG BX,* ☎ *441/236–3615; in U.S., 800/637–4116;* 𝔽𝔸𝕏 *441/236–2427. 3 rooms and 8 apartments, all with bath; 9 have kitchens. CP, EP. AE, MC, V.*

$$ **Paraquet Guest Apartments.** These apartments (pronounced "parakeet") are in an ideal location—a mere five-minute walk from Elbow Beach. Ideal for budget travelers, they are spartan but spic-and-span, spacious and well-lit, with TVs, clock/radios, and small refrigerators. Nine units have kitchens. Rooms, which were spruced up in 1995, are done in simple, functional furnishings reminiscent of a motel. Efficiency units have full baths, while the rest have only shower baths. The three units in the Paraquet Cottage share a patio. There is a market nearby for supplies, and the fine restaurants at Horizons and the Stonington Beach Hotel are within walking distance. The bus stops right in front of the Paraquet's diner-style restaurant that serves a delicious traditional breakfast on Sunday morning. ☎ *Box PG 173, Paget PG BX,* ☎ *441/236–5842,* 𝔽𝔸𝕏 *441/236–1665. 12 rooms with bath. EP. Restaurant. No credit cards.*

$$ **Pretty Penny.** A three-minute walk from the ferry dock at Darrell's Wharf
★ and 10 minutes by scooter from the south-shore beaches, this upscale lodging has one of the friendliest, most helpful staffs on the island. The

grounds are small and offer no good views, but guest cottages are surrounded by trees and shrubs. Each room is brightened by a colorful tile floor and has a dining area and private patio. A small kitchen area features a microwave oven, refrigerator, and cupboards well-stocked with china, cooking utensils, and cutlery. TVs can be rented. A general spruce-up of the rooms was made in 1995; the Shilling, a newly renovated room in a quaint cottage across from the main building, is a charmer. If you want absolute privacy ask for the Play Penny, which is tucked away by itself. ☎ *Box PG 137, Paget PG BX,* ☏ *441/236–1194; in U.S., 800/637–4116;* ☒ *441/236–3290. 9 apartments with shower bath. EP. Pool. AE, MC, V.*

$–$$ **Barnsdale Guest Apartments.** Budget travelers who want to be near the south-shore beaches and the ferry to Hamilton would do well to consider the small apartments in this two-story, yellow house. In a residential neighborhood very close to a grocery store, the apartments are nestled in a garden with an orchard of loquat, banana, orange, and peach trees, which guests are encouraged to sample. All are clean and neat studio efficiency units, each with a private entrance. Annually spruced up, each room is tastefully decorated, and sleeps up to four guests on pullout sofa beds. All have a fully equipped kitchen, TV, iron and ironing board. Apartment Number 5 is a charmer with a light, airy feeling—but it's next to the pool area, which can become noisy. An outdoor barbecue gives guests a chance to escape from the kitchen and enjoy those balmy Bermuda evenings. ☎ *Box DV 628, Devonshire DV BX,* ☏ *441/236–0164,* ☒ *441/236–4709. 7 efficiency studio apartments with bath. EP. Pool. AE, MC, V.*

$–$$ **Sky Top Cottages.** This aptly named hilltop property has spectacular
  ★   views of the island's southern coast and the azure ocean beyond. Its steep grade is not appropriate for those people who have cardiac problems or arthritic joints, but runners and walkers will appreciate its proximity to Elbow Beach, one of the best stretches of sand for a workout. Neat sloping lawns, carefully tended gardens, paved walks bordered by seasonal flowers, and a nearby citrus grove provide a pleasant setting for studios and one-bedroom apartments. The individually decorated units have attractive prints and carefully coordinated colors. Studio apartments have shower baths, and one-bedroom apartments have full baths. Fully equipped kitchens are in nearly every unit. Frangipani is furnished in white wicker and rattan and has an eat-in kitchen, a queen-size bed, and a sofa bed. Honeysuckle is a three-level apartment with a sitting room, kitchen, dining room, and a bedroom with king-size bed and bathroom upstairs. All units have phones; TVs can be rented. Barbecue grills are available for guests' use. ☎ *Box PG 227, Paget PG BX,* ☏ *441/236–7984. 11 apartments with bath. EP. MC, V.*

$ **Whale Bay Inn.** Golfers approaching the 14th hole of the Port Royal Course are sometimes baffled to find golf balls other than their own dotting the green. Little do they know that it's a mere chip shot from the front lawn of this inn, and some guests can't resist the challenge to play through. Vacationers who want to be near Hamilton's shops are better served elsewhere, but if you are looking for an area that offers uncrowded, peaceful beaches this West End property is the place to be. Whale Bay Beach is a short walk away; the beaches of Church Bay (for some of the island's best snorkeling), Horseshoe Bay, and Somerset Long Bay are easily reached by moped. Apart from the annual painting of the rooms, new furniture, TVs, and attractive area rugs were some of the additions made in 1995. The ocean is visible beyond beds of flowers and the rolling lawn that surrounds the Bermuda-style pink building. Guest rooms are contemporary, with rattan and muted prints. All five ground-floor units have a bedroom, a separate sitting room with sofa beds, phone, and a private entrance. The two end units have larger bathrooms and are better suited to families. Small, modern kitchens are equipped with microwave ovens, two-burner stoves, refrigerators, cutlery, dinnerware, and cooking utensils. Groceries can be delivered from nearby markets. ⌖ *Box SN 544, Southampton SN BX,* ☎ *441/238–0469,* ℻ *441/238–1224. 5 apartments with bath. EP. Beach. No credit cards.*

Guest Houses

$$ Edgehill Manor. Atop a high hill surrounded by gardens and shrubs, this large colonial house is within easy walking distance of downtown Hamilton and less than 15 minutes by scooter from the best south-shore beaches. The staff is friendly and helpful, and guests are guaranteed plenty of personal attention. In the morning, feast on home-baked muffins and scones in the cheery breakfast room, which is decorated with white iron chairs, glass-top tables, and vivid wallpaper. The individually decorated guest rooms feature French provincial furniture, colorful quilted bedspreads, large windows, and terraces. All rooms have air conditioning and cable TV. A large poolside room has a kitchen and is suitable for families. Anyone traveling alone on a tight budget should ask for the small ground-level room that offers a kitchen and private terrace. ⌖ *Box HM 1048, Hamilton HM EX,* ☎ *441/295–7124,* ℻ *441/295–3850. 9 rooms with bath. CP. Pool. No credit cards.*

$$ Little Pomander Guest House. A little jewel in a quiet residential area
★ near Hamilton Harbour, this is a find for budget travelers seeking accommodations near Hamilton. The two cottages were professionally decorated with a keen eye for detail—nothing here is out of place. The registration area, with its soft colors, fresh flowers, and comfortable arrangement of sofas and chairs, is spacious and airy. In the main house, guest rooms are cheerily decorated: Plump pastel-colored comforters cover the beds, and the shams, dust ruffles, drapes, headboards, and shower curtains are made of matching fabrics. Continental breakfast is served family-style to guests in the main house in a sunny room where tables are set with china in a blue-and-white floral design. There are three apartments in the neighboring cottage; of particular interest is the spacious Captain's apartment, with its white wicker furniture, coordinated blue-and-white decor, and balcony overlooking Hamilton Harbour. All units have microwaves, cable TV, phones, and refrigerators. Guests congregate at sunset on the waterside lawn to enjoy views of Hamilton Harbour, and often stay to cook dinner on the barbecue grill. For a $10 fee, guests can play tennis across the road at the Pomander Tennis Club. ⌖ *Box HM 384, Hamilton HM BX,* ☎ *441/236–7635; in U.S., 800/637–4116;* ℻ *441/236–8332. 5 rooms, 3 apartments with bath. CP. AE, MC, V.*

$$ Oxford House. This is the closest you can get to downtown Hamilton
★ without pitching a tent—it's less than a five-minute walk from the shops, ferries, and buses. A family-owned and operated two-story establishment, it's popular with all age groups and is an excellent choice for shoppers. Just off the small entrance hall, a fireplace, crisp linen tablecloths, and pastel-colored curtains lend warmth to the breakfast room, where guests sample scones, English muffins, fresh fruit, and cereal in the morning. The bright, airy rooms (doubles, triples, and quads) are individually decorated with bold fabrics. Each room has a coffeemaker and ironing board (irons are available on request). Two rooms have full baths; the rest have showers only. A small bookcase in the upstairs hall is crammed with paperbacks and serves as a library for guests. ⌖

Box HM 374, Hamilton HM BX, ☎ *441/295–0503; in U.S., 800/548–7758;* FAX *441/295–0250; in Canada,* FAX *800/272-2306. 12 rooms with bath. CP. AE, MC, V.*

$–$$ **Loughlands Guest House & Cottage.** Built in 1920, this stately white mansion on a hill above South Road is loaded with fine antiques and European china. Lladro figurines grace the mantelpiece in the formal parlor; antique grandfather clocks stand in corners; and handsome breakfronts display Wedgwood china, and Baccarat and Waterford crystal. Less than a five-minute walk from Elbow Beach, the guest house offers welcome amenities such as a guest refrigerator, Continental breakfast of cereals, fruit juice, prunes, croissants, danish pastries, and coffee, all served in the enormous, well-appointed dining room. Although the guest rooms are not filled with fascinating objets d'art, they are tastefully decorated. No two are alike—there are singles, doubles, triples, and quads—and most include large comfortable chairs and cotton spreads. A large cottage near the main house has additional rooms. ⌨ *79 South Rd., Paget PG 03,* ☎ *441/236–1253. 18 rooms with bath, 6 with shared bath. CP. Pool, tennis court. No credit cards; personal checks accepted.*

$ **Hillcrest Guest House.** Set back from quaint Nea's Alley in St. George's, behind a gate and manicured gardens, this green double-gallery house dates to the 18th century. It's been a guest house since 1961, but owner Mrs. Trew Robinson says her father took in shipwrecked sailors in 1914, when this was a private home. Today, Mrs. Robinson offers personal attention and helpful advice to budget travelers. The upstairs and downstairs lounges are spacious and homey, decorated with Oriental rugs, treasured family pictures, and heirlooms. Guest rooms are spotlessly clean, but they lack the charm of the public rooms. No meals are served, but guests can keep refreshments in the refrigerator. The house is far from Hamilton and many of the beaches, but nearby Tobacco Bay Beach and the adjoining, secluded coves are some of the island's best snorkeling spots; and the St. George's golf course is almost within putting distance. ⌨ *Box GE 96, St. George's GE BX,* ☎ *441/297–1630,* FAX *441/297–1908. 10 rooms with bath. No credit cards.*

$ **Salt Kettle House.** Set behind a screen of palm trees on a bay adjoin-
★ ing Hamilton Harbour and just a two-minute walk from the Salt Kettle ferry that goes to Hamilton, this small secluded guest house attracts repeat visitors year after year and is popular with boating enthusiasts. Just to the left of the entrance is a cozy lounge with a fireplace where guests gather for cocktails (BYOB) and conversation. A hearty English breakfast is served family-style in the adjacent dining room, which offers water views. Two guest rooms are located in the main house, and an adjoining apartment features a double bedroom, bathroom, living room, and kitchen. The best accommodations are in the four waterside cottages, which have shaded patios and lounge chairs, bed/sitting rooms, and kitchens. The Starboard, which accommodates four people, is a two-bedroom, two-bathroom unit with a living room, fireplace, and kitchen. Guest rooms are small, though the decor is charming. Owner Mrs. Hazel Lowe makes improvements every year, and in 1995 rooms were spruced up with paint and new bedspreads. All of the units are air-conditioned. Guests can swim in a cove outside. ⌨ *10 Salt Kettle Rd., Paget PG 01,* ☎ *441/236–0407,* FAX *441/236–8639. 3 rooms, with bath, in main house; 1 cottage accommodates 4 guests; 3 cottages each accommodate 2 guests. BP. Lounge. No credit cards.*

9 The Arts and Nightlife

THE ARTS

AVAILABLE IN ALL HOTELS and tourist information centers, *This Week in Bermuda, Preview of Bermuda,* and *Bermuda Weekly* are free publications that list what's happening around the island. The Bermuda Department of Tourism gives away copies of its "Bermuda Calendar of Events" brochure at all of its offices. The informative *Bermuda* ($3.95), a quarterly magazine, describes upcoming island events and carries feature articles on what visitors can do. *The Bermudian* ($4) is a glossy monthly magazine that also carries a calendar of events. In some hotels there is a TV station that broadcasts a wealth of information about sightseeing, restaurants, cultural events, and nightlife on the island. Radio VSB, FM 1450, gives a lineup of events on its Community Calendar daily at 11:15 AM. Or you can dial 974 for a phone recording that details information about nature walks, tours, cultural events, afternoon teas, and seasonal events. The island is so small, however, that virtually everyone knows what's going on. In truth, the arts scene in Bermuda is not extensive, and many of the events and performing groups listed below operate on a casual or part-time basis. If you see a bulletin board, inspect it for posters describing events. **City Hall Theatre** (City Hall, Church St., Hamilton) is the major venue for a number of top-quality cultural events each year, although performances and productions are staged elsewhere on the island, too. Contact the **Box Office** (Visitors Service Bureau, ☎ 441/295–1727) for reservations and information about all cultural events on the island. American Express, MasterCard, and Visa are accepted at the theater and the box office.

Some good amateur acting is done by members of the **Bermuda Musical & Dramatic Society,** whose plays are scheduled throughout the year in their Daylesford headquarters a block north of City Hall. A Christmas pantomime at City Hall is always a sellout, as are most performances. Contact their box office for reservations and information (Daylesford, Dundonald St., Hamilton, ☎ 441/292–0848 or 441/295–5584).

In January and February, the **Bermuda Festival** brings internationally renowned artists to the island for a series of performances. The 2½-month program includes classical and jazz concerts and theatrical performances. The 1996 program is set to include performances by the Harlem Spiritual Choir, Russian pianist Ignat Solzhenitsyn, and the internationally acclaimed Royal College of Music. Most of the performances take place in City Hall and other locations. Ticket prices range from $20 to $35. For information and reservations, contact Bermuda Festivals, Ltd. (Box HM 297, Hamilton HM AX, ☎ 441/295–1291, FAX 441/295–7403) or the Bermuda Department of Tourism (*see* Important Contacts A to Z *in* the Gold Guide).

Visitors who want to meet local painters and see some of their work are welcomed by members of the **Bermuda Society of Arts** to the **Harbour Gallery** (Front St. W., Hamilton, ☎ 441/296–2232), where Irish coffee is sometimes served in the evening.

Concerts

Beat Retreat Ceremony and **Regimental Musical Display** are separate performances by the Bermuda Regiment Band and the Bermuda Isles Pipe Band with Dancers, arranged by the Bermuda Department of

Tourism once or twice a month, except in August. They perform on Front Street, Hamilton; King's Square, St. George's; or the Royal Naval Dockyard, Ireland Island.

The **Bermuda Philharmonic Society** presents several programs throughout the year, including classical music concerts by the full Philharmonic and by soloists. Students of the Menuhin Foundation, established in Bermuda by virtuoso violinist Yehudi Menuhin, sometimes perform with the orchestra; visiting musicians often play in these events. Concerts take place in the Cathedral of the Most Holy Trinity in Hamilton (*see* Chapter 3, Exploring Bermuda), King's Square in St. George's, or at the Royal Naval Dockyard.

The **Gilbert & Sullivan Society of Bermuda** mounts a musical production each year, usually in October. In addition to Gilbert and Sullivan operettas, the group occasionally does Broadway shows.

Dance

One of the many **Bermuda Gombey troupes** performs each week as part of the off-season (Nov.–Mar.) festivities organized by the Bermuda Department of Tourism. Gombey (pronounced "gum-bay") dancing is a blend of African, West Indian, and American Indian influences. The Gombey tradition in Bermuda dates to the mid-18th century, when costumed slaves celebrated Christmas by singing and marching through the streets. The masked male dancers move to the accompaniment of skin-covered drums and the shrill whistle commands of the captain of the troupe. The ritualistic, often frenetic movements of the dancers, the staccato drum accompaniment, and the whistle commands are passed from generation to generation. Dancers wear colorful costumes that include tall headdresses decorated with peacock feathers and tiny mirrors. On all major holidays different troupes of Gombeys dance through the streets to many of the hotels, attracting large crowds of followers. It's traditional to toss coins at the feet of the dancers.

The **Bermuda Civic Ballet** performs classical ballets at various venues during the year. Internationally known artists sometimes appear as guests.

The **Dance Theatre of Bermuda** gives its audiences a blend of classical, modern, and jazz dancing. Performances are staged at various places throughout the year.

Movies

Bermuda has four cinemas showing first-run movies: Two are in Hamilton, one is in St. George's, and the fourth is in the West End. Check the listings in the *Royal Gazette* for movies and show times.

Neptune Cinema (The Cooperage, Dockyard, ☎ 441/291–2035) is a 118-seat cinema that shows feature films at night. Features are usually shown at 7:30 and 9:30 nightly, and 7:30 only on Sunday.
The Little Theatre (Queen St., Hamilton, ☎ 441/292–2135) is a 173-seat theater across the street from Casey's Bar. Show times are usually 2:15, 7, and 9:30.
Liberty Theatre (corner Union and Victoria Sts., Hamilton, ☎ 441/291–2035) is a 270-seat cinema in an unsavory section of Hamilton. The area immediately outside the theater is safe during the day, but visitors should not loiter in this neighborhood after dark. Show times are usually at 2:30, 5:30, 7:30, and 9:30 daily, and 2:30 and 7:30 on Sunday.

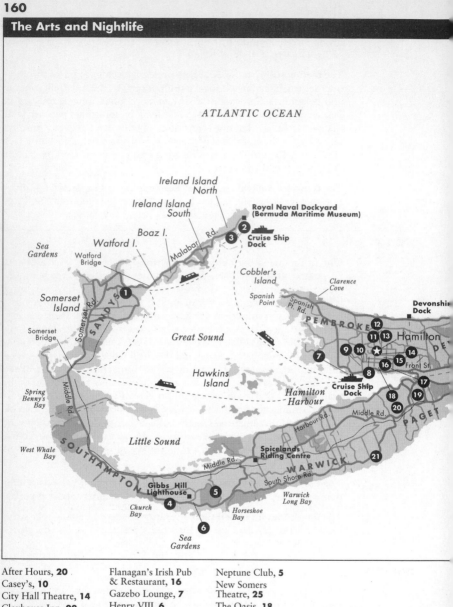

ATLANTIC OCEAN

Ireland Island North

Ireland Island South

Royal Naval Dockyard
(Bermuda Maritime Museum)

Boaz I.

Watford I.

Cruise Ship Dock

Sea Gardens

Watford Bridge

Cobbler's Island

Clarence Cove

Spanish Point

Spanish Pl. Rd.

Devonshire Dock

Somerset Island

PEMBROKE

Somerset Bridge

Great Sound

Hamilton

Front St.

Spring Benny's Bay

Hawkins Island

Cruise Ship Dock

Hamilton Harbour

Middle Rd.

West Whale Bay

SOUTHAMPTON

Little Sound

Harbour Rd.

PAGET

Spicelands Riding Centre

Middle Rd.

WARWICK

Gibbs Hill Lighthouse

Church Bay

Horseshoe Bay

Warwick Long Bay

South Shore Rd.

Sea Gardens

Tobacco Bay
Fort St. Catherine
St. Catherine Beach
ST. GEORGE'S
24
25 Town of St. George
St. George's Island
St. George's Harbour
Cruise Ship Dock
Ferry Rd.
St. David's Rd.
Conoy Island
Kindley Field Rd.
Bermuda Airport
23
The Causeway
St. David's Island
Sea Gardens
Bermuda Perfumery
Crystal Caves
Blue Hole
Leamington Caves
St. David's Lighthouse
Crawl Hill North
Harrington Sound Rd.
Castle Harbour
HAMILTON
TUCKER'S TOWN
Aquarium, Museum, and Zoo
Harrington Sound
Sea Gardens
...hire
North Shore Rd.
22
Harrington Sound Rd.
SMITH'S
John Smith's Bay
VONSHIRE
South Shore Rd.

N

KEY
⛴ Cruise Ship
⛴ Ferry
— Railway Trail

0 · · · 2 miles
0 · · · 3 km

New Somers Theatre (York St., St. George's, ☎ 441/297–2821) is a 248-seat cinema at the entrance to the town of St. George's, just below the St. George's Club. Show times are usually 7 and 9 Monday through Thursday, with an additional viewing time scheduled Friday through Sunday.

Theater

Dinner theater has become popular over the past few years in Bermuda. In 1996 the **Jabulani Repertory Company** (☎ 441/295–3000) will stage a new lineup of contemporary plays on weekends from November to April at the Hamilton Princess. The hotel offers patrons a specially priced dinner before each show.

Bermuda is the only place outside the United States where **Harvard University's Hasty Pudding Theatricals** are performed. For almost 30 years, the satirical troupe has performed on the island during Bermuda College Weeks (March–April). Produced by the estimable Elsbeth Gibson, an American-born actress/producer who lives in Bermuda, each show incorporates political and social themes and issues of the past year. The Hasty Pudding Theatricals are staged in the City Hall Theatre (*see above*); ticket prices are about $20.

NIGHTLIFE

During high season all hotels and cottage colonies feature entertainment—barbecues, steel bands, dinner dancing, and other diversions. Otherwise, the island's nightlife is fairly subdued; there are no casinos and only a few nightclubs and discos. Much of the action occurs in the pubs and lounges, which range from hotel bars to local hangouts. Some places close during the off-season, so check *This Week in Bermuda and Preview of Bermuda* (*see above*) for the latest information about what's happening each night. As a general rule, men should wear a jacket and tie to clubs; for women the dress code is casual but smart. Pubs and discos begin to fill up around 9:30 or 10.

The music scene is dominated by local acts and bands playing the island's hotel and pub circuits. Occasionally, outside performers are billed, particularly during the Bermuda Festival (*see above*). The island superstar is **Gene Steede,** a guitarist, singer, and comedian who has been described as Tony Bennett, Harry Belafonte, and Johnny Carson rolled into one; his performances at The Princess hotel in Pembroke draw large crowds. Among the other popular entertainers to watch for are the **Coca-Cola Steel Band** and the **Bermuda Strollers. Jimmy Keyes** is a popular pianist/comedian who holds forth at the Southampton Princess Hotel's Neptune Lounge. **Sharx** is a rock band; the **Travellers** straddle country and rock music.

Around 3 AM, when the bars and discos close, head for the **Ice Queen** (Middle Rd., Paget, ☎ 441/236–3136). This place is like a drive-in movie without the movie—the parking lot is jammed with cars and mopeds. The main attraction is the $2.75 burgers, which taste terrific after a night on the town. Order them from the take-out window and enjoy them at the beach, where drunk and disorderly crowds won't bother you. Open from 11 AM, it's also a good place to stop for an ice-cream cone break.

Another late-night spot is **After Hours** (117 South Rd., Paget, ☎ 441/236–8563), just past the intersection of South and Middle Roads. Good curries, suppers, hamburgers, and sandwiches are served until the wee hours.

Bars and Lounges

Those who like to drink in a hard-core bar will enjoy **Casey's** (Queen St., across from the Little Theatre, Hamilton, ☎ 441/293–9549). It's not fancy, nor is it touristy by any means. It's just a bar—a narrow room with a jukebox and a few tables—but the place packs them in, especially on Friday night. It's open 10–10 every day except Sunday. **The Colony Pub** (The Princess, 76 Pitts Bay Rd., Hamilton, ☎ 441/295– 3000), where the lights are low and the piano music soft and soothing, is a popular meeting place for young professionals. The **Neptune Club** at the Southampton Princess Hotel (South Shore Rd., Southampton, ☎ 441/238–8000) is wildly popular because of its British comedian/pianist Jimmy Keyes, whose hilarious show airs nightly except Sunday. There is always local or visiting entertainment scheduled at the ever-popular watering hole, **Henry VIII** (South Shore Rd., Southampton, ☎ 441/238–1977). **Flanagan's Irish Pub & Restaurant** (Front St., Hamilton, ☎ 441/295–8299) is a great bar with live entertainment most nights. **Ye Olde Cock & Feather** (Front St., Hamilton, ☎ 441/295–2263), which draws both locals and tourists, hosts happy hour Monday through Saturday from 5 to 7, and a mixed bag of live entertainment. **Docksider Pub & Restaurant** (Front St., Hamilton, ☎ 441/292–4088) attracts a young crowd with live entertainment. **Spazzizi's** (Elbow Beach Hotel, South Shore Rd., Paget, ☎ 441/236–3535) offers nightly entertainment by local performers. **Loyalty Inn** (Somerset Village, ☎ 441/234–0125) is a very casual neighborhood bar, where laid-back locals sometimes dare to do the karaoke bit. There's no cover, and dinner and snacks are served nightly. In the Bailey's Bay area, the **Swizzle Inn** (Middle Rd., Hamilton Parish, ☎ 441/293–9300) is strictly for the young, with a dartboard, a jukebox that plays soft and hard rock, and business cards from all over the world tacked on the walls, ceilings, and doors. The yachting crowd gathers at the **Wharf Tavern** (Somers Wharf, St. George's, ☎ 441/ 297–1515) for rum swizzling and nautical talk.

The Club Scene

Calypso

Bermuda legend **Gene Steede** is top banana for an island revue at the 280-seat **Gazebo Lounge** (The Princess, 76 Pitts Bay Rd., Hamilton, ☎ 441/295–3000). The $30 cover includes two drinks and the show, which runs from April through October. The **Clayhouse Inn** (North Shore Rd., Devonshire, ☎ 441/292–3193), packs in locals and tourists for a rowdy show involving limbo dancers, The Bermuda Strollers, The Coca-Cola Steel Band, and an occasional top-name entertainer. Shows are at 10:15 Monday through Thursday; about $23 covers the entry fee plus two drinks. A range of entertainment is laid on for the weekend.

Rock/Soul

Greg Thompson's Hitsville Bermuda at the Palm Reef Hotel's Gombey Room (Harbour Rd., Paget, ☎ 441/236–1000) is a musical salute to Motown and a tribute to the island's show-business traditions. Featuring music by everyone from the Mills Brothers to the Vandellas to En Vogue and the Drifters, this new singing and dancing revue is action packed. The Bermuda Gombeys put on a special performance, too. Show time is 10 PM, and the cost is $29; the dinner-show package is $55.

Folk

The only place to hear folk music is at The **Bermuda Folk Club's** monthly get-togethers, which usually take place on the first Saturday of the month at 8:15 at the Old Colony Club, Trott Rd., Hamilton (☎ 441/293–9241). Entry is $5, and the drinks have happy-hour prices. For specifics about dates and venues, contact Rab Craig (☎ 441/293–0010 or 441/292–2210) or Paul Maccoy (☎ 441/236–8070 or 441/295–9208), or write to the Bermuda Folk Club, Box WK 158, Warwick, WK BX. Entertainment is provided by local and visiting musicians, and covers many musical styles besides folk.

Rock and Roll

Club 21 (16 Ireland Island, Sandys, Dockyard, ☎ 441/234–7037 or 441/234–2721) is a sophisticated spot where the lights are low and the live music is loud. High-season shows are Tuesday through Saturday at 9:30 and 11:30, and there are Sunday jam sessions from 9 PM to 2 AM. There's a $12 cover.

Jazz

Hubie's Bar (Angle St., Hamilton, ☎ 441/293–9287), off Court Street, attracts fun-loving locals and visitors who appreciate good live jazz, which is played only on Friday 7–10 PM; live bands perform Wednesday and Saturday nights. It's best to take a cab to this club, since the area can be dangerous at night. Under new management, **Oscar's** (9 Victoria St., Hamilton, ☎ 441/292–0348) has daily happy hour from 3 to 7, live jazz every Sunday evening, a casual local clientele, and no cover.

Contemporary

Club 21 (16 Ireland Island, Sandys, Royal Naval Dockyard, ☎ 441/234–2721) is a sophisticated spot where the lights are low and the music loud. Lots of action and a fun crowd make this a popular place for locals and visitors.

Discos

After extensive renovations, **The Club** (Bermudiana Rd., Hamilton, ☎ 441/295–6693) recently became a sophisticated nightspot. By day, it caters to the business crowd and can be rented for private meetings; special menus are available. When meetings are not being held, lunch and dinner are served, and cocktail happy hours from 5 to 7 keep the place hopping. With dancing every night until 3 AM, this is a favorite nightspot among locals and visitors, who appreciate its comfort and elegance. The entry fee is $15. **The Oasis** (Emporium Bldg., Front St., Hamilton, ☎ 441/292–4978 or 441/292–3379) is a hot spot with a karaoke bar and disco, and a slightly younger crowd that gladly pays the $15 cover charge. There is dancing nightly from April through October in the chic **Palm Court** at the Sonesta Beach Hotel & Spa (off South Rd., Southampton, ☎ 441/238–8122).

10 Portraits of Bermuda

BERMUDA AT A GLANCE:
A CHRONOLOGY

1503 Juan de Bermudez discovers the islands while searching for the New World. The islands are eventually named after him.

1603 Diego Ramirez, a Spanish captain, spends several weeks on Bermuda making ship repairs.

1609 An English fleet of nine ships, under the command of Admiral Sir George Somers, sets sail for Jamestown, Virginia, with supplies for the starving colony. Struck by a hurricane, the fleet is scattered, and the admiral's ship, the *Sea Venture,* runs aground on the reefs of Bermuda. The colonization of Bermuda begins.

1610 After building two ships, *Deliverance* and *Patience,* from the island's cedar trees, the survivors depart for Jamestown, leaving behind a small party of men. Admiral Sir George Somers returns to Bermuda a few weeks later but dies soon afterward. He requests that his heart be buried on the island.

1612 Asserting ownership of the islands, the Virginia Company sends 60 settlers to Bermuda under the command of Richard Moore, the colony's first governor. The Virginia Company sells its rights to the islands to the newly formed Bermuda Company for £2,000.

1616 The islands are surveyed and divided into shares (25 acres) and tribes (50 shares per tribe). The tribes, or parishes, are named after investors in the Bermuda Company. The first slaves are brought to Bermuda to dive for pearls and to harvest tobacco and sugarcane.

1620 The Bermuda Parliament meets for the first time, in St. Peter's Church in St. George's, making it the third oldest parliament in the world after those of Iceland and Great Britain.

1684 The Crown takes control of the colony from the Bermuda Company. Sir Robert Robinson is appointed the Crown's first governor.

1775 The American Continental Congress announces a trade embargo against all colonies remaining loyal to the Crown. Dependent on America for food, Bermuda negotiates to give the rebellious colonies salt if they will lift the embargo. The colonies refuse, but state that they will end sanctions in exchange for gunpowder. Without the knowledge of Governor George Bruere, a group of Bermudians breaks into the magazine at St. George's and steals the island's supply of gunpowder. The gunpowder is delivered to the Americans, who lift the embargo.

1780 The "Great Hurricane" hits Bermuda, driving ships ashore and leveling houses and trees.

1784 Bermuda's first newspaper, the *Bermuda Gazette & Weekly Advertiser,* is started by Joseph Stockdale in St. George's.

1804 Irish poet Thomas Moore arrives in Bermuda for a four-month stint as registrar of the admiralty court. His affair with the married Hester Tucker was the inspiration for his steamy love poems to her (the "Nea" in his odes), which have attained legendary status in Bermuda.

1810 The Royal Navy begins work on Dockyard, a new naval base on Ireland Island.

1812 In response to American raids on York (now Toronto) during the War of 1812, the British fleet attacks Washington, DC, from its base in Bermuda.

1815 Hamilton becomes the new capital of Bermuda, superseding St. George's.

1834 Slavery is abolished.

1846 The first lighthouse in the colony, the 117-foot-high Gibbs Hill Lighthouse, is built at the western end of the island in an effort to reduce the number of shipwrecks in the area.

1861 Bermuda enters a period of enormous prosperity with the outbreak of the American Civil War. Sympathetic to the South, Bermudians take up the lucrative and dangerous task of running the Union blockade of southern ports. Sailing in small, fast ships, Bermudians ferry munitions and supplies to the Confederates and return with bales of cotton bound for London.

1883 Princess Louise, daughter of Queen Victoria, visits Bermuda. In honor of her visit, the new Pembroke Hotel changes its name to the Princess.

1901 Afrikaner prisoners from the Boer War are incarcerated in Bermuda. By the end of the war, approximately 5,000 prisoners are housed on the islands.

1915 A 120-man contingent of the Bermuda Volunteer Rifle Corps (B.V.R.C.) departs for service in France during World War I. In action at the battles of the Somme, Arras, and the Third Battle of Ypres, the unit loses more than 30% of its men. In 1916, the Bermuda Militia Artillery also heads for France.

1931 Constructed at a cost of £1 million, the Bermuda Railway opens years behind schedule. Maintenance problems during World War II cripple train service, and the whole system is sold to British Guiana in 1948.

1937 Imperial Airways begins the first scheduled air service to Bermuda from Port Washington in the United States.

1940 During World War II, mail bound for Europe from the Americas is off-loaded in Bermuda and taken to the basement of the Princess Hotel, where it is opened by British civil servants trying to locate German spies. Several spies in the United States are unmasked. As part of the Lend-Lease Act between Prime Minister Churchill and President Roosevelt, the United States is awarded a 99-year lease for a military base on St. David's Island. Construction of the base begins in 1941.

1944 Women landowners are given the vote.

1946 For the first time, automobiles are permitted by law on Bermuda.

1951 The Royal Navy withdraws from Dockyard and closes the base.

1953 Winston Churchill, Dwight D. Eisenhower, and Prime Minister Joseph Laniel of France meet on Bermuda for the "Big Three Conference."

1959 NASA opens a space tracking station on Coopers Island, which is part of the American base.

1971 Edward Richards becomes Bermuda's first black government leader (a title later changed to premier).

1973 Governor Sir Richard Sharples and his aide, Captain Hugh Sayers, are shot dead. In 1976, Erskine "Buck" Burrows is convicted of the murder, as well as several other murders and armed robberies. He is hanged in 1977.

1979 Gina Swainson, Miss Bermuda, wins the Miss World Contest. An official half holiday is announced and Gina Swainson postage stamps are released in 1980.

1987 Hurricane Emily hits Bermuda, injuring more than 70 people and causing millions of dollars in damage.

1990 President Bush and Prime Minister Thatcher meet on Bermuda.

1994 Her Royal Highness Queen Elizabeth II and Prince Philip make an official visit to Bermuda.

1995 The Royal Navy closes its Bermuda headquarters after having maintained a presence on the island for 200 years.

The U.S. Naval Air Station base closes; it had operated since September 1940.

BERMUDA'S HIDDEN LANDSCAPES

AT THE PUB ON THE SQUARE in St. George's, Bermuda, there is a sign on the second-floor veranda that everyone ignores. "Do not feed the birds," it says, but the clientele keeps handing out crumbs to the sparrows that dart through the open railings.

I sat on that veranda on a sultry October afternoon, finishing a pint of Watney's and looking out over King's Square. I had just enjoyed my first cup of Bermuda fish chowder, which the Pub, like most local restaurants, lets you fine-tune with cruets of dark rum and a fiery concoction called sherry peppers.

At the next table an English toddler was singing a song about a little duck. The 18th-century square below was quiet, partly because it had just rained and partly because at the moment there was no cruise ship anchored at St. George's. I crumbled a few morsels from the bun of my fish sandwich, tossed them to the sparrows, and made up my mind on another Watney's. After all, I wasn't playing golf that afternoon.

Not playing golf? The Bermuda Islands, conventional wisdom has it, are a place where you live on the links. But I was after a different place—a traveler's Bermuda, if I could find it.

On an archipelago roughly 22 miles long and seldom more than a mile wide, traveling can be a difficult order—unless you severely limit your pace. Fortunately, automobiles are out of the question. Visitors can't rent them (even residents weren't allowed to own cars until 1946), and the only option for exploring Bermuda on four wheels is to engage a taxi driven by an accredited guide. But why risk seeing the whole place in a day? If you move at a speed faster than a walk, you miss details like the sign I saw on a small, shuttered yellow building: "Dot & Andy's Restaurant. Operated by Barbara and Donna."

Until recently, walking in Bermuda has meant edging gingerly along the nearly nonexistent shoulders of narrow lanes, ready to press yourself into the hibiscus hedges when a car comes by. A few years ago, though, some enterprising Bermudians got the idea of turning the right-of-way of the abandoned Bermuda Railway into an island-length hiking trail. (The entire railway, down to the spikes, was sold to British Guiana, now Guyana, in 1948.)

My first choice, as a rail enthusiast, would have been to have the narrow-gauge locomotive and cars still rattling along the tracks. But being able to walk the route, or part of it, is clearly the next best thing. My problem was that I chose a section that skirted a residential district along Bailey's Bay, near the northeastern end of the main island. Here the old roadbed was frequently severed by sharp inlets of the sea, and the trestles that had once bridged them had long since gone to South America. I'd walk a hundred yards or so and have to go back to the road, often finding no signs to tell me when I could pick up the trail again. (Farther west on the islands, the old route is less frequently broken.) On one side was the ocean, on the other a series of relentlessly suburban backyards—there are no raffish little shacks here like the ones you find on other islands. Finally, after I had inadvertently wandered into my fourth backyard, it began to rain. It was the kind of rain that makes you so wet in the first couple of minutes that there's no sense in hurrying out of it. I walked to a bus shelter and admitted defeat . . . and some success, having got into a situation in which I could hardly be mistaken for a tourist, even in Bermuda.

It was in the bus shelter that I met a young American who was waiting out the storm with his two toddlers. He was a civilian worker at the U.S. naval air station, a submarine-watching facility now largely dedicated to operating the islands' commercial airport. His most telling comment had to do with his younger child, who had been born in Hamilton: "She's a real Bermuda Onion."

He knew, of course, that genuine Bermudian citizenship requires at least one native parent, or jumping through more bureaucratic hoops than most people would care to deal with, but the fact that he liked thinking of his little girl as a Bermudian meant that he wasn't just serving a remunerative sentence in a far-away place. To a wet traveler like me, the message was that there was a community here, and foreigners could become part of it.

THE RAIN THAT ENDED MY railway trail walk was part of the tail end of Hurricane Nana, which had threatened to strike the island in full force before being pushed off track by a continental cold front. "We don't have hurricanes in Bermuda," a hotel bartender had told me with a wink, obviously remembering 1987's Emily, with her 116-mph winds, 50 injuries, and $35 million damage.

"No," I replied. "I live in Vermont, and we don't have snow."

Nana was a hurricane that missed, although she faded and veered away with great theatrical effect. By nine that evening the rain returned, sheeting sideways against the windows of the hotel restaurant while tall palms thrashed in wild abandon. From the hotel bar the storm was a terrific backdrop—the room was all Key Largo atmosphere heightened by the adrenal tingle that comes with a sudden pressure drop. It didn't last long. Within an hour, all that remained of Nana in Bermuda was a random gusting among the palm tops, and it was fine outside for a walk down to the bay.

The next day I reverted to the vehicle of choice for covering ground in Bermuda. Motorized or "auxiliary" cycles, and the more modern motor scooters—none for rent with engines larger than 50cc, but powerful enough for islands with a 20-mph speed limit—have become a virtual post-card cliché in Bermuda, and to strap on your de rigueur white helmet is to feel as if you've somehow become part of the landscape.

A lot of visitors are afraid the scooters can too easily help them accomplish just that, but the bikes aren't all that dangerous, once you learn the controls and remember to stay on the left, British style. There is, however, a common motorbike injury the locals call "road rash," a nasty abrasion of whatever appendage happens to meet with the road, or with one of Bermuda's limestone walls, during a badly executed turn.

What I most wanted the bike for was exploring the Bermuda hinterlands. I had already visited St. George's, the islands' oldest settlement and former capital, with its narrow meandering streets, lovely State House (built in 1620), and cedar-beamed, 18th-century church of St. Peter. I had been particularly intrigued with a local attraction called the Confederate Museum, headquarters of blockade-running operations during the U.S. Civil War. (What really caught my interest there was the attitude of the black docent, "proud," as she put it, of a building that housed the branch office of a desperate effort to keep her ancestors in chains. In Bermudian race relations, bygones are bygones to a remarkable degree.)

TOWNS ARE BEST EXPLORED on foot, even though it did get to be great fun to breeze into the capital for dinner after dark and have maître d's take my helmet. The bike, though, would let me discover the countryside, with its quiet lanes and tended meadows and fragments of old estates. One of those estates—Verdmont, in Smith's Parish, now a Bermuda National Trust property—lay at the end of a delightfully convoluted route I had devised, one that was designed to take me buzzing along as many back roads as possible.

It was on St. Mark's Road, rounding Collector's Hill, that the essence of this miniature landscape suddenly came clear: I was looking, I realized, at a near-perfect combination of Martha's Vineyard and the Cotswolds. On the Vineyard account was the gently rolling countryside with the sea not far away, as on a New England sea-coast farm; the Cotswolds element was provided by a little jewel of a limestone Gothic church, by narrow byways with names like Pigeon Berry Lane, and by the faultless juxtaposition of every stand of trees, half-acre of greensward, and carefully clipped hedgerow.

As it turned out, I wasn't the first to get this feeling about the place: I saw later that two of the local streets were named Nantucket Lane (close enough) and Cotswold Lane. And why not? The Cotswold Hills, Bermuda, and the Massachusetts islands are all essentially English places, the latter two offering their settlers an Englishness of landscape even before any art was applied to it. And that art, in all three locales, was the particular English genius for conjuring tremendous diversity within the most compact of areas. Consummately ordered yet always romantically picturesque, the English landscape aesthetic depends on constant variety and small surprises, and never upon great vistas.

THE RESULT IS A SENSE of much in little, of no space wasted; the effect in Bermuda is to shrink the visitor into the islands' scale, rather than to leave him feeling like a scooter-mounted giant in a hibiscus garden.

There was another aspect of Bermuda to consider, one that counters the islands' persona as a serene, ocean-borne fragment of English countryside. This is its past history as fortress Bermuda, a 21-square-mile dreadnought permanently anchored in the Atlantic. Fort St. Catherine, at the colony's extreme northeastern tip, is now decommissioned and restored to reveal its vast warren of tunnels, built to feed shells to guns commanding the northern and eastern approaches to the islands. St. David's Island, too, has its battery, a rusting line of World War II–era shore artillery where feral house cats pad about the empty magazines.

From the 17th to the 20th century, dozens of promontories and harbor entrances throughout Bermuda bristled with guns, reflecting Britain's confrontations with forces that ranged from imperial Spain to the newly independent United States to the U-boats of the Third Reich. And no single installation loomed so mightily as the Royal Navy Dockyard, at the barb of Bermuda's fishhook-shaped western end.

From 1810 to 1950 the dockyard was the "Gibraltar of the West," providing a heavily fortified anchorage for British warships and a citadel of massive limestone support structures. Approaching by ferry from Hamilton, I immediately was struck by the orderliness and permanence of it all, by the twin towers of the main building with clock faces showing the time and the hour of the next high tide, and by the ubiquitous initials VR—"Victoria Regina," shorthand for one of history's most remarkable imperial achievements. The dockyard looks as if it were built to last a thousand years, and it may, though now it houses a cluster of museums, craft galleries, restaurants, and boutiques. Like the rest of Bermuda's defenses, the dockyard was never tested by a serious attack; its bristles were too formidable a challenge.

Time and again in Bermuda, one encounters the opposing tidal pull of British and American influences. This, after all, is a place where they still refer to the panorama of harbor islands as seen from the top of Gibbs Hill as the "Queen's View," because Elizabeth II admired it in 1953. But this British colony also conducts its financial affairs in dollars, not sterling, and nearly 90% of its visitors are American.

THERE IS A CONTINUING Bermudian tradition that many residents link with the long British military presence, and that is a certain formality of dress. I was reminded of it one day in downtown Hamilton, when I saw a white-haired gentleman wearing a blue blazer, a white shirt, and a rep silk tie, along with pink Bermuda shorts, white kneesocks, and pink tassels on his garters. The shorts themselves are a throwback to the military, and got their start as a local trademark when Bermuda tailors began refining officers' baggy khaki shorts for civilian wear. They are now ubiquitous as Bermudian business attire, but the most striking thing about them is not the fact that they expose gentlemen's knees but that they are integrated into a very correct, very formal men's civilian uniform. I never once saw a businessman's collar and tie loosened on a hot day in Bermuda—a sure sign that the stiff upper lip can outlast even the presence of the Royal Navy.

I thought about where I might find the quintessence of Bermudian formality and local tradition, and concluded that the place to look was probably afternoon tea at the venerable Hamilton Princess Hotel. I was staying elsewhere, and thought it might be appropriate to call the Princess first to see if outsiders were welcome. "Are you serving tea at four?" I asked the English-accented woman who answered the telephone.

"Yes."

"Is it all right to come if you're not registered at the hotel?"

"Are you registered at the hotel?"

"No. That's why I'm asking."

"I'll switch you to dining services."

"Hello?" (Another Englishwoman's voice.)

"Hello, I'm wondering if I can come to tea if I'm not registered at the hotel. "

"What is your name, sir?" I gave her the name and spelling. At this point, I was tempted to add "Viscount."

"I don't have you listed as a guest."

"I know that. I'm calling to ask if it's all right to come to tea if I'm not a guest."

"No, sir."

Now we were deep in Monty Python territory, and I had the John Cleese part. Clearly, there was nothing to do but get dressed, scoot into Hamilton, and crash tea at the Princess. But when I sauntered into the hotel with my best ersatz viscount air, all I found was a small antechamber to an empty function room where a dozen people in tennis clothes stood around a samovar and a tray of marble pound cake slices. I poured a cup, drank it, and was gone in five minutes. Crashing tea at the Princess had been about as difficult, and as exciting, as crashing lunch at my late grandfather's diner in New Jersey.

Hamilton is a tidy, cheerful little city, but as the days drew down I returned more and more to the countryside, particularly to the back roads where small farms survive. Bermuda was once a mid-ocean market garden, in the days before the United States restricted imports, and property values skyrocketed beyond the reach of farmers; now, an occasional neat patch of red earth still produces root crops, broccoli, cabbage, and squash. I even saw a truck loaded with onions go by—a reminder of a Bermuda before golf.

— *By William G. Scheller*

William G. Scheller is a contributing editor to National Geographic Traveler. His articles have also appeared in the Washington Post Magazine, Islands, *and numerous other periodicals.*

AMERICA'S REBEL COLONIES AND BERMUDA: GETTING A BANG FOR THEIR BUCKWHEAT

WHEN THE War of American Independence began, Bermudians at first felt little personal concern. There was some sympathy for the colonists; quarrels between arbitrary executive power and people, which in America had now led to real trouble, had also been part of Bermuda's history, and besides this there were ties of blood and friendship to make for a common understanding. But for all that, Bermudians, while expressing discreet sympathy, were chiefly concerned for their ships and carrying trade, and realizing their helpless position, they believed their wisest course lay in continued loyalty to the Crown. The wisdom of this policy was suddenly brought into question when the Continental Congress placed an embargo on all trade with Britain and the loyal colonies, for as nearly all essential food supplies came from the Continent, the island faced starvation unless the decree was relaxed. Thus there was a swift realization that Bermuda's fate was deeply involved in the war.

The drama now began to unfold and soon developed into a struggle between the governor, George Bruere, and the dominant Bermuda clique led by the Tuckers of the West End. Bruere's chief characteristic was unswerving, unquestioning loyalty, and the fact that two of his sons were fighting with the royalist forces in America—one of them was killed at Bunker Hill—made the ambiguous behavior of Bermudians intolerable to him, both as a father and as an Englishman.

Of the Tuckers, the most prominent member of the family at this time was Colonel Henry, of the Grove, Southampton. His eldest son, Henry, colonial treasure and councillor, had married the governor's daughter, Frances Bruere, and lived at St. George's. There were also two sons in America, Thomas Tudor, a doctor settled in Charleston, and St. George, the youngest, a lawyer in Virginia. The two boys in America, caught up in the events around them and far removed from the delicacies of the Bermuda situation, openly took the side of the colonists.

Up to the time of the outbreak of the war there had been warm friendship between the Tuckers and the Brueres, a relationship made closer by the marriage of Henry Tucker to Frances Bruere. But when it became known in Bermuda that the Tuckers abroad were backing the Americans, Bruere publicly denounced them as rebels and broke off relations with every member of the family except his son-in-law. But Colonel Henry was more concerned with the situation in Bermuda than he was with the rights and wrongs of the conflict itself, and he believed that unless someone acted, the island was facing serious disaster. So, privately, through his sons in America, he began to sound out some of the delegates to the Continental Congress as to whether the embargo would be relaxed in exchange for salt. This move, never in any way official, had the backing of a powerful group, and before long it was decided to send the colonel with two or three others to Philadelphia to see what could be arranged. Meanwhile another but less powerful faction took form and likewise held meetings, the object of which was to oppose in every way these potential rebellions.

Colonel Henry and his colleagues reached Philadelphia in July 1775 and on the 11th delivered their appeal to Congress. Though larded with unctuous flattery, the address met a stony reception, but a hint was thrown out that although salt was not wanted, any vessel bringing arms or powder would find herself free from the embargo. The fact that there was a useful store of powder at St. George's was by now common knowledge in America, for the Tucker boys had told their friends about it and the information had reached General Washington. Thus, before long, the question of seizing this powder for the Americans was in the forefront of the discussions.

Colonel Henry was in a tight corner. Never for an instant feeling that his own loyalty was in question, he had believed himself fully justified in coming to Philadelphia to offer salt in exchange for food. But these new suggestions which were now being put to him went far beyond anything he had contemplated, and he was dismayed at the ugly situation that confronted him. It is evident that the forces at work were too strong for him. The desperate situation in Bermuda, verging on starvation, could only be relieved by supplies from America, and an adamant Congress held the whip hand. After some agonizing heart-searching, he gave in and agreed with Benjamin Franklin to trade the powder at St. George's for an exemption of Bermuda ships from the embargo.

COLONEL HENRY RETURNED home at once, arriving on July 25. His son St. George, coming from Virginia, arrived about the same time, while two other ships from America, sent especially to fetch the powder, were already on their way.

On August 14, 1775, there was secret but feverish activity among the conspirators as whaleboats from various parts of the island assembled at Somerset. As soon as it was dark, the party, under the command, it is believed, of son-in-law Henry and a Captain Morgan, set off for St. George's. St. George, lately from Virginia and sure to be suspect, spent the night at St. George's, possibly at the home of his brother Henry, and at midnight was seen ostentatiously walking up and down the Parade with Chief Justice Burch, thus establishing a watertight alibi. Meanwhile the landing party, leaving the boats at Tobacco Bay on the north side of St. George's, reached the unguarded magazine. The door was quickly forced, and before long, kegs of powder were rolling over the grass of the Governor's Park toward the bay, where they were speedily stowed in the boats. The work went on steadily until the first streaks of dawn drove the party from the scene. By that time 100 barrels of powder were on the way to guns that would discharge the powder against the king's men.

When Bruere heard the news he was frantic. A vessel which he rightly believed had the stolen powder on board was still in sight from Retreat Hill, and he determined

to give chase. Rushing into town, the distraught man issued a hysterical proclamation:

POWDER STEAL
Advt
Save your Country from Ruin, which may hereafter happen. The Powder stole out of the Magazine late last night cannot be carried far as the wind is so light.
A GREAT REWARD
will be given to any person that can make a proper discovery before the Magistrates.

News of the outrage and copies of the proclamation were hurried through the colony as fast as riders could travel. The legislature was summoned to meet the following day. Many members of the Assembly doubtless knew a good deal, but officially all was dark and the legislature did its duty by voting a reward and sending a wordy message expressing its abhorrence of the crime.

BUT NO PRACTICAL HELP WAS forthcoming, and after several days of helpless frustration Bruere determined to send a vessel to Boston to inform Admiral Howe what had happened. At first no vessels were to be had anywhere in the island; then, when one was found, the owner was threatened with sabotage, so he withdrew his offer. Another vessel was found, but there was no crew, and for three whole weeks, in an island teeming with mariners, no one could be found to go to sea. At last, on September 3, the governor's ship put to sea, but not without a final incident, for she was boarded offshore by a group of men who searched the captain and crew for letters. These had been prudently hidden away in the ballast with the governor's slave, who remained undiscovered. The captain hotly denied having any confidential papers, so the disappointed boarders beat him up and then left.

In due course the ship reached Boston, and Admiral Howe at once sent the *Scorpion* to Bermuda to help Bruere keep order. Thereafter for several years His Majesty's ships kept a watchful eye on the activities of Bermudians, and in 1778 these were replaced by a garrison. It has always seemed extraordinary that no rumor of this bargain with the Americans reached Bruere before the actual robbery took place. It is even more amazing that within a stone's throw of Government House such a desperate undertaking could have continued steadily throughout the night without discovery.

The loss of the powder coincided with the disappearance of a French officer, a prisoner on parole. At the time it was thought that he had been in league with the Americans and had made his escape with them. But 100 years later when the foundation for the Unfinished Church was being excavated, the skeleton of a man dressed in French uniform was disclosed. It is now believed that he must have come on the scene while the robbery was in progress and, in the dark, been mistaken for a British officer. Before he could utter a sound he must have been killed outright by these desperate men and quickly buried on the governor's doorstep.

—By William Zuill

A native Bermudian who was a member of the Bermuda House of Assembly, William Zuill wrote several historical works about the island. This excerpt about the role of Bermuda in the American War of Independence is taken from his book, Bermuda Journey. *William Zuill died in July 1989.*

FOLLOWING IN THE TRACKS OF THE BERMUDA RAILWAY

BERMUDA IS lovely, but a walk along its narrow roads can involve close encounters with countless madcap moped drivers and a stream of cars. A more serene way to sample Bermuda's lush terrain, stunning seascapes, and colorful colonies of island homes is to follow the route of the railroad that once crossed this isolated archipelago. The Bermuda Railway Trail goes along the old train right-of-way for 18 miles, winding through three of the several interconnected islands that make up Bermuda.

Opened in 1931, the railway provided smooth-running transportation between the quiet village of Somerset at the west end and the former colonial capital of St. George's to the east. But by 1948 it had fallen victim to excessive military use during World War II, soaring maintenance costs, and the automobile. The railroad was closed down, and all its rolling stock was sold to Guyana (then called British Guiana). In 1984, Bermuda's 375th anniversary, the government dedicated the lands of the old railway for public use and began to clear, pave, and add signs to sections of its route.

The trail's most enchanting aspect is that it reveals a parade of island views hidden from the public for nearly 30 years, scenes similar to what the first colonists must have found here in the early 1600s. In a few places the trail joins the main roads, but mostly it follows a tranquil, car-free route from parish to parish, past quiet bays, limestone cliffs, small farms, and groves of cedar, allspice, mangrove, and fiddlewood trees. Short jaunts on side trails and intersecting tribe roads (paths that were built in the early 1600s as boundaries between the parishes, or "tribes") bring you to historic forts and a lofty lighthouse, coral-tinted beaches, parks, and preserves.

I explored the Railway Trail on foot, moped, and horseback, using an 18-page guide available free at the Visitors Service Bureau in Hamilton. (You can also find the guide at some of the big hotels.) The booklet contains historical photos, a brief history of the railroad, maps, and descriptions of seven sections of trail, which range from 1¾ to 3¾ miles.

Sporting a pair of proper Bermuda shorts, I revved up my rented moped and headed out to the Somerset Bus Terminal, one of eight former railroad stations and the westernmost end of the trail. From there I followed the paved path to Springfield—an 18th-century plantation house used by the Springfield Library. A leisurely stroll in the adjoining five-acre Springfield & Gilbert Nature Reserve took me through thick forests of fiddlewood. I also saw stands of Bermuda cedars that once blanketed the island but were nearly wiped out by blight in the 1940s.

Back on the trail I spotted oleander, hibiscus, bougainvillea, and poinsettia bursting through the greenery at every turn. In backyards I could see bananas, grapefruit, oranges, lemons, and limes growing in profusion, thanks to Bermuda's consistent year-round subtropical climate.

I parked the moped at the trailhead to Fort Scaur—a 19th-century fortress built by the Duke of Wellington, conqueror of Napoleon at Waterloo—and strolled up to its mighty walls and deep moat. Through a dark passage I reached the grassy grounds with their massive gun mounts and bunkers. A telescope atop the fort's walls provided close-up views of the Great Sound and Ely's Harbour, once a smuggler's haven. A caretaker showed me around the fort, one of the three largest in Bermuda.

On my moped again, I motored past Skroggins Bay to the Lantana Colony Club, a group of beachside cottages. I stopped to sip a Dark and Stormy—a classic Bermudian rum drink—and to enjoy the view of the sail-filled Great Sound. My post-swizzle destination: Somerset Bridge. Only 32 inches wide, this tiny bridge was built in 1620 and looks more like a plank in the road than the world's smallest drawbridge—its opening is just wide enough for a sailboat's mast to pass through.

I ended my first Railway Trail ride at the ferry terminal near the bridge, where I boarded the next ferry back to Hamilton. Had I continued, the trail would have taken me through what was once the agricultural heartland of Bermuda. The colony's 20 square miles of gently rolling landscape, graced by rich volcanic soil and a mild climate, once yielded crops of sweet, succulent Bermuda onions, potatoes, and other produce. But tourism has become bigger business here, and today only some 500 acres are devoted to vegetable crops.

Just west of Sandys Parish the trail runs for some 3¾ miles through Warwick Parish. The path, now dirt, overlooks Little Sound and Southampton, where fishing boats are moored. Here the Railway Trail begins to intersect many of Bermuda's tribe roads, which make interesting diversions. Tribe Road No. 2 brings you to the Gibb's Hill Lighthouse, built around 1846. This 133-foot structure is one of the few lighthouses in the world made of cast iron. You pay $2 for the dubious privilege of climbing 185 steps to the lens house, where you're rewarded with far-reaching views of the island and Great Sound. The 1,500-watt electric lamp can be seen as far away as 40 miles.

Spicelands, a riding center in Warwick, schedules early-morning rides along sections of the Railway Trail and South Shore beaches. I joined a ride to follow part of the trail where it cuts deep into the rolling limestone terrain—so deep that at one point we passed through the 450-foot Paget Tunnel, whose walls are lined with roots of rubber trees.

We rode through woodlands and fields, past stands of Surinam cherry trees and houses equipped with domed water tanks and stepped, pyramid-shaped roofs designed to catch rainwater. As we trotted through the cool darkness beneath a dense canopy of trees it was hard to imagine a time when noisy rolling stock rattled along the same route, carrying some of the 14 million passengers who rode the railway while it was in operation. Finally, a tribe road led us through tropical vegetation to the clean, coral-pink beaches of Bermuda's beautiful South Shore.

East of Hamilton, the Railway Trail follows the North Shore, beginning in Palmetto Park in the lush, hilly parish of Devonshire. It hugs the coastline past Palmetto House (a cross-shaped, 18th-century mansion belonging to the Bermuda National Trust) and thick stands of Bermuda cedar to Penhurst Park, where there are walking trails, agricultural plots, and good swimming beaches.

Farther east the trail hits a wilder stretch of coast. The Shelley Bay Park and Nature Reserve along here has native mangroves and one of the few beaches on the North Shore. After a short walk on North Shore Road, the trail picks up again at Bailey's Bay and follows the coast to Coney Island. The park here has an old lime kiln and a former horse-ferry landing.

The remaining sections of the trail are in St. George's. Start at the old Terminal Building (now called Tiger Bay Gardens) and stroll through this historic town. The trail passes by Mullet Bay and Rocky Hill Parks, then heads to Lover's Lake Nature Reserve, where nesting long tails can be seen amid the mangroves. The end of the trail is at Ferry Point Park, directly across from Coney Island. In the park there's a historic fort and a cemetery.

Evenings are perhaps the most enchanting time to walk along the Railway Trail. As the light grows dim, the moist air fills with songs from tiny tree frogs hidden in hedges of oleander and hibiscus. The sound sets a tranquil, tropical mood that, for nearly a half century, has been undisturbed by the piercing whistle and clickety-clack of Bermuda's bygone railroad.

—By Ben Davidson

A former travel editor for Sunset Travel magazine, Ben Davidson specializes in travel writing and photography.

MORE PORTRAITS

THE WELL-RESPECTED HISTORIAN William Zuill wrote extensively about the island. Published in 1945 and now somewhat outdated, Zuill's 426-page *Bermuda Journey: A Leisurely Guide Book* provides a fascinating look at the island and its people, with historical notes and anecdotes. The book is out of print; check with the Bermuda Book Store in Hamilton (☎ 441/295–3698) to see if used copies are available. Zuill's other books include *The Wreck of the Sea Venture*, which details the 1609 wreck of Admiral Sir George Somers's flagship and the subsequent settlement of the island, and *Tom Moore's Bermuda Poems*, a collection of odes by the Irish poet who spent four months on Bermuda in 1804.

W. S. Zuill, the son of the historian, wrote *The Story of Bermuda and Her People,* a recently updated volume tracing the history of the island from the *Sea Venture* wreck to the present. *Bermuda*, by John J. Jackson, contains an abundance of facts on Bermudian business, economics, law, ecology, and history, as well as tourist information. John Weatherill's *Faces of Bermuda* is a marvelous collection of photographs, and those curious about the legendary Bermuda Triangle can read about its history in *The Bermuda Triangle Mystery Solved,* by Larry David Kusche.

For a charming account of growing up in Bermuda during the 1930s and 1940s, refer to *The Back Yard,* by William Zuill's daughter Ann Zuill Williams. *"Rattle and Shake": The Story of the Bermuda Railway,* by David F. Raine, tells the tale of the fabled narrow-gauge railroad in photos and prose. The island's traditions and the unique culinary lineup that accompanies special holidays are the highlight of *The Seasons of Bermuda* by Judith Wadson. The island is showcased in several coffee-table books of color photographs, such as *Bermuda,* by Scott Stallard, *Bermuda Abstracts,* by Graeme Outerbridge, and *Bermudian Images,* by Bruce Stuart. Among the books for younger audiences are Willoughby Patton's *Sea Venture,* about the adventures of a young boy on the crew of the ill-fated ship; E. M. Rice's *A Child's History of Bermuda,* which tells the story of the island in terms children can readily understand; Dana Cooper's illustrated book, *My Bermuda ABC's* and *My Bermuda 1,2,3,;* and Bermudian artist Elizabeth Mulderig's three *Tiny the Tree Frog* books.

INDEX

✗ = *restaurant*, ⊞ = *hotel*

NOTES

NOTES

NOTES

NOTES

NOTES

NOTES

NOTES

NOTES

NOTES

NOTES

Your guide to a picture-perfect vacation

Kodak and Fodor's join together to create the guide that travelers everywhere have been asking for—one that covers the terms and techniques, the equipment and etiquette for taking first-rate travel photographs.

The most authoritative and up-to-date book of its kind, **The Kodak Guide to Shooting Great Travel Pictures** includes over 200 color photographs and spreads on 100 points of photography important to travelers, such as landscape basics, under sea shots, wildlife, city street, close-ups, photographing in museums and more.

$16.50   ($22.95 Canada)

At bookstores everywhere, or call 1-800-533-6478.

Fodor's. The name that means smart travel.™

Escape to ancient cities and

 *journey to* *exotic islands with*

CNN Travel Guide, a wealth of valuable advice. Host

Valerie Voss will take you to

all of your favorite destinations,

 *including those off the beaten*

path. Tune-in to your passport to the world.

CNN TRAVEL GUIDE
SATURDAY 12:30 PM ET   SUNDAY 4:30 PM ET

Fodor's Travel Publications

Available at bookstores everywhere, or call 1–800–533–6478, 24 hours a day.

Gold Guides

U.S.

Alaska

Arizona

Boston

California

Cape Cod, Martha's
Vineyard, Nantucket

The Carolinas & the
Georgia Coast

Chicago

Colorado

Florida

Hawaii

Las Vegas, Reno,
Tahoe

Los Angeles

Maine, Vermont,
New Hampshire

Maui

Miami & the Keys

New England

New Orleans

New York City

Pacific North Coast

Philadelphia & the
Pennsylvania Dutch
Country

The Rockies

San Diego

San Francisco

Santa Fe, Taos,
Albuquerque

Seattle & Vancouver

The South

U.S. & British Virgin
Islands

USA

Virginia & Maryland

Waikiki

Washington, D.C.

Foreign

Australia &
New Zealand

Austria

The Bahamas

Barbados

Bermuda

Brazil

Budapest

Canada

Cancún, Cozumel,
Yucatán Peninsula

Caribbean

China

Costa Rica, Belize,
Guatemala

The Czech Republic
& Slovakia

Eastern Europe

Egypt

Europe

Florence, Tuscany
& Umbria

France

Germany

Great Britain

Greece

Hong Kong

India

Ireland

Israel

Italy

Japan

Kenya & Tanzania

Korea

London

Madrid & Barcelona

Mexico

Montréal &
Québec City

Morocco

Moscow, St.
Petersburg, Kiev

The Netherlands,
Belgium &
Luxembourg

New Zealand

Norway

Nova Scotia, New
Brunswick, Prince
Edward Island

Paris

Portugal

Provence &
the Riviera

Scandinavia

Scotland

Singapore

South America

South Pacific

Southeast Asia

Spain

Sweden

Switzerland

Thailand

Tokyo

Toronto

Turkey

Vienna & the Danube

Fodor's Special-Interest Guides

Branson

Caribbean Ports
of Call

The Complete Guide
to America's
National Parks

Condé Nast Traveler
Caribbean Resort and
Cruise Ship Finder

Cruises and Ports
of Call

Fodor's London
Companion

France by Train

Halliday's New
England Food
Explorer

Healthy Escapes

Italy by Train

Kodak Guide to
Shooting Great
Travel Pictures

Shadow Traffic's
New York Shortcuts
and Traffic Tips

Sunday in New York

Sunday in
San Francisco

Walt Disney World,
Universal Studios
and Orlando

Walt Disney World
for Adults

Where Should We
Take the Kids?
California

Where Should We
Take the Kids?
Northeast

Special Series

Affordables
Caribbean
Europe
Florida
France
Germany
Great Britain
Italy
London
Paris

Fodor's Bed & Breakfasts and Country Inns
America's Best B&Bs
California's Best B&Bs
Canada's Great Country Inns
Cottages, B&Bs and Country Inns of England and Wales
The Mid-Atlantic's Best B&Bs
New England's Best B&Bs
The Pacific Northwest's Best B&Bs
The South's Best B&Bs
The Southwest's Best B&Bs
The Upper Great Lakes' Best B&Bs

The Berkeley Guides
California
Central America
Eastern Europe
Europe
France
Germany & Austria
Great Britain & Ireland
Italy
London
Mexico

Pacific Northwest & Alaska
Paris
San Francisco

Compass American Guides
Arizona
Canada
Chicago
Colorado
Hawaii
Hollywood
Las Vegas
Maine
Manhattan
Montana
New Mexico
New Orleans
Oregon
San Francisco
South Carolina
South Dakota
Texas
Utah
Virginia
Washington
Wine Country
Wisconsin
Wyoming

Fodor's Español
California
Caribe Occidental
Caribe Oriental
Gran Bretaña
Londres
Mexico
Nueva York
Paris

Fodor's Exploring Guides
Australia
Boston & New England

Britain
California
Caribbean
China
Florence & Tuscany
Florida
France
Germany
Ireland
Italy
London
Mexico
Moscow & St. Petersburg
New York City
Paris
Prague
Provence
Rome
San Francisco
Scotland
Singapore & Malaysia
Spain
Thailand
Turkey
Venice

Fodor's Flashmaps
Boston
New York
San Francisco
Washington, D.C.

Fodor's Pocket Guides
Acapulco
Atlanta
Barbados
Jamaica
London
New York City
Paris
Prague
Puerto Rico

Rome
San Francisco
Washington, D.C.

Rivages Guides
Bed and Breakfasts of Character and Charm in France
Hotels and Country Inns of Character and Charm in France
Hotels and Country Inns of Character and Charm in Italy

Short Escapes
Country Getaways in Britain
Country Getaways in France
Country Getaways Near New York City

Fodor's Sports
Golf Digest's Best Places to Play
Skiing USA
USA Today The Complete Four Sport Stadium Guide

Fodor's Vacation Planners
Great American Learning Vacations
Great American Sports & Adventure Vacations
Great American Vacations
National Parks and Seashores of the East
National Parks of the West

Before Catching Your Flight, Catch Up With Your World.

Fueled by the global resources of CNN and available in major airports across America, CNN Airport Network provides a live source

of current domestic and international news,

sports, business, weather and lifestyle programming. Plus two daily Fodor's features for the facts you need: "Travel Fact," a useful and creative mix of travel trivia; and "What's Happening," a comprehensive round-up of upcoming events in major cities around the world.

With CNN Airport Network, you'll never be out of the loop.

HERE'S YOUR OWN PERSONAL VIEW OF THE WORLD.

Here's the easiest way to get up-to-the-minute, objective, personalized information about what's going on in the city you'll be visiting—before you leave on your trip! Unique information you could get only if you knew someone personally in each of 160 destinations around the world. Everything from special places to dine to local events only a local would know about.

It's all yours—in your Travel Update from Worldview, the leading provider of time-sensitive destination information.

Review the following order form and fill it out by indicating your destination(s)

and travel dates and by checking off up to eight interest categories. Then mail or fax your order form to us, or call your order in. (We're here to help you 24 hours a day.)

Within 48 hours of receiving your order, we'll mail your convenient, pocket-sized custom guide to you, packed with information to make your travel more fun and interesting. And if you're in a hurry, we can even fax it.

Have a great trip with your Fodor's Worldview Travel Update!

Fodor's WORLDVIEW TRAVEL UPDATE

Customized to your interests and dates of travel

Time-sensitive

Insider perspective

DESTINATIONS

Worldview covers more than 160 destinations worldwide. Choose the destination(s) that match your itinerary from the list below:

Europe
Amsterdam
Athens
Barcelona
Berlin
Brussels
Budapest
Copenhagen
Dublin
Edinburgh
Florence
Frankfurt
French Riviera
Geneva
Glasgow
Lausanne
Lisbon
London
Madrid
Milan
Moscow
Munich
Oslo
Paris
Prague
Provence
Rome
Salzburg
Seville
St. Petersburg
Stockholm
Venice
Vienna
Zurich

United States (Mainland)
Albuquerque
Atlanta
Atlantic City
Baltimore
Boston
Branson, MO
Charleston, SC
Chicago
Cincinnati
Cleveland
Dallas/Ft. Worth
Denver
Detroit
Houston
Indianapolis
Kansas City
Las Vegas
Los Angeles
Memphis
Miami
Milwaukee
Minneapolis/St. Paul
Nashville
New Orleans
New York City
Orlando
Palm Springs
Philadelphia
Phoenix
Pittsburgh
Portland
Reno/Lake Tahoe
St. Louis
Salt Lake City
San Antonio
San Diego
San Francisco
Santa Fe
Seattle
Tampa
Washington, DC

Alaska
Alaskan Destinations

Hawaii
Honolulu
Island of Hawaii
Kauai
Maui

Canada
Quebec City
Montreal
Ottawa
Toronto
Vancouver

Bahamas
Abaco
Eleuthera/
 Harbour Island
Exuma
Freeport
Nassau &
 Paradise Island

Bermuda
Bermuda Countryside
Hamilton

British Leeward Islands
Anguilla
Antigua & Barbuda
St. Kitts & Nevis

British Virgin Islands
Tortola & Virgin
 Gorda

British Windward Islands
Barbados
Dominica
Grenada
St. Lucia
St. Vincent
Trinidad & Tobago

Cayman Islands
The Caymans

Dominican Republic
Santo Domingo

Dutch Leeward Islands
Aruba
Bonaire
Curacao

Dutch Windward Island
St. Maarten/St. Martin

French West Indies
Guadeloupe
Martinique
St. Barthelemy

Jamaica
Kingston
Montego Bay
Negril
Ocho Rios

Puerto Rico
Ponce
San Juan

Turks & Caicos
Grand Turk/
 Providenciales

U.S. Virgin Islands
St. Croix
St. John
St. Thomas

Mexico
Acapulco
Cancun & Isla Mujeres
Cozumel
Guadalajara
Ixtapa & Zihuatanejo
Los Cabos
Mazatlan
Mexico City
Monterrey
Oaxaca
Puerto Vallarta

South/Central America
Buenos Aires
Caracas
Rio de Janeiro
San Jose, Costa Rica
Sao Paulo

Middle East
Istanbul
Jerusalem

Australia & New Zealand
Auckland
Melbourne
South Island
Sydney

China
Beijing
Guangzhou
Shanghai

Japan
Kyoto
Nagoya
Osaka
Tokyo
Yokohama

Pacific Rim/Other
Bali
Bangkok
Hong Kong & Macau
Manila
Seoul
Singapore
Taipei

INTERESTS

For your personalized Travel Update, choose the eight (8) categories you're most interested in from the following list:

1.	**Business Services**	Fax & Overnight Mail, Computer Rentals, Protocol, Secretarial, Messenger, Translation Services
	Dining	
2.	**All-Day Dining**	Breakfast & Brunch, Cafes & Tea Rooms, Late-Night Dining
3.	**Local Cuisine**	Every Price Range—from Budget Restaurants to the Special Splurge
4.	**European Cuisine**	Continental, French, Italian
5.	**Asian Cuisine**	Chinese, Far Eastern, Japanese, Other
6.	**Americas Cuisine**	American, Mexican & Latin
7.	**Nightlife**	Bars, Dance Clubs, Casinos, Comedy Clubs, Ethnic, Pubs & Beer Halls
8.	**Entertainment**	Theater—Comedy, Drama, Musicals, Dance, Ticket Agencies
9.	**Music**	Classical, Opera, Traditional & Ethnic, Jazz & Blues, Pop, Rock
10.	**Children's Activites**	Events, Attractions
11.	**Tours**	Local Tours, Day Trips, Overnight Excursions
12.	**Exhibitions, Festivals & Shows**	Antiques & Flower, History & Cultural, Art Exhibitions, Fairs & Craft Shows, Music & Art Festivals
13.	**Shopping**	Districts & Malls, Markets, Regional Specialties
14.	**Fitness**	Bicycling, Health Clubs, Hiking, Jogging
15.	**Recreational Sports**	Boating/Sailing, Fishing, Golf, Skiing, Snorkeling/Scuba, Tennis/Racket
16.	**Spectator Sports**	Auto Racing, Baseball, Basketball, Golf, Football, Horse Racing, Ice Hockey, Soccer
17.	**Event Highlights**	The best of what's happening during the dates of your trip.
18.	**Sightseeing**	Sights, Buildings, Monuments
19.	**Museums**	Art, Cultural
20.	**Transportation**	Taxis, Car Rentals, Airports, Public Transportation
21.	**General Info**	Overview, Holidays, Currency, Tourist Info

Please note that content will vary by season, destination, and length of stay.

Name

Address

City   **State**   **Country**   **ZIP**

Tel #   (   )   -   **Fax #**   (   )   -

Title of this Fodor's guide:

Store and location where guide was purchased:

INDICATE YOUR DESTINATIONS/DATES: You can order up to three (3) destinations from the previous page. Fill in your arrival and departure dates for each destination. **Your Travel Update itinerary (all destinations selected) cannot exceed 30 days from beginning to end.**

		Month	Day	Month	Day
(Sample) **LONDON**	From:	6	/ 21	To: 6	/ 30
1	From:		/	To:	/
2	From:		/	To:	/
3	From:		/	To:	/

CHOOSE YOUR INTERESTS: Select up to eight (8) categories from the list of interest categories shown on the previous page and circle the numbers below:

1 2 3 4 5 6 7 8 9 10 11 12 13 14 15 16 17 18 19 20 21

CHOOSE WHEN YOU WANT YOUR TRAVEL UPDATE DELIVERED (Check one):

❑ Please send my Travel Update immediately.

❑ Please hold my order until a few weeks before my trip to include the most up-to-date information.

Completed orders will be sent within 48 hours. Allow 7–10 days for U.S. mail delivery.

ADD UP YOUR ORDER HERE. SPECIAL OFFER FOR FODOR'S PURCHASERS ONLY!

	Suggested Retail Price	Your Price	This Order
First destination ordered	$ 9.95	$ 7.95	$ 7.95
Second destination (if applicable)	$ 6.95	$ 4.95	+
Third destination (if applicable)	$ 6.95	$ 4.95	+

DELIVERY CHARGE (Check one and enter amount below)

	Within U.S. & Canada	Outside U.S. & Canada
First Class Mail	❑ $2.50	❑ $5.00
FAX	❑ $5.00	❑ $10.00
Priority Delivery	❑ $15.00	❑ $27.00

ENTER DELIVERY CHARGE FROM ABOVE: +

TOTAL: $

METHOD OF PAYMENT IN U.S. FUNDS ONLY (Check one):

❑ AmEx ❑ MC ❑ Visa ❑ Discover ❑ Personal Check (U. S. & Canada only)
❑ Money Order/International Money Order

Make check or money order payable to: Fodor's Worldview Travel Update

Credit Card __/__/__/__/__/__/__/__/__/__/__/__/__/__/__/__/ **Expiration Date:**__/__

Authorized Signature

SEND THIS COMPLETED FORM WITH PAYMENT TO:
Fodor's Worldview Travel Update, 114 Sansome Street, Suite 700, San Francisco, CA 94104

OR CALL OR FAX US 24-HOURS A DAY
Telephone **1-800-799-9609** • Fax **1-800-799-9619** (From within the U.S. & Canada)
(Outside the U.S. & Canada: Telephone 415-616-9988 • Fax 415-616-9989)

(Please have this guide in front of you when you call so we can verify purchase.)
Code: FTG   Offer valid until 12/31/97